After the Vows Were Spoken

After the Vows Were Spoken

MARRIAGE IN AMERICAN LITERARY REALISM

Allen F. Stein

Ohio State University Press: *Columbus*

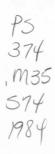

PS
374
.M35
S74
1984

An earlier version of "William Dean Howells" appeared, under the title "Marriage in Howells's Novels," in *American Literature* 48 (1977), copyright © 1977 by Duke University Press. It is reprinted herein by permission.

Library of Congress Cataloging in Publication Data

Stein, Allen F.
  After the vows were spoken.
  Bibliography: p.
  Includes index.
  1. Marriage in literature.   2. American fiction—19th century—History and criticism.   3. American fiction—20th century—History and criticism.   4. Realism in literature.   I. Title.
PS374.M35S74   1985   813'.009'354   84-16552
ISBN 0-8142-0382-5

To Gale, Philip, Wendy, and Ethan

CONTENTS

ACKNOWLEDGMENTS

I WISH TO THANK the English Department of North Carolina State University for allowing me a semester's leave for writing and research at an important stage in the development of this book. I am grateful to Charlene Turner, who typed my manuscript with accuracy, intelligence, and unfailing helpfulness. I am indebted as well to my former office mate Carmine Prioli, who, with his usual wit, patience, and good cheer, put up with my chronic moroseness and complaining as I worked through this project. Finally, Robert S. Demorest, the editor of the Ohio State University Press, edited my manuscript with care and thoughtfulness, for which I will always be appreciative.

After the Vows Were Spoken

INTRODUCTION

*A*T THE CONCLUSION of *Tom Sawyer*, Twain comments, "When one writes a novel about grown people, he knows exactly where to stop—that is with a marriage."[1] For those of us accustomed to reading novels about grown people (at times, perhaps, only ostensibly grown people) by such writers as Updike, Bellow, Mailer, Philip Roth, Lurie, Heller, Cheever, and a panoply of other observers of the complex and multifarious intimacies of American married life, Twain's remark is a curious one because it excludes from fiction—and cavalierly at that—not only a crucial realm of adult experience but a central subject of some of the better American fiction of recent decades. But curious as it may be, it reflects an attitude long held by American authors in the nineteenth century and only beginning to change in Twain's own day. Once begun, though, the change was rapid. Thus, had Twain made his statement ten years later, the publication, in the interim, of *The Portrait of a Lady, A Modern Instance*, and *The Rise of Silas Lapham* would have made the idea that married life was beyond the purview of American fiction seem a badly dated one; and had he made it thirty years later, it would, in the light of the careers of Howells, James, Chopin, Wharton, and Herrick, have been incomprehensible.[2] The marriage fiction that comprises much of the best work in those five careers is the subject of this study, one that attempts to show how effectually these writers worked to prove the truth of W. H. Auden's assertion in our own day that "any marriage, happy or unhappy, is infinitely more interesting and significant than any romance, however passionate."[3]

To be sure, Twain's comment is an overstatement for comic effect. Neither he nor his predecessors among American authors would concur with the notion, implicit in his remark, that the central experience of adult life is courtship and its complications and that all the years following the wedding ceremony are of little interest to anyone save, perhaps, the married couple. Indeed, any survey of major American fiction before 1876, when Twain made his statement, makes clear that areas of adult experience other than courtship were thought suitable for literary delineation. But the same survey would show, however, that whatever these areas might be, in a given work, it was more than likely that married life would not be one of them—thus revealing a foundation of truth underlying Twain's humorous exaggeration. In effect, then, although what William Wasserstrom describes as the "Puritan conviction that marriage rather than celibacy is the approved state of man"[4] never really waned on the American scene in the first three-quarters of the nineteenth century, there was little, as Twain implied, in the way of an effort in American fiction of adult life to depict this "approved state." One, for example, never sees Ahab with the young wife he left back on shore. Chillingworth and Hester's life as man and wife before their fateful separation can only be inferred in retrospect, and Phoebe's life with Holgrave and Hilda's with Kenyon can only be anticipated. Arthur Mervyn, Edgar Huntly, Natty Bumppo, Roderick Usher, Taji, Ishmael, Pierre, Coverdale, the Reverend Mr. Hooper, even Thoreau's fictional reconstruction of himself at Walden pond are all unmarried and in most cases unimaginable as married.

The few glimpses of American marriage afforded readers before the 1870s neither show how most married Americans lived nor make one believe that the authors who presented them were interested in the subject in its own right. Irving's Van Winkles, Cooper's grim lower-class marrieds like the Bushes or Spikes, Hawthorne's Aylmers, Browns, and other misunited unfortunates, and Poe's couples enmeshed in the dubious gratifications of spiritual and psychological vampirism all seem, perhaps, to convey an implicit encomium to celibacy; and though in the cases of Irving and Poe, at least, the pairs might, in part, be meant to do so, the major impulse behind these depictions finally has little to do with a delineation of marriage. Irving's love of humor and local color and his profound ambivalence about the desire for repose and for escape from a world too much with one, Cooper's conservative political, religious, and social views, Hawthorne's emphasis on the need to maintain a feeling heart, and the mixed yearning and horror with which Poe pursued his personal vision of transcendent beauty in the universe that he found to be so dark yet so strangely lovely all take primacy over their presentations of marriage, which become, invariably, little more than vehicles or symbols for conveying these overriding concerns. Similarly, even the few ostensibly pleasant unions seen, like Cooper's elegant matings of highborn folk and the cozy pairs inhabiting Hawthorne's "The Great Carbuncle" and "The Ambitious Guest," are the vaguely limned, idealized, unconvincing affairs they are because, their pronuptial intentions notwithstanding, the authors involved are more concerned with delineating their overriding visions than with marriage itself and any types of behavior it may, in fact, engender. Nor, one might note, was this tendency to subordinate the treatment of marriage in fiction to other concerns peculiar to the major writers. Even the producers of the popular sentimental fiction of the mid-nineteenth century, the E. D. E. N. Southworths, Susan Warners, and Maria Cumminses, "rarely offer a portrait of marriage," as Alfred Habegger notes, though their works so often depict heroines in singleminded search of the nuptial altar.[5]

Unlike their counterparts elsewhere, then, who, to quote David Daiches on the British Victorian novelists, were exploring the "moral and psychological adequacy of the institutions through which social and economic life was organized" and who, like the British writers described by Daiches, found their imaginations "most directly engaged" by the institutions of marriage and family,[6] American fiction writers of all levels of competency through the first three-quarters of the nineteenth century rarely looked at the actual dealings between husbands and wives any more closely than Emerson did when he declared marriage "the perfection which love aimed at, ignorant of what it sought" and "a relation of perfect understanding, aid, contentment . . . which dwarfs love to green fruit."[7] Though Emerson's enthusiasm for matrimony is a little more restrained in "Illusions," in which he speaks of marriage as an experience that has its consolations and educative possibilities despite being an "especial trap" that is "laid to trip up our feet with,"[8] the fact remains that his response to marriage whether unreservedly affirmative or relatively somber is, like that of the fiction writers of his day, the typically American one through much of the nineteenth century of quickly looking past matrimony—or, indeed, any institution—to something else: a moral truth, a political or social theory, a cosmological vision. This is by no means to imply that a close scrutiny of marriage cannot lead to these things. In fact, for the five writers whose marriage fiction we shall examine, it actually does; but these writers look at marriage far more closely than did their predecessors, see it, as their frequent accounts of marriage reveal, as fascinating in its own right, and reach whatever conclusions or visions they do reach, consequently, through their delineations of marriage rather than by leaping beyond the marriages in their works.

The reasons for this relative lack of interest in depicting matrimony on the part of American writers for most of the nineteenth century are not terribly hard to discern, of course. As commentators have long noted, institutions mattered far less to these writers, society itself mattered far less to them for the most part, than individuals, the universe, and those abstractions that might help define the relationship between the two. The influence of the Calvinist emphasis on the necessity for lonely self-scrutiny on the path to one's spiritual destiny, the premium on rugged individualism in frontier life, the glorification of the self-made man in American economic ideals, the commitment to individual freedoms built into the American political framework, and, certainly, the lack of a long-established, stable, hierarchical social order—all, along with, doubtless, other features of the American scene, distracted most nineteenth-century American writers from a close look at marriage. Not surprisingly, this mélange of influences made them far more interested in defining the nature of man and man's place in the universe and establishing those values for the individual, and even the myths to ground them in, that precede and prepare for the establishment of a society, than they were in observing day-to-day existence and those institutions, such as marriage, so intimately tied to it.[9] Whatever the underlying causes, there was indeed nothing in American fiction until the 1870s comparable to the close examination marriage underwent in the works of English writers as diverse as Dickens, Thackeray, Gaskell, Eliot, Trollope, or Meredith.

Just as a whole complex of influences kept American writers from looking at marriage closely for most of the nineteenth century, there was no single factor that brought about the interest in delineating marriage that developed in American fiction in the latter part of the century. Clearly, all the elements on the American scene leading to the rise of literary realism generally and the close look at social relations it inspired helped turn American writers to the specific social relation of marriage as a subject. The Civil War, urbanization, industrialization, Darwinian theory, and advances in knowledge in the sciences generally, the development of pragmatism, the rise of sociology and of a new awareness of social and economic inequities, drew a number of American writers, as all know, to increased concern with relations among people and away from a narrow if intense concern with the individual in relation to absolutes, abstractions, and the cosmological context. More specifically, the rise of the so-called new woman—vocal, independent, and deeply inclined to question the traditional roles assigned her—the rapidly rising divorce rate, and the falling birthrate among the "better sort" brought about widespread concern among the American public about the condition of marriage and the family. Christopher Lasch notes in this connection that "by the end of the nineteenth century, American newspapers and magazines brimmed with speculation about the crisis of marriage and the family."[10] Given the high level of concern, then, among sensitive Americans in the latter part of the century with social relations generally and married life in particular, it is in no way surprising, of course, that American writers would turn readily to close observation of marriage in their fiction. Finally, perhaps the most crucial factor turning American writers of fiction in the latter part of the century to close scrutiny of marriage was, one suspects, the fact that if one were committed to examining social relations and examining them particularly, as the realists usually did, with an eye to ascertaining and promulgating patterns of social behavior conducive to humane dealings among people and the generating of a more humane social situation at large, one might find oneself almost of necessity turning to a close look at marriage. As a social relation more intimate and intense than most, and demanding more of those in it than most, marriage is not only an eminently suitable subject but even the most logical place to begin for such writers as the realists, who hoped to reveal ranges of behavior among people in close conjunction with one another in fiction that their readers might find both compelling and educative.

Nor, obviously, were James and Howells, whose first works of fiction are, in fact, marriage stories, and Chopin, Wharton, and Herrick, whose earliest work includes marriage stories, alone among those writers usually associated with literary realism in depicting married life. Harold Frederic's *Seth's Brother's Wife* and *The Damnation of Theron Ware*, for example, present sardonic looks at marital faithlessness in the cases of Seth's sister-in-law and the would-be philanderer, the Reverend Mr. Ware, respectively, and the latter work offers a no less sardonic view of the comradeship and affection achieved in matrimony by the roving evangelical hucksters, the Soulsbys. Henry Blake Fuller's *The Cliff-Dwellers* and *With the Procession* reveal how vulnerable marriage is to the pressures exerted on it by the pernicious commitment of all too many late-nineteenth-century Americans to the pursuit of wealth, possession, status, and power. E. W. Howe in *The Story of a Country Town* presents a grim picture of marital conflicts, suffering, and infidelity in a stark rural setting, and Hamlin Garland in stories set in scenes similar to Howe's portrays the hard economic lot confronting many rural married folk and the capacity of some to endure it together with a deeply moving quiet courage. Writers linked to the naturalist tradition, too, did not ignore marriage as a subject. Norris's McTeagues and Zerkows reveal a brutishness that becomes all the more horrifying within the context of marriage that so exacerbates it, and the difficulties of the Jadwins in *The Pit* and the destruction visited upon the Derricks and Annixters in *The Octopus* show, as do the problems undergone by Fuller's married characters, the ugly and ruinous impact on married life of conflicts over money and power. Dreiser's Eugene Witla in *The Genius*, Hurst-wood in *Sister Carrie*, Lester Kane in *Jennie Gerhardt*, and Rufus Haymaker in "Free" all reveal the desperation felt by men finding themselves in marriages they consider repressive and unfulfilling. Not surprisingly, utopian novelists also include accounts of marriage in their programs for the perfection of society. Edward Bellamy in *Looking Backward* and *Equality* envisions a future in which matrimony in its traditional form will persist but within the framework, of course, of a more humane social atmosphere generally; and his brother Charles in *An Experiment in Marriage* espouses the development of a new form of matrimony based on perfect equality between the sexes and on the conviction of both husband and wife that the legal bonds of their marriage shall be easily set aside should love fail to last as long as life.

Clearly, as this brief survey of some of the portrayals of marriage in late nineteenth-century and early twentieth-century American fiction shows, an extensive literary history might be written on the subject. It is not my purpose to attempt such a comprehensive study here. Instead, I have confined myself, as I have noted, to five authors—Howells, James, Chopin, Wharton, and Herrick. I have chosen these five in particular because their portrayals of marriage are more fully delineated than those of their contemporaries and because, more than for their contemporaries—especially the utopians, naturalists, and regional realists—marriage is central to their work in terms both of the proportion of their fiction in which it figures and its significance in conveying their most pivotal themes. In Howells's fiction, for example, it is marriage that is intended to provide many of the most telling instances of how the overwhelming commitment to self that in its various manifestations Howells saw as ravaging the American scene might best be overcome. It is marriage too in his work that offers some of the most painful instances of the very social breakdown he lamented and worked against. Finally, for Howells, it is often delineations of marriage that convey with the greatest force the havoc wrought by those terrors in existence itself that transcend the failures of any given society, and it is delineations of marriage through which he means to show with the greatest affection the fragile havens of comfort and decency men and women can establish in the very midst of those terrors. For James, whose well-known "imagination of disaster" made him no less aware, obviously, of the terrors lurking in existence than was Howells, it is marriage that reveals, more intensely and consistently perhaps than any other human relationship, the dangers and, too, the faint possibility for a hard-won triumph of a rare, highly personal form that are attendant upon an intimate confrontation with experience. Nor is marriage any less significant in the works of Chopin, Wharton, and Herrick. Underlying the local color, the humor, the striking ironies in Chopin's fiction is her exceedingly deterministic vision of the total inability of people either to resist or, more often than not, even understand the deeply rooted impulses that drive them; and it is in her marriage works that this central feature of Chopin's outlook becomes most apparent. Similarly, it is her marriage stories that most evidence Wharton's awareness of human imperfection and of the consequent necessity for the maintenance of an essentially restrictive social order as a means of limiting the destructive capacity inherent in the folly of individual men and women. Further, as one might suspect, it is her stories of wedded life that show Wharton's awareness of just how large a part marriages can play either in preserving or pulling down such a social order. Finally, Herrick's distaste for an America that he viewed as increasingly corrupt and his inability when conveying his visions of what a fulfilling life and fulfilling relations between the sexes might be to ground them in anything much akin to the America around him is evident most poignantly in his fiction of marriage, the institution that engendered in him his profoundest hopes and his deepest disappointments in regard to the American scene.

Certainly, then, these five writers share a concern with delineating marriage, a concern that permeates their careers, but they are linked by something else too. All are, as I noted, figures usually considered to be realists—writers who in Edwin Cady's words are "especially concerned with persons in their relations with other persons."[11] Consequently, a look at their depiction of marriage, perhaps the quintessential social relation, reveals a great deal not only about their brightest expectations for mankind and, as well, their most troubling doubts and disturbing fears but a great deal too about realism itself as practiced in late nineteenth- and early twentieth-century America. Obviously, students of the "realism" of this period generally recognize that the mode is neither easy to define nor manifested in any entirely consistent manner in the works of those usually thought of as realists or as strongly linked to the realist tradition; nevertheless, discussions of realism have always suffered from a failure to look at a large body of material closely. A careful examination, therefore, of these five writers as they reach widely varying conclusions about an institution that seems in such a basic manner to epitomize that fundamental object of realist interest, human relations in a commonplace social context, does portray freshly and vividly, I think, just how exceedingly disparate from one another the realists often were in their aims, methods, and central values.

However, along with presenting vividly the multifariousness of approaches and values that one finds under the rubric of "realism," a study of the marriage fiction of these five writers shows certain surprising similarities apart from their mutual interest in marriage, similarities that reflect tendencies in realism of which commentators have never taken adequate note. Edwin Cady and Harold Kolb, perhaps the commentators who have provided the most painstaking and extensive accounts of what realism in America was, find themselves in general agreement both with each other and with other writers on the subject in their view of the realists' overriding orientation. Unlike "the romantic," who, Cady notes, is "in the long run . . . concerned with the ideal, the transcendent, the superhuman" (p. 7), the realist's impulse, he asserts, is "toward the common, democratic, mock heroic, and novelistic" (p. 64). Further, realism, in fact, as typified for

Cady by Howells's work, "attacks superhumanism," for it is "anti-idealistic, anti-organicist, anti-egoistic" (p. 180), and, in short, maintains as "essential" to its "moral vision" an "active disbelief in the health or safety of romantic individualism" (p. 11). Similarly, Kolb observes that "the realists cannot accept supernaturalism, Platonic idealism, and the worlds of the spirit,"[12] for "in their best work the realists were pragmatic, relativistic, democratic, and experimental" (p. 39); and, more, typically concentrating "on what people are rather than what they ought to be, on men rather than Man" (p. 40), they "believed in an open, anthropocentric universe in which men might control their destinies" (p. 104).

As Mark Twain said in another context, there is nothing wrong with all this, except that it ain't so. Ain't entirely so, anyway, I might note; for although one can readily take carefully selected works by each of the five authors treated here and prove line for line and point for point the validity of these accounts by Cady and Kolb, a study of the realists' work on marriage—a very large body of work clearly of high importance to them—reveals something quite different. It reveals, for example, that decidedly nonpragmatic outlooks are evident in marriage works by James, Chopin, and Herrick and that doubts about the pragmatic orientation surface even in the works of Howells himself, the most explicit spokesman among the realists for pragmatic modes of solving human problems.[13] Similarly, the belief in free will that is presupposed both by pragmatism and the concept of an "anthropocentric universe in which men might control their destinies" is not evident in Chopin's marriage fiction or apparent without some severe qualifications in marital fiction by James, Wharton, and, again, Howells himself.[14] Finally, idealism, absolutism, sympathetic depictions of personal quests after obscure goals, and even "romantic individualism" are not foreign to the marriage fiction of these five.[15]

Thus, a major similarity that emerges as one studies the marriage fiction of these five authors is that the outlook of none of them really conforms consistently to the prevailing notions of what the outlook of a realistic writer is. Doubting more than has heretofore been thought the orientation toward social relations that commentators have posited as central to their work, valuing more than has heretofore been realized the individualistic orientation that has been posited as vehemently eschewed by them, these realist writers do not seem so "realistic" after all. In light of this, it should not be too surprising to see that another striking similarity among them becomes apparent when one studies their marriage fiction, namely, that to a degree that would be wholly unanticipated by any who accept standard notions of realism, they portray marriage as an exceedingly bleak relationship characterized by blighted hopes, stunted lives, and a misery that is often unremitting.

This is not to say that they see benefits as never to be derived in wedded life. One may learn through the suffering that marriage often brings—a crucial point in some works by James and Wharton and one at least touched on by Howells and Herrick. Further, one may by enduring a trying marriage serve as a bulwark against social disorder—an idea of more than a little significance in Wharton's marriage fiction particularly, but evident as well in marriage works by Howells and Herrick. Finally, one can even find happiness as a husband or wife—there are indeed figures who do in the works of all five authors. But the marriages in which such benefits are, in fact, derived are in a decided minority here. And, ultimately, even when they are delineated, they only infrequently inspire especially sanguine thoughts about matrimony as experienced by American men and women. For one thing, whatever the intentions of the authors, those relatively few marriages in which benefits accrue are too often simply rendered unconvincingly, the depictions marred by a sentimentality or ideality reflecting, one suspects, lack of real conviction on the writers' parts. For another, the benefits are often arrived at by individuals acting with "idealistic," even "romantic" and perhaps rather idiosyncratic codes of conduct, codes that may be shaped by the absolutist imperatives operative in their own personal makeups. Finally, even those marriages, such as one occasionally sees in Wharton's works, in which benefits are derived, the delineation is convincing, and the protagonist follows a morality that reaches beyond the personal, are unions so tinged with the darkness of the surrounding world, so somber in their affirmations as to offer prospective marrieds bleak prospects at best for their future state as husband and wife. The benefits of marriage, then, as envisioned by these five authors are not often presented as within the reach of most marrieds, linked as these advantages almost customarily are to a context of sentimental ideality or described as garnered only through the development of a highly personal moral vision. And even when they are in reach, they only rarely do more than palliate slightly the pain in existence of which marriage invariably makes these authors aware.

A decided pessimism thus characterizes the marriage fiction of these five figures although they generally value the institution of marriage itself. It is a pessimism about the human capacity to establish and maintain successful intimate social relations. And it is this pessimism, I think, that is especially revelatory in terms of understanding these writers and the realism to which they are linked. Implicit in the accounts of realism by Cady and Kolb and many others is the notion that realism by and large is a body of literature reflecting an optimistic stance toward life. Surely, this is the message when words like "pragmatic," "democratic," and "experimental" are used to characterize the realists, who are further described as believing that man can "control" his destiny. It is a message asserting that the realists have faith that persons can work together rationally, humanely, flexibly, *socially*, and resolve their differences, thereby making themselves happier and in some tangible way improving the common lot. But examination of the marriage fiction presents, as I have noted, a different message, one that asserts that in a central, perhaps *the* central, social relationship humaneness, happiness, and moral development are exceedingly elusive. It is a message too that points up, despite what the commentators have seen, the human capacity for growth far less than the human capacity for futility; and it is a message that implies that such growth as may occasionally occur is often of a highly individualistic nature and to be measured on an absolutist rather than "relativistic" scale, one perhaps even "transcendent" rather than mundane. Obviously, it is a message that should prompt yet further definitions of realism.

One reason for the prevailing pessimism of the marriage fiction may well be that conventionally happy marriages are probably less interesting to depict than unhappy or idiosyncratically happy ones. But far more important, I suspect, is the continuing tradition of romantic individualism in America. Harold Kolb himself notes that "it is a mistake to simplistically oppose realism to romanticism, and it is unhistorical" (p. 133) and observes the realists' "debt to the romantic emphasis on personal experience and the individual" (p. 136). As far as this goes, it is an apt reminder; but the debt is larger than Kolb observes, for part of the romantic emphasis on personal experience and the individual was the romantic suspicion of all that would restrict the individual, impinge on personal freedom of movement and development, and this too was manifestly passed on to the realists. This legacy for which they are indebted undercuts at every turn the faith they usually seek to maintain in marriage and, by extension, in personal improvement through social relations generally. Therefore, should one wish to begin to understand in depth both the legacy of romanticism that makes itself felt in realism and the surprising extent of the pessimism about social relations that this legacy prompts in realistic literature in America, one might best begin with the realists' studies of husbands and wives.

These, then, are the aims of my study: an illumination of the central ideas of five prominent realist writers through an examination of their marriage fiction—a body of material that bulks large in their careers in terms of quantity and significance; an observation of the multifarious nature of realism by focusing on the widely varying responses among the five to what may be the quintessential social relation; and observation too, though, of similarities among the five that offer surprising insights into the nature of realism in practice, showing that the realists were far less "realistic" and more "romantic" than commentators have shown and, strikingly, far more pessimistic than heretofore thought about the possibility of personal growth through nourishing social relations.

My focus, therefore, is literary. Consequently, it is not my purpose to judge these writers in terms of whether or not their views on marriage were conducive to creating an atmosphere in which more equitable conditions for women, less ruthless business practices, and a less rigidly stratified social and economic structure might develop. Valuable as studies leading to such judgments may be, my primary concerns here are literary, and, because an examination of marriage and literary realism has never before been attempted, the topic is fresh enough as well as rich enough to demand my full attention. Again, I should be immensely pleased, however, should such literary matter as I present be useful to anyone dealing with the relations between American literature and social change.

Carl Jung once asserted that "viewed as a psychological relationship, marriage is the most complicated of structures."[16] One might add that viewed as a social relationship it is no less an exceedingly complicated one. And because it is so complex psychologically, socially, and often spiritually as well, and clearly so fascinating to so many, from the writers we look at here to psychologists, economists, sociologists, reformers of all stripes, and even comedians, who persistently get laughs with gags of the "Take my wife—*please!*" variety, I seek to focus primarily on marriage itself as presented in the works we shall examine. More often than not, courtship is beyond my purview unless a given courtship bears significantly on the form a subsequent marriage takes or unless the delineation of the courtship in some significant manner reflects the outlook of the author on marriage itself. Similarly, relations between parents and children, unless they bear on an author's view of marriage, are touched on only slightly in this study. Finally, I should add that in seeking to get at what is most of import in the marriage fiction of these five authors, I have found it most useful to employ a variety of approaches. Because the marriage fiction of Howells, for example, is of interest more in terms of the overriding ideas Howells advances on matrimony and the way they develop over his career than in terms of the working-out of these ideas in any particular work, I have opted for a survey approach to his marriage fiction in which no work is dealt with at great length. On the other hand, Herrick's marriage fiction is most fruitfully explored, I find, through close scrutiny of the stylistic and philosophical difficulties into which he is led in his accounts of matrimony by the conflict in his own nature between realistic and romantic impulses. Consequently, the Herrick chapter focuses on a few central works and examines them at length. I found too that the sheer mass of marriage stories by James and Wharton and the complexity with which they frequently render both their ideas on wedlock and the themes with which they connect it, necessitated three chapters on each of this pair, chapters in which some works are treated only cursorily and others are discussed extensively. The Chopin chapter, like those on James and Wharton, is an effort to combine survey with close, extended analysis. Though I began this work with approximate symmetry and uniformity of approach as my expectation, it was not long before I found that, like marriage itself, a study of marriage can make demands on one that are never anticipated at the outset.

1. Mark Twain, *The Adventures of Tom Sawyer* (New York: Harper & Brothers, 1922), p.292.

2. Howells's *Their Wedding Journey*, a significant depiction of married folk published in 1871, anticipates the spate of marriage fiction to come.

3. Quoted in Joseph Epstein, *Divorced in America: Marriage in an Age of Possibility* (New York: Dutton, 1974), p. 28.

4. William Wasserstrom, *Heiress of All the Ages: Sex and Sentiment in the Genteel Tradition* (Minneapolis: University of Minnesota Press, 1959), p. 124.

5. Alfred Habegger, *Gender, Fantasy, and Realism in American Literature* (New York: Columbia University Press, 1982), p. 17. For another study of this sentimental fiction, see Helen Papashvily, *All the Happy Endings* (New York: Harper & Brothers, 1956).

6. David Daiches, Preface to Jenni Calder's *Women and Marriage in Victorian Fiction* (New York: Oxford University Press, 1976), p. 9.

7. Ralph Waldo Emerson, *Journals of Ralph Waldo Emerson 1849–1855*, ed. Edward Waldo Emerson and Waldo Emerson Forbes (Boston: Houghton Mifflin, 1912), pp. 87–88.

8. Ralph Waldo Emerson, *The Conduct of Life* (Boston: Houghton Mifflin, 1904), p. 316.

9. James Fenimore Cooper in such works as *Home As Found* and *The Crater* is an exception to this tendency.

10. Christopher Lasch, *Haven in a Heartless World: The Family Besieged* (New York: Basic Books, 1977), p. 8. Also see in connection with these changes Ernest Earnest, *The American Eve in Fact and Fiction 1775-1914* (Urbana: University of Illinois Press, 1974), and Judith Fryer, *The Faces of Eve: Woman in the Nineteenth-Century American Novel* (New York: Oxford University Press, 1972).

11. Edwin H. Cady, *The Light of Common Day: Realism in American Fiction* (Bloomington: Indiana University Press, 1971), p. 21. Subsequent page references to this work appear in the text.

12. Harold Kolb, *The Illusion of Life: American Realism as a Literary Form* (Charlottesville: University of Virginia Press, 1969), p. 38. Subsequent page references to this work apper in the text.

13. Although Richard A. Hocks, in *Henry James and Pragmatistic Thought* (Chapel Hill: University of North Carolina Press, 1974), argues cogently that "William James's pragmatistic thought is literally *actualized* in the literary art and idiom of his brother Henry James, especially so in the later work" (p. 4), a study of Henry's marriage fiction reveals, I believe, a commitment in Henry James to romantic individualism that such influence as he may have felt from William's philosophy could never really shake.

14. Habegger notes in this connection that "one of the reasons realism was often 'pessimistic'" was that "it insisted that the self was limited and conditioned and not capable of the apotheosis promised by mass fantasy" (p. 109). Similarly, Anthony Channell Hilfer, in *The Ethics of Intensity in American Fiction* (Austin: University of Texas Press, 1981), asserts that in Howells's *A Modern Instance* "choice is shown to be a complex process in which vague and not fully acknowledged impulses have a major role" (p. 56), a situation that Hilfer does not see as eliminating free will, but that does severely limit it nonetheless. Finally, Gordon O. Taylor, speaking of Howells's *A Hazard of New Fortunes* in *The Passages of Thought* (New York: Oxford University Press, 1969), observes "a latent sense of determinism" in "the fictive psychology of the novel" (p. 109).

15. For discussions of the significance of the romantic quest motif in James's work, see my "Lambert Strether's Circuitous Journey: Motifs of Internalized Quest and Circularity in *The Ambassadors*," *ESQ* 22 (Fourth Quarter, 1976): 245-53, and Daniel Mark Fogel's *Henry James and the Structure of the Romantic Imagination* (Baton Rouge: Louisiana State University Press, 1981). For a discussion of James's essentially romantic commitment to capturing the unique intensity of highly personal experience in his fiction, see the chapter on James in Charles Schug's *The Romantic Genesis of the Modern Novel* (Pittsburgh: University of Pittsburgh Press, 1979). Also see Hilfer's chapters on Howells and James for studies of their tendency toward affirmation of the self's ability to respond intensely to experience in its quest for fulfillment and identity, and see Taylor for his discussions of Howells and James as writers who aimed at "intensifying and extending analysis of the mind in process" (p. 7), an aim not at all at odds, certainly, with the goals of a Hawthorne, a Melville, a Poe, or an Emerson as each focused on the self in its process of self-formulation and self-definition.

16. Quoted in Epstein, pp. 40-41.

WILLIAM DEAN HOWELLS

CALLED BY ONE COMMENTATOR "pre-eminently the novelist of late nineteenth century American mating and marriage,"[1] William Dean Howells is also the first American author to explore in any detail in his fiction the actual "ever after" in which newlyweds presumably live happily once their vows are spoken. From his first novel, *Their Wedding Journey* (1871), which depicts newlyweds (no longer terribly young or passionate ones, at that), until his last, *The Vacation of the Kelwyns* (1920), which delineates three marriages and closes with a fourth in the offing, a major portion of Howells's work examines marriage in America.[2] Further, unlike those who touched on married life before him—Hawthorne, Poe, Cooper, and Irving among them—marriage for Howells is neither nightmarish nor treacly but, as Wendell Stacy Johnson, describing marriage as presented in English Victorian poetry, puts it, "an institution and an experience to be analyzed, questioned, perhaps redefined, and an idea that has deep social . . . implications."[3] In his analysis of these implications, Howells concludes initially with his first two significant treatments of wedded life that matrimony can be of inestimable worth to society in that by providing a man and woman with the comforts of a relationship built on quiet affection and civility it educates them to an awareness of their responsibilities to men and women at large. This initial view is one that Howells still maintains at the end of his long career, but with a significant difference. Having passed through a period in which he was troubled deeply by the suspicion that marriage might be for many a relationship actually retarding the growth of either a profound social conscience or a mature awareness of the existential chaos generally of which social inequity is one manifestation, Howells could never maintain as unquestioning a commitment to the institution as his earlier career indicated he might. Consequently, the later works affirming marriage, even though largely no longer marked by explicit doubts about the institution, reflect some uneasiness in their inability to depict convincingly that marriage can bring about any substantive diminution of evil and in their penchant for casting over the happy marriage a haze of ideality, an aura of the idyllic, as if Howells did not fully believe, finally, that a marriage at once happy and productive of social good was realizable as a sharply delineated *fact* of common life. Thus his career manifests a gradual darkening of his views of what husbands and wives are capable of in reality both toward each other and toward society, a darkening that leads him to what is little less than a consignment of marriage in his fiction to the realm of sentimentality, divorced from failure but also from life.

For Howells marriage can offer, above all, a means of liberation from the prison of self. This is the burden of perhaps the most explicit characterization of marriage to appear in Howells's work, one offered by a minister in the minor novella *The Day of Their Wedding* (1896), when he declares that "heaven is imaged in every true marriage on earth; for heaven is nothing but the joy of self-giving, and marriage is the supreme self-giving." The "self-giving" he describes has little in common with those grandiose acts of self-sacrifice so typical of the popular sentimental fiction that Howells loathed. Rather, it involves "the adjustment of temperaments, the compromise of opinions, the reconciliation of tastes" that day-to-day living together over the years demands.[4] Hence, the successful marriage is an unending, basically pragmatic process of mutual accommodation between the partners, conveying to each the lesson that the welfare of one is finally indistinguishable from that of the other. This relationship, which Howells usually characterizes as more one of "affectionate comradery"[5] than one of passion (which he regards as having self-gratification as its goal), fashions for the fortunate couple a little sphere of civility and order in a world that otherwise is often chaotic and threatening.

Moreover, as Howells comes increasingly to see, by teaching the pair that they are responsible for each other, marriage can render them far more receptive to the doctrine that they are responsible for others in the community. So crucial is this aspect of marriage to Howells that in his utopian society of Altruria the state tries to ensure that prospective marrieds are well-matched, warning them repeatedly "against the danger of trusting to anything like a romantic impulse," which ultimately is antisocial in its promptings.[6] Good marriages make it more probable that the Altrurian system, based on a pervasive sense of complicity among the citizenry, will continue to flourish. Conversely, Howells, like his Altrurians, is fully cognizant that bad marriages not only fail to help the community but indeed wreak pernicious effects on it by bringing ever-increasing numbers of those nearby into their disruptive orbits of unhappiness.

Though Howells doubtless feels that escape from mere concern with self can occur without marriage, and for a period is troubled by the suspicion that even good marriages might retard the development of selflessness, it is apparent that he regards marriage both early and late in his career as the most likely means "poor Real Life" has to offer for this personal growth to occur. More often than not, the characters he most admires in his work—such persons as Basil and Isabel March, Silas Lapham, Judge and Mrs. Kenton—are happily married and continue to grow through their marriages. On the other hand, the characters about whom he has the greatest misgivings—the Bartley Hubbards, Angus Beatons, James Langbriths, and Clarence Bittridges—are all either unmarried or caught up in bad marriages. Indeed, in Howells's work the extent to which a character is presented as worthy of respect is usually in direct proportion to the success his or her marriage enjoys (or is likely to enjoy if he or she is a newlywed or soon to marry). Similarly, rare in Howells's novels is a good person who is trapped in a bad marriage or a bad person fortunate enough to be in a good one.[7] Thus, although other routes out of the prison of self do exist, so often for Howells's characters "marriage," as Isabel March notes sententiously, "is all that there is."[8]

Not surprisingly, given his sense of the potential of marriage for good or ill, Howells throughout his career regards the institution with a sense of wonder and fascination. Like Dorothea Brooke in George Eliot's *Middlemarch*, he might conclude, "Marriage is unlike anything else. There is something even awful in the nearness it brings." Certainly, Howells too approaches marriage with the awe that the presumably sacred, totally intimate union of two people ought to inspire, awe that is apparent despite his realization that so much of every marriage is inextricably bound up in the pedestrian. Indeed, the notorious lack of passion in most of Howells's happier marriages may well result less from his supposed priggishness, or capitulation to the taboos of the market, or even from his belief that the passions are inevitably linked with selfishness, than from a fundamental awe in the face of the intimacy of the marriage union. In any case, so significant a relationship is marriage to Howells that in shaping and refining his vision of it over the years, he is shaping and refining as well, to a great extent, his vision of what men and women are capable of.

Their Wedding Journey and *Doctor Breen's Practice* (1881), Howells's first significant treatments of marriage, are widely dissimilar in plot and tone, but both works have as their central themes the notion that marriage enables one to deal with disorder and hence makes one happier and more civil. Failure to note Howells's intentions in them long led critics to misinterpret both works, regarding the first as a pleasant but largely insipid travelogue and the second as a poorly executed and finally evasive problem novel on the question of whether a woman ought to be a doctor.[9] Only recently have commentators noted the inherent grimness of the scenes through which the honeymooning Marches travel and the moral hysteria at the root of Grace Breen's decision to become a doctor, an emotional instability that ought to disqualify *this* woman from the medical profession but that clearly is not presented by Howells as typical of women doctors as a group.[10] In each of these novels, marriage is presented by Howells as a key means of mitigating the threat of the confusion that lurks both in the external world and within oneself.

The disorder that the Marches confront may well seem out of place on a wedding journey, but Howells's point here is that despite sentimental views, coming through a stormy courtship as the Marches have done (anti-romantically enough, before the novel begins) and choosing to live together forever after does not exempt a couple from misfortune. Indeed, one might almost see the Marches' less than idyllic honeymoon as little more than a telescoping of years of marriage and the exigencies attendant upon them. Further, he wants to show that although marriage cannot render people invulnerable, it can make it easier to bear what must be borne. And, from the first, he keeps constantly before his readers reminders of just how much there is to be borne. He begins by even declaring it "not particularly sane" to take a wedding journey or, in fact, any journey, in a world as chancy as ours. Certainly the prospect facing the Marches is, as Howells describes it, not an enticing one: "The drawbridges that gape upon the way, the trains that stand smoking and steaming on the track, the rail that has borne the wear so long that must soon snap under it, the deep-cut where the overhanging mass of rock trembles to its fall, the obstruction that a pitiless malice may have placed in your path."[11]

The Marches manage to survive their journey, but not before undergoing experiences which show that Howells's litany of the dangers of traveling across America (and obviously of traveling through life generally) does not overrate the possibilities of unpleasantness. New York City, where they spend a miserably hot day, is a disquieting urban wasteland peopled by belligerent multitudes whose daily routine involves carrying out mindless tasks without purpose or respite, even under a merciless summer sun. Their nightboat trip up the Hudson to Albany is marred first by the "cheap spectacle" (p. 45) of their sordid fellow passengers and then by a collision with a smaller vessel in which a man is mortally wounded. Niagara Falls, mecca of honeymooners, strikes them as less beautiful than menacing, "an awful homicide" (p. 88). So menacing is it, in fact, that the suggestible Isabel succumbs briefly to hysteria, and exasperates Basil by refusing fearfully to leave a little island near the falls because it would involve recrossing some (perfectly safe) bridges over which they have strolled just minutes before.[12] Later, at Montreal the irrationality unleashed in Isabel by the ominous beauty of the falls momentarily traps both of them as they have their first quarrel, one sparked by the inconsequential question of how many horses the carriage they hire for a tour ought to have. Finally, after dangers, irritations, and disappointments, the Marches return, "dustier than most of us would like to be a hundred years hence," to a Boston that "was equally dusty," where "the trees . . . before their own door [were] gray with dust" and the Virginia creeper under their window "hung shrivelled upon its trellis" (p. 178).

Little as there is in all this that bespeaks affirmation either in marriage or life, *Their Wedding Journey* is nevertheless not a pessimistic work. Keeping it from becoming so is the Marches' marriage itself, which, although not without its own difficulties, as glimpsed at Niagara and Montreal, is a good one because Basil and Isabel are always willing to reconcile their differences with love, common sense, and an ability to laugh at themselves—traits that ensure a civility that will inevitably serve them well in their dealings not only with each other but clearly with all the rest of the world. Consequently, punctuating his account of the grimmer aspects of life the Marches encounter are reminders by Howells that their relationship with each other keeps them from being unduly cast down. In New York City, as they stroll past a small churchyard, they smile at "the absurdity" of the thought that they shall ever join those in the ground whose "wedding-journeys are ended" (p. 20). Later, trudging through the midtown tumult, they regard themselves as "in it" but not "of it" (p. 33). Even on the nightboat, after the accident, Basil stands apart from the other passengers, "amused and shocked" to see that his pity for the injured man is merely "quite an abstraction." He tries "dutifully" to "imagine another issue to the disaster of the night, and to realize himself suddenly bereft of her who so filled his life," but to no avail; his effort turns into a "revery" (p. 50) that concludes with a long catalogue of Isabel's charms.

Although Howells's portrayal of Basil and Isabel as believing they are somehow invulnerable to the dark forces of life simply because they love each other adumbrates his suspicion in subsequent works that married life too often turns a pair inward, away from the world and social responsibility, here his tone is affectionate and untroubled, as he sees merely a fond delusion of newlyweds and their touching faith that marriage makes life better, a faith that he himself shares unabashedly at this point. And thus, with no misgivings, he simply establishes that when two persons come to accommodate themselves to each other's foibles, petulances, and even foolishness, and learn to question themselves and make the necessary compromises, they do, in fact, learn to bear more easily the grimmer aspects of life.[13] In this vein Howells declares of the Marches, "I find nothing more admirable in their behaviour than their willingness to make the very best of whatever would suffer itself to be made anything at all of" (p. 59). This applies, of course, not merely to the events of their journey but to those of their marriage as well. Thus, their ability to come through their less than idyllic wedding journey with their good natures intact augurs well for the years ahead. Fittingly, Howells notes on the Marches' return to Boston and home, "Their holiday was over to be sure, but their bliss had but begun; they had entered upon that long life of holidays which is happy marriage" (p. 179).

The idea that existence might be regarded as a "long life of holidays" would be utterly alien to Doctor Grace Breen, whose "New England girl's naturally morbid sense of duty" keeps her "in the irritation of perpetual self-question."[14] Rejected in love, she considers her misfortune somehow a failure of character on her part and has become a physician because of an ill-conceived notion that the profession will serve an expiatory purpose; "I wished to become a physician," she confesses, "because I was a woman, and because—because—I had failed where—other women's hopes are" (p. 43). Grace's self-accusatory nature and her idiosyncratic motivations reveal that Howells's primary focus in *Doctor Breen's Practice* is not on the controversial issue of whether women should enter professions that hitherto have been the preserves solely of men. Rather, it is on Grace Breen herself and the means by which she might become a less tormented woman. In examining Grace's problem, however, Howells *is*, in fact, dealing with a large social question, one that actually encompasses the controversy over women doctors, and that is whether women (and, by implication, men) stand much of a chance of leading fulfilling lives if unmarried or if isolated from their husbands.

Setting *Doctor Breen's Practice* at a fashionable resort as he does, Howells is able to present a sufficient number of dissatisfied unattached women in addition to Grace to justify his conclusion that a close marital relationship affords the best possibility of fulfillment for most people. Although none of the other women are under the obvious nervous strain that Grace is, being unattached has nonetheless had unfortunate effects on them. Her friend, Mrs. Maynard, separated from her husband and considering divorce, is hypochondriacal, flirtatious, and chronically dissatisfied. Though ostensibly happy in their marriages, the other wives at the resort are content to vacation, idling away their days in gossip and silly chatter about clothing and hairstyles, while their husbands remain in the city, laboring at their desks in careers about which the wives have little knowledge and less interest. The only unmarried young woman in the novel, apart from Grace, is the unremittingly romantic Miss Gleason, who idolizes Grace as a feminist heroine and is given to such febrile declarations as that it would be better for Mrs. Maynard to die in Grace's care than to be given over to a male physician as the terrified woman desires.

The likelihood that a good marriage can rescue women from either hysteria or frivolity is stressed through Howells's portrayal of the changes brought about in Mrs. Maynard and Grace by their commitments to marriage that end the novel. Mrs. Maynard's husband effects a reconciliation with her, and, almost immediately, she seems more sensible, as revealed in her statement to Grace about the difficulties of dissolving a marriage:

> "We had broken into each other's lives, and we couldn't get out again with all the divorces under the sun. That's the worst

of getting married: you break into each other's lives. . . . We don't either of us expect we can have things perfectly smooth, but we've agreed to rough it together when we can't. We've found out that we can't marry and become single, any more than we could die and come to life again." (P. 265)

Mrs. Maynard's new level-headedness foreshadows the improvement in Grace after she weds Libby. The brief glimpse Howells provides of their marriage indicates that it is a successful one and, as such, one that benefits not only wife and husband but society at large. Grace, though still a daughter of the Puritans, no longer lacerates herself. She has found repose, is happy with Libby, and is even practicing medicine contentedly by treating the sick children of her husband's employees. Although some who think "that she ought to have done for the sake of women what she could not do for herself" regard her as "sacrificed in marriage" (p. 271), neither she nor Howells thinks this way.

It is important to note too that Libby has grown through the marriage. A rather light sort when single, with his marriage he has taken over his father's factories, which he runs intelligently and humanely. Thus, Howells's doctrine in *Doctor Breen's Practice* that a good marriage makes for happier, more useful people is, ultimately, not limited in its application solely to women. Nor in dealing with this larger question of the effect of a good marriage on the people in it has Howells evaded or forgotten the specific aspect of the "Woman Question" with which the work at first seems to deal. Grace, as noted, is still practicing medicine (at her husband's suggestion, significantly) after her marriage, so Howells obviously finds nothing untoward about women in the professions. His major point, however, is that, regardless of a career, regardless of sex, being well-married is better than being alone.

After *Their Wedding Journey* and *Doctor Breen's Practice*, with their portrayals of marriage as virtually an unmitigated good for the married and all with whom they come into contact, Howells's significant marriage fiction for the next decade suggests that he is caught up in a deeper analysis than heretofore of American morality and its ramifications for the social and economic scene.[15] Beginning with *A Fearful Responsibility* in 1881 and reaching fuller fruition in *A Modern Instance* (1882), *The Rise of Silas Lapham* (1885), *The Minister's Charge* (1887), and *A Hazard of New Fortunes* (1890), Howells shifts his major emphasis in his depiction of marriages almost exclusively to an inquiry into the effects of matrimony (both at its best and worst) on society. During this period he seems increasingly to doubt that even the best of American marriages can do anything to ameliorate the crisis in American morality reflected in an inhumane social and economic structure. Still more pessimistically, he suspects at times that even the ostensibly good marriage—the union of a pair who love and comfort each other—only perpetuates the crisis by turning the pair away from active participation in the cause of social reform.

A Fearful Responsibility, the short novel with which this period of social inquiry in Howells's career begins, is less a study of any specific social problems than an examination of what Howells sees as a particularly troubling orientation toward the world, one that, though it manifests itself in a narrow context here, has far larger implications. In his ironical account of the timid Professor Owen Elmore, a man whose deadening influence blights the lives of those around him, Howells presents not only his first predominantly bleak novel but his first indication of profound doubts about marriage and its effects on society.[16] Though Elmore seems constitutionally a weak, self-indulgent man who, single or married, would be incapable of vital commitment to the welfare of others, it is clear in any case that his marriage exacerbates his shortcomings by providing him with a context of comfort and solace into which he can readily retreat to avoid responsibilities to others. More, the particular nature of his marriage is significant here, for it is manifestly an unromantic one, built on an essentially pragmatic accommodation by each mate to the needs of the other—a marriage, in short, that seems, like that of the Marches, to avoid the passions that Howells thinks such dangerous lures to destructive selfishness. When this sort of marriage becomes, as it does here, a producer and perpetuator of sterility for all of those whom it touches, it is an indicant of the strength of Howells's doubts about both marriage and the largely prudential, commonsensical assumptions about life on which he bases his views of what matrimony is at its best.

From start to finish, Elmore's sojourn in Venice, where the central action of *A Fearful Responsibility* takes place, marks him as a man singularly unresponsive to life and the needs of people. The sojourn begins with an escape from commitment, when Elmore, who "almost volunteered" to join the mass of his colleagues and students in the Union Army, decided prudentially that his "bronchitis was a disorder which active service would undoubtedly have aggravated."[17] His stay is characterized throughout by his ineffectuality, as Elmore, who attempts to convince himself that his service to his nation though not active is yet valuable, works desultorily on his *Story of Venice in the Lives of Her Heroes* and in conversation "fought for our cause against the English, whom he found everywhere all but in arms against us" (p. 5). And, ultimately, it is a sojourn destructive of love and vitality, as ironically the only efficacy manifested by Elmore in Venice or elsewhere is a life-denying one. Thrust, even amid the comforting beauty of Venice, into what he regards as a "fearful responsibility"—that of taking charge for some weeks, with his wife, of the beautiful, vibrant Lily Mayhew, younger sister of the woman who brought the Elmores together, Elmore destroys the romantic possibility in the girl's life and with it her vibrancy. Frightened by the possibility of complication in his own life when the girl and a young Austrian officer to whom she has not been properly introduced fall in love, Elmore chooses to disregard the Austrian's obvious personal merits (and even the further credential, a disquieting one to Elmore, of having a brother who is a volunteer in the Union Army) and puts the quietus on the blooming love by drily refusing it his approval. Because he desires to live "in that safety from consequences which he chiefly loved" (p. 104), Elmore opts for the comforts of rigid formalism and avoids the real involvement and the necessity of showing some real courage that allowing the unconventional love to have a chance would demand. From this time on, Lily is changed. A sober young woman for the rest of her stay, a sober young woman she remains on her return to America and through a long spinsterhood, which ends at last with an unexceptionable, if unexceptional, marriage to a clergyman.

With the end of the war, Elmore, back in America, remains as he was, dead and deadening and comfortable. Though his *Story of Venice in the Lives of Her Heroes* is completed only in a version much scaled-down from his original plans and "fell into a ready oblivion," with its sole reviewer noticing it "with three lines of exquisite slight" (p. 155), his career has nonetheless advanced, as his college, now a university and military institute, has named him president—the former president "fell at Fort Donelson" (p. 4). As the years pass, he has occasional misgivings about the part he played with Lily and the Austrian, wondering whether he may have "spoiled two lives" by venturing to "lay sacrilegious hands upon two hearts that a divine force was drawing together, and put them asunder" (p. 159); but he is quick to conclude that since "Lily could console herself" with a marriage, then maybe the Austrian too had "'got along'" (p. 164) and is just as quick to remind himself that he "had really acted the part of a prudent and conscientious man" and "was perfectly justifiable at every step" (p. 162).

Thus is Professor Owen Elmore revealed as a man whose conscientiousness seems unfortunately to reside most in his prudence about his own welfare, a man whose ability to commit himself to his country, his profession, his friends or acquaintances is highly suspect. Significantly, in light of Howells's developing views on matrimony, Elmore's marriage is not a troubled one. Typically, though he is a Casaubon sort who can "endure *ennui*" that makes his wife "frantic" (p. 11), he and she do not jar—they merely accommodate by accepting, largely with good humor, each other's ways. Part of his wife's habitual accommodation to Elmore's needs is her effort to keep him comfortable, even if this means kissing him "patronizingly . . . on the top of the head" or patronizing him when he is troubled about the part he has played in Lily's life by telling him reassuringly that "he has done the best anyone could do with the responsibilities that ought never to have been laid upon a man of his temperament and habits" (p. 162). It is also, in part, her comforting persuasiveness that helps convince Elmore that remembering his tendency to bronchitis is the better part of valor during the Civil War. This is a marriage, then, that retards the development of any possibility within Elmore for real commitment to anyone outside the marriage. By fostering a basically prudential and narrowly pragmatic orientation toward human relations, one devoid of idealism and a capacity for romantic commitment, this relationship encourages a selfish, timid isolation from life and from the responsibilities that being a member of the human community thrusts upon one. The lifelessness of this marriage and its effects is pointed up by the childlessness of this pair, often a sign for Howells of a union that in some signal way is a failure.[18] Certainly, idealism and romance are always exceedingly dangerous as Howells sees them, but in *A Fearful Responsibility*, as he embarks on a decade of close scrutiny of social problems, it is clear that he fears that marriages of the sort he most values may by totally eschewing idealism and romance have blighting effects on the capacity of those in them to make the courageous commitments necessary to effect social good in a time of moral difficulty for the nation.

A Modern Instance, a larger scrutiny of American social problems than *A Fearful Responsibility*, focuses on a whole society in moral chaos. The old religious life of New England and, apparently, of America itself is nearly extinct, and with it has gone a major means of leading man to a higher love than love of self. In this novel, at once a chief manifestation of this chaos and an exacerbation of it is the unhappy marriage, one that bears little resemblance to any marriage heretofore presented by Howells. The dismal union of Bartley Hubbard and Marcia Gaylord reflects the shortcomings of the society from which Bartley and Marcia spring, indeed, is virtually predestined to failure by those shortcomings; but it in turn has its own damaging effects on the social fabric by harming those unfortunate enough to come in close contact with it. Thus, their marriage is indubitably a "modern instance," a knot of misery that may well involve particular strands of sorrow all its own, but whose general configuration Howells sees as all too indicative of the way his countrymen live. He planned at one point to call the novel *An American Marriage*, a revealing title in that it makes the pain of the Hubbards no less representative and reveals once more his growing realization in this period of the pivotal relationship between society and marriage.

Always in judging the Hubbards, therefore, and in trying to assess how accountable they are, together and individually, for the ugliness in which they become entangled, one must bear in mind that at least partially extenuating their culpability is the social background that helps shape them, one with no lasting values.[19] The town of Equity in which Marcia grows up and in which her destructive passion for Bartley is spawned is one that has put behind itself the legacy of religious faith and moral seriousness that is the worthwhile part of its otherwise stultifying Puritan heritage. Instead, it has embraced a fashionably modern, liberal religious outlook that seems compounded of little more than church socials, "popular lectures," and the cheerfully held dogma "that the salvation of one's soul must not be made too depressing, or the young people would have nothing to do with it."[20] No less incapable of offering Bartley and Marcia real guidance is the more complex world of Boston in which they settle after their elopement. The city is heartless and fragmented, a mélange of disparate lives, all going their own feckless ways. Moreover, Bartley's career with the venal Boston newspapers that pander to the worst elements of the urban scene is as unfortunate a one as he could have fallen into, encouraging as it does his cynicism about human nature and cheapening his goals.

Even the few with whom the Hubbards come in contact who have values are incapable of serving as moral guides. The most vigorous moralists in the novel, Squire Gaylord and Eustace Atherton, apply their codes too rigidly and uncharitably, having long since lost a compassionate Christian basis for their ethical beliefs (though Atherton, unlike the squire, still professes to be a Christian). More poignantly, the Hallecks, who indeed reveal qualities of compassion and

grace that seem to mark them as the last remnants of an earlier, more admirable period, are able to maintain their way of
life solely by avoiding extensive participation in the contemporary scene. When Ben Halleck becomes involved with that
most typically "modern" of couples, the Hubbards, he is destroyed.

Consequently, given the bleakness of their society, it is not
surprising that increasing numbers of morally rudderless
characters like Bartley and Marcia meet and mate. But as
much an outgrowth of the *Zeitgeist* as these marriages may
be, they too wreak pernicious effects that will make the scene
even grimmer. Lest this point be missed, Howells makes it
twice in *A Modern Instance*. One of the most important aspects of this novel that has gone largely unnoticed is that it
contains two bad marriages, each of which hurts those who
come in contact with it and indirectly damages the larger social body.

Though it is the Hubbard marriage on which the work cen-
ters, this union has been in large measure blighted even before it begins by a disastrous earlier marriage, that of
Marcia's parents, Squire and Mrs. Gaylord. The inability of
this ill-matched pair to maintain a real marriage makes it all
but impossible for Marcia ever to establish a relationship of
mutual accommodation with Bartley. The headstrong, passionate, yet oddly withdrawn father who rarely leaves his office and the cowed, quietly selfish mother who has
"involuntarily come to live largely for herself" (p. 102) are
present psychologically and spiritually in every confrontation their daughter has with Bartley, even as they are absent
in her younger years, when they find it more convenient to
allow Marcia her own way rather than to guide her. As a result of the influences exerted on her by her parents' marriage, Marcia's demeanor as wife becomes a series of
pendulum-like swings between slavish submission and passionate outbursts of possessiveness, reflecting her desperate
desire for the affection that she never received in adequate
measure from her parents and revealing as well her curious
inheritance of both her father's overweening will and her
mother's humiliating self-effacement.

Marcia is thus rendered incapable of giving the morally weak Bartley (himself an orphan, with no worthwhile example of marriage before him to emulate) the probing, compassionate criticism he needs. With a less unstable wife, Bartley might have turned out better, as Howells notes several times. Early in the novel, when Bartley is with the decent, honorable drifter, Kinney, Howells comments, "A curious feeling possessed him; sickness of himself as of someone else; a longing to be something different; a sense of captivity to habits and thoughts and hopes that centered in himself and served him alone" (p. 116–17). And shortly after Bartley marries Marcia, her father warns her, "You can make him worse by being a fool" (p. 189). Undoubtedly, then, for all his failings, Bartley at the start of his marriage is capable of being both better and worse. With a wife less hampered by the failed marriage of her parents, a wife who could regard him not as a possession to be at once jealously guarded and humbly worshipped, Bartley might grow, might rise beyond a love of mere comfort. Instead, he becomes ever more corrupt, ever more deeply immured in the prison of self-gratification, where he is joined by his wife, who, damaged by the past and betrayed by the weak husband whom she is powerless to aid, is no more able to free herself than he.[21]

Pursuing their mutually destructive courses of self-gratification, Bartley and Marcia have deleterious impact on those about them, as Howells shows that the effects of a bad marriage are visited not merely on the children conceived in it and their future mates. Others too are immediately caught up in the disaster of the Hubbards and hurt by it. Kinney's idea for an autobiographical narrative is stolen by Bartley. Ben Halleck, whose unrequited, illicit passion for Marcia is fired by her evident unhappiness, ends miserably as a fundamentalist minister afraid to think. Finally, Marcia's own father destroys his health with his virulent attack on Bartley at the divorce trial. Though less obvious than the pain brought to those close to the Hubbards, the indirect effects of the wreckage of their marriage are no less sinister. It is almost impossible to note what all the unfortunate manifestations might be, but some are readily apparent. The Halleck family and Atherton are deeply troubled by Ben's unhappiness, Mrs. McAllister's dangerous flirtatiousness is encouraged by Bartley, the readers of Bartley's newspaper articles presumably have their baser instincts encouraged by them, thereby lowering further the general social tone. Some such catalogue as this might be drawn up of the cancerous effect of one failed marriage on the people around it, and even this cannot nearly be all-inclusive. What, for instance, of the future effect on Bartley's own child? Do the ripples circling out from a bad marriage ever cease? Howells seems to have his doubt that they do.

Also given to such doubts is Atherton, who alone in *A Modern Instance* sees that it is the crucial role of marriage to help maintain the well-being of society by repressing the "natural man," who is little more than a "wild beast" (p. 472). Marriage does this, Atherton believes, by promoting the "implanted goodness that saves—the seed of righteousness treasured from generation to generation, and carefully watched and tended by disciplined fathers and mothers in the hearts where they have dropped it" (p. 472). Should any marriage fail to do this, all of society is damaged, for "no one sins or suffers to himself in a civilized state. . . . Every link in the chain feels the effect of the violence, more or less intimately. We rise or fall together . . ." (p. 474). Hence, divorce, to which the Hubbards resort, is for Atherton a heinous modern innovation that tempts "people to marry with a mental reservation," and weakens "every marriage bond with the guilty hope of escape whenever a fickle mood, or secret lust, or wicked will may dictate" (p. 451). Though Atherton is more than a little pompous and unyielding through much of the novel, the dire consequences for society wrought by an unhappy marriage are all too apparent a confirmation of his dark vision for one to dismiss it lightly.

It is worthy of note that the only mitigation of the dominant bleakness of *A Modern Instance* resides in a successful marriage, that of Atherton himself, to the Boston socialite Clara Kingsbury. The marriage is a good one, for, like all of Howells's happy couples, they are already obviously caught up in a process of mutual accommodation. They talk out their ideas freely and affectionately criticize each other's foibles and crotchets, indicating that together they will learn and grow. Clara, gaining some ballast from Atherton's conservatism and solemnity, no longer resembles the flighty, slightly fatuous, rich girl do-gooder she seemed to be early in the novel. Atherton, under the influence of Clara's constitutional warmth and kindness, is no longer the arbitrary moralist he was before the marriage. Nevertheless, the mitigation here is slight at best, for the marriage is seen but briefly, a flicker of brightness in the midst of an overwhelming gloom. Consequently, Atherton's final words, "Ah, I don't know! I don't know!" (p. 514), which close the novel, though perhaps a healthy acknowledgment on his part of the folly of attempting to apply his long-held principles categorically and without charity, are also a sign of his inability even in the midst of what seems to be a good marriage to see any applicable system of values for coping with the wreckage caused by bad marriages and the moral emptiness that spawns them.

Thus, both the ostensibly happy marriage of the Elmores in *A Fearful Responsibility* and the hideously unhappy one of the Hubbards in *A Modern Instance* reflect Howells's growing worry about the impact of marriage on American life in a time of moral difficulties. Further doubts surface in *The Rise of Silas Lapham*, in which Howells explores at greater length the possibility touched on in *A Fearful Responsibility* that even loving husbands and wives may lead each other farther astray from a healthy social consciousness than the general moral decline has already led them.

That the Lapham marriage has long been a good one is obvious. In its early years, Persis, a former schoolteacher with a strong Puritan resolve, was Silas's moral and commercial mentor. It was she who both encouraged him in starting his business and persuaded him to set it aside to fight for the Union during the Civil War. It was Persis too who instilled in Silas his crucial sense of moral compunction about having forced Rogers out of the partnership with him. Thus, the marriage was indeed, as Howells puts it, "a rise in life for him."[22] Nor has Silas alone risen. Persis's comment that she wishes Irene "was going to marry such a fellow as *you* were, Si, that had to make every inch of his own way" (p. 181) reveals how fully she admires her husband and derives comfort from his strength. Moreover, their openness with each other, their frequent banter, and their willingness to share the responsibility and grief for Irene's unhappiness and for their imminent financial ruin all indicate a strong marriage. Lest readers overlook its success, Howells begins the novel by quickly contrasting the Lapham marriage with the disastrous Hubbard marriage, in which there is no such close communion between a pair of equals as there is here.

Nevertheless, for all of the happiness of this marriage, there are, increasingly, disquieting elements in it. George N. Bennett notes aptly that the strong mutual affection of the Laphams has contributed to their social ignorance.[23] This seems at first to manifest itself merely in terms of comic gaucherie (witness their house furnishings, described in lavish detail by Howells for full humorous effect), but ultimately its results are far more sinister. For Howells, the probing social observer, manners are often reflective of morals, and Silas's lack of the social amenities is ultimately a function of parochialism, a commitment solely to himself and his family. His crass patronizing of Bromfield Corey when that Brahmin visits his office, his boorish bragging at the Corey dinner, even his frenetic buggy driving are of a piece with his painting of his name all over the landscape, his forcing of Rogers out of the partnership, and his willingness at least to consider a shady deal. All indicate that Silas is so devout a husband and father that he has never gained an adequate awareness of the necessity of concern with others outside the family (save for Zerilla Dewey, whose father once did him and his the service of saving his life).

Further pointing up how effectively strong commitments to one's spouse and to a pleasant marriage may have antisocial tendencies are the other marriages glimpsed in *The Rise of Silas Lapham*. The comfortable Corey marriage offers Bromfield every incentive to continue his easy course of wry dilettantism and to ignore the promptings of his own incipient social conscience, which is manifested by his remark that if he were poor he would break into a rich person's home that is vacant for the summer "and camp out on the grand piano" (p. 194). Similarly unmoved by a social conscience is Milton Rogers, who uses his wife's illness as an excuse for his dishonest business scheme. Even Zerilla Dewey is contemplating a divorce so that she can marry Mr. Wemmel, who "stands ready" to "provide a comfortable home" (p. 296) for her and her mother.

In this vein, it is particularly noteworthy that, despite the closeness of Silas and Persis, Silas's climactic moral rise is initiated not by his marriage as it currently exists but by the atavistic promptings within him of the waning Puritan moral heritage that Persis instilled in him in the early days of their marriage. The "economy of pain" doctrine that Silas adopts from the resolution of the Pen-Tom-Irene triangle and applies to the moral question in the business sphere is simply a renaming of the old New England moral imperatives. (This is why the "Wrestling Jacob" allusion used to describe Silas in the throes of moral struggle is so apposite, establishing as it does a traditional religious frame of reference otherwise absent in this novel.) Moreover, Persis herself has long since lost this heritage with the rise in Lapham prosperity and wavers crucially on the question of Rogers's shady proposal, while revealing mere querulousness and undue suspicion in dealing with Silas's relationship to Zerilla. Despite her devotion to Silas, then, Persis offers him little help when the moral crisis comes; and this makes for some disquieting implications in what, finally, is an otherwise affirmative novel. One is left to ponder gloomily whether most Americans, who are farther removed than Silas from the old religious doctrines, might have the capacity to rise that he has, particularly if they are devoted to wives similarly out of touch with those doctrines.[24]

Certainly no reassurance on this score is offered in Howells's next novel, *The Minister's Charge*, in which the inequities, the ugliness, and the pervasive failure in compassion that characterize the Boston scene lead the Reverend Mr. Sewell to deliver his compelling sermon on "complicity" (adumbrated earlier, as we have seen, by Atherton in *A Modern*

Instance). In it Sewell admonishes his congregation that "no man sinned or suffered to himself alone" and, further, that it is "the virtuous who fancied themselves indifferent spectators" who are most blameworthy.[25] Admirable as his declaration of this principle may be, it is obvious nonetheless that Sewell, a modern, liberal minister with no ties to the earlier New England zeal, lacks the moral energy to bring himself to act on it. Moreover, it is significant that the major force discouraging Sewell's efforts to live up to the demands of his own sermon is the influence exerted on him by his doting wife.

Nowhere is the necessity for Sewell to act with a sense of complicity more apparent than in his dealings with his "charge" Lemuel Barker, who has come to Boston from the country on the strength of Sewell's ill-advised and dishonest praise of his poetry. Unfortunately, Sewell's commitment to Lemuel is an uneasy and intermittent one at best, and one with which his wife has little sympathy. Convinced (probably wrongly) that her husband taxes himself too much with the concerns of others, she refuses one evening to allow Barker to see him for advice, an action that leads to devastating repercussions. Impulsively, Barker leaves Bromfield Corey's employ and goes to work as a streetcar conductor by way of irrevocably committing himself to marry Statira Dudley. On his new job, he suffers a severe injury that nearly kills him. Thus, Mrs. Sewell's intervention, regret it though she subsequently does, reveals just how damaging a failure to acknowledge one's complicity can be.

In his vacillating on the question of complicity, Sewell contrasts most markedly with Lemuel himself, before whose rigorous latter-day Puritan vision of morality the minister quails, confessing, "He has an eye of terrible and exacting truth. I feel myself on trial before him. He holds me up to a standard of sincerity that is killing me" (p. 143). Given Howells's continuing concern with the relations between marriage and society, it is not surprising that the contrast between the two is most clearly delineated in their differing views about a promise of marriage. Trying to convince Lemuel that it is an act of misguided self-sacrifice to honor his engagement to the seriously ill factory girl, Sewell is arguing from an awareness of what makes for a pleasant marriage. To him Lemuel's refusal to break the engagement obviously seems little more than quixotic. However, it is nevertheless the only example in *The Minister's Charge* of someone attempting, at the real cost to himself that the doctrine demands, to put complicity into action. Though the marriage might not be as comfortable a one as Sewell's, it would be one in which Statira's presumably brief life might run its final course without the pain of rejection, and one in which Lemuel might advance even further in character and in his sense of complicity through the test imposed by renunciation. Though in modern New England such a decision would make him as incongruous a figure as his old diehard feminist mother is in her militant bloomer costume, it also would reveal him as a man of moral stature surpassing that of most of his contemporaries. In any case, Howells, perhaps unable to face the bleakness of such an affirmation, has Statira beg off in a totally unconvincing ending that does not do credit to the discomfiting implication of the rest of the work.

Consequently, those commentators who believe that *The Minister's Charge* is flawed because of the apparent absence in its plot of an application of the doctrine of complicity have been looking in the wrong place.[26] Lemuel, who reveals a sense of what complicity involves, is the very character toward whom the minister should be directing more wholeheartedly his own sense of complicity. In fact, as Corey notes ironically, Lemuel "could formulate Sewell's theology a great deal better than Sewell could" (p. 387). Unfortunately, Sewell, somewhat reminiscent of Owen Elmore, is a fundamentally weak man whose lack of conviction and love of ease are encouraged by his wife and who is unable to learn fully his own lesson. As with *The Rise of Silas Lapham*, then, Howells reveals here that in fallen times even as potentially redemptive a relationship as marriage can hinder the growth of an active social consciousness.

With *A Hazard of New Fortunes*, Howells's examination of the impact of marriage on society takes on an added dimension as the novel reflects his strong suspicion that the social and economic chaos of late-nineteenth-century America is perhaps a manifestation of cosmic disorder or mismanagement.[27] Though Howells continued in the face of this realization to fight the good fight for social reform, as his personal activities and his Altrurian novels reveal,[28] *A Hazard of New Fortunes* and other non-utopian novels to come, such as *The Shadow of a Dream, The World of Chance* (1893), and *The Landlord at Lion's Head* (1898), display a deep sense that much of the pain, injustice, and evil in life is inexplicable and irremediable. Thus, in *A Hazard of New Fortunes,* Howells turns to the existential question of how a person should live in a world in which suffering seems unavoidable and large-scale reform inevitably ineffectual. In answering this question, nowhere does Howells pull back from his advocacy of his central doctrines of complicity and the economy of pain. However, he does emphasize that their application, if it is to be even marginally successful, must be limited in scope, that is, limited to those within one's immediate ken.[29] If *A Hazard of New Fortunes* proves anything, it proves that one's legitimate sense of responsibility for others must be channeled toward those for whom one can have some real prospect of doing good. One suspects that the large hope behind this thinking for Howells, one that he would readily admit is a slim one in an inequitable universe, is that if enough people are decent to those nearby them, in the long run a more humane society—like that of Altruria—might evolve.

With this new awareness of the limited scope in which complicity must be operative comes for Howells a renewal of his faith in marriage, which he now presents for the first time as a union that at its best instills in the partners not merely a sense of comfort in a troubled world but an awareness of complicity. In learning to care for each other, they can see more readily that they need to care for others about them. Certainly this is what occurs for the Marches through their extended initiation into the facts of life as they move to the most chaotic, most modern, hence most American of cities, New York.

Though the house-hunting adventure with which the Marches' New York residence begins is probably overlong, as most commentators have noted, it is not as devoid of significance as it might at first seem.[30] Rather, the mutual support of husband and wife (apparent even under the badinage) as they look for a stable home in a cold and menacing city establishes the central tension that Howells portrays throughout the novel: complicity and an attempt to establish order in conflict with chaos and selfishness. Moreover, the mutual support manifested by the Marches in this episode prefigures the tenor of their relations as they confront a more important crisis later, Basil's threat to resign if Lindau is fired from the staff of *Every Other Week*. At first, Isabel, full of misgivings about their economic future, berates Basil shrilly for his decision; but almost immediately thereafter she defends him, acknowledging, "I had to have my say out."[31] Her response and Basil's refusal to indulge in recriminations of Isabel for her outburst display vividly how marriage encourages a sense of complicity, as a willingness to help each other makes them more receptive to the notion that they must help others with whom they come in contact. Presumably, had Basil not learned this lesson through years of marriage to Isabel he would be less likely to fight for Lindau.

The stability and the sense of what complicity involves that are developed in the Marches' marriage contrast strongly with the chaos and irresponsibility in which many of the other characters are caught up and which they, in fact, tend to perpetuate. Significantly, each of the more troubled (and troublesome) characters is either unmarried or trapped in a bad marriage. The selfish ass Beaton, the incurably romantic and histrionic Miss Vance, the dilettante writer Kendrick, and the absolutist exponents of apocalyptic reform Lindau and Conrad are all unmarried. The Dryfoos marriage has long since gone to pieces, with Dryfoos so dominating his wife that, like Mrs. Gaylord in *A Modern Instance*, she retreats from ties to others, leaving her daughters, Christina and Mela, to grow up with no guidance that will inculcate goals greater than self-gratification. Conrad, the one member of this unfortunate family who attempts to act with a sense of complicity, sees no evidence at home of how it can be operative in a limited context and mistakenly comes to believe that the doctrine is applicable only on a grandiose scale.

Through much of the novel, Fulkerson reveals a commitment to self as glaring as that shown by some of the most misguided characters in the book, but his willingness (albeit halfhearted) to heed Miss Woodburn's urging and stand by March during the Lindau crisis convinces her to marry him and leads one to suspect that his long-dormant good traits will continue to awaken and grow under her wifely tutelage. (Somewhat heavy-handedly, Howells notes that the honeymooning Fulkersons take the same "line of travel that the Marches had taken in their wedding journey" [p. 429].) Thus, Howells again suggests that a successful marriage will probbly serve to make one more humane, more civil, more responsible in a disordered world. The existential chaos, doubtless, is real for Howells, but he nevertheless does not intend Basil's hope that somehow all that occurs "means good" (p. 423) to be mere sentimentalism. Basil's own marriage is calculated by Howells to indicate that people can attain some order and goodness here, and if this does not ensure that in the long run the universe means good, it is meant to offer one grounds for at least the encouragement offered by a slender hope.

The problem with all this, though, is, I suspect, that the hope here may just be too slender. For all his obvious intentions to turn this exceedingly grim novel somewhat in the direction of affirmation through the March marriage and the implicit prospects of the Fulkerson marriage, the effect just does not come off. As with the Atherton union in *A Modern Instance*, one perceives at best a terribly slight mitigation of the prevailing darkness, but nothing more. The pointless deaths of Conrad and Lindau, the destruction of the Dryfoos family and, symbolically, of the whole stable rural way of life that produced them, the growth of huge cities that, permeated by injustice, are a place of apparently overpowering instability and lovelessness, and, finally, the universal absurdity of which all of these may ultimately be manifestations cannot in any meaningful way be offset by the marriage of Basil and Isabel March. Further, the effect of their marriage, paradoxically, is to heighten the horror here rather than to lessen it as Howells obviously wishes to. By establishing with the March marriage what is essentially an ideal standard of behavior that most are unable to meet, Howells inadvertently makes the human failures in this work all the more telling and painful. Clearly, the March marriage is meant to represent countless numbers of similar marriages that exist, presumably, even in the America of *A Hazard of New Fortunes*, and perhaps, taken together, countless numbers of them might balance or offset the absurdity and horror depicted here; but we do not see these marriages. We see only one in this novel, and it is not enough. And, one suspects, we do not see more because Howells at this stage of his career is too overwhelmed by the darkness to really believe in such marriages or their efficacy save as ideals. Finally, despite his efforts to present the March marriage as an unadulterated good, Howells does reveal some continuing suspicion that the good marriage might restrict one's full development, as Basil, seeking to follow a line of bleakly deterministic thought at the close, a line that might lead to some insights of moral significance, is warned away from his possibly heterodox speculations by a fearful Isabel, forcing him to his response, "*I* don't know what it all means, Isabel, though I believe it means good." Viewed in this context, his remark seems less the affirmation that Howells probably intended than a sentimental sop that Basil throws his wife—and himself, really—at her urgings. *A Hazard of New Fortunes*, then, remains a dark novel, its darkness in no way substantially lessened by Howells's essentially unconvincing reaffirmation of the value of marriage.

After *A Hazard of New Fortunes*, Howells restricts his treatments of major social injustice and of plans for social reform to his utopian novels. Responding, it seems, to his suspicion that the larger-scale suffering, injustice, and evil in the world are inexplicable and irremediable—a suspicion he held despite his continuing personal efforts for various reforms and despite his utopian novels[32]—Howells in the main body of his fiction after 1890 focuses on the timeless failings of men and women and explores ways in which individuals can make an often painful existence more tolerable for themselves and those close to them. In keeping with this shift of emphasis, Howells, as with his first marriage works, *Their Wedding Journey* and *Doctor Breen's Practice*, seeks to show simply that marriage at its best can make those in it more comfortable as well as more humane to those with whom they come into contact. However, the problems evidenced in that reaffirmation in *A Hazard of New Fortunes* persist, as Howells is not always quite as convincing from this time on as he intends to be in portraying marriage as a force for good.

Though *The Shadow of a Dream* presents the Marches at a stage of their lives before their move to New York, it was written after *A Hazard of New Fortunes* and shows its influence. The sense of complicity Howells depicts as awakened in the Marches during their experience in New York is in evidence here, as Basil and Isabel find themselves increasingly drawn into the torment caused the Faulkners and Nevil by Faulkner's recurring dream that his wife and his best friend Nevil are only waiting for his death to declare their love for each other and marry. At first the Marches have misgivings about their involvement, but Isabel's remark that perhaps they have held themselves "too much aloof—tried to escape ties"[33] is a reminder of Howells's conclusion in the earlier novel that a good marriage can readily encourage an awareness of complicity. Though the Marches cannot retard the seemingly inevitable process of disaster in which Faulkner, Hermia, and Nevil are all at last caught up, their effort to do so is clearly intended by Howells to speak well for the effect their pleasant union has on their sense of responsibility for others.

Unfortunately, the Faulkners have no such marriage. Kept from it as they are by their excessive romanticism, obscure psychological difficulties,[34] and (perhaps initiating all) what appears to be nothing less than a dark fate in a frightening universe,[35] they serve in their married relations, like the Hubbards, as a telling example of how a bad marriage can increasingly turn a pair not only from each other but from all meaningful contact with the world about them. Though the Marches themselves finally do not know what to make of the Faulkner marriage and its horrible aftermath and even disa-

45

gree in their tentative attempts to come to some understanding, with Basil wanting to absolve the unfortunate trio from all responsibility for what has occurred and Isabel tending to believe that the Faulkners and Nevil are indeed morally accountable, their effort to struggle to meaning together is a reminder at the close of the work of the sort of shared relationship a good marriage can develop, one that, further, may lead the married pair to a sense of close ties with others.

Consequently, the March marriage here, as in *A Hazard of New Fortunes*, is calculated to provide a modicum of affirmation in a work of otherwise unremitting bleakness. However, here as in the earlier work and as with the Atherton marriage still earlier, Howells's effort is not entirely successful.[36] Because the horror Howells presents is again so overwhelming, involving as it does here the awful destruction of three essentially good persons, the quintessentially commonplace March marriage once more is dwarfed in its impact on the reader by the darkness with which it comes into contact. And, ironically, it again works—against, one assumes, Howells's intentions—to enhance the grimness by grounding the horror in which the Faulkners and Nevil are caught up in a context of everyday reality and making everyone and every marriage seem all too vulnerable to the terror that can lurk in life. Further, this marriage once again seems to blunt Basil's efforts to confront painful truths and to grow, perhaps, by doing so. When he suggests, contemplating the pain undergone by his unfortunate trio of friends, that "existence" may be "all a miserable chance, a series of stupid, blundering accidents" (p. 59) and, later, that "they were all three destined to undergo what they underwent, and . . . what happened to them was not retribution, not penalty . . . but simply fate" (p. 114), Isabel will have none of it and cuts off his speculations effectually. So, as before, Howells does reveal some residual suspicions that even the good marriage might keep one so insulated from hard clashes with reality as to prevent the development that might make even a good man a better one. Certainly, the last March tales, the late minor works, *A Circle in the Water* (1895), *A Pair of Patient Lovers* (1901), *An Open-Eyed Conspiracy* (1897), and

Their Silver Wedding Journey (1899), reveal no further development in the Marches. In them they are a contented and kind but essentially uninspiring couple, reflective of Howells's regained faith in the power of matrimony to lead a pair to happy and moderately useful lives, and portrayed in a pleasant haze of sentimental affection and gentle amusement as a likable pair who have their silly but lovable foibles and crotchets.

Like *A Hazard of New Fortunes, The Shadow of a Dream*, and the final March narratives, Howells's last extended treatments of marriage, *The Kentons* (1902), *Miss Bellard's Inspiration* (1908), and *The Vacation of the Kelwyns*, all are geared to present the regained faith in marriage as a potential means of benefiting society by providing people with comfort and stability in an often chaotic world, restraining their dangerous impulses of romantic individualism, and encouraging the growth of a sense of complicity. Also, given Howells's renewed faith in marriage, it is not surprising that each work ends with either a marriage or one impending that should bode well for those in it (though Lillias Bellard's marriage may be more liable to pitfalls than Ellen Kenton's or Parthenope and Emerance's, which close the other two novels).

In each of these three works, characters given to dangerously romantic outlooks or unrestrained, destructive self-assertiveness are contrasted with those in long-established happy marriages, whose learned willingness to support each other lends itself to a sense of social responsibility. In *The Kentons* Ellen Kenton, who pines morbidly for the worthless suitor Bittridge; her younger brother, Boyne, who is prone to fairy-tale fantasies of performing chivalric deeds; and her younger sister, the frivolous and flirtatious Lottie—all are incapable of the self-restraint and sense of commitment to others that their level-headed parents, Judge and Mrs. Kenton, have attained through years of marriage. How marriage operates to instill these traits is shown vividly when Judge Kenton wants to horsewhip Bittridge for his insufferably insolent behavior: his wife talks him out of it. However, his son, Richard, who fails to talk to his own wife beforehand, administers the public whipping and then must face the physical and spiritual revulsion this ugly act inspires in him (and face, as well, his wife's quiet disapproval as she comforts him). Hence, as usual, marriage restrains the irrational and works for social decency. In like manner, the Crombies in *Miss Bellard's Inspiration* attempt to minister to the Mevisons, whose marriage is being destroyed by the unfortunate Mrs. Mevison's crazed behavior; and they counsel Lillias Bellard, whose own future is endangered by her penchant for romantic self-dramatization. Finally, in *The Vacation of the Kelwyns*, the somewhat silly idealist, Parthenope, and the impulsive Emersonian individualist, Emerance, differ distinctly from the Kelwyns and Kites, who, whatever limitations they may have, are not foolishly romantic. Moreover, the "mundane working relationship" as George N. Bennett calls it,[37] that these two couples establish in their marriages renders each pair better able to be at least civil to the other despite their differences and their lack of understanding of each other's ways. Like all the successfully married couples in Howells's later works, then, they learn (however imperfectly) to consider more than just themselves.

All of these last three major marriage novels are conceived by Howells to be, as he wrote of *The Kentons*, "flowers picked from the fruitful fields of our common life";[38] and through them he seeks to teach, as Judge Kenton tells his daughter, that "wherever life is simplest and purest and kindest, that is the highest civilization."[39] Certainly, the happy marriages that he depicts in them are made of husbands and wives who are basically simple, pure, and kind persons, men and women whose marriages do reflect well on the institution—and yet the works just do not convince. *The Kentons*, in great part a tribute to the Ohio and Ohioans of Howells's youth,[40] is imbued with an affection for Judge and Mrs. Kenton and the bucolic, Midwestern values that shaped them that is touching but that also consigns them and their marriage and all both represent to a realm of ideality linked inextricably with an earlier, less complex America than that of 1902. Obviously sincere and unstinting in his approval of this pair (and their son and his wife, as well) as Howells is, his own conviction here is never in doubt. But even if such mar-

riages as those of the Kentons do exist, he fails nonetheless
to convince that they do, that the sort of marriage depicted
here, compounded as it is of unfailing mutual understanding
and accommodation and unfading love, is a product of anything but his own fond, idealizing memories. The Crombies,
in *Miss Bellard's Inspiration*, whom George N. Bennett notes
"might be described as cousins to Isabel and Basil March,"[41]
are rendered with some affection and with a quiet, humorous
tolerance for their ineffectuality and their penchant for self-
isolation. But they are a palely drawn and rather tedious couple withal, and the Mevisons in their collapsing marriage are,
unfortunately, despite Howells's obvious intentions otherwise, a far more telling argument against marriage than the
Crombies are for it. Finally, *The Vacation of the Kelwyns*,
subtitled *An Idyl of the Middle Eighteen-Seventies*, does
present two moderately successful marriages; but, like the
marriages in *The Kentons*, they are presented in a haze of
ideality that renders them less than entirely convincing.
Nearly forty years before this novel, Howells presented a
union similar to that of the Kelwyns. It was the marriage of
the Elmores in *A Fearful Responsibility*. Here as there, a
fumbling, timid, pedantic type is secured from having to confront things as they are by a patronizing wife. In the earlier
work, the marriage was treated with a probing irony and
helped initiate a decade of close scrutiny of marriage and its
role in society. Here, in Howells's final treatment of matrimony, the marriage is, like that of the Kites, only a mildly
diverting bit of gentle comedy in an "idyl" of long ago.

In *The Vacation of the Kelwyns*, his last published novel,
Howells presents a Shaker preacher who delivers a vitriolic
attack "on marriage and giving in marriage."[42] One who
seems most likely to concur with this diatribe is Mrs. Allison,
the much put-upon wife of the town drunkard; but she does
not. Instead, she tells Parthenope, who is considering marriage with Emerance, "Don't you let them Shakers get
around you with their talk. I've had a hard time as any, but
it's more of an even thing than they say, marryin' is. *I* know,
and they don't" (p. 168). For Howells too, both at the start of

his career and the close, marriage is "more of an even thing" than any of its detractors might say. As early as 1869, in a review of Horace Greeley's *Recollections of a Busy Life*, Howells regards marriage as central to "all that really holds human society together for good."[43] And this is a view to which he seeks to return with *A Hazard of New Fortunes*, striving to admire the institution as a source of comfort, order, and, most importantly, of the moral strength that can enable one to rise above humanity's chief besetting evil, the unrestrained commitment to self. His inability to be entirely convincing in portraying this view is obviously in no way attributable to lack of effort, as he returned to it again and again. It *is* attributable, one suspects, to his development in the eighties of a real sensitivity to the horror in human existence, a horror that overweighed, as he rendered it in his works, the affirmation of his happy marriages. As a concomitant of this, his failure to be entirely convincing is also perhaps attributable to his tendency to retreat from the horror to the creation of an essentially sentimental perspective of marriage—a highly romantic, highly personal vision of an enduring relationship built on quiet happiness, gentle humor, willing accommodation, and unfailing love. The vision is poignant but, unfortunately, one that as he presents it fails to compel belief.

1. Kenneth Eble, "Howells' Kisses," *American Quarterly* 9 (Winter 1957): 441.

2. Howells worked on *The Vacation of the Kelwyns* periodically over many years and may have finished it several years before leaving it as a completed manuscript at his death.

3. Wendell Stacy Johnson, *Sex and Marriage in Victorian Poetry* (Ithaca, N.Y.: Cornell University Press, 1975), p. 38.

4. William Dean Howells, *The Day of Their Wedding* (New York: Harper, 1896), pp. 86–87. Howells's thinking here is not far from what Richard McGhee describes as the perception of Victorian writers that marriage must keep the "notions of duty and desire in balance" (*Marriage, Duty, and Desire in Victorian Poetry and Drama* [Lawrence: Regents Press of Kansas, 1980], p. ix).

5. William Dean Howells, *A Pair of Patient Lovers* (New York: Harper, 1901), p. 52.

6. William Dean Howells, *Through the Eye of the Needle* (1907; Bloomington: Indiana University Press, 1968), p. 397. This point is also made in Howells's novel *April Hopes*.

7. Two of these rare exceptions are Arthur Mevison (in *Miss Bellard's Inspiration*) and Mrs. Royal Langbrith (in *The Son of Royal Langbrith*), both of whom are good (though rather weak) people who have had miserably unhappy marriages because of difficult mates.

8. William Dean Howells, *Their Silver Wedding Journey* (New York: Harper, 1899), p. 156.

9. Among the studies that, I believe, underrate Howells's achievement in *Their Wedding Journey* are William M. Gibson, "Materials and Form in Howells' First Novels," *American Literature* 19 (May 1947): 158–66, and John K. Reeves, "The Limited Realism of Howells' *Their Wedding Journey*," *PMLA* 77 (December 1962): 617–28. Two writers who see Howells as failing to answer the woman-as-doctor question satisfactorily in *Doctor Breen's Practice* are Oscar W. Firkins, *William Dean Howells* (Cambridge, Mass.: Harvard University Press, 1924), p. 96, and Edwin H. Cady, *The Road to Realism* (Syracuse, N.Y.: Syracuse University Press, 1956), p. 207.

10. For *Their Wedding Journey*, see Marion W. Cumpiano, "The Dark Side of *Their Wedding Journey*," *American Literature* 40 (January 1969): 472–86, and David L. Frazier, "*Their Wedding Journey*: Howells' Fictional Craft," *New England Quarterly* 42 (September 1969): 323–49. For *Doctor Breen's Practice*, see George N. Bennett, *Wiliam Dean Howells: The Development of a Novelist* (Norman: University of Oklahoma Press, 1959), pp. 108–13.

11. William Dean Howells, *Their Wedding Journey* (1872; Bloomington: Indiana University Press, 1968), p. 13. For this and the others of Howells's novels, all page references after the first to each will be to the edition cited and will appear in the text.

12. Gary Hunt argues, with little real evidence, I think, that this scene reflects Isabel's fear of sexuality and is one of several in the work that reveal the sexual terror of both Marches ("'A Reality That Can't Be Quite Definitely Spoken': Sexuality In *Their Wedding Journey*," *Studies in the Novel* 9 [Spring 1977]: 17–32).

13. Alfred Habegger suggests that in the nine works in which the Marches appear, "Isabel finds more of a refuge than does Basil," who usually "acts as the senior partner, protector, rescuer" (p. 83). Actually, I suspect, *Their Wedding Journey* and the subsequent works show that Basil finds marriage to be as much of a refuge as does Isabel and that Basil's assumption of the senior partner's role is far less consistent than Habegger asserts it to be. Certainly, Basil seems anything but a "senior partner" when, in *A Hazard of New Fortunes*, he returns home to tell Isabel of his refusal to submit to Dryfoos's demand that Lindau's work be dropped from *Every Other Week*.

14. William Dean Howells, *Doctor Breen's Practice* 1881; rpt. Westport, Conn.: Greenwood, 1969), p. 13.

15. Bennett aptly notes that it is a mistake to assume that Howells's social consciousness developed only after 1885, when he first read Tolstoy (p. 114). For Howells to have been as affected by Tolstoy as he was, there must have been a number of ideas he held to which Tolstoy's teachings had a kinship, ideas that inevitably shaped the works of the early eighties.

16. For an extended discussion of *A Fearful Responsibility* as a reflection of Howells's doubts about the pragmatic orientation, see my "A New Look at Howells's *A Fearful Responsibility*," *Modern Language Quarterly* 39 (June 1978): 121–31.

17. William Dean Howells, *A Fearful Responsibility and Other Stories* (Boston: James R. Osgood, 1881), p. 5.

18. For instance, Isabel March notes in *The Shadow of a Dream* that because the Faulkners have no children they "are not really a family."

19. Ellen F. Wright, in "Given Bartley, Given Marcia: A Reconsideration of Howells' *A Modern Instance*," *Texas Studies in Literature and Language* 23 (Summer

1981): 214–31, has a dissenting view here. Regarding the Gaylord marriage as "to some degree salutary" (p. 216), she notes that it, the Halleck marriage, which she sees as "definitely successful" (p. 216), and the Atherton marriage, which, she suggests, is "a direct counterpoint to the Hubbard marriage," all indicate that the quality of American life in *A Modern Instance* is not in any significant way to blame for the failure of Bartley and Marcia's marriage. "The blame for the Hubbards' divorce," Wright observes, "lies squarely with the Hubbards" (p. 226).

20. William Dean Howells, *A Modern Instance* (Cambridge, Mass.: Houghton-Mifflin, 1910), p. 27.

21. Elizabeth Stevens Prioleau observes that "rather than regulating [Bartley and Marcia's] unbridled appetites, marriage only encourages darker, crueler, more pathologic expressions of them" (*The Circle of Eros: Sexuality in the Work of William Dean Howells* [Durham, N.C.: Duke University Press, 1983], p. 58). Hilfer notes perceptively that all that holds this hideous marriage together is the "powerful force of habit" (p. 64).

22. William Dean Howells, *The Rise of Silas Lapham* (1885; Bloomington: Indiana University Press, 1971), p. 49.

23. Bennett, p. 154.

24. Howells's personal difficulties at the time of the composition of *The Rise of Silas Lapham*, when, as he put it, the "bottom dropped out," give one further reason to believe that the novel is a grimmer one than it usually has been taken to be. For the fullest discussion of these difficulties, see Cady, *The Road to Realism*, and Kenneth S. Lynn, *William Dean Howells: An American Life* (New York: Harcourt Brace Jovanovich, 1971).

25. William Dean Howells, *The Minister's Charge* (Cambridge, Mass.: Houghton-Mifflin, 1914), p. 458.

26. Among those who see the novel as flawed because it fails to dramatize complicity effectively are Firkins, p. 121, and Bennett, pp. 164–71.

27. For the fullest discussion of *A Hazard of New Fortunes* as a work depicting existential chaos, see George C. Carrington, Jr., *The Immense Complex Drama: The World and Art of the Howells Novel* (Columbus: Ohio State University Press, 1966), pp. 82–100.

28. For the fullest treatment of Howells as a reformer, see Robert L. Hough, *The Quiet Rebel: William Dean Howells as Social Commentator* (Lincoln: University of Nebraska Press, 1959).

29. This is the point made implicitly through Annie Kilburn's marriage to Morrell and their adoption of Idella Peck in another of Howells's novels of social criticism, *Annie Kilburn*.

30. Among the few commentators who see this episode as significant is Carrington, who regards the house-hunting adventure—rightly, I think—as the Marches' initiation into a sense of existential chaos.

31. William Dean Howells, *A Hazard of New Fortunes* (1890; rpt. New York: New American Library, 1965), p. 309.

32. Typifying this suspicion are some remarks in a letter Howells wrote to Howard Pyle in 1891, responding to Pyle's laudatory comments on *The Shadow of a Dream*. Howells answers, "Happy for all if [like Nevil] they could die out of their difficulties! But even this is not permitted to many, to most. Perhaps we can only suffer into the truth, and live along, in doubt whether it was worth the suffering. It may be an illusion, as so many things are (maybe all things). . . ." The letter appears in Mildred Howells's compilation, *Life in Letters of William Dean Howells, Volume Two* (New York: Doubleday, Doran, 1928), p. 11.

33. William Dean Howells, *The Shadow of a Dream* and *An Imperative Duty* (1890, 1893; Bloomington: Indiana University Press, 1970), p. 44.

34. See, for example, George Spangler, "*The Shadow of a Dream*: Howells' Homosexual Tragedy," *American Quarterly* 23 (Fall 1971): 110–19, and Prioleau's discussion of this novella.

35. For provocative discussions of this aspect of the work, see John W. Crowley, "The Length of Howells' *Shadow of a Dream*," *Nineteenth-Century Fiction* 27 (September 1972): 182–96, and Barbara L. Parker, "Howells's *Oresteia*: The Union of Theme and Structure in *The Shadow of a Dream*," *American Literature* 49 (March 1977): 57–69.

36. *The Quality of Mercy* (1892), which closes with the marriage of Northwick's daughter, and *The World of Chance* (1893), which contains the successful marriage of the Brandreths, are also bleak novels whose bleakness Howells attempts to mitigate somewhat with these happy unions. Both are only briefly glimpsed marriages, though, and the horrible marriage of the Dentons in the latter work—though also seen only briefly —is conveyed with greater force than the Brandreth union.

37. George N. Bennett, *The Realism of William Dean Howells 1889–1920* (Nashville, Tenn.: Vanderbilt University Press, 1973), p. 241.

38. Quoted in William Dean Howells, *The Kentons* (1902; Bloomington: Indiana University Press, 1971), p. xi.

39. Howells, *The Kentons*, p. 206.

40. See George C. Carrington, Jr., on this in his Introduction to the edition of *The Kentons* cited above.

41. *The Realism of William Dean Howells 1889–1920*, p. 213.

42. William Dean Howells, *The Vacation of the Kelwyns* (New York: Harper, 1920), p. 140.

43. William Dean Howells, *Atlantic Monthly* 23 (February 1869): 261. Particularly difficult to credit in the face of this and of all we have seen are the remarks in passing by Earnest that "Howells regarded marriage as more of an ordeal than a joy" and that "marriage to a man with Howells's views on women and sex could be a major disaster" (p. 245).

HENRY JAMES

THE EARLY SHORT FICTION

*I*N HENRY JAMES'S first marriage story, "A Tragedy of Error" (1864)—which is also his first story—a faithless wife tries vainly to have her unsuspecting husband murdered; in his last, "Mora Montravers" (1909), a plodding, ineffectual fellow attempts futilely to brighten his loveless marriage by idealizing and sharing vicariously in the romantic misadventures of his shallow, even morally questionable, niece. Not only is neither story likely to make readers any more eager to rush to the nuptial altar than was their creator, but neither, as well, differs significantly from the great majority of the many portrayals of marriage James presented in the forty-five years between these two works.[1] For James marriage was invariably a relationship with an inordinately high potential for conflict, confusion, and the disillusionment that can forever blight a life. That it should be so for him is not surprising, for marriage inevitably is shaped by, and inextricably bound up in, the world of conventional experience, a world that James himself regarded with suspicion and that his protagonists for whom he cared most come to see as providing the invaluable materials for the forging of a personal moral vision but nonetheless as a realm, finally, in which they cannot live. Peter Brooks's contention that "from the very beginning" James was attempting to delineate "dilemmas of moral consciousness" involving "meanings that could not be grounded and justified, either in any known system of manners or in any visible and universally accepted code of moral imperatives"[2] points up that James was indeed, in Jacques Barzun's words, going "back over the realists' heads, to the romanticists, whom he wished to purge and renovate."[3] James, then, by the very nature of his endeavor to define a moral vision not grounded in conventional experience—in fact, one transcending and even inimical to it—

would not be likely to contemplate marriage with anything approaching the enthusiasm that a Howells tried with varying success to maintain.

But suspicion, predominant as it is, is only one side of James's response to marriage; and to see this response in its totality, one might begin by recurring to Barzun's thesis that James in going back to the romanticists hoped to "purge and renovate" them. Clearly, what such a process involved for James was an effort to follow the romantic course of establishing a personal moral vision with oneself as the sole arbiter of its validity without falling into the error, lurking for romantics, of losing all ties to the quotidian.[4] To avoid such error, James was aware, one must know the world, frightening as it is, and never forget either its reality or its grimness. That James never did forget the reality of pain is evidenced in what he himself called his "imagination of disaster," which is rarely far removed from any work of note he ever created. Perhaps the most striking description of just how stark a perception of the bleakness in existence James did maintain is in Theodora Bosanquet's comment on what her employer perceived when "he walked out of the refuge of his study." There, she notes, he observed unflinchingly "a place of torment, where creatures of prey perpetually thrust their claws into the quivering flesh of the doomed, defenseless children of light."[5] Frightening as he saw the world to be, though, James believed that one comes to moral growth through contact with it rather than avoidance of it. More, his works reveal his conviction that the movement through interaction with the world to moral development is not simply a linear one in which, finally, all significant contact with experience is left behind. Rather, he held, a valid moral awareness is maintained by remaining in nourishing contact with the perilous world of experience. One must be, then, in a condition akin to Whitman's stance in *Song of Myself,* being "both in and out of the game and watching and wondering at it." Thus, one notes the ambivalence toward experience that makes for a major tension in all of James's fiction,[6] a tension that is felt with particular keenness in the marriage stories; for if there was one area of experience that aroused particularly strong feelings of ambivalence in James, it was the dealings of husbands and wives.

That the latter should be the case is eminently understandable, for with the intimacy it establishes, marriage brings one into perhaps a closer contact with the world outside oneself than one usually finds with any other human relation. Consequently, the possibilities both for pain and growth that are inherent in any confrontation with experience are increased multifold, a fact that may account for James's description of marriage in *The Portrait of a Lady* as a "form" that is both "ghastly" and "magnificent."[7] Given James's view of the human capacity for evil and folly, the sort of difficulties he envisioned as endemic to marriage are not hard to imagine. Clearly, the predatory selfishness of some and the pathetic vulnerability of others frequently grow when the selfish and the vulnerable become increasingly enmeshed in experience, especially in a relationship that demands as much of limited beings as marriage inevitably does. Somewhat less obvious, but no less real for James, are the opportunities—opportunities, of necessity, intimately linked with pain—that he believed marriage offers. These derive from the fact that marriage, as James saw it, by generating for the married person a confrontation with experience outside the self ultimately can generate an enormously significant confrontation with self. As Robert Seidenberg has pointed out, one can be forced to find very quickly how tolerant, how generous, how unselfish, how brilliant, one *really* is. He asserts, "Only in marriage is one likely to experience . . . day-in-day-out *confrontation* with oneself through another, and it is this unavoidable confrontation that makes all the difference," a difference possibly destructive of "illusions about self-importance, courage, honesty, integrity, and generosity,"[8] and, hence, to one with James's moral concerns, of surpassing significance.

In a letter to Grace Norton, James once stated, "One's attitude toward marriage is a fact—the most characteristic part doubtless of one's general attitude toward life." He could say this, of course, because he knew marriage is experience—life—writ large. Because he was aware of how painful experience, how painful life, could be, he added to Norton, "If I were to marry I should be guilty in my own eyes of inconsistency—I should pretend to think quite a little better of life than I really do." Nonetheless, he also declared, in a letter to his brother William congratulating him on his engagement, "I believe almost as much in matrimony for most other people as I believe in it little for myself."[9] This is apparently a manifestation of his awareness that though he felt unsuited personally for marriage and was cognizant of the limitations of human nature, he saw in the confrontations of matrimony exceptional opportunity for union not merely between two persons but between the individual and the world, a vital communion, in other words, between the self and all outside it in which is attained nothing less than a transcendent love that can redeem a life.[10] Since the stakes are thus so high and the odds against victory so great, the rare marriages in James's fiction that result in this redemptive vision for one or both partners make for perhaps the most striking affirmations in his work, and the rest of the marriages often rank among the most poignant and painful losses he delineates. Indeed, James's attitude toward marriage, then, is revelatory of his most characteristic attitude toward life.[11] Like the marriages that evidence its central facts with singular vividness, life as James saw it is steeped in defeat yet worth the living because of the possibility of attaining a triumph of surpassing beauty.

Though there are no clearly marked stages in the development of James's view of marriage, for his conception of it as an almost invariably bleak experience that is never entirely devoid of potential value for a sentient few is maintained consistently throughout his career, the marriage fiction before 1881 and *The Portrait of a Lady* is marked by blatant, even lurid, qualities of melodrama that largely disappear from his subsequent depictions of wedded life. That James would resort to melodrama at all in depicting an aspect of existence as inherently tied to the commonplace as is marriage is significant in itself. It reveals, obviously, how pervaded by menace he felt matrimony to be, but it shows something else of import too, as Peter Brooks notes. "Melodrama," he asserts, "starts from and expresses the anxiety brought by a frightening new world in which the traditional patterns of moral order no longer provide the necessary social glue." He goes on to point out that the mode, however, "demonstrates over and over that the signs of ethical forces can be discovered and can be made legible" and that it "strives to find, to articulate, to demonstrate, to 'prove' the existence of a moral universe which, though put into question, masked by villainy and perversions of judgment, does exist and can be made to assert its presence and its categorical force among men."[12] Though for James, early and late, "proof" of a moral universe would always be exceedingly hard to come by, the effort to define a highly personal moral vision that might be used in adducing a transcendent ground for ethical behavior was nonetheless not to be evaded. Thus, he turned to melodrama to convey implicitly just how arduous the pursuit of value and how frightening the confrontation of good and evil are in a seemingly disordered universe. The very blatancy with which the melodrama of the pre-1881 stories is conveyed therefore becomes symptomatic not merely of the heavy-handedness of the apprentice author but of the vehemence of his concern that marriage, one of the "traditional patterns of moral order" of which Brooks speaks, was, even more than other such patterns, perhaps, failing to "provide the necessary social glue."

What the early marriage stories also clue one to is that the melodramatic persists in James's marriage fiction after 1881, albeit in a much more subtle manner, one frequently involving internalization of modes of melodramatic behavior and conflict rather than overt manifestations of them. James's penchant for melodrama is, of course, evident in many of his works both before and after 1881 having little to do with marriage, and almost invariably his handling of the genre reflects his commitment to those concerns out of which, as Brooks notes, the genre developed. However, it is in the marriage stories that the arduous pursuit of value takes on especial significance and poignance. Again, this doubtless manifests that the intimacy in marriage makes the potential failures and triumphs inherent in the relationship exceedingly intense ones.

Further, the pre-1881 stories make clear early in James's career that, characterize marriage though he does in *The Portrait of a Lady* as both "ghastly" and "magnificent," the latter aspect of matrimony would be exceedingly rare in James's fiction. The few genuinely pleasant marriages in his work—those, for example, of the Freers in "Lady Barberina" (1884) and the Assinghams in *The Golden Bowl* (1904)—are marked by qualities of affectionate accommodation that James, like Howells, might find admirable but that clearly fall short for James, finally, of the moral grandeur that, because it is attainable in marriage, makes the institution "magnificent." This is especially evident in those pre-1881 marriage works in which James's use of such marriages in shaping apparently affirmative conclusions is so unconvincing as to call his intentions into question. That "magnificent" marriages would be even rarer in his works than the merely happy ones is again obvious from the tenor of James's pre-1881 marriage fiction. But, oddly enough, though both the blatancy of his melodrama in this period and the paucity of sufficiently sentient protagonists work with his predominant use of the short story form for his depictions of marriage to preclude the possibility of any sort of magnificence such as Isabel Archer and Maggie Verver attain through their extended confrontations with the consequences of their singular marriages,[13] adumbrations of their victories are evident even in the early works. However, evident as they may be, the prevalent note in the pre-1881 marriage fiction is one of ghastliness, as it would be for the remainder of James's career, to be relieved only occasionally in the works to come by a few, generally uncompelling, pleasant marriages and two darkly triumphant ones.

Of course, just as melodrama is not restricted by James merely to his marriage fiction, neither is the ghastliness that he observed in life. Stark conflicts of will, innocence (often innocence culpable in its ignorance and egotism) preyed upon by the experienced, children suffering because of the cruelty and stupidity of adults, art in mortal conflict with philistinism, love in conflict with lust, liberty in conflict with confinement—these obviously are the staples of all of James's significant work, not just of his marriage fiction. However, in the stories of wedded life, they are presented with a power that is, if not greater than in the fiction not involving marriage, at least different in kind, marked, as I have noted, by a peculiar intensity. That intensity is doubtless more marked in the marriage works of 1881 and beyond, but it is there early as well; and to appreciate the greatness of the later marriage fiction, it is useful to begin by observing its origins in the earlier, which, for all its imperfections, reveals some small successes even at the start.

"A lurid and fanciful melodrama," as one commentator has called it,[14] "A Tragedy of Error" is not a terribly auspicious beginning for James's marriage works or for his fiction generally. The tale of a French adulteress who hires a cutthroat boatman to drown her loving husband, only to have her plan miscarry when the villain, mistaking her lover for his prey, kills him instead, has all the earmarks of apprentice work. Overly predictable, one-dimensional in its characterizations, unvaryingly lurid in tone, the story is an undeniably tedious one. But, for all this, there are two aspects of the work that are relatively effective, both bearing on James's ambivalent response to marriage. By establishing economically and graphically, first, just how dark, frightening and disordered the realm of experience can be and then implicitly both linking marriage to it and showing how a violated marriage merely exacerbates the chaos, James imparts to "A Tragedy of Error" a thematic significance that transcends the imperfections of the work and an intensity that, though not enough to offset the banality of much in the story, redeems it from total failure.

James's metaphor for the terror of experience in "A Tragedy of Error" is the sea. The woman's lover declares in a statement that is contradicted by nothing that occurs in the tale that life is essentially a situation in which "we are all afloat on a tumultuous sea . . . struggling toward some *terra firma* of wealth or love or leisure."[15] The cutthroat boatman, formerly a sailor, is one who, having ranged far literally and figuratively over the seas of experience, can tell many a tale capable of confirming the lover's dark vision. The world he knows, one in which a man might "drive a knife up to the hilt into your back, with an oath, and slice open a melon with it, with a song, five minutes afterward" (1:37), is one touched by a palpable evil of which James would never doubt the reality.

Marriage, rather than being somehow inviolate and isolated from this realm of experience tied metaphorically to the sea, is intimately linked with it, as James establishes in several ways. First, of course, the faithless wife lives in a home overlooking the sea. Further, her choice of a boatman to do the killing of her husband, her plan that the murder be by drowning, and James's presentation of her literally in a boat scheming with the hired killer all serve to point up that marriage is inextricably bound up in experience, partaking of all its menace. Finally, the boatman's contemptuous reply, when asked by the wife if he is married, "No, I thank you. I'm not cursed with that blessing" (1:34) conveys the inescapable impression that in his various excursions into the darkest reaches of experience he has seen enough of marriage to make the relationship seem a singularly appalling one. Nowhere, then, does James present any reason, as Howells attempts to, for believing that marriage offers something better than experience at large or that, in fact, it is not part and parcel of experience itself.

James does point up vividly, however, that a violated marriage only aggravates the disorder and menace that experience is. Thus, in debasing and seeking to destroy her marriage, the wife here not only becomes a plotter with a low-life villain but, in effect, his equal. The narrator comments darkly, "You cannot touch upon certain subjects with an inferior but by the sacrifice of the barrier which separates you from him. There are thoughts and feelings and glimpses and foreshadowings of thoughts which level all inequalities of station" (1:40). That she has indeed become his equal is rendered graphically when the boatman (certainly no subtle villain) grabs a jug of milk away from his young nephew, downs it, and when told it was for an infant in the family, mutters,

"I wish the baby'd choke" (1:31). His abrogation of familial ties and responsibilities obviously parallels the wife's and links her with him in a realm of utter formlessness and chaos. Typifying this condition further is the wife's vulnerability to the gossip of her spying servants. Their delighted chatter of her name being bandied about in the streets, their excited accounts of her gulping "brandy by the glassful" (1:28) as she becomes increasingly agitated at the prospect of the impending return of her long-absent and unsuspecting spouse, all reveal a social order gone topsy-turvy, with servant elevated over employer. Finally, even the mistaken identity murder itself, with all of its implications of randomness and gratuitous horror, emphasizes the aggravation of the confusion in an already chaotic world that occurs when marital commitments are violated.

"A Tragedy of Error," then, is no paean to marriage. Not only does the central situation itself here make it impossible to see marriage as other than frightening, but the conclusion, when the shocked wife sees a figure emerge from the distance and (her husband being lame) "come limping toward her with outstretched arms" (1:47), drives home the horror with a terribly effectual final turn of the screw. His damaged leg, at once a reminder on James's part of the vulnerability of one mate to another and of the possibly unpleasant physical intimacy that marriage involves, makes the limping figure both pathetic and threatening, an all too accurate embodiment of a fragile relationship too rarely sustaining and ordering and yet one from which it is disastrous to seek escape. As the latter point reveals, therefore, "A Tragedy of Error," although not a paean to matrimony, is not a single-minded rejection of it. By establishing with some vividness and even subtlety the menace of marriage as inextricably part of a menacing world and, as well, the inherent dangers of leaving the relationship, James reveals the complexity of his response to matrimony, a complexity that is inevitably a feature of the many marriage works to come.

James's next two marriage stories, "My Friend Bingham" (1867) and "A Problem" (1868), ostensibly at least, present marriage in far more affirmative terms than does "A Tragedy of Error." In them marriage seems a means of reconciling conflicts, assuaging sorrows, and either initiating growth of character or signifying that it has taken place. In each a melodramatic tale involving the death of a child and the weakness of adults is brought to an apparently happy conclusion through the healing offices of marriage. But, as a brief look at both reveals, there is much in them that undercuts the seeming affirmations of the virtues of matrimony, much that makes the marriages presented seem little better than that delineated in the earlier story. Ultimately, indeed, the endings of these two stories strike one as sufficiently suspect to make one question James's intentions. He may be attempting consciously to show with more than a little irony that typically "happy" marriages can exist only if human failings and the terrors of existence are glossed over or blithely ignored. On the other hand, these stories may, in fact, present a situation in which either James's shortcomings as a youthful author or his deeply rooted misgivings about the benefits to be derived from seemingly pleasant marriages lead him to undercut inadvertently his own conclusions. Another possibility, finally, is that James, though still a relatively unsophisticated writer at this stage of his career, fully intends that these stories be ambiguous ones, thereby calling into question the implicit case for marriage with which each closes. Unfortunately, neither story gives one enough to go on to resolve the question of James's intentions with any degree of certainty. Whether he means them to be or not, consequently, the tales are not without their ambiguities, and the affirmative visions of marriage in them are not entirely convincing.

Viewed from one angle, "My Friend Bingham" does actually seem to be a story in which the title character's moral growth is linked to the marriage he makes.[16] At the outset of the tale, Bingham is apparently one bent on going through life without significant involvement or commitment. His having "forsworn marriage" after being jilted, his "fastidiousness of mind" and "formalism of manner" are all cited as betokening that he is "one who has not been obliged to address himself to practical questions" (1:168) and who, presumably, is well pleased that he has not been. All this seems to change, however, when, walking along the shore one day and hunting aquatic birds, Bingham accidentally shoots and kills the only child of a young widow. Before long his sympathy for the woman turns to admiration of her quiet courage and strength of character, and this, in turn, leads to love, marriage, and the development of a Bingham less inclined to superficiality. Nothing mars the couple's subsequent happiness, not even the fact, which the narrator, Bingham's friend, attributes to a "fantastic principle of equity," that Bingham's wife "has never again become a mother" (1:190). When last seen, Bingham, in the final words of the story, is described as a "truly incorruptible soul," a "confirmed philosopher," and, lastly, as one who "has grown quite stout" (1:190). Thus, from the angle of vision at which we are presently regarding it, "My Friend Bingham" seems to delineate a sort of Emersonian system of compensation, with marriage here providing the reward. Horror, then, is real; but within it, so the story appears to suggest, lie the seeds of solace and spiritual growth. By precipitating suffering and not seeking to evade the consequences of his action, by, in fact, wedding the grieving mother and entering into extended involvement with her sorrow, Bingham matures. No longer is he an uncommitted or "light" man; even his new stoutness seems to bespeak an increase in his substantiality. Marriage, hence, from this almost Howellsian perspective, is seen to provide solace in a difficult world as well as a means of both fostering and signifying moral growth.

But, as I have noted, there is a good deal in "My Friend Bingham" which shows that the work may be something quite different from the story just limned, that it may indeed be a troubling account of human shallowness as not the least frightening aspect of a world replete with inexplicable horror. Seen from this perspective, there is no compensation, only loss, and there is no growth on Bingham's part, only the too quick accommodation to things as they are of a man who is irremediably insubstantial. Clearly, even the narrator himself (perhaps speaking for James) has doubts over how the story is to be taken, suggesting at the outset of his account that he has often asked himself "whether in the events here set forth, the element of pain is stronger than that of joy." He avers that "an affirmative answer . . . would have stood as a veto upon the publication of my story for . . . the literature of horrors needs no extension." On the other hand, though, he notes that he hesitates to "assume the responsibility of a decided negative" and has "therefore determined to leave the solution to the reader" (1:165).

Should the reader wish to, he would have little trouble in reaching the "affirmative answer" that the speaker suggests would shift this tale into the realm of the "literature of horrors," for James gives one more than ample opportunity to do so. One has difficulty, for example, in accepting the notion that any marriage can palliate or offset significantly the horror of the child's death, which is made all the more terrible to contemplate by the circumstances surrounding it. These include, first, a setting in which all pleasant views are "so completely obstructed by the rank, coarse herbage, that [the] prospect was reduced to a long narrow band of deep blue ocean traversing its black fibres, and to the great vault of the sky" (1:169); second, an awful coincidence in that Bingham fires just as the narrator is reciting the lines in which Coleridge's Ancient Mariner declares that he shot the albatross with his crossbow; and last, the pathetic behavior of the child at the moment of the shooting, as, suddenly rising up with "his little hands extended and his face raised toward the retreating bird," he takes the shot directly in the head and throws his hands back to it, reeling "downwards out of sight" (1:172). The resultant impression here of a universe in which weird, inexplicable disaster is all too common makes Bingham's subsequent behavior and marriage seem something less than the response of a deeply feeling individual. Certainly, Bingham's initial outpouring of grief is short-lived, and it is not long before he is eating voraciously and seeing in the immensity of the nighttime sky something reassuring, "a sight for bereaved mothers." He asserts to the narrator as he looks at it, "Somehow, my dear boy, I never felt less depressed in my life. It's none of my doing" (1:178). The distances between stars, then, the desert places without, open in him no sense of corresponding desert places within. Instead, they simply lead him, apparently, to the comfortable conclusion that nothing matters enough ultimately to warrant one's taking things, even the death of a child, too seriously. Viewed from this angle, then, Bingham's ostensibly happy marriage to the mother of the deceased boy, a marriage that for many men in his situation might be an intolerable, constant reminder of that hideous moment on the beach, becomes an indicant not of moral and spiritual growth but of a lack of human responsiveness. Similarly, his increased stoutness and his "incorruptibility" might be construed as signs of an imperviousness to spiritual and emotional torment and a sinister capacity for thriving in the midst of suffering, and the reference to his being "a confirmed philosopher" only an ironic comment on his propensity for suppressing any incipient stirrings of personal guilt, personal feelings.

The marriage of such a man as is revealed when the story is read from this second vantage point would presumably serve no worthwhile purpose as far as James is concerned. Rather than enabling him to grow through providing a realm of both valuable experience and solace, marriage in this case would serve merely as a means by which an inveterately shallow man avoids a useful confrontation with himself. In the context of this reading of the tale, the childlessness of the Binghams is less a sign that some finally equitable system of compensation is at work (or a means by which James prevents an affirmative ending from being saccharine) than it is merely one more inexplicably unpleasant event in a universe pervaded by inexplicable unpleasantness.

Whether it is by design that "My Friend Bingham" lends itself to such diametrically opposed readings is, as I have noted, impossible to ascertain. Suffice it to say, whatever James's intentions, his seeming affirmation in it of marriage as a context of comfort, order, and moral growth is open to question. Nor in "A Problem" is James's presentation of the supposed salutary effects of marriage any more convincing, for in this work, which James Kraft characterizes as "one of James's oddest and most banal tales,"[17] the estranged young husband and wife who finally reach an accommodation with each other, presumably growing in the process, are such a childish, insipid pair that one finds it difficult to believe them capable of the growth that their reaffirmed marriage seems to bespeak. Again, consequently, an apparently happy union is depicted, purposely or not, as tinged with more than a little ghastliness and with none of the magnificence that, alone in marriages, could win James's full loyalty.

In this work a pair of newlyweds find their marriage haunted by dark prophecies. First, an old, drunken, evil-looking, Indian squaw fortune-teller declares with a certain relish that their firstborn will be a daughter who will die in early childhood. Later, although their first child—indeed a girl—weathers a critical illness, their vague unease about ominous predictions remains and is aggravated disastrously when the wife's confession to her husband that a fortune-teller predicted long before her marriage that she would wed twice brings a confession from him about an identical prediction for his own future. Racked by jealousy over loves envisioned for the surviving mate, the pair turn on each other bitterly, creating a rancor that leads the wife into unabating querulousness and suspicion and the husband into increasing dissipation and self-indulgence. Inevitably, a separation ensues, which ends when their little girl does, in fact, die of a sudden illness. Shaken, standing together now in a communion of grief before a clergyman to view the remains of their child, the pair realize their affection for each other and embrace as the minister, raising his hand "with a pious sacramental gesture," bestows his approval. Thus, as a friend comments later, "the terrible problem is at last solved" and each has "been married twice" (1:386).

The problem of this young couple may indeed be solved to their own satisfaction, but severe difficulties remain for the concerned reader. Is one to believe that the "remarriage" of this pair brings the story to a satisfyingly happy ending? If so, James apparently expects his readers to overlook a good deal. The viciousness of the squaw, the death of the child, the fatuity and irrationality of the couple, even the eerie possibility that the fortune-teller may somehow have some efficacy, all raise questions about the nature of existence and the capacity for human folly that are never addressed adequately by the conclusion of the story. If indeed James believes that married love conquers all, he has hardly made a plausible case for that conviction and has, in effect, presented virtually a parody of it. The reunion of husband and wife here betokens no effort—at least no effort that James delineates—on the part of either at self-examination or the mature scrutiny of the human condition generally that can lead to self-control and moral development. Consequently, the ostensible point that marriage brings one into a framework of difficulty that can finally engender both personal growth and the formation of a pleasant union that offers comfort in a troubled world never compels the reader to belief; and thus the marriage here seems little more than an evasion of painful realities. Again, as with Bingham's perhaps similar marriage, it is impossible to say whether this apparent undercutting of his conclusion is intended by James as an ironic commentary on the notion that all difficulties can be resolved by a happy marriage with all living happily ever after. But even if it is not so intended, the conclusion is so weak as to manifest a lack of real conviction either that happiness can be found in most marriages or that, if found, it is not ignoble.

James's first three marriage stories, then, establish matrimony as a relationship that he regards as inevitably linked with death, conflict, confusion, and evasion. Though he touches on the possibility of mutual accommodations occurring in marriage that manifest personal growth and ensure at least a modicum of happiness for a couple, he seems unconvinced that marital happiness is anything but exceptional and that it and genuine development of character are not mutually incompatible. His next three marriage tales of the period before 1881, "The Last of the Valerii" (1874), "Madame de Mauves" (1874), and "Crawford's Consistency" (1876), show a narrowing of James's focus. Sensing, perhaps, that happiness in marriage is more often than not beyond the reach of the people with whom he is most concerned, the sensitive ones, James in these stories explores more closely than in the first three the possibility that marriage as an experience generating particularly intense responses can lead one with especial efficacy to a fuller awareness of oneself and of the nature of existence generally—an idea of particular significance in treatments of marriage, as, in different ways, it is also explored by Howells, Wharton, Herrick, and Chopin. The results he presents are no more auspicious than those depicted in the first three works, and once again they occur in a context of often blatant melodrama. As yet, James does not perceive states of internalized melodrama or the quiet, essentially romantic, and highly personal triumphs that can be derived from even the most painful confrontations with experience.

Heightening the reader's sense that the wedding altar is the entrance to alien territory is the fact that each of the marriages presented in these stories unites disparate types. Differences of nationality, class, sensibility are central, of course, to much of James's fiction having little to do with marriage and are used often, like marriage, to delineate areas of experience foreign to the protagonist into which he or she is initiated with valuable educative results sometimes ensuing; however, when James ties these differences, as he does here, to marriage itself, the most consistently intimate confrontation with otherness he can imagine, the focus on whether or not the experience is suitably educative is particularly close. And what James seems to conclude at this stage of his career is that, unfortunately, the initiation that marriage involves frequently brings one to know pain, but little else. Such moral or spiritual development as the protagonists do undergo is slight, stunted, quickly blighted, and certainly not worth the suffering to which they are exposed. In the future the sufferings undergone by his protagonists in markedly similar situations would strike James in at least two cases as bringing more than sterile pain, as being, in fact, nothing less than prods to a growth of character that would come for these figures, one suspects, in no other relationship than matrimony. But here, in these three stories, finally, marriage seems only a form shrouded in a ghastliness that is unremitting.

"The Last of the Valerii" is a story that at once looks back to Hawthorne's *The Marble Faun* and ahead to *The Golden*

Bowl. In it a childlike, sluggish Italian count is aroused from his lethargy by his young wife, an energetic American prone to romantic visions of self-sacrifice; and he thus comes into possession of his mature, authentic identity. Did the story end here with the count, like Hawthorne's Donatello, rescued from a charming but debilitating and unduly prolonged state of youthful fecklessness and, perhaps, like Amerigo, ready to be awakened to the rewards of marital love, it would be James's first genuinely convincing depiction of marriage as precipitating growth of character. However, the story does not end on anything like so positive a note as this. Threatened by her husband's newfound identity, one that marks him as a man who, like his ancestors before him, has a fierce, pagan devotion to beauty and the art that seeks to shape it and do it reverence, the wife takes measures that render him once again the tractable, ineffectual, mildly uxorious fellow she married; and the story closes with the count vaguely troubled over what he has lost but with no hope of getting it back. In effect, then, James shows here, as he will in several subsequent works, that marriage often is not merely unproductive of valuable development in the married but is inherently inimical to the love of beauty and the creativity that give life meaning to so many, married or not.

When first glimpsed, the newlyweds, Count Valerio and Martha, are thoroughly pleased with each other. But happiness in marriage for James is, as we have seen in the earlier tales, suspect, the result, possibly, of husband and wife being somehow insensitive or undeveloped. That such may indeed be the case with this pair is apparent on closer observation of them. Their typical daily activities, described by the narrator, a painter who is Martha's godfather, are revealing:

> She played dominos with him after dinner, and carried out in a desultory way a daily scheme of reading him the newspapers. This observance was subject to fluctuations caused by the Count's invincible tendency to go to sleep,—a failing his wife never attempted to disguise or palliate. She would sit and brush the flies from him while he lay picturesquely snoozing, and, if I ventured near him, would place her finger on her lips

and whisper that she thought her husband as handsome asleep as awake. (3:95)

The unmistakable impression here of an unnaturally child-like individual being mothered by his doting bride is rein-forced when the narrator notes that the count has "no beliefs, nor hopes, nor fears,—nothing but senses, appetites, and serenely luxurious tastes" (3:95) and that he carries in his pocket a collection of "fragments of antique pavement" (3:97) that by the half-hour he tosses in the air and catches on the back of his hand. Nor is Martha, for all her maternal air with the count, without a certain disturbingly childlike quality herself, as manifested by the sentimental romanticism that leads her both to marry so unlikely a fellow as the count in the first place largely because of the dark, exotic past of his family and to wish vaguely and grandiosely to do "something more for him than girls commonly do for their lovers,—to take some step, to run some risk, to break some law, even!" (3:92). Her inchoate longings in this line lead her, comically enough, considering her husband's indifference to his reli-gion, to declare heroically that she will even become a Cath-olic if he wishes her to, a resolution that grows out of no religious devotion but simply out of a propensity for self-dramatization and an attraction to what she considers to be the strange foreignness of the church.

That such happiness as their marriage has brought this pair presupposes an almost culpable denial both of the grim lessons of human history about the ephemerality of happi-ness and of their own capacities to achieve something more than the unnatural prolongation of adolescent pleasures is evidenced through the setting and the misgivings of the nar-rator about this marriage. The walks of the count's villa, lined with "disinterred fragments of sculpture" standing in "the perpetual twilight like conscious things, brooding on their gathered memories" and seeming to "whisper heavily the whereabouts of their mouldering fellows, still unrecov-ered from the soil" (3:94), are a visible reminder that life is not all pleasant naps, domino games, and the reciprocal joys of doting, maternal wife and amiable, childlike husband. The very fragments of ancient paving stone with which the count habitually plays are, if not *memento mori*, at least small tokens of the limitations imposed on human dreams and plans rather than the mere toys that the count makes of them. Hence, when the narrator, who believes his goddaughter to be a "creature susceptible of the finer spiritual emotions," asks himself "what was becoming of her spiritual life in this interminable heathenish honeymoon" (3:96) with a man asleep to whatever potential for maturity he has, the setting itself reinforces his sense that the couple are leading too light a life, a spiritually atrophied one based on a mutual refusal to acknowledge the somber burden of human history and put aside childish things.

The implicit question running through James's account of the strange happiness of these newlyweds, obviously, is whether their marriage can bring them to fuller awareness of their mature identities and thereby evolve into a union based on acknowledgment rather than denial of their authentic natures and ties to human history. In the context of this question, Martha's urging her husband to hire a crew to undertake a series of systematic excavations on his grounds seems symptomatic less of a desire to add some sculptures to the count's already extensive collection aboveground than of a response to what the narrator perceives as a "dawning sense . . . that she was the least bit strangely mated" (3:97). Her efforts to fathom the nature of her husband by delving into his ancestral past—and, perhaps, in doing so to find out more about herself and why she married him—indeed bring both of them to knowledge of themselves. Unfortunately, this new knowledge is so inimical to the continuation of their marriage that Martha feels compelled to suppress it, thereby both reestablishing their former condition so redolent of overripe pleasures and implicitly conveying James's grim vision at this stage of his career that marriage and real growth through the confrontation with experience that wedlock affords are incompatible.

The crisis for both Martha and the count is precipitated when the unearthing of a lovely statue of Juno awakens the pair to the count's true nature, which has been lying as dor-

mant in him as was the statue in the earth. No longer a som-
nolent child jokingly referring to himself as a pagan, the
count awakens to the dread but exhilarating truth that underlying his twinges of "superstitious" (3:98) awe of the
secrets buried in his ancestral grounds have been the
promptings of a nature that is genuinely and atavistically pagan. Unleashed in the count by the sight of the Juno is a devotion to ancient beauty and to the worship of the old Roman
divinities that is so passionate as to make all aspects of contemporary life seem empty to him. Before long he keeps the
severed hand of the statue in a silver box as a relic, and the
Juno itself he keeps under lock and key and visits alone for
private nocturnal devotions in which he actually prostrates
himself before it. Detesting now the Christianity he used to
accept nominally with mild amusement, the count declares of
believers, "I should like to pull down their pictures, overturn
their candlesticks, and poison their holy-water!" (3:110).
More, the count seems constantly to be making "invidious
comparisons" between the marble goddess and his contemporaries that result in his "despising mankind"; and, notes
the narrator, "from this untender proscription his charming
wife was not excepted," for soon he is glimpsed responding
to her "persuasive caress" with "an ill-concealed shudder"
(3:106). Thus has the count's marriage brought him to a new
knowledge of himself, one, unfortunately, that unfits him
for the relationship that prompted his self-perception.

Attempting to restore the marital condition destroyed by
the unearthing of the Juno, Martha, more willing to be the
conventional nineteenth-century wife than she earlier would
have thought possible, again acts, this time ordering work-
men to reinter the statue. Results are immediate; finding the
Juno gone, the count is no longer the proud pagan. Hesitating
before his wife only a moment, "as if her very forgiveness
kept the gulf open between them," he then "strode forward,
fell on his two knees and buried his head in her lap"
(3:121–22). Years later, when next seen, the count is responding to the question of a guest about the Juno's hand,
still unburied but now on view in his cabinet. Asked if it is "a
Roman," he replies "with a frown," in the last words of the

story, that it is "a Greek" (3:122). All, then, thanks to Martha's second initiative, seems to be as it was before. Though now, as his frown indicates, less than perfectly happy, the count has once again denied his authentic identity; and, as his tearful genuflection before Martha implies, he has given up the adoration of his goddess for a childlike surrender to devotion to his motherly wife. Martha too has given up something significant. By reinstituting her "interminable heathenish honeymoon," she robs herself of the opportunity to grow through confronting the suffering and loss inherent for her in her husband's change. Renouncing her husband might well have been the gift of love for which she had wished so romantically, and, though painful, it might have ensured the spiritual growth that eludes her.

The marriage of this pair endures, consequently, marked by a happiness that is still essentially childish, though now ever so slightly tinged with faint discontent. The pain is not severe, however; were it so, it might be a stimulant to growth. Instead, it is merely sterile, unproductive.[18] There will be no change, no development in this marriage ever again; nor will there be passion or beauty, for at this stage in his career (as well as in many works long after), James sees the demands of marital domesticity as incompatible with passion, beauty, art or growth, as incompatible with all potential value save a highly suspect happiness for the inadequately sentient and a pain for the rest that is only too rarely educative. Clearly, Valerio is the "Last of the Valerii," the last in his line, that is, to hear and heed, however briefly, the timeless call to the demanding but joyous worship of beauty. With all this said, it is difficult, therefore, to agree with the assessment of one commentator that this story is "slight in content."[19] Though marred by a slightly clumsy melodramatic treatment of the count's adoration of the Juno and his scorn for the modern world and all in it, the story certainly is devoid neither of craftsmanship nor content. The implicit conflicts it embodies, its devastating ironies, its somber Italian atmosphere, all are manipulated skillfully by the narrator, himself an artist who has remained a bachelor, to show misgivings on James's part about marriage that are anything but inconsequential either in terms of his future work or in terms of any sensitive inquiry into problems inherent in marriage.

No less strange a union than that of the count and Martha and certainly no more likely to allay misgivings about marriage is the tie between the couple in "Madame de Mauves," an American girl of stringent morality and the philandering French nobleman she marries. Though James's concern here is as much with the often dangerous clash of distinctive national types as it is with the difficulties of husbands and wives, he sees, as I have noted, that the dangers in this clash are particularly marked for one who finds himself or herself married to one from a different culture that has ways that are often impervious to the understanding of an outsider. For James, of course, both a different culture and a marriage are simply exceedingly intense types of experience, carrying, therefore, in acute form all the dangers and potential benefits that are inherent in any confrontation with experience. But as "Madame de Mauves" reveals, the chances of gaining something of value from the often painful contact with things foreign diminishes appreciably if one's marriage is the central means of the contact, for the demands established by the special intimacy of marriage are too great, James believes, for most to be capable of meeting with fullest sensitivity in the best of circumstances, much less when they are from different backgrounds. In this tale, an even darker one than "The Last of the Valerii," there is not even a pretense of accommodation, happiness, or valid insight growing out of the conflict between the married pair. Unable to win his wife's love or forgiveness, even when he gives up his philandering, the shamed, unhappy baron finds no recourse but suicide. Unbending, incapable of compassion, his widow goes on unchanged, deriving what chilly comfort she can from her implacable rectitude. Again, the entrance into the alien realm, the experience writ large that is marriage, brings only pain, pain the more hideous for being unremunerative.

That the marriage of this couple will demand adjustments from both is apparent immediately. In a manner anticipatory of that of Isabel Archer and Gilbert Osmond, they misread each other from the first, entering into a marriage that neither would make were the other's traits clearly understood. Euphemia Cleve (her name, apparently, an allusion to Madame de LaFayette's Princesse de Clèves, similarly a blind devotee of duty)[20] lives absolutely committed to romantic ideality. Convinced that "Americans were vulgar" (3:128), she seeks to bestow in marriage her not inconsiderable fortune on "a son of the Crusaders who was to suffer her to adore him," a "gentleman rather ugly than handsome, and rather poor than rich" whose "ugliness was to be nobly expressive, and his poverty delicately proud" (3:130). Her conviction that the Baron de Mauves is just this man, one who would accept her fortune only with "a world of stifled protestations" (3:130), needs merely her glance at his decrepit ancestral home to be complete. Finding it "as delightful as a play" (3:132), Euphemia, who enjoys imagining herself in a drama fully as much as the young Isabel Archer likes fancying herself in a novel, decides to marry this *chevalier sans peur et sans reproche* she takes the baron to be and live with him in perfect communion at the shrine of romantic devotion to principle. For his part the baron, an urbane, likable fellow, but a feckless and impecunious sybarite nonetheless, fails to see Euphemia's single-mindedness, regarding her, instead, as a pliant young thing whose naïveté and beauty will charm him while her fortune solves his financial difficulties. "He found," James states, "that he needed pastimes, and, as pastimes were expensive, he added heavily to the list of debts to be cancelled by Euphemia's millions" (3:143). Neither, obviously, perceives that the other has been shaped by cultural influences incomprehensible to one from a different background. The narrow puritan resolve at the core of Euphemia's romantic attachment to the ideal is as alien to the baron as his notion that a man may have dissolute pleasures and still be a good fellow and acceptable husband is to her. In depicting the dismal union of this misled pair, James shows that the marriage prompts them neither to the accommodations that can make for happiness in marriage nor to the educative pain that can make for magnificence.

Though neither mate, obviously, is without fault in the marriage of this luckless pair, the main obstacle to any hope for success in their marriage is Euphemia. Deaf to the time-honored arguments of her sister-in-law and the baron's grandmother about the necessity of both accepting the world as she finds it and facing all with a tolerance that will allow her to maintain her dignity, to make all comfortable, and to keep a proud family name from being laughed at, Euphemia isolates herself behind her monolithic moral code, regarding her husband with a cool disdain that baffles this hapless lover of ease, pleasure, and good cheer. So baffled is he, in fact, that he blunders to the egregious conclusion that Euphemia simply needs an affair of her own to set all right and adopts desperately the crass and abortive expedient of trying to initiate a liaison between his wife and Longmore, another naïvely moralistic and romantic young American, who clearly is infatuated with her. Failing in this when Longmore's uneasy, tentative overtures are coolly rebuffed by Euphemia as unworthy of her compatriot, the baron is moved to a perplexed reverence and, perhaps, even love for his intransigent spouse. He repents of his ways, appeals to her for forgiveness, and, when she "inexorably" (3:208) refuses to give it, kills himself in despair.

The repeated inability of Euphemia to make any sort of accommodation with her mate or with things as they are imparts to the failure of this marriage to bring her either happiness or education an aura of terrible inevitability. All (including, as we have seen, even her maiden name) argues against any capacity for change in her. Her own admission that her "conscience" will "effectually prevent" her "from ever doing anything very fine" (3:171), her propensity for arguing for reason and restraint with a manner so "strangely intense" as to reflect "a kind of passion" (3:195), and her persistent refusal to accept the fact that she is in France, married to a baron rather than, as she comes to wish fondly, "the daughter of a poor New England minister, living in a little white house under a couple of elms, and doing all the housework" (3:169), all are symptomatic of her tenacious refusal to dwell anywhere else, finally, than in what she calls "a nameless country of my own" (3:146). As an unyielding inhabitant of this rarefied, unanchored realm, she becomes implacably as chilling a figure to her husband as his sister was to his brother-in-law, who, in an action foreshadowing the Baron's own death and helping to generate the sense of inevitability permeating the work, committed suicide rather than continue having to face her. Though it is crude, certainly, to characterize her, as one observer does at the end of the work, as "the charming little woman who killed her husband" (3:208), it is true nonetheless that it is no more in her to forgive him as a reformed philanderer than it is in her to accept him, or indeed any actual man, as a tolerable substitute for the hero of her romantic-cum-puritanical imaginings.[21]

Heightening one's sense of Euphemia's intractability and of the failure of marriage to initiate improvement in her is the development of her countryman, Longmore, a fellow who, luckier than the baron, remains single. Initially Longmore comes to France with a Woollett-like destestation of things foreign and particularly of things French—regarding the Baron, for example, as an "unclean Frenchman" (3:127)—and he quickly falls into a naïve infatuation with Euphemia in which he virtually canonizes her; but he gradually develops into one capable of real insight. The passions aroused in him by his adulation of Euphemia as a lady of sorrows do not abate barrenly, therefore. Instead they lead him to an unsettling appreciation of the pleasures of a French painter and his lovely mistress, an obviously contented pair whom he observes vacationing together at a country inn amid scenes of sunlit bucolic beauty that are far removed in space and mood from the dim, chill, terraced gardens in which he usually sees Euphemia. Newly receptive to the possibilities of life because of what he observes while in the countryside, Longmore, though certainly never to become a licentious man (James, of course, is advocating not promiscuity but humanity), is capable by the close of the tale of regarding Euphemia with a highly equivocal "awe" (3:209). Such regard implies a willingness to keep one's distance from its object, and the story ends without the slightest implication that Longmore now or at any time in the future is any longer the sort who would consider closing that distance.

Edward Wagenknecht speaks of James in this story as presenting more "impressively" than any Catholic novelist the "ideal of indissoluble marriage."²² It is difficult to see where in fact this ideal is presented save in the mind of Euphemia Cleve de Mauves, a woman whose defense of the ideal seems calculated by James to make it suspect to most readers. Such happiness as one sees in the story—that of the artist and his lover—is extramarital. Such real growth as one sees—that of Longmore—occurs in one who is single. That the baron does change through his confrontation with his wife argues no defense of marriage here, for were his growth significant rather than a ploy of James to attack Euphemia and emphasize the grimness of this union, James would doubtless focus on it more closely and show the baron to have gained a capacity for a renunciatory mode of existence that would preclude the possibility of suicide. Rather than bringing, then, either the happiness or the personal development that might conceivably derive from a confrontation with significant experience, this marriage brings only pain, death, and, for the survivor, confirmed blindness to her own shortcomings. More, the very inevitability with which, as we have observed, all this occurs itself argues implicitly against a fundamental assumption underlying marriage: the notion that a capacity for personal improvement is inherent in most and that marriage can help foster it. For many, apparently, James believes, devastating shortcomings are ineradicable and, in fact, only exacerbated by marriage, leading to a situation in which matrimony brings far more suffering for those involved than remaining single would have. Nor, despite the arguments of the baron's sister-in-law, does marriage here serve as a form bringing social stability. Suicides rarely help maintain social order, and the two marriages touched on in this work both end, of course, with the self-destruction of the husband. (That the baron's suicide is not at all in keeping with his character as developed by James up to this point testifies to James's willingness here to subvert even literary form to convey his grim vision of matrimony.) James, then, in "Madame de Mauves" as in "The Last of the Valerii," sees the entrance into the alien territory of marriage as resulting in an unhappiness that carries with it no compensations.

Similarly lacking in significant compensations is the pain that the title character in "Crawford's Consistency" brings upon himself by entering into an incongruous marriage that he knows will be disastrous and that does turn out to be probably the most grotesque of James's many marital horrors. Crawford, a mild-mannered young New York gentleman of scholarly pursuits, is jilted by the only girl he has ever loved, the vapid, mindless beauty Elizabeth Ingram, who, automaton-like, accedes to her mercenary parents' demand that she seek a more lucrative match. Immediately thereafter, for reasons that the narrator, who is Crawford's friend, confesses he finds inexplicable, Crawford weds himself to a blowzy, coarse, cheaply attractive, lower-class woman whom he picks up at a third-rate restaurant, a woman, moreover, whose faults are perfectly obvious to Crawford himself. Predictably the marriage is a torture for the poor man. In the best of circumstances, his wife is a greedy boor with a taste for liquor and for loud, ungrammatical self-congratulation who makes him the joke of good society; but when Crawford loses the greater part of his money in a bank failure, she turns into a shrill virago who abuses her pathetic mate verbally and physically, actually breaking his leg and leaving him with a permanent limp when she pushes him down a flight of stairs. Through it all, until his wife's death (not surprisingly, of delirium tremens) and beyond, Crawford is thoroughly consistent, a perfect, uncomplaining gentleman and the wonder of his friends.

Crawford's motive in all this, though the narrator sees it as shrouded impenetrably in obscurity, is not indiscernible. Behind this hideous marriage lies contempt, contempt for conventional notions of matrimony in good New York society and contempt for himself for ever putting aside when he first met Elizabeth his long-held dictum that "a man should only marry in self-defense" (4:17). His marriage is a backhanded swipe at Elizabeth, her parents, and all those who maintain a social order that helps foster the link between financial considerations and notions of what makes for an acceptable marriage.[23] By marrying this boardinghouse denizen, Crawford implies that the Ingrams and the society that shaped them are of no greater worth than his harridan bride—indeed, that, stripped of all social graces, they are identical to her in their underlying coarseness, avarice, and identical to her in their underlying coarseness, avarice, and unjustifiable self-esteem. He notes, in fact, that she "resumes a certain civilization," that she is its "last word—the flower" (4:34)—in other words, the final product of her class and its chief beauty, just as Elizabeth is of hers. Further, this linking himself to this woman may be, paradoxically enough, at once a manifestation of deep sexual longings (she exudes a strong, almost animal, sensuality) and of his contempt for himself for having them and for having allowed his responsiveness to Elizabeth's beauty to blind him to her mindlessness. The role of marriage, then, as a crude financial arrangement, as a means by which a spuriously "good" society maintains itself, and as a chance for the legal release of animal drives are all bitterly parodied by Crawford in the union he makes, one that enables him at the same time to inflict on himself the cruelest of punishments.

A "shameless potboiler," as James himself characterized it,[24] "insignificant," as, more recently, Peter Buitenhuis has called it,[25] a clumsy melodrama lacking in subtlety or sufficiently delineated and believable character, as is obvious to any reader, "Crawford's Consistency," nonetheless, ought not to be ignored, for it brings to a stark conclusion the skein of James's troubled response to matrimony in the pre-1881 marriage stories. Its very crudeness of conception—particularly at a stage of his career in which James was gaining some real control of his craft—manifests graphically his doubts and fears about wedlock. Elizabeth, for example, ends the story a homely spinster, all her beauty and her parents' hopes of a lucrative marriage for her blasted when smallpox cruelly scars her face, a conclusion to her husband-hunting career barely justifiable as a gross form of poetic justice but far more understandable as an expression of the vehemence of James's distaste for her and the form of conventional marriage to which she and her parents are committed. Similarly, although Crawford's physical abuse at the hands of his wife is a perhaps too lurid touch, it is simply the brutal culmination of a pattern in which husbands are defeated by their mates that runs through the marriage fiction before *The Portrait of a Lady* and seems, despite the plethora of unhappy wives in his work, a manifestation of especially terrible fears on James's part about the husband's lot in matrimony. Count Valerio gives up his pagan identity and heritage for his wife; the Baron de Mauves gives up his illicit pleasures and then, literally, his life for his unyielding mate; Elizabeth Ingram's father is dominated by his overbearing spouse; and Crawford, finally, whose marriage to Elizabeth would presumably have been no happier than Mr. Ingram's or the marriage he does, in fact, make, is left physically impaired, with a limp recalling that of the vulnerable, schemed-against husband in "A Tragedy of Error." Further, the very shrillness of James's portrayal of Crawford's wife conveys more vividly than in either "The Last of the Valerii" or "Madame de Mauves" that the sufferings undergone in this uneasy union of disparate types are horribly lacking in adequate compensation. Crawford may well be even more "agreeable" than previously, as "a clever old lady" (4:45) of the narrator's acquaintance suggests; but this, unlike such profound moral growth as Isabel Archer will undergo in her own horrible marriage, which this work, like "Madame de Mauves," oddly prefigures, seems little more than a manifestation of Crawford's willingness to be hurt while proving that he remains above the turmoils of involvement in marriage, the relationship for which he has come to have such contempt. Indeed, what one sees most in this failed but frightening tale is waste—the waste of Crawford's potentially useful life as he ensnares himself in a deadening marriage and, one suspects, the waste of a potentially good story as James, apparently ensnared in his own terrible personal misgivings regarding marriage and unable yet to envision such unique triumph through matrimony as Isabel will attain, allows useful material to be marred by an unduly shrill treatment.

Thus, "Crawford's Consistency" portrays in extreme form James's suspicion permeating "The Last of the Valerii" and "Madame de Mauves" that although all initiations into alien realms of experience are dangerous, marriage is the one most fraught with peril, particularly when it involves the union of mates from widely different backgrounds. Needless to say, the unhappiness running through all James's pre-1881 marriage fiction also culminates with particular intensity in "Crawford's Consistency," making the story in this area too a fitting capstone to the depiction of wedlock before *The Portrait of a Lady*.[26] For all this, though, nothing in the tale so epitomizes the tenor of James's marriage fiction in this period as the passage in "Madame de Mauves" in which Euphemia recapitulates for Longmore the process of initiation that her marriage vows set in motion for her:

> "My marriage vows introduced me to people and things which seemed to me at first very strange and then very horrible, and then, to tell the truth, very contemptible. At first I expended a great deal of sorrow and dismay and pity on it all, but there soon came a time when I began to wonder whether it was worth one's tears." (3:169–70)

The poignance of this statement of marital pain, this inadvertent confession of Euphemia's that in failing to bring her happiness marriage also caused the atrophy of her capacity for warm emotional response, bespeaks something more in James than a detestation of marriage. It makes clear that underlying the ghastliness of the marriages in both "Madame de Mauves" and "Crawford's Consistency," as well as in the other pre-1881 marriage fiction, there is a terrible sense of loss on James's part, as a context of experience that he sees to be rich with the potential for both happiness and spiritual growth leads all too often to mere unhappiness. The very frequency with which James writes of marriage both before 1881 and thereafter and, as well, his continuing propensity to depict it in terms of melodrama reveal his continuing hope, however tenuous, that marriage might indeed be a relationship that redeems for some the sad wastage that is so much of human experience.

---

1. Noting the great number of marriage works James wrote, Munro Beattie, in his essay "The Many Marriages of Henry James," asks, "Might it not appear that of the major story-tellers in our language marriage was especially of the essence for Henry James?" (Marston LaFrance, ed., *Patterns of Commitment in American Literature* [Toronto: University of Toronto Press, 1967], p. 93).

2. Peter Brooks, *The Melodramatic Imagination: Balzac, Henry James, Melodrama, and the Mode of Excess* (New Haven, Conn.: Yale University Press, 1976), p. 5. Also useful to see in this context is Leo B. Levy, *Versions of Melodrama: A Study of the Fiction and Drama of Henry James, 1865-1899* (Berkeley: University of California Press, 1957).

3. Quoted in Brooks, p. 97.

4. Perhaps an example close to home of this sort of romantic would be Emerson, whom James's father characterized as a "man without a handle."

5. Quoted in Brooks, p. 5.

6. For the fullest discussion of this facet of James's work, see Philip M. Weinstein, *Henry James and the Requirements of the Imagination* (Cambridge, Mass.: Harvard University Press, 1971).

7. Henry James, *The Portrait of a Lady*, vol. 2 (Boston: Houghton Mifflin, 1881). Though it is Goodwood who uses the term "ghastly" (p. 433) and the narrator, describing Osmond's view of the "form," who uses the term "magnificent" (p. 356), the words are both apt characterizations of James's view of matrimony.

8. Robert Seidenberg, *Marriage between Equals* (Garden City, N.Y.: Anchor Books, 1973), pp. 29-30.

9. F. O. Matthiessen, ed., *The James Family* (New York: Knopf, 1947), pp. 294-95.

10. For a discussion of this aspect of marriage as evidenced in *The Golden Bowl*, see Quentin Anderson, *The American Henry James* (New Brunswick, N.J.: Rutgers University Press, 1957).

11. Less typical of James's view of matrimony is his statement in a letter to Grace Norton in 1883 that "singleness consorts much better [than matrimony] with my whole view of existence (of my own and of that of the human race) . . ." (quoted in Leon Edel, *Henry James: The Middle Years* [Philadelphia: Lippincott, 1962], p. 80).

12. Brooks, p. 20.

13. James's only novel touching on married life before 1881 is *Confidence* (1879). In this exceedingly slight work, the briefly seen marriage of the Wrights, supposedly a happy one (though unconvincingly so) after some difficulties, gives no evidence of any capacity for magnificence.

14. James Kraft, *The Early Tales of Henry James* (Carbondale: Southern Illinois University Press, 1969), p. 1.

15. Henry James, *The Complete Tales of Henry James*, vol. 1, ed. Leon Edel (Philadelphia: Lippincott, 1962), p. 25. This edition of the tales, published (1962-64) in twelve volumes, is the text for all of James's short fiction that I cite. All subsequent volume and page references for the short fiction are to this edition and appear in the text.

16. One who views the story from this angle is Fogel, who, apparently untroubled by the complex ambiguities in "My Friend Bingham," see Bingham's marriage as "the act and sign of reconciliation" (p. 146).

17. Kraft, p. 20.

18. In light of the count's obvious self-suppression, it is difficult to credit Fogel's contention that he "has been saved by his wife from his enthrallment to a statue of Juno . . ." (p. 148).

19. Kraft, p. 77.

20. Kraft, pp. 55-56. Also worth noting, I suspect, is the fact that the name "Euphemia" is derived from a Greek source meaning "good repute."

21. One who admires Euphemia and would take strong exception to my characterization of her is Edward Wagenknecht, who has a provocative chapter on this tale in his *Eve and Henry James* (Norman: University of Oklahoma Press, 1978). Among

those whose view of Euphemia is closer to my own are J. A. Ward, "Structural Irony in 'Madame de Mauves,'" *Studies in Short Fiction* 2 (Winter 1965): 170–82, and Charles T. Samuels, *The Ambiguity of Henry James* (Urbana: University of Illinois Press, 1971).

22. Edward Wagenknecht, "Our Contemporary Henry James," *College English* 10 (December 1948): 131.

23. Kraft, pp. 86–87.

24. Quoted in James, *Complete Tales*, 4:7.

25. Peter Buitenhuis, *The Grasping Imagination* (Toronto: University of Toronto Press, 1970), p. 84.

26. Revealingly, perhaps, the most convincing untroubled marriage in the works of this period occurs in "Longstaff's Marriage" (1878), in which the bride, wed while on her deathbed, quickly expires.

HENRY JAMES
THE LATER SHORT FICTION

ESPITE THE TRIUMPHS attained by Isabel Archer and Maggie Verver in the midst of troubled marriages, isolated triumphs that provide virtually the sole justification of James's persistent but always tenuously held hopes for wedlock, the great part of his marital fiction from 1881 on presents as bleak a vision of matrimony as that in the earlier works. One still sees marriage presented predominantly as a relationship of perhaps irremediable difficulties and as disturbingly linked to, if not engendering, danger for children, suffering, death, and the failure to achieve or to maintain a humane social order. One still sees too all this presented in what is often an essentially melodramatic context. But nonetheless there is a change. As a result, doubtless, of James's increased sophistication in observing and depicting character, the melodrama is now internalized, subtilized. The action, though often as lurid as in the works before 1881, is distinctly subordinated to examination of the motives that prompt it and of its impact on those concerned, figures who are more extensively delineated and often far more sentient than their counterparts before 1881.[1] Further, the depiction of marital difficulties is now directed intensely at answering the crucial question that, implicitly at least, was central to the marriage fiction before 1881 but never adequately perceived or developed by James—and that is whether a marriage is indeed a relationship that, as its defenders assert, can promote legitimate self-expression and personal development and repress mere selfishness or is simply a relationship, more often than not, in which an ugly clash of wills culminates not in wisdom but in wrecked lives. James's increased subtlety and new clarity of focus make his many tales of failed marriages after 1881 more poignant and troubling than any of those before, but they make possible, as well, his portrayal of such quiet victories as those attained in their marriages by Isabel Archer and Maggie Verver, victories that, reflecting the development of James's exceedingly rarefied romantic sensibility in a context of ostensibly "realistic" social observation, would earlier in his career have been out of his ken.

Before turning to *The Portrait of a Lady*, which, of course, marks these major changes in James's marriage fiction, and to the other novels significantly involving marriage, I shall examine some of James's depictions of marriage in the short fiction after 1881. Because there is no chronological pattern of development either in thought or style to James's marriage fiction in this period (other than the movement in the marriage works as in all of his fiction to the prose style of the later phase) I can do this for the sake of convenience and, for the same reason, treat the short works themselves in terms of their different marital subjects rather than in terms of chronological sequence. Further, by looking at the short works first, we can come to perceive more fully, perhaps, the highly personal framework of values in which the palpable marital horrors of *What Maisie Knew* (1897) and *The Awkward Age* (1898) and the complex affirmations of matrimony in *The Portrait of a Lady* and *The Golden Bowl* (1904) are operative. Though certainly the conflicting demands of marriage and art, the complications to which the disparate national backgrounds of husband and wife give rise in marriage, and the self-deception that James believes marriage often breeds are neither mutually exclusive topics nor ones that exhaust James's concerns in his post-1881 short fiction of marriage, they are nonetheless the major themes of these works. Moreover, they afford a representative range of stories, showing clearly their dominant grimness as they delineate movingly and powerfully the painful and usually futile struggles of married characters to attain valid means of self-expression, struggles, of course, central to the novels at which we shall look later.

Conflicts about the legitimate limits of self-expression are, needless to say, most explicit in the stories dealing with the relations between art and marriage. Though in a number of stories not concerned with marriage James presents the commitment to artistic achievement primarily as bespeaking an unquestionably admirable devotion to beauty and integrity in an often shabby world, in the marriage stories the situation is somewhat different. Aware, apparently, as was Hawthorne, that a commitment to art might of necessity be at odds with commitments to people, James in these works treats art primarily as simply a particularly demanding form of the desire for self-expression, one by its very nature likely to engender conflicts between the artist and others, conflicts, obviously, that have devastating impact in as intimate and intense a relationship as marriage. The point of all this for James is not merely to show that artists do not do well in marriage but that the penchant for self-expression generally is, given the shortcomings of human nature, almost inevitably a source of difficulty in marriage. Thus, when artists in "The Author of 'Beltraffio'" (1885) and "The Lesson of the Master" (1892) and an incipient artist in "The Birthplace" (1903) have trouble in their marriages and when a marriage is assailed by the egos of two artists in "The Liar" (1888), James's efforts are directed less at making a case for or against art in relation to marriage than at showing how rarely the drives of one mate or the other for self-expression fail to lead to wrenching problems between them, as inevitably they bring about the jarring combat of fully aroused and bitterly opposed wills.

Consequently, "The Author of 'Beltraffio,'" though it has all the earmarks of an account of the conflict between art and philistinism in the context of marriage, is in reality a story having far less to do with the problems of the artist or, for that matter, those of the philistine than it does with the hideous effects of egotism in that same context. The egotism here resides specifically in the efforts of two artists (Ambient and the narrator), a frustrated would-be artist (Ambient's sister), and a woman bitterly suspicious of all art that is lacking in conventional morality (Ambient's wife) to impose their own private sense of what is fitting onto reality and to deny the others and the pathetic, ill-fated Dolcino an opportunity to be anything but dehumanized figures compliantly imprisoned in this personal vision. Such egotism, of course, is found in all areas of experience, but it has particularly virulent effects when it makes itself felt in a situation involving marriage.

Just how virulent these effects and sad the losses they wreak can be is evident from the very opening of the story, as a scene of deceptive attractiveness quickly becomes the first in a series of examples of the disturbing propensity of the adult characters to force reality to their own specifications. To a quick, uninitiated glance, the prospect that presents itself to the narrator as he arrives with his celebrated host at Ambient's home seems redolent with unalloyed marital good fortune. The lovely wife awaiting her famous husband, with their child of surpassingly delicate beauty in her "maternal embrace" (5:308), the well-appointed garden tea table, the spacious English lawn, the picturesque cottage, the marvelously time-worn steps on the grounds, the "magnificent beeches," the "garden walls of incalculable height" (5:307), all seem to bespeak a matrimonial ideal often envisioned but rarely attained, a vision of all that marriage should be in terms of sentient, loving mates who are also loving parents of charming children and who live graceful lives amid circumstances of quietly restrained beauty. Almost immediately, however, it is apparent that this marriage approaches this brilliant ideal only in external appearance. It takes only Ambient's oddly intoned "She has got the boy" (5:308), his wife's refusal to let go of the child when his father bids him to come, and Dolcino's ineffectual efforts to break from his mother's arms to make one see that this marriage is one flawed by deep conflict.

Nonetheless, that conflict is largely dormant until the arrival of the narrator, which precipitates an active struggle in which, finally, not only Mark and Beatrice but Gwendolen and the narrator himself are caught up, a struggle involving the effort of each of the adults to turn the Ambient marriage into a private fiction of his or her own creation with Dolcino as the virtually foredoomed victim. Ambient's assertion that he and his wife "shall probably kill [Dolcino] between us, before we have done with him!" (5:317) sparks in him no effort at accommodation with Beatrice that might save the boy but merely the detached stance of the observant author who becomes, paradoxically enough, a willing, passive participant in the story that he has set in motion and then stepped back to watch quietly as it develops to the awful end he has foreseen. Similarly, Beatrice, who, as her name implies, is committed totally to the view that life must be spiritually and morally untainted, chooses, ultimately, to create a drama of personal salvation for herself and her son, with Dolcino as unwitting martyr to her ideal of unsullied purity. Though husband and wife bear the major culpability for the death of the boy in that each is violating solemn commitments as mate and parent to avoid the egregious self-indulgence into which they lapse, neither Ambient's sister nor the narrator is without blame for what occurs. Posing as eccentric genius and uncanny prophetess of dire happenstance who plays the vital role of chorus in an exotic tragedy of misalliance, Ambient's sister merely aggravates Beatrice's distrust of her husband's art by establishing an atmosphere in which the artistic and the perverse seem one. No less responsible for reinforcing Beatrice's misgivings about Ambient's work is the narrator, who, regarding all about him as "reproductions of something that existed primarily in art or literature" and believing, further, that the Ambient home "had . . . a general aspect of being painted in water-colors and inhabited by people whose lives would go on in chapters and volumes" (5:307), decides unconsciously to ensure that this story into which he envisions himself as thrust will have the formal integrity so fitting for any work associated with the author of the beautifully shaped *Beltraffio*, even if that integrity demands the death of a child and the destruction of a marriage.

Unlike his would-be acolyte the narrator, Mark Ambient himself may well be, as he declares, beyond the stage at which he "always arranged things too much," did "everything to them that life doesn't do" (5:331–32); but he is not beyond the "gospel" of the "aesthetic war-cry" of "art for art" (5:303) that he sounded in *Beltraffio*. Consequently, although he no longer holds that formal control implies the rigid symmetry that would ensure the death of a child if his father asserts that he sees it looming ahead, he does still hold to the doctrine that saving the child in the name of some moral vision imposed on the work is a violation of all that artistic integrity demands. More, what such integrity demands, as he now sees it, is the presentation of "an impression of life itself" (5:331), a vision of things as they are, unshaped and unconstrained either by the shibboleths of morality or the formalistic imperatives of structure itself. Unfortunately, so given over to this doctrine is Ambient by the time at which the events of the story take place that he is living his life in the state of detached observation warned against so often by Hawthorne, a condition in which, as the narrator notes, "he looked at all things from the standpoint of the artist, felt all life as literary material" (5:333)—a condition, in other words, that one might call "life for art's sake." Therefore, as the conflict with his wife develops, he is less concerned with ameliorating the situation than with observing what its denouement will be. As potential literary material, it must not, given his theory, be shaped in the direction of any resolution, aesthetic or moral, but must be merely recorded in the honing, clarifying sensibility of the artist. If it is this point of view in its earlier "art for art's sake" form that initially prompted the conflict with his wife, this, presumably, for Ambient merely adds a dash of paradox to the material, making it potentially more interesting. If the wife herself sees things differently and wishes to regard herself and her husband and child as something other than figures in a book in progress, well, then, for Ambient the response can only be, as he puts it succinctly to the narrator, "Damn her point of view!" (5:324).

Thus does Ambient, "impregnated—even to morbidness—with . . . the love of beauty and art," as James puts it in his notebook sketch for the story,[2] disastrously conflate art and life and assume for himself the dual role of observer and character in a story that, whether he is fully aware of it or not, can only have an unhappy ending, an ending that, in spite of all his professed desire for detachment, he cannot escape helping to shape. As character, Ambient lives to the hilt the role he perceives to be assigned to him by the terms in which his conflict with his wife is couched. If these define him as the faintly decadent bohemian apostle of Art, standing lithely and gracefully yet with a seemly, nondemonstrative strength against the forces of philistinism embodied in her, he accepts them unquestioningly and with the observing artist's detachment watches himself play out this role. Though, as Donald Reiman suggests, Ambient is not without some taste for respectability and convention,[3] he breaks the tenuous truce that he and Beatrice have imposed on their struggle,[4] precipitating the events that bring on the conclusion to the story in which as observer he is so interested. By having as a guest a young man whose avowedly artistic predilections and adoration of him and his work cannot help but strike Beatrice as flattering his worst traits and cannot fail to call to mind for her all that she does not want her son to become under Ambient's influence,[5] Mark arouses in her the antagonism that his disciple's actions will channel in the direction of the destruction of Dolcino. Further, by treating this adoring and impressionable young man as little less than an intimate confrere, he inevitably puts the narrator in mind of doing something to resolve the conflict into which he has so recently been initiated. Hence, Ambient, by turning the fellow, in effect, into at once another character in his life-story and, oddly enough, another creator-observer as well,[6] makes the death of his son a foregone conclusion.

Though Ambient neither wishes his son to die nor knows that the narrator will, virtually under his aegis, lead Beatrice to bring about the boy's death, he does little to prevent the catastrophe from occurring. Such behavior as he manifests in yielding to the narrator's blandishments to "trust a mother—a devoted mother, my dear friend!" (5:352), though grotesquely inconsistent with one's notion of the way a devoted father should act when his overwrought wife will not allow a doctor to see their seriously ill child, is, on the other hand, all too consistent, as is his behavior throughout the story, with his whole theory of the literary calling. Unwilling to be more than an observer watching himself play the part of sensitive artist in a body of "literary material" that most men know as life, Ambient lets things happen. Having, that is, conceived of his situation less as a part of life than as a literary event, he is bound by his sense of what literary craftsmanship involves to keep his shaping hand off the action and let the characters play out their roles as their makeups demand. If, in his character as the much put-upon author of *Beltraffio*, he cannot avoid exerting a certain effect upon an impressionable younger character with whom he comes into contact, that character, in turn, must be allowed the freedom to give that effect natural consequences in the action. Again, if those consequences themselves generate further, perverse ones, in this case in the wife of the celebrated author who figures so centrally in the "literary material" Ambient observes, this is simply a natural outgrowth of character interaction, which, of course, must be allowed to follow a logic of its own, as Ambient has come to believe. Thus, Ambient does not simply "abdicate familial responsibility and authority," as Viola Hopkins Winner suggests,[7] but actually abdicates his role in the human community. Though his sudden outbursts, "Is he dying—has she killed him?" and "I'll save him, please God!" (5:352) in response to his sister's urgent statement that both she and Beatrice want the doctor to come may well reveal a more typically paternal response than one has seen heretofore in Ambient, any genuinely fatherly feeling here is mingled inextricably with his odd double consciousness as literary character–authorial observer. The theatrical gesture as he utters these lines of "flinging away his cigarette" (5:353), that standard prop of his nocturnal bohemian talks with the narrator, presents a touch of pathos and humanity so perfectly apt to the role of cultivated artist shocked into predictably futile action by the brutal excesses of his philistine wife as, presumably, to elicit the approval of Ambient the observant seeker after material for art. The story he observes, obviously, is the account, so neatly played out, of the martyrdom of the high priest of art-craft, Mark Ambient. That Dolcino is the unfortunate who dies matters not; the martyr remains Ambient and, apparently, "making the most out of life" (5:334), to which he tells the narrator that he but not his wife is dedicated, involves sacrificing life itself, in terms of his son and his own humanity, to the necessity of gaining material for his self-expression through art.

Irretrievably ensconced in his own story as Ambient may conceive his wife to be, she, for her part, tells the narrator when he remarks ingenuously that the Ambient home and grounds have the "tone" of the author of *Beltraffio*'s work, that "I don't in the least consider that I am living in one of his books; I shouldn't care for that at all" (5:314). So averse is she, in fact, to regarding herself as in one of his works, expressing as they do that gospel of "art for art" which is so repugnant to her, that she is prompted finally to try to impose her own vision on reality in opposition to her husband's. In this vision, obviously, she bravely saves her son from such decadence as she sees embodied in her misguided husband and his work, in his disciple the narrator, whom she finds so noxious that she ensures that he never even touches Dolcino, and in her sister-in-law, whose desperate desire to establish the fiction that she is "original" (5:319) despite her lack of real talent or insight leads her to the pathetic expedient of always posturing as "pictorial and melancholy" (5:318). The story into which Beatrice forces her marriage is clearly a didactic one, teaching that heroic sacrifice is demanded if purity is to be defended. Her realization with the imminent demise of her child that this tale is not without its terrors causes her to relent in her efforts to impose her vision on her marriage and makes her beg for the doctor to hurry to the child's side. Her loss of will here and the fact that "she failed rapidly after losing her son" (5:355) show her to be less the devoted artist than is her husband, a fact, obviously, that would be no surprise to Beatrice Ambient. Nevertheless, though, in her effort to impose her own perception of things on the reality about her, she expresses herself in a manner analogous to that of the artist and, ironically enough, inadvertently plays the role all but assigned to her in the private fictions of the others.

No less concerned with bringing his fictional imposition on reality to a suitable conclusion is, as we have seen, the narrator. Convinced that he has "seized Mark Ambient's point of view" (5:323), which he characterizes as that "of the artist to whom every manifestation of human energy was a thrilling spectacle, and who felt forever the desire to resolve his experience of life into a literary form" (5:323), he seeks throughout to turn the disastrous marriage of the Ambients into the stuff of fiction. Because he is still tied, unlike Ambient, to the notion, as Donald Reiman points out, that art must "unfold in artistically satisfying symmetry," this "young American apostle of aestheticism sees in his mind's eye the logical, artistic resolution of the struggle"[8] and takes measures to bring it to fruition. He precipitates the climax of his work by giving Ambient's manuscript to Beatrice and then ensures that events will flow smoothly to their clearly foreshadowed conclusion by quieting Mark long enough for Beatrice to do her worst. By persuading Gwendolen to suppress her suspicions about Beatrice's behavior, the narrator establishes a perfect intimacy with his readers, as he makes certain that he alone can bring them into close communion with the facts behind events long shrouded in romantic secrecy. Thus, although Ambient himself never writes the story that he both observed and participated in so intimately, the narrator has done so, working in his master's tradition. That he consciously intended the boy to die is doubtful. He is not a blatant villain out of crude melodrama. But that he sacrificed his concern for the boy's well-being and for that of his parents, as well, to force a logical resolution because he had more interest in them as figures in a story of his own crafting than as people in their own right is clear.[9]

Though much of any discussion of "The Author of 'Beltraffio'" must be directed at analyzing the makeup of the narrator, all that one brings to light about him bears, finally, on the marriage that is central to the work. His behavior throws further light on the failings of Ambient and his wife, making clear the main reasons for the failure of their marriage. Significantly, as Ora Segal notes, this marriage is never seen directly—never seen, that is, in terms of extended dialogue between husband and wife. The pair never being seen alone, one learns of their strained marriage mainly through Gwendolen's comments about them and through their comments about each other, making their marriage one seen only from the outside.[10] This not only heightens one's sense of their estrangement from each other but imparts to their marriage a pervasive sense of loss, for, pathetically enough,

Ambient *knows* his wife is a woman of singular beauty and virtue and Beatrice *knows* that her husband's works have their own beauty and are the result of rigorous labor. Yet each, like the narrator, and like poor Gwendolen as well, cannot yield up the absolute commitment to a private vision of how reality ought to be ordered; and, as a result, disaster ensues. Whether either mate learns from the loss of Dolcino is impossible to say. One hopes that Beatrice's dipping into *Beltraffio* and Ambient's long delay in publishing the manuscript that led to his son's death are signs of development, but the manuscript *is* published and Beatrice *is* merely dipping into *Beltraffio*. Because of the intensity of the commitment each makes to self-expression, then, a commitment so intense as, in effect, to demand that all around one express oneself, the marriage of this pair becomes a battleground. Because most people, James believes, manifest a like commitment, particularly in situations of close confrontation with others, most marriages, he suspects, go in one form or another the route of the Ambients'. If one or both of the mates is an artist, this grim story points up, so much the worse.

Although the marriage of the Capadoses in "The Liar" is not destroyed, as was the Ambients', by art, which is again presented as a particularly acute outcropping of the desire for self-expression, it is, James makes clear, debased by it. More specifically, Colonel Capadose's wife, so ingenuous and authentic as a young woman that Oliver Lyon, the portrait painter who regrets that she did not marry him, once considered her a perfect model for a painting of Werther's Charlotte, is shown to have become a willing accomplice in her husband's prevarications. Though Capadose is a likable fellow whose lies seem, for the most part, harmless ones—even something of an art form—the situation seems more than a little unsavory, as the last lie in the story, which they tell together, particularly reveals. Capadose's desire to recast reality in order to satisfy his obscure need for self-expression, then, rather than restricted or suppressed within the confines of marital demands, overwhelms his marriage, carrying all, including his wife, before it. Ultimately, his marriage, as he refashions it, becomes an insidious bastion out of which he forays to do battle with facts and into which he retreats for comfort and support when facts and their consequences rise up against him.

James's strategy throughout the tale is to link Capadose, whose name, fittingly, may be derived from the Italian for "masterpiece" (*capodopera*), to the painter Lyon in order to show that both are artists singularly devoted to their crafts. One possible purpose for this linkup is to show that Lyon is, not unlike Ambient, an artist of the heartless sort, incapable of the warmth or the genuine affection that his Doppelgänger, Capadose, is fully capable of manifesting. Seen in this light, the story is primarily a character study of Lyon as a liar, in this case a liar who deludes himself by overestimating his capacity for human feeling. More likely a purpose for the linkup, however, is James's effort to establish that Capadose himself is indeed an artist, though assuredly of a unique sort, and, like Lyon, is not at all averse to using and shaping people, even his wife, to his own ends. Thus, a grim story develops in which, once again, marriage is not proof against the chaotic egotism endemic to human nature.

Lyon's propensity for subordinating people to the uses he might make of them at first makes itself felt in relatively innocuous ways. A fellow guest at dinner he mentally dismisses as "just not a subject," and that luckless fellow's wife he regards airily as having an unfortunate "sort of appearance of fresh varnish . . . so that one felt she ought to sit in a gilt frame, suggesting reference to a catalogue or a pricelist," a "bad though expensive portrait" (6:385–86). Such quiet cataloguing of types, though somewhat cold and smug, seems understandable in a portrait painter who takes his craft seriously. What is not legitimate, however, is the desire to manipulate that Lyon manifests as he becomes increasingly involved with the Capadoses. In his dealings with the prevaricating colonel and his wife, Lyon's motives, though mixed, all bespeak this desire to use others that James, like Hawthorne, sees as often intimately bound up in the artist's motivation.[11] Lyon's portrait of Capadose is a means of furthering his career and of humiliating the feckless colonel for his wife's audacity in not marrying Lyon. Further, it is an effort to humiliate Mrs. Capadose herself in Lyon's presence by forcing her either to tell an obvious falsehood on her husband's behalf or acknowledge before the painter that she has married a pathological liar. And underlying these aims is, even worse, an utterly malignant curiosity, itself bound up inextricably with a desire to manipulate another for the sheer joy of asserting one's power to do so.

Capadose himself, though clearly a far less subtle man than Lyon, is, as noted, likened to the painter throughout. Not only was the colonel, of course, drawn to the same woman whom Lyon so admired—though from start to finish the colonel's commitment to her has been stronger—but the colonel is pointedly described as an artist in his own right. Like any artist he has not really chosen his calling but has, in a sense, been chosen by it. As one acquaintance remarks of Capadose's tale-telling, "It's a natural peculiarity—as you might limp or stutter or be left-handed" (6:407). Indeed, Lyon tends typically to regard Capadose as an artist, perhaps sensing vaguely the similarities between them. Characterizing Capadose for himself, he muses, "He is the liar platonic . . . ; he is disinterested, he doesn't operate with a hope of gain or with a desire to injure. It is art for art and he is prompted by the love of beauty. . . . He paints, as it were, and so do I!" (6:411–12). Elsewhere, in the same vein, he speaks of the freedom with which Capadose "handled the brush" when indulging himself as "*raconteur*" (6:405). Even closer ties between the two are developed by James when, during the painting of Capadose's portrait, Lyon derives the impression that "no one drew the Colonel out more than he" (6:415) and soon comes to feel, in fact, that he and the colonel are virtually partners in the creation of the work. When the colonel in his storytelling "had his intermissions, his hours of sterility, . . . then Lyon felt that the picture also languished. The higher his companion soared, the more gyrations he executed, in the blue, the better he painted . . ." (6:420). Together, then, the two do the portrait, and together too they are drawn into lies; for if Capadose's willingness to sacrifice fact to his farfetched stories makes him more than a little bit an artist, Lyon's willingness to sacrifice others to the overweening demands of what he conceives to be legitimate artistic interest marks him increasingly as a liar. Masking his purpose in painting the portrait, declaring that it will remain in his hands when he secretly intends to send it to the Academy, Lyon reveals himself to be a liar of a particularly nasty, self-serving sort, just the sort Capadose finally becomes once the portrait has carried out its appointed office.

But there is another way, finally, in which these two are alike. Each uses Capadose's wife and debases her in doing so. By putting her in a position in which the woman feels compelled to lie in order to protect her husband, Lyon satisfies his curiosity, his manipulative urge, and his desire to see brought low someone who apparently is satisfied after having rejected him as a prospective husband. Nor does Capadose seem much more appealing than Lyon at the close. By linking the pair as closely as he does, James prepares the reader at last to see how heinous is Capadose's treatment of his wife. Without the Doppelgänger motif, Capadose's lying would seem little more than a foible quietly tolerated by a loving wife. But once James has established through the association with Lyon that the lying, like any manifestation of the creative urge, may bespeak an urge to self-assertion that overpowers all concern for the autonomy of others, the full implications of the lying and of Mrs. Capadose's response to it can be seen. In essence, this once unsullied, genuine woman has been forced to give up her moral autonomy and become little more than an appendage to her husband, useful in buttressing up any private vision he wishes to impose on reality.

That the unloving Lyon, himself taken aback by the coolness with which she is now capable of lying, is, as Leon Edel notes, "unable to grasp the simple truth that she loves her husband"[12] is obvious; but no less obvious is the fact that the total aplomb with which the Capadoses give each other support as they create their ludicrous fantasy attempting to mask their destruction of the portrait marks them both as practiced liars, experienced not merely in spinning yarns for the sake of yarns but yarns for the sake of self-protection. The love that brought a girl who once seemed Werther's

Charlotte to this seems too easily subverted by the coercive pressures of a demanding spouse to ever serve as an appealing example of marital affection. Unfortunately, of course, it is this very feature of marriage, this propensity of the relationship to be wracked by the demanding self-assertiveness of one or the other of the mates—self-assertiveness that is particularly acute when linked with artistic predilections—that makes marriage such a frequently grim proposition as James sees it, so likely a context for such sad little melodramas as the one he subtly shows working itself out here to its tawdry conclusion.

As anyone who has read "The Death of the Lion," *The Tragic Muse*, or "The Next Time," among other tales of the artistic life by James, knows, James does not always associate art with the dangers of undue self-assertion. He values art too highly and defends the freedom of the artist too often for anyone to believe that the suspicions about the artistic sensibility that he reveals in "The Author of 'Beltraffio'" and "The Liar" are ones he holds consistently. Given James's dedication to art, it is not surprising that his fears for the integrity of any marriage when it is faced with the too fervent desire for self-expression on the part of those in it would be matched by his fears for the legitimate aims of the artist when they conflict with the demands made by marriage. These fears are central to his treatment of the Gedges in "The Birthplace," another of James's post-1881 stories showing the difficulties that he envisions as inevitably arising from the close confrontation of art and marriage.

That timid, dun-colored, middle-aged Morris Gedge, erstwhile librarian at Blackport-on-Dwindle and now resident guide at the "birthplace" of England's greatest writer, becomes an artist at all is a surprise. Seemingly trapped forever in a dreary domestic realm that is characterized mercilessly by James as one of flies in the butter dish and of tins of biscuits "that refused to squeeze in the cupboard" piled shabbily on the sofa or on top of the "cottage-piano" (11:407–8), Gedge, like his chronically worried, thoroughly pedestrian wife, strikes one as unlikely to gain more from his work at the shrine than perhaps a few more shillings a week. However, from the first, James does make clear that although the Gedges seem to meet the qualifications set by the controllers of the "Birthplace" that they be a "united couple" (11:403), there lurks within Morris a sensitivity that sets him apart from his wife. In the dismal days at Blackport, "the tears came into his eyes sooner still than into his wife's while he looked about with her at their actual narrow prison, so grim with enlightenment, so ugly with industry, so turned away from any dream, so intolerable to any taste" (11:405). The tenacity with which he clings in the face of opposition to his "dream" of "enlightenment" and "taste" once he forges it at the "birthplace" under the influence of late genius of the place shows once and for all that under his unpromising milquetoast demeanor he has the stuff of the artist in him.

Throughout, Gedge's development is resisted by his wife. Satisfied with the extra money and with what she conceives pretentiously and foolishly to be an elevation in social status, undisturbed by the mendacious spiel demanded of her and her husband by the managers of the shrine and the tourists, Mrs. Gedge fears lest her husband's increasing disenchantment with the lies they must tell will lead him into a rebellious course that will cost them their position. Assuring herself that she is in good relation to the writer they ostensibly venerate at the "Birthplace," she declares with self-serving sentimentality, "We see Him because we love Him—that's what we do. How can we not, the old darling—with what He's doing for us? There's no light . . . like true affection" (11:411). And when her husband, troubled by his part in what he calls "the Show" (11:421), in which they turn "Him" into that "old darling" in whose name they pander to the most sophomoric impulses of willingly deceived visitors, embarks on a series of "nightly prowls" (11:418) in which he seeks genuine "Communion" with the "enshrined Presence," she can only see in this the "danger" that he may become "affected" (11:422). In fact, of course, he is "affected," though not in the purely nonremunerative sense of being addled that his wife fears. "The point was," James notes, "that he was on his way to become two quite different persons, the public and the private—as to which it would somehow have to be managed that these persons should live together" (11:425). That his way of managing this ultimately is to bring both selves together in a new, higher identity as artist is at this point still as inconceivable to him as it would be to his wife; and were the forging of this new identity to hinge on the encouragement of his spiritually and aesthetically lifeless mate, it clearly would remain unimaginable to him and unachieved.

The vital inspiration that Gedge does receive comes, significantly, from outside his marriage, through his contact with the Hayeses, a deeply sensitive, aesthetically alert, young married couple who achieve a perfect union rare among married folk in James's work. Unlike the Gedges, they are admirably attuned not only to the promptings of beauty but to each other, as is strikingly apparent when they discuss their perception that the spirit of the great writer whose memory they revere is too all-encompassing to be snugly in residence at the "Birthplace." The wife declares to her husband, "It's rather a pity, you know, that He *isn't* here. I mean as Goethe's at Weimar. For Goethe *is* at Weimar." To which her husband replies, "Yes, my dear; that's Goethe's bad luck. There he sticks. *This* man isn't anywhere. I defy you to catch Him," prompting her laughing response, "Why not say, beautifully, that, like the wind, He's everywhere?" (11:436). It is such happiness and intelligence as seen in what Gedge feels to be this "tone of pleasantry, though of better pleasantry, . . . and more within his own appreciation than he had ever listened to" (11:436), which causes him to unburden himself to this pair about his difficulties.

Having done so, Gedge is left with much to ponder about his career and his marriage. The sympathy that he receives from this young pair obviously intensifies his internal conflict about his position at the shrine. Further, the image of marital fulfillment they present contrasts so obviously with the lack of identity of purpose flawing his own marriage that he finds himself looking at Mrs. Hayes and thinking, "If poor Isabel could only have been like that!—not as to youth, beauty, arrangement of hair or picturesque grace of hat—these things he didn't mind; but as to sympathy, facility . . . !" (11:437). Finally, what, in effect, his unburdening himself to the Hayeses and his admiration for them lead him to is a tendency for the first time to view his marriage from outside its dreary context, from the vantage point of that "private" half of himself who now knows not only that the "Birthplace" is fraudulent but that there is at least one marriage that makes his own seem as fraudulent as the shrine. And this new perspective, in turn, enables Gedge to see his way through to the opportunity of forging his new identity. This incarnation as artist, interestingly, gives the "Birthplace" an odd legitimacy by ensuring that at any rate one brilliant creator has been born on its premises.

The second visit of the Hayeses, after Gedge has assumed his new identity, is a means by which James enables the reader to see that no irony is being directed at Gedge and at his triumph. If this pair, sensitive and alert as they are, see him not as a humbug but as having achieved something grand, then clearly he has. This pivotal role played by the Hayeses both as inspirers of Gedge's growth and certifiers that the growth has, in fact, taken place might well make one wonder whether marriage is, for James, as inimical to art as Mrs. Gedge's demeanor initially makes it seem. Indeed, it is the very conflict within him between his desire not to take "the bread from [his wife's] mouth" (11:443) and his hatred of the lies that she wants him to feel no compunction in telling that leads him to develop his special art form of delivering the lies with an accomplished raconteur's grand flourishes. Too, the Gedges end up thoroughly reconciled to each other—"just as we were," as his wife puts it—but better off too because of the addition of a raise voted for their "sweet little stipend" (11:465) as acknowledgement by the managing committee of Gedge's ability to please the hordes of guileless tourists. Marriage, consequently, seems, at least for Gedge, to have become a relationship that can serve variously as catalyst for artistic achievement and a realm of easy domestic comfort in which he can savor his triumph. And if it can be this for Gedge, one might wonder whether it perhaps could be a means by which others would be enabled to come into full possession of their talents for self-expression and similarly flourish.

Unfortunately, despite the happy turn of events for Morris Gedge, there is really little in "The Birthplace" to convince one that James has come to see marriage as a relationship consistently conducive to the nurturing of the artistic impulse. The marvelously successful Hayes marriage is thoroughly atypical, of course, of most marriages poor Gedge has seen and, indeed, of most marriages found in James's work:

> They were children of fortune, of the greatest, as it might seem to Morris Gedge, and they were of course lately married. . . . Somehow the world was theirs. . . . The thing was that the world was theirs not simply because they had money—he had seen rich people enough—but because they could in a supreme degree think and feel and say what they liked. They had a nature and a culture, a tradition, a facility of some sort—and all producing in them an effect of positive beauty—that gave a light to their liberty and an ease to their tone. (11:433)

Clearly, the Hayes union is exceptional, presented by James more as an ideal of what marriage ought to be, and hence as an educative contrast for both Gedge and the reader to the Gedge marriage, than as a representation of what most, or even many, marriages are. Rather than inspiring Gedge by showing him what he can hope his marriage will become, it instills in him a dissatisfaction with his matrimonial lot that prompts him to his subtle rebellion against his wife and all the shabby, conventional mendacity to which she seeks to tie him. Nor is even the ideal Hayes marriage presented without some reservation, for Gedge does observe that "they were of course lately married," a cautionary note thrown in by one who has seen, apparently, too much marriage to believe that in the long run more marriages turn out to be like the early stages of the Hayeses' wedded life than the middle stages of the Gedge union. Finally, there is little reason to believe that the latter segment of the Gedge union will be much better than the part James presents. What reconciliation James observes at the close is prompted more by Mrs. Gedge's fervent gratitude for the raise in their stipend than by any epiphany through which she comes to understand what her husband is doing and his motivations for doing it. The frenzied, frightened tone she manifests when she fears that Gedge has gotten himself cashiered gives ample evidence of what sort of response Gedge might have expected from his wife over the years ahead had he in fact lost his job. Doubtless, even as she thankfully and bewilderedly stays beside him through the years to come, Gedge's lot will indeed be a lonely one.

Thus, the major impression with which one is left at the close of "The Birthplace" is that Gedge's curious triumph is achieved more through the influence of a long-dead genius, the encouragement of a virtually unique couple, and, perhaps most importantly, Gedge's long-dormant talent for artistic expression than through the influence of his marriage, a relationship in which he had long stagnated. Gedge's ability to use the peculiar circumstances in which he finds himself, then, is a singular happenstance, bespeaking no affirmation of marriage as an encourager to legitimate self-assertion through art. Though central to the particular art form that Gedge creates for himself are, James notes, a totally spurious "clerical unction" and the affectation of a "priestly character" (11:452), there is nonetheless running through James's stories of art and marriage the underlying notion that the celibacy that one identifies with the priest's calling may well be necessary for those who hope to create art.

Certainly, this view is central to "The Lesson of the Master." In fact, the very lesson that the celebrated author Henry St. George conveys to his admirer, the promising young writer Paul Overt, is that for the artist "one's children interfere with perfection. One's wife interferes. Marriage interferes" (7:264). If the artist marries, St. George declares, "he does so at his peril—he does so at his cost" (7:264). And what that cost is precisely is the artist's opportunity to attain the "great thing," as he calls it, "the sense of having done the best—the sense, which is the real life of the artist and the absence of which is his death, of having drawn from his intellectual instrument the finest music that nature had hidden in it, of having played it as it should be played" (7:263). St. George attained this "great thing" once, early in his career. His failure to achieve it since, a failure sensed not by the literary world at large but only by a few who count, such as St.

George himself and Overt, to whom he confesses his sense of defeat, is attributed by St. George to his marriage. His wife, whose frail health and delicate good looks belie her iron will in matters fiscal, has been, St. George confides to Overt, the bane of his career, a veritable dragoness laying waste his work. Pressuring him to provide her and their strapping sons with all the advantages of fashionable English life, she sets St. George to work, as if turning out "a few" (7:220) novels, as she puts it, were simply a matter of diligently applied sound business practices. Put to his task in a windowless chamber before a tall desk at which he can only write standing, "like a clerk in a counting-house" (7:258), St. George cranks away at his suitably remunerative works with machinelike regularity from eleven till two each day. Thus does St. George do his obeisance to what he characterizes as the "the idols of the market—money and luxury and 'the world,' placing one's children and dressing one's wife—everything that drives one to the short and easy way" (7:239). If his devotion to these idols necessitates that he let his wife force him to burn a "bad book" (7:219) on which he is at work— one, presumably, that is too fine to sell well or that, perhaps, touches too closely on the Master's sense of artistic loss—it is something he does without demur. Such, then, is the price, teaches the Master, that marriage exacts from his art; and, as "The Last of the Valerii," "The Author of 'Beltraffio,'" and "The Birthplace" all show, this innate antipathy of a wife for art is virtually a given in James's marital fiction.

There is, to be sure, some ambiguity in "The Lesson of the Master" that does, perhaps, cast Mrs. St. George's role as dragoness into doubt. St. George's marriage after his wife's death to the very girl he warned Overt not to imperil his career by marrying does raise some interesting questions. For example, is St. George's impassioned attack on matrimony for the artist merely a smokescreen thrown up by a man who knows that his frail wife will not last long and is himself looking longingly at the girl Overt wishes to wed? Further, will St. George now, after scaring Overt away from the girl and winning her for himself, give the lie to his own thesis and write a new masterpiece, as Overt fears he will? Or, finally, is St. George's warning, whether he seeks to win the girl for himself or not, merely the sleazy self-extenuation of an author who either chose willfully to prostitute his talent or found after his fine early work that he had tapped dry the vein of his talent? An affirmative answer to any of these questions, of course, reduces greatly the responsibility of Mrs. St. George and of marriage generally as destroyers of art.

However, there is, finally, little reason to believe that either any such affirmative answer or reduction of responsibility is intended by James. The apparent ambiguity serves the purpose of making Overt, who did, in fact, write a brilliant work while in self-imposed exile from the girl, question whether such renunciation as he endured and will, apparently, have to continue enduring at least as far as *this* girl is concerned, is indeed necessary for the true artist. As such, James makes vivid for his readers the agonizing self-doubts about his lonely course that the artist must inevitably confront and that impart to his calling its quality of awful heroism. To share Overt's doubts is to know, however briefly, the absence of comfortable signposts that the artist must know all his life. Further, there is little reason to believe that St. George will ever turn out any work again, much less any work of note. His demeanor at the close, "almost *banal*" and "almost smug" (7:280) as he confronts Overt at the celebration of his engagement, and his bride-to-be's appearance of being "happy with a kind of aggressiveness of splendor" (7:279) do not seem to suggest that literature is in the offing. Thus, although one cannot be sure, the likelihood is that St. George's lesson on behalf of the artist's celibacy is a sound one as James sees it; and, one might note, even if it were in this case meant to be taken ironically, the very fact that James here as in the stories we have looked at previously would think to associate terrible hindrances to art with marriage is another significant indication of his recurring fears that marriage may be inimical to self-expression through art.

Two other stories that make this same association and thus reflect the same fears are "The Real Thing" (1892) and "The Next Time" (1895). Though the lack of malleability for artistic purposes revealed by Major and Mrs. Monarch in the former is the result more of their social training and absence of innate talent than of any other factors, the fact remains that they *are* married and that in their touching mutual support each reinforces the other's shortcomings as model. Nor is it merely coincidence, one suspects, that the painter and his models Oronte and Miss Churm, all skilled in their own ways in the artistic calling, are all, apparently, single. In the latter story, although Ray Limbert's wife does not keep him from producing his brilliant fiction, his misery as impecunious genius is increased by his knowing that he is failing to support adequately his wife and children. Moreover, his works are successful only in spite of his abortive efforts to prostitute his genius so that he can be a better provider.

Repression and overly aggressive self-expression are, as we have noted, evident as problems not merely in stories in which one of the mates is an artist. As "The Last of the Valerii" and "Madame de Mauves" manifest, international marriages are particularly prone to difficulty in James's fiction, so much so, in fact, that Leon Edel notes, "Implicit in these tales" is James's "sense that there could be no happy marriages between American and European."[13] And the chief difficulty that these marriages have in the short fiction involves this very question, so prevalent in the stories of the relation of art and marriage, of whether matrimony, typically, is compatible with legitimate self-expression or simply a relationship too often marked by repression and immoderate efforts at self-assertion. Certainly, the suppression by his wife of Count Valerio's pagan heritage and the mutual misunderstanding of the Baron de Mauves and his unyieldingly American wife as they manifest traits instilled in them by their different national backgrounds reflect this question implicitly. Nowhere, however, in James's short fiction are the problems of manifesting one's own identity while married to someone of foreign birth and training explored more extensively and explicitly than in the sardonic "Lady Barberina," a tale that delineates all the difficulties perceived in the two earlier short tales of international marriage but, avoiding the somewhat heavy-handed melodrama of both through subtle wit, conveys more tellingly the loss that James sees as ensuing all too frequently in such marriages.

Unmarried, free to live in manners that their national backgrounds have trained them to, Lady Barberina and Doctor Jackson Lemon are happy and no threat to each other's happiness and way of life. Married, they are caught up in conflict that is irremediable save for the sacrifice of one or the other's sense of identity and purpose. When first seen, before the marriage, Lady Barberina seems one of the fortunate ones. Glimpsed riding proudly and happily with her family, among friends and social peers amid "the deep, dark English verdure" (5:200) of Hyde Park, Lady Barb seems little less than the finest example in England of the beauty and self-assured grace that centuries of upper-class breeding in a stable, hierarchical social order can produce. Lemon, the young American galloping in the park the same day on a horse too large for him, seems no less fortunate and no less an admirable product of his national culture. Wealthy, as Lady Barb is not, Lemon has nonetheless, in the best American manner, pursued a career anyway, becoming a physician. Though his money has to some extent dulled his appetite for achievement in his field, a friend asserts, "He takes a great interest in medical science, and . . . he will always be doing something in the way of research" (5:211). The very picture of him sitting a horse too large for him denotes his American aggressiveness and irrepressible desire to overcome odds and assert himself, if not in medicine then certainly elsewhere. That such a pair might make a brilliant marriage is the fond wish of Lady Beauchemin, who thinks "English and American society ought to be but one— . . . the best of each—a great whole" (5:219). Unfortunately, though, it is a wish that James sees as having virtually no chance of becoming reality.

Ironically, James shows, it is those very traits that make Lady Barb and Lemon the "best" of English and American society that doom their marriage from the start. Lemon's determination "to marry Lady Barb and carry everything out" (5:262) against the advice of his American friends and after confronting disquieting difficulties with her parents over the marriage "settlement"—a British arrangement that he finds offensive—grows as much out of Yankee determination, stubbornness, and the will to assert himself socially as out of affection for the girl or understanding of her makeup. His blithe statement "If she likes me, she'll like my country" (5:237) reveals not only his culpable ignorance of his prospective bride's nature but an optimism and a faith in the power of love and the charm of his native land that James sees as peculiarly, quaintly, and rather dangerously American. Obviously, determination, optimism, and even the will to achieve social grandeur can be admirable traits, but, symptomatic as they are of the still raw, still new, democratic way of life in America, they are incomprehensible and vaguely irritating to the quintessentially English Lady Barb, particularly when, living in the United States with her husband, she finds herself cut off from the world she has known and in which she has flourished. Similarly, when her father characterizes Lady Barb succinctly as "a clever, well-grown girl, [who] takes her fences like a grasshopper" (5:234), he is marking those traits that make her the fine product of the upper-class English way of life who attracted Lemon in the first place but also revealing inadvertently the narrow range of her accomplishments and interests, a narrowness that will lead to her unhappiness in America and to the exasperation of her husband.

More knowing than her son, Lemon's mother, "who had never thought of matrimony without a community of feeling in regard to religion and country" (5:285), treats her daughter-in-law from the first on her arrival in America "with the greatest gentleness—all the gentleness that was due to a young woman who was in the unfortunate position of having been married one couldn't tell why" (5:274). Though certainly anything but brutal and overbearing with his unhappy wife, Lemon has little understanding of her situation. Unable to regard Central Park as a suitable substitute for Hyde Park, finding American conversation too intense and continuous, loath to visit among democrats, whose manners she detests, whose recreation she abhors, and whose propensity to measure themselves against her she finds at once ludicrous and vaguely baffling, Lady Barb is as out of place in New York as Lemon unknowingly was in London. Consequently, she spends her time wishing only to return to England or, as a miserably inadequate substitute for it, to talk of her homeland with her husband. This, the only real source of satisfying intimacy she has with him, apparently, is not enough finally to make a marriage. More often than not, in fact, Lady Barb feels that with Jackson absent only when he is doing research or reading a paper to a medical society, she has "more of her husband's company than she counted upon at the time she married" (5:276). Moreover, such few warm moments as they have are never seen, and the conversation between them that is directly presented is almost akin to stichomythia in its prevalence of short, clipped utterances, conveying an intense coldness and repressed hostility under its calm that show little sympathy on Lemon's part and augur badly for the future of their union. Indeed, when last seen, Lemon, having taken permanent residence with his wife in England, seems as miserable as did his wife in America. No longer doing research, unwilling to see either Mrs. Freer, an old American friend who warned him against the marriage, or her husband, who encouraged him to marry the girl, Lemon has become a repressed, ineffectual man. Too, he has a little daughter "with features that [he] already scans for the look of race—whether in hope or fear" (5:301) is not known, though one has dark suspicions, of course, of his feelings should the girl show marked signs of her mother's background. This is particularly ironic in view of the fact that it was the English racial traits of the child's mother "which were after all what he had married her for, thinking that they would be a fine temperamental heritage for his brood" (5:297). Thus concludes the effort by the "best" of each culture to achieve a union. Instead of mutual accommodation to each other's identities, there is merely suppression of one or the other, as husband or wife must become an unassertive married stranger in a confusing foreign land.

There are two other marriages in this story, one an international union that does achieve happiness of a sort, the other a marriage of Americans that is conventionally happy in a way that one rarely sees in James's works. The former is the union between Lady Barb's younger sister, Lady Agatha, a flighty, flirty, too pliant girl, and Herman Longstraw, a loud, genial, essentially spurious fellow of dubious origins. Neither is a particularly admirable example of his or her national type, and James's point in bringing the pair into the story seems to be to show that only such overly adaptable types, devoid of developed identities, settled tastes, principles, or substance can have a happy international marriage. Significantly, James points out "it is as good as known that Jackson Lemon supports them" (5:301), a further indicant, one suspects, that this pair lack substance and that such happiness as they know neither ought to be sought after nor thought to bespeak any faith on James's part that international marriages might be a success. The latter marriage is that of the aptly named Freers, a distinctly American couple highly reminiscent of Howells's Marches in their openness, friendly badinage with each other, and essentially pragmatic orientation. Such happiness as they know is hard-won, for they lost a child in the distant past and still feel that loss keenly. Though Freer's desire to see Lemon marry Lady Barb so that he and his wife can observe how the young pair will do is troubling, the Freers do seem, by and large, likable and even admirable. What James includes them for, apparently, is not to present through them a paean to the typically Howellsian sort of marriage but a contrast to the international marriage. Whereas such marriages as that of the Freers rarely interested James, probably striking him, as we have noted, as rather pedestrian, the very terms of their success, with mutual accommodation implicit in every relaxed bit of conversation reported, points up the reasons for the difficulties undergone by Lemon and Lady Barb, two whose rigid commitments to the countries of their birth will not allow for a marriage in which both mates can assert their identities.

Hence, in international marriages, as in marriages involving artists, James's short fiction presents more difficulties involving self-assertion than it does solutions. In a number of other short tales written after 1881, he shows that another difficulty stifling mature assertion of self in all too many marriages is self-deception. As we have noted with regard to other problems that James depicts, self-deception is not peculiar to marriage in his fiction. But, again as with the others, self-deception, James shows, is, if not more prevalent in marriage than elsewhere, more intense, more prolonged, and more prone to blight lives irremediably. Bearing on this aspect of James's misgivings about marriage, though not, strictly speaking, a marriage story, is the strange "Maud-Evelyn" (1900). When Marmaduke gives up his plans to marry and instead spends his young manhood irretrievably caught up in venerating the memory of a dead young girl he never knew, convincing himself with the aid of her bereft parents that she grew up and that he loved her and married her, only to have their happy union ended by her untimely death, his indulgence in this life-denying self-delusion is merely a disquieting literalization of what a number of James's characters do when, tying themselves to a relationship highly productive of self-delusion, they marry and incur personal disaster. No less damaged by a life-denying self-delusion is the widowed Mrs. Warren Hope in "The Abasement of the Northmores" (1900). Her unwillingness to acknowledge that her late husband was a man of far less ability in his career of government service than was his friend Northmore, the man she rejected for him (and subconsciously wishes she had not), has led her into a joyless existence compounded of envy and a sense of undeserved obscurity while both men lived and to virtual paranoia[14] now that both are gone. Her futile, frenzied efforts to build up her husband's posthumous reputation (if possible, at the expense of Northmore's and to the chagrin of his widow) are obviously the pathetic expedients of a woman who sought vicarious achievement through her marriage and could not find even that paltry fulfillment. But, even more, they are again symptomatic of the destructive self-deception to which James finds so many of his married characters prone.

More humorous in tone is "The Path of Duty" (1884), but the humor does not belie the fact that the marriage depicted in it is one ruined by the self-serving self-deception of the husband. Devoted to a woman other than his fiancée, Ambrose Tester renounces, out of ostensible fidelity to his engagement vows, all possibility of either an affair or marriage with her. Though such a decision might seem strikingly high-minded, it is soon apparent that Ambrose has gained more than he has given up. Before long he is spending innumerable intimate hours after his marriage with his renounced love, basking in the glow of her approval of his moral strength and rewarding her with similar admiration. That his poor wife, consequently, finds herself with little to do other than puzzle in loneliness over her husband's behavior seemingly has no effect on him, caught up as he is in this exercise of mutual congratulation. Again, then, marriage, a breeder of self-deception, results in either unhappiness or groundless self-satisfaction. For one such as James who so values consciousness and self-awareness, this aspect of marriage is, needless to say, particularly unfortunate.

Perhaps the short work after 1881 epitomizing this specific failing in marriage is the late, unduly neglected novella "Mora Montravers" (1909), a sardonic account of the multiple self-deceptions engendered by an especially luckless union. As middle-aged, ineffectual "poor Traffle" (12:267) contemplates his orphaned niece Mora's decision to live with the little "painter-man" (12:268) Walter Puddick instead of in the dreary house in which he and his stolid wife, Jane, have raised her, the quiet desperation that unbeknownst to him and his wife has characterized their marriage makes itself felt for him. "Living on their sufficient means in their discreet way, liked, respected, and even perhaps a bit envied, in the Wimbledon world . . ." (12:268) has not been enough, he comes suddenly to see, to make a marriage, to compensate for "their thin ideals, their bloodless immunity, their generally compromised and missed and forfeited frankness . . ." (12:273). However, this revelation that he has been mired in self-deception comes too late in the game for Traffle. Unaware, though, that he is too long accustomed by now to the yoke of convention and too timid by nature and ingrained habit to make good an escape from the stultifying marriage he has come so suddenly to despise, Traffle does not perceive that it is too late and seeks to use his niece's flight as a means to his own, thus embarking on a self-deception every bit as pathetic as the one from which he has only just been awakened and far more ludicrous.

The particular form that his effort at reform takes is that of regarding himself as a sophisticated, sentient person long immured in Philistia with an insensitive mate but now gradually and gracefully asserting his identity and winning his way, through the example of the gloriously "Bohemian" (12:313) Mora and Puddick and such contacts with them as he has, into his rightful realm. Here, one assumes, he and the erring couple can regard each other as loving comrades in the task of keeping alight the flames of beauty and freedom. Several facts, however, undercut Traffle's escapist vision. First, Puddick may not have nearly as much talent as Traffle is so quick to believe he does, may, in fact, be little more than a ne'er-do-well who finally marries his mistress Mora only to get the money offered him by Jane to do so. Second, Mora, rather than the exotic apostle of bohemianism Traffle takes her to be, may only be a rather selfish, shallow, little thing whose avowed desire to be "free" consists of little more than the wish to partake of a good time whenever she can find it. Certainly, it is with no compunction whatever that she deserts her new husband to take up with the "smart," obviously nonbohemian Sir Bruce Bagley, Bart. And, finally, Traffle himself probably is motivated more by an illicit, unconscious passion for Mora (no blood relation to him) than by genuine avuncular affection. Thus, embarked on the pursuit of nothing less than a new identity that he cannot hope realistically to achieve, seeking to feel at one with people whom he more than likely misunderstands and overrates, and driven by an illicit longing that may well have precipitated his awareness of his marital dissatisfaction in the first place, Traffle pursues his course of self-deceit.

Though, as evidenced by Arthur Miller's *A View from the Bridge*, a depiction of another uncle's troublesome attachment to his niece, there is much in Traffle's situation susceptible of tragic delineation, James sees no tragic potential in his protagonist here. More dreamer and bumbler than doomed hero, Traffle maunders along comically. He tacitly admits to Mora "that her aunt was a goose of geese—compared to himself and her" (12:291); vaguely identifies with Puddick because he too once dabbled in painting and is, of course, drawn more powerfully to Mora than he knows; coyly alludes, to Puddick's horror, to certain unnamed "realities" of which "you must be having your full share" (12:277); and, finally, dreams that the pair of lovers will some day see their way clear to "invite him, their humble admirer, to tea" (12:293). All the while, he assures himself, he is "becoming under the precious initiation opened to him by Mora, whether directly, or indirectly, much more a man of the world" (12:290). His illusions about his new identity and about any special affection his niece may have for him are effectually dispelled when, virtually overcome with emotion at coming upon her by chance after not having seen her for a long while, he finds himself treated with no warmth from her but only informed airily that she is now Mrs. Puddick but is leaving her husband. Thus does Traffle learn to his chagrin that, all his efforts and dreams notwithstanding, for Mora he will inevitably "stand or fall with fatal Jane"and that "it was in fact with fatal Jane tied as a millstone round his neck that he at present knew himself sinking" (12:307–8). He has the clear sense too now, perhaps hardest of all for him to take, "of having seen the last of Mora as completely as if she had just seated herself in the car of a rising balloon that would never again descend to earth" (12:313). He soon finds, however, that he has not seen the last of poor, rejected Puddick. Coming home, he finds the fellow bohemian of his imaginings all too comfortably ensconced with "fatal Jane," who, having undertaken without her husband's knowledge a search for new identity and new freedom all her own, is providing the little "painter-man" with a solace prompted by underlying motivations the nature of which Traffle is exceedingly well-equipped by now to guess. Abashed, Traffle can only muse enviously, "Lord, the fun some people did have. Even Jane . . . unmistakably, was in for such a lot" (12:333).

As one follows Traffle through his misguided course of self-deception, one is inevitably reminded of Lambert

Strether, another man who belatedly tried to live all he could, and of Strether's vicarious and ultimately painful involvement with Chad and Madame de Vionnet. Indeed, like Strether, Traffle even has an embassy to carry out, as he acts as his wife's intermediary, offering Mora and Puddick money set aside by Jane if they are willing to marry. However, there is a major difference between the luckless Traffle and Mrs. Newsome's ambassador. Strether finally attains a redemptive renunciatory vision that, James believes, will enable him to face all that lies ahead with grace and courage. Traffle, on the other hand, the victim of his marriage, learns little. Left fruitlessly envying "fatal Jane," for "even" she will now have "fun," Traffle, clearly, has grown little. Leon Edel's characterization of this tale as one of "human waste, mistaken lives, wrong decisions, lost opportunities"[15] seems applicable to no one in the work as much as Traffle, who, finding that he has deceived himself for years into believing that his empty marriage is fulfilling, rushes desperately into what are merely new, more humiliating self-deceptions. His failure to realize that he has been shaped too effectively by his marriage to be a type other than he is or to live more fully than he does will, one suspects, be repeated by his wife, who will doubtless learn as little from the experience with Puddick as Traffle did with Mora about the power of marriage to enmesh one inextricably in a web of self-deception. Apparently, then, James, here as elsewhere, sees the frustrations of marriage as often breeding self-deceit of such staying power as to make the clear, illusion-free thought of a grown Strether impossible to achieve.

Breeding repression, self-deception, lacerating conflicts, feverish attempts at self-assertion, marriage in James's shorter fiction after 1881 is a relationship pervaded invariably by loss and pain. Little in this is, of course, different from what occurs in the earlier short fiction of marriage; but all here is heightened, as we have noted, because of James's greater subtlety and intensity of focus. As before, much here is the material of melodrama, always, as Peter Brooks notes, a sign in James's work of deep concern over the implications of social disorder inherent in the flawed lives he depicts. The bitter struggle of father and mother over their beautiful, frail son, the plight of a woman married to a pathological liar who himself is pathetically vulnerable to the devious attack of his wife's former suitor, a young man wedding himself to a dead girl he never knew, an uncle amorously pursuing his wayward niece, the conflict between a wealthy American and the English noblewoman he married over where they will make their home, the attempt of a virtually paranoid widow to humble the family of the dead man she did not marry but wishes unconsciously that she did—all this, needless to say, is the stuff less of "realism" than of melodrama; but James by emphasizing event less than the internal makeup of those involved, as he did not do in the marriage works before 1881, save, perhaps, in "Madame de Mauves," gears all in the post-1881 marriage works, melodramatic or not, to the overriding question of whether marriage is compatible with legitimate self-assertion and valid self-development. Inevitably, as we have seen throughout this chapter, he concludes that they are not.

1. An exception to this is the weak "Georgina's Reasons" (1884), a shallow, rather silly tale of a flighty, selfish girl's bigamy and her first husband's continuing commitment to the vow he made her. Because of the weakness of the tale, his renunciation of personal happiness in order to maintain his loyalty to his vow carries none of the moral authority of Isabel's similar renunciation and seems merely a somewhat foolish, quirky thing to do.

2. F. O. Matthiessen and Kenneth B. Murdock, eds., *The Notebooks of Henry James* (New York: Oxford University Press, 1947), p. 57.

3. Donald Reiman, "The Inevitable Imitation: The Narrator in 'The Author of Beltraffio,'" *Texas Studies in Literature and Language* 3 (Winter 1962): 507.

4. Speaking of the state between the Ambients that I have characterized as a "truce," the narrator notes (5:336), "[Ambient] had the art, by his manner, by his smile, by his natural kindliness, of reducing the importance of [the difference between himself and his wife] in the common concerns of life, and Mrs. Ambient, I must add, lent herself to this transaction with a very good grace."

5. James Scoggins makes this point effectively in "'The Author of *Beltraffio*': A Reapportionment of Guilt," *Texas Studies in Literature and Language* 5 (Summer 1963): 265–70.

6. Scoggins suggests that Ambient is Frankenstein-like in the effect he has on the narrator (p. 267).

7. Viola Hopkins Winner, "The Artist and the Man in 'The Author of *Beltraffio*,'" *PMLA* 83 (March 1968): 108.

8. Reiman, p. 506.

9. This is borne out, as Ora Segal notes, in the "wry" and "amused" tone, as she describes it, that predominates in the closing passages of the tale (*The Lucid Reflector* [New Haven, Conn.: Yale University Press, 1969], p. 124).

10. Segal, p. 120.

11. For a discussion of ties between this story and Hawthorne's conception of the artist, see Edward Rosenberry, "James's Use of Hawthorne in *The Liar*," *Modern Language Notes* 76 (March 1961): 234–38.

12. James, *Complete Tales*, 6:11.

13. James, *Complete Tales*, 5:9.

14. For an excellent account of Mrs. Hope's difficulties, see Robert L. Gale, "The Abasement of Mrs. Warren Hope," *PMLA* 78 (March 1963): 98–102.

15. James, *Complete Tales*, 12:10.

HENRY JAMES

THE NOVELS

*E*XCEPT FOR THE MARRIAGES delineated at length in *The Portrait of a Lady* and *The Golden Bowl,* such significant glimpses of married life as James offers in the novels are no more calculated to convey an affirmative vision of the institution than are those presented in the shorter works. Indeed, even most of the unseen marriages, those ended by the times in which the novels they figure in are set, are generally unappealing to contemplate. The terrors of being the husband of either Madame de Bellegarde or Mrs. Newsome are doubtless ineffable. Similarly, the shabbiness of the Condrip marriage, the deceits and quiet viciousness of the Merle union, and the tepid pleasures derived from being the wife of the young Lambert Strether are all readily perceivable though the marriages themselves are long since past. In marriages that to the dubious fortune of the husbands are still extant, Guy Brissenden, who, if the narrator's theory in *The Sacred Fount* is to be believed, is being slowly drained of vitality by his vampire wife, and Jim Pocock, gurgling his joy in *The Ambassadors* at being allowed a chance to go to the Varieties and other Parisian hot spots and thus for a few evenings get out from under the pressures of being the husband of Sarah and the son-in-law of Mrs. Newsome, convey ample evidence of James's continuing fears that marriage engenders domination, self-deception, and self-repression. However, the marriages seen at greatest length, other than those in *The Portrait of a Lady* and *The Golden Bowl,* are presented in *What Maisie Knew* (1897) and *The Awkward Age* (1899); and these, though singularly unappealing, convey (implicitly and indirectly to be sure), as the shorter fiction does not, the benefits that can be derived from marriage, even in the midst of the predominant pain.

The marriage between Maisie's parents and the subsequent one of her father and her quondam governess, Miss Overman, are seen as Maisie sees them and, hence, are all the more disturbing, even frightening, than they would be if seen from an adult perspective. The figures in them, like all adults in Maisie's world, "approach and fade," in Tony Tanner's words, "like fish in a murky aquarium." More, when they are near, again to quote Tanner, "they change their relationship with her most capriciously . . . and show her annoyance and affection, attention and indifference in an arbitrary manner which Maisie is at a loss to comprehend." Literally and figuratively, then, "people in general" are for Maisie "never where you might expect them to be."[1] To put it another way, they appear to her much as figures do to a child caught in nightmare. They are imbued so luridly with preternatural, even supernatural, capacities for ill, for shape-changing, for sheer starkness of being as to make one pity the poor child trapped in intimate confrontation with them. Thus, all that Maisie sees is disturbingly "phantasmagoric—strange shadows dancing on a sheet," cruelly intensified as if, James notes, "the whole performance had been given for her—a mite of a half-scared infant in a great dim theatre,"[2] attempting to see just how she fits into the performance, which is the playing-out of perhaps the meanest marriage James ever depicts.

By her estranged parents, for whom marriage "had mainly suggested . . . the unbroken opportunity to quarrel," Maisie was wanted "not for any good they could do her, but for the harm they could, with her unconscious aid, do each other" (p. 5). So might one with a bit of experience characterize the relation of the Faranges with their daughter; but, unable to perceive as a detached, sentient adult might that her mother and father are a promiscuous, hypocritical, lust-ridden pair, deterred neither by common decency nor fear of notoriety from their vicious pursuit of pleasure and their childish hatred of each other, Maisie sees them merely in terms of the vivid images and stark experiences that she connects with them and that she tries feebly to shape into some sort of order understandable to herself. Thus, to Maisie her father is most of all a man with "shining fangs" (p. 180) and a broad expanse of gleaming shirt-front who blows smoke in her face, pinches her thin calves in cruel sport, swears at her mother present and absent, belabors Maisie with being variously "a dirty little donkey" (p. 156) or "a little ass" (p. 183), and, finally, who deserts her and his second wife to run off with a rich American woman who seems to Maisie "a dreadful human monkey in a spangled petticoat" with a "nose that was far too big and eyes that were far too small and a moustache that was, well, not so happy a feature as Sir Claude's" (p. 193). Her mother, who speaks brutally in Maisie's presence of the girl's father, and finally deserts Maisie and Sir Claude to run off with a new lover, is a garish, billiard-playing virago, quick to belabor her little daughter with her "falsity" when Maisie fails to grasp either her attacks on her husband or her tawdry plans. Invariably, she is as bewildering and threatening to Maisie as is the girl's father. Pulled to her mother's breast when the woman makes a self-serving show of maternal affection, the child finds herself "amid a wilderness of trinkets, . . . as if she had suddenly been thrust, with a smash of glass, into a jeweller's shop-front" (p. 145). As one would expect, this pair and their subsequent mates and lovers confront Maisie with an unending succession of the strange: a trip to a seedy exhibition hall in which devotees of anthropology can observe the "Flowers of the Forest," the flowers being a "large presentment of bright brown ladies—they were brown all over—in a medium suggestive of tropical luxuriance" (p. 171); the sundry study rooms with the fantastic Mrs. Wix and her omnipresent "straighteners"; a sudden meeting in a verdant park with her mother and a mysterious "Captain"; a hurried, obscure journey across the channel to a quaint French town—all of these, along with the moustachioed American "Countess," the quarrels, the coach rides as she is shunted between parents, former parents, and soon-to-be parents, the smoke-filled rooms in which her father holds forth about her thin calves to his sporting friends, and the billiard rooms in which her mother dominates the table become the clutter of disorienting scenes, places, and people that is her childhood.

The voracity, vulgarity, depravity, the sheer nastiness forming this Sargasso Sea of her youth are lost upon Maisie. Similarly lost upon her is the propensity of the adults around her to use her for their own sleazy purposes as, among others, bearer of ugly epithets that she fails to know the meanings of, go-between, pretext for illicit liaisons, and butt of coarse, lewd humor. Clearly, it is through the mistreatment of this child, all the more painful to observe, perhaps, because she is so unaware of it, that James shows the ugliness he finds so often attendant upon marriage. Nonetheless, Maisie's life is not blighted. Despite her youth and naïveté, she attains genuine moral stature, and attains it not merely in spite of the corruption that surrounds her but because of the experiences that it presents her. When Maisie, confronting Sir Claude in the presence of the second Mrs. Beale Farange in the French seaside town, demands of him nothing less than love, commitment, and courageous renunciation not only of Mrs. Beale but of his whole way of life, she has become, of course, the "abominable little horror" (p. 354) that Mrs. Beale calls her; but she is so only from the perspective of that irretrievably corrupt woman and the others like her who are used to Maisie solely as pliant and passive, an easy mark. From the perspective of James, Maisie has become, wondrously enough, the only character in the work capable of speaking with moral authority, the only one who, because she loves, cares, and demands honesty of others and herself, has really attained the freedom about which the others prate whenever they wish to justify their low courses of self-indulgence.[3] When Sir Claude, rising to an appreciation of Maisie's moral grandeur but otherwise incapable of breaking from the chains of lust forged by the lure of Maisie's stepmother, fails to leave with Maisie, the girl's new will does not shatter. "By this time . . . afraid of nothing" (p. 352), loath to yield to her old governess and become again merely a means by which a sordid affair can be made to seem respectable, Maisie will now chart her own course. Encouraged by Sir Claude's appreciation of her integrity and bravery, ready now to live genuinely the moral life about which her nominal protectress, the ineffectual and all too corruptible Mrs. Wix, merely cants and maunders, Maisie sails back to England in control of her future, gliding over waters in which, figuratively speaking, all the others are merely submerged and thrashing viciously about.

Prompting Maisie's growth has been not merely her real love for Sir Claude but the very pain into which the chaotic lives of her parents have immersed her. Somehow, through the welter of sharp, grotesque images and bizarre places and events that she has been unable to shape into ideas she can articulate, Maisie has discerned the outlines of right and wrong, love and hate. Perhaps in seeing and knowing intimately these opposites, she has, by virtue of her innate worth, gravitated ineluctably to the good. Had she not known the pain, she might not finally feel so repelled by it; had she not been subjected to its grips so intensely, her final hold on her moral vision might not be so tenacious. What this all amounts to, of course, is no striking affirmation of marriage on James's part but an awareness that one does not find in the shorter fiction that the pain associated with any given marriage *can* be educative, if not for the married persons themselves at least for one tied intimately to marriage (an ironic reversal, this, of Howells's fond wish that the good effects of a happy marriage will ripple outward into society and, for that matter, of Herrick's view, later, that the bad effects of unhappy marriages will ripple outward). For James to envision marriage as educative for the marrieds, he needs the fuller scope provided by a more extensively delineated marriage than one perceives here or in *The Awkward Age.*.

Such education as is derived from the wrecked marriages dotting the London landscape of the Brookenham circle in *The Awkward Age* again is not to be found in the married folk themselves but in others—in this case, the bachelor Longdon, too old to marry, and the slightly shopworn ingenue Nanda, regarded by Vanderbank, the man she could love, as too tainted for him to marry. The affection, understanding, and depth of communication achieved by Longdon and Nanda not only grow out of their painful contacts with the marital disasters about them but serve as examples, oddly enough, of what some of the dimensions of a good marriage might be. Indeed, through all of James's account of this circle and its disastrous marriages what one is left with, finally, is not so much a sense of revulsion from marriage on James's part as a longing that it might be more often all that it should be. Though this, of course, is implicit in the melodramatic mode in which the shorter marriage fiction is written, it never makes itself felt as explicitly as it does here. Thus, in *The Awkward Age* one perceives less of a sense on James's part of marriage as a relationship pricking human failings into action than of marriage as a potentially worthwhile relationship beset by human failings. Though James may well regard marriage in these terms in the shorter works, the emphasis there seems inevitably to be on marriage as breeding ground of problems rather than on marriage as vulnerable to problems inherent in those who wed.

Certainly, at first glance, marriage in *The Awkward Age* seems nothing but an unpleasant opportunity to lapse into corruption or to be hurt by a partner who does. Edward Wagenknecht's succinct account of the adulteries permeating the work gives a vivid sense of just how inescapable the marital pitfalls seem:

> Cashmore is having an affair with Carrie Donner, whom he drops (or so he claims) when he is attracted to Nanda, shamelessly avowing his new interest to Mrs. Brook herself, who expresses no indignation; his wife, Lady Fanny, is involved with Captain Dent-Douglas; and Lady Fanny's brother, Lord Petherton, is having an affair with the Duchess. Later Petherton switches to Little Aggie [Mitchy's wife and the Duchess's niece] and Lady Fanny to Harold Brookenham, who is mature only in his vices.[4]

Nor is there any reason to believe, apparently, that, given the views on matrimony of those depicted in this novel, adulterous relationships and a gradually widening network of corruption are anything but virtual inevitabilities to which marriage among them gives rise. J. A. Ward notes that for Longdon, "who represents the mores of a previous age," marriage "is a matter of sacred trust and devotion." For the others, though, who seem to epitomize the failings of the present age for James, marriage, Ward points out, is something quite different: "To Mrs. Brook and the Duchess, marriage is a matter of political intrigue; . . . to Cashmore, Petherton, Lady Fanny, and Mrs. Donner . . . it is a matter of frivolity; to Vanderbank, it is a matter of self-effacement."[5] Marriage, then, regarded variously as means to power, subject for mirth, titillating opportunity for illicit pleasures, and possible threat to self-indulgence, does not offer these characters anything approximating "sacred trust and devotion." Sadly, the closest they come to attaining what Longdon sees as inherent in a good marriage is in their formation of Mrs. Brook's "circle," a group that, in achieving an ephemeral intimacy, arouses in Mitchy and, perhaps as well, in Mrs. Brook herself, a capacity for commitment that approaches what Longdon has in mind as the goals and rewards of matrimony. However, that the fulfillment Longdon envisions can be achieved in any marriages made on the modern scene James depicts here seems even more improbable than that such transient virtues as are shown in the "circle" can be made permanent, compelling forces in the lives of those who make up this group.

Nevertheless, what predominates here for all the adultery, dishonesty, and pain associated with marriage is, as I have noted, not an attack on the institution but a poignant sense of what is lost when marriages fail or when matrimony itself is not respected sufficiently. One senses this in what is perhaps the dominant force in the novel, the talk of the circle itself. Dorothea Krook notes that the conversation, "oblique, allusive, elliptical" as it is, bristling with "crucial implications of which not one must be lost on pain of losing the thread of a whole scene, if not of the whole story," is clearly "the speech of a homogeneous, closely-knit social group sharing common standards, attitudes, forms of behavior." Further, she points out, "precisely because so much is shared, no part of what is shared need ever be explicitly referred to."[6] Such talk as this engenders certain expectations, of course, expectations of shared commitments, shared concerns, a sense of community. Nowhere, finally, are these expectations met by the group. As Mrs. Brook perceives at the close, their talk has been "mere talk," and it has been "mere, mere, mere," as Vanderbank rejoins, because, Mrs. Brookenham states, the talkers "haven't had the excuse of passion."[7] Unfulfilled by the circle, these expectations are met, surprisingly, for a moment anyway, in the Brookenham marriage, the only union at which James affords his readers an inside look in *The Awkward Age*. What is so surprising in this is that the Brookenhams' talk usually shows them to be far less on the same wavelength than are the members of the group. The uncomprehending rejoinders, the unresponsive "ohs" tendered Mrs. Brook typically by her "dry and decent and even distinguished" but pedestrian and unimaginative husband prompt her at one point, in fact, to think "she would no more have appealed to him seriously on a general proposition than she would, for such a response, have rung the drawing-room bell" (p. 56). Briefly, though, this poorly mated pair do in their talk achieve the affection and the sense of community at which the talk of the circle merely points. This occurs when, in the course of discussing Nanda's future, Mrs. Brook confesses that she feels herself the chief obstacle to her daughter's making a good marriage. Hearing this, her husband asks with real affection, "And what's the matter with 'you'?" To which Mrs. Brook, touched, replies, "That's the nicest thing you ever said to me. But ever, *ever* you know," and goes on to declare poignantly, "Consider that fact well, and, even if you only said it by accident, don't be funny—as you know you sometimes *can* be—and take it back. It's all right. It's charming isn't it? When our troubles bring us more together?"(pp. 384–85). This moment in which their talk has been touched for once by some degree of deep affection is not enough, obviously, to redeem the continuum of lesser moments that is the Brookenham marriage, but it *is* enough to show that marriage is a relationship in which the unfulfilled promise of the circle's talk *can* be fulfilled, even such a marriage as that of deeply flawed people like the Brookenhams.

The idea that marriage is a relationship of potential value subverted by human failings that is conveyed implicitly in the Brookenhams' brief moment of genuine affection and indirectly in the vision of shared concerns and commitments engendered by the circle's talk is reinforced elsewhere in the novel. When Longdon's declaration to Nanda that "you shall never be anything so sad" as one who does not marry prompts her query "Why not—if *you've* been," his rejoinder "Exactly because I have" (p. 193) makes eminently clear that from the standpoint of one who, however old-fashioned his tastes may be, is in a position to know, marriage is a definite good. Similarly, Nanda's own declaration that in marriage "the great thing is to be helpful" (p. 445) provides a compelling reminder of all that a marriage can be when those in it have it in them to seek to be of aid to each other. Finally, the sad retreat from the modern rout undertaken together by Longdon and Nanda, though the palest of matrimonial imitations to be sure (Longdon far in the past had sought to marry Nanda's late grandmother, whom Nanda strongly resembles), does nonetheless provide a hint of what a real marriage might offer in the way of mutual comfort and support in a difficult world.

The wisdom that Maisie, Longdon, and Nanda attain is, as we have seen, a wisdom that comes outside marriage though closely linked to it. In *The Portrait of a Lady* and *The Golden Bowl*, James's most extensive delineations of marriage, it comes within wedlock itself. In the former, in fact, it is virtually the only reward that Isabel's marriage offers her, for love in any usual sense, comfort, and joy are not to be hers with Gilbert Osmond. Nevertheless, what Isabel does derive at last from her marriage is enough to make it a successful, even a triumphant, one for her. Needless to say, it is so only in a very special sense. To understand fully the terms in which her triumph is operative, it is useful, I think, to turn to an account offered in the 1920s by Count Herman Keyserling of the highest benefits that can be derived from marriage. In his essay "The Correct Statement of the Marriage Problem," Keyserling never refers to James and probably does not even have him in mind; but his unconventional theories are, in any case, of admirable aid in enabling one to appreciate the no less unconventional victory that James romantically envisions Isabel as attaining. Writing of those who are sufficiently sentient to be capable of achieving more than commonplace gratifications in their marriages, Keyser-ling notes that "the fulfillment of marriage and its happiness entail the acceptance of the suffering pertaining to life. It gives the latter a new and deeper meaning."[8] His subsequent assertion that marriage without intimate knowledge of pain is incompatible with real personal growth seems so in tune with James's thinking at the close of *The Portrait of a Lady* as almost to have been written by James himself in explana-tion and defense of Isabel's behavior at the end of the work:

> Marriage is essentially an ideal common to all humanity, for, if properly understood and carried out, it *precludes* the possi-bility of attaining satisfaction on a low plane, and conse-quently establishes a higher one. Its intention is not to slacken but intensify conditions. That is why unhappily married peo-ple more rarely do harm to their souls than those who are happily married. Not only does an unhappy marriage promote self-development more positively than does a state of ease due to lack of experience, but it leads more readily to that inward happiness which is the necessary consequence of achievement than any harmony can do which fails to make life more in-tense.[9]

This, then, is a characterization of matrimony as the inevi-tably painful but potentially triumphant, drawn-out confron-tation with experience that is what James envisions marriage at its best as being and that, within the narrower scope of the short fiction and of the briefly delineated marriages in *What Maisie Knew* and *The Awkward Age*, is never developed.

Keyserling's statements do, obviously, take us a bit ahead of ourselves; for Isabel's triumph, as James manifestly sees her decision to return to Osmond to be, is only comprehen-sible as the final stage of a completed action, the culmination of her seemingly idiosyncratic decision to marry Osmond in the first place. However, the key terms for understanding that earlier decision are again to be found in Keyserling's ac-count of the grim triumph attainable in marriage. When he speaks of the need to "intensify conditions in order to pro-mote self-development," he is dealing in assumptions that are central to James's portrayal of Isabel's needs and her un-derlying reasons for marrying Osmond. For James, inevitably, living in "intensified conditions" implies living in intimate confrontation with experience, which, in turn, finally implies the opportunity to confront oneself and thereby undergo the "self-development" of which Keyserling speaks. For a young woman in the nineteenth century, even a young woman as independent and even willful as Isabel is, James realizes—as Kate Chopin and Edith Wharton later will—the major chance to achieve such a confrontation can only come with marriage and, perhaps, with a marriage none too happy at that. Now obviously Isabel does not marry Osmond with the idea in mind of having a bleak marriage and thereby growing. She marries him, as Tony Tanner notes, for entirely other reasons, reasons involving her own youthful egotism and devotion to what she considers to be her freedom. "Like many another character in American fiction," Tanner points out, "[Isabel's] energy goes into avoiding any commitment which might serve to define and arrest her." Thus, obscurely feeling the need for involvement with life and the chance to put her financial power to use, Isabel seeks marriage; but desiring, as well, to soar over the world that lies all before her and, in good American Emersonian fashion, loath, as she declares to Madame Merle, to let anything express her but herself, she seeks a marriage offering her the largest area in which to be her unencumbered self. And wedding Osmond, Tanner asserts, presents itself for Isabel as the most obvious means of achieving just such an ideal marriage in which involvement and unrestricted free play of self are happily combined because, as she unconsciously perceives, she and Osmond, despite all appearances to the contrary, are markedly alike.[10] Her marriage to one greatly like herself turns out far differently, of course, from what she had imagined—the aspects of herself reflected in Osmond had indeed been, to use the term she applies to her husband, "unimaginable"—but it is, finally, a means by which she comes to know herself and attain the growth of which Keyserling speaks.

Had Isabel wed Goodwood, Warburton, or such unexceptionable young men as her sisters do, she never would have found herself thinking of herself and her husband that "they were strangely married at all events, and it was a horrible life";[11] but she also would not have undergone the confrontation with experience and, ultimately, with herself into which marriage with Osmond has led her. What one sees of Isabel in her married life until her decision to go to Ralph is a woman who, in many ways akin to her husband from the first, seems to become even more strikingly like him as the marriage wears on. Similar to Osmond initially in her weaker traits, including propensities for paying "excessive attention to appearances rather than realities," for preferring art to life, for having "more theories than feelings, more ideals than instincts,"[12] Isabel when first seen after several years of marriage seems like Osmond even in manner. The clipped answers and distant tone underlying the facade of merriment in her meeting with Rosier in chapter 38, a style of conversation generally that, as Ralph observes, reveals that she has lost her "discrimination" and "fallen into exaggerations," even the very "mass of drapery" drawn behind her "light step" and the "majesty of ornament" sustained by her "intelligent head," all manifest "that she appeared now to think that there was nothing worth people's either differing about or agreeing upon" (2:143). All of this, of course, bespeaks a rather uncomfortable likeness to Osmond that is all the more apparent the first time the pair are shown in conversation since their marriage. Their talk is of a tautness never heretofore glimpsed in marital conversation in American literature, as husband and wife jockey intently for the psychological edge over each other, alert to each shifting nuance of menace in the other's words, and it shows unsparingly how completely akin to Osmond's Isabel's demeanor has become. As her husband unfolds his hopes that Warburton will propose to Pansy, who, he wishes, will reject Rosier's blandishments, Isabel's replies are no more calculated to give him pleasure than his obvious quiet relish in the fact that her former suitor now seems interested in his daughter is meant to give Isabel. Her quiet comment that "it matters little" to one in love, as Rosier is, whether she encourages him or not or whether Osmond "turns him out" or not because "a lover outside's always a lover" gives Osmond little joy. Nor do her replies in response to his cool assurances that his daughter "wishes above all to please" and will "do what I like." To the former she rejoins, "To please Mr. Rosier perhaps"; to the latter the quietly sinister line, "If you're sure of that, it's very well" (2:181, 183). Thus James shows that Isabel now, so like her husband, "was not accommodating, would not glide" (2:182). Were she "accommodating," of course, she certainly would not ask of Osmond as she does, when he speaks of Pansy becoming Lady Warburton, "Should you like that?" (2:181); for the very essence of Osmond's self-esteem is his maintenance of the appearance that he seeks little from the world, and her question is a frontal assault on this pose—as, doubtless, she well knows.

Hence, all evidence presented in the early chapters depicting the married life of the Osmonds shows that the general similarities between the pair before their marriage are reproduced now in the smallest, most intimate details of their demeanor together. Consequently, Isabel, in effect, by confronting in her marriage this sort of mocking mirror image of her own worst traits, responds, paradoxically enough, by exaggerating these traits as she combats them when they are manifested by her spouse. Though, to be sure, this does not make for a happy marriage, it makes for one in which the growth of which Keyserling speaks and that James clearly values is possible. It is possible, finally, because, despite all similarities between them, Isabel is not a female Osmond but someone far better than he. Were she not so, one suspects, neither James nor Ralph would concern himself so much about her development as he does, nor would characters as admirable in their different ways as Ralph, Warburton, Goodwood, and Henrietta be as devoted to her as, in their different ways, all of them are. And what makes her better than Osmond is the capacity for commitment, compassion, for sheer openness to life and its vicissitudes—the capacity, in short, as all these imply, for moral growth, which she never loses despite all her errors and which is never evinced in her husband.

Though the major difference between Isabel and Osmond can be perceived most clearly when one looks at their thoughts on marriage itself, these seem at first, like so much else described thus far, to reflect more similarities between them than differences. Typically, Osmond's remark to Goodwood that "being married's in itself an occupation" (2:314) obviously echoes (although he has not heard it) Isabel's comment to Ralph, shortly before, that "when one's married one has so much occupation" (2:305). More significantly, Osmond's assertion that the "disagreeable proximity" in which he and Isabel find themselves is of their "own deliberate making" and that therefore they "should accept the consequences" of their action because what he values "most in life is the honour of a thing" (2:356) is markedly similar to Isabel's earlier statement to Henrietta (again unheard by Osmond), "One must accept one's deeds. I married him before all the world; I was perfectly free, it was impossible to do anything more deliberate. One can't change that way" (2:284). Also, the motivation underlying Isabel's words here seems markedly similar to the egotism reflected in everything her husband says and does. Her remark to Henrietta "I can't publish my mistake. . . . I'd much rather die" (2:284) seems like nothing so much, in this vein, as verbalization of an attitude that her husband has never quite put into words. But James's purpose, here and elsewhere, in showing similarities between this husband and wife is not, finally, to show that they are lastingly of a piece. Rather, as we have seen, it is to show both the process by which Isabel must confront and even exhibit in aggravated form her worst traits before she can grow beyond them and the terrible intimacy in which she exists with Osmond as she undergoes this process.

More, for all the apparent similarity of their statements on marriage that I have just quoted, their motivations in making them are not identical at all; for though there may be some residual egotism inherent in Isabel's desire to maintain the facade of a good marriage before the world, her marriage has taught her enough of herself and life to lead her to see that matrimony is in and of itself to be defended and maintained. It has taught her this because, unlike her husband, whose professed concern with the "honour of a thing" and with "the observance of a magnificent form" (2:356) starts and ends virtually with his concern for the image of himself that he presents to the world and the world's response to that image, Isabel is, finally, capable of caring for things outside herself—for concepts, relationships, institutions, and people. Thus, when she speaks of the necessity of maintaining her marriage, it reflects her concern for personal integrity, her awareness of the worth of the institution, and even, strangely enough, her devotion to Osmond himself more than it reflects egotism.

Several other passages conveying reflections about marriage make this distinction between Isabel and her husband clear. In the course of his conversation with Goodwood in which he speaks of marriage as an "occupation," Osmond notes too that it is so because "my wife and I do so many things together." He goes on to relate with a deceptive air of amiability, "We read, we study, we make music, we walk, we drive—we talk even, as when we first knew each other. I delight, to this hour, in my wife's conversation"; and he concludes with an Iago-like show of offering friendly counsel: "If you're ever bored take my advice and get married. Your wife may indeed bore you . . . ; but you'll never bore yourself. You'll always have something to say to yourself—always have a subject of reflection" (2:314). Knowing what the Osmonds' marriage is like, aware that Osmond, finding Isabel resistant to his efforts at repression, has decided "there was nothing left but to hate her" (2:201), one perceives the menace and mockery permeating these words. Quietly taunting Goodwood, who still is devoted to Isabel, Osmond reveals at the same time the perverse pleasure he seems genuinely to take in being with her and thereby having the continual chance to hate and punish her for her independence. Marriage for him, then, a relationship in which, to use the sinister phrase he uses earlier in conversation with Goodwood, he and his wife are an "united" as "the candlestick and the snuffers" (2:420), is an opportunity for subtle refinements of sadism at the expense of his baffled wife and for self-dramatization before a world at large that, he hopes, is similarly baffled and suitably intrigued.

For Isabel, on the other hand, marriage is less a matter of indulging one's own egotism than it is a matter of obligation. Curiously, she sees this most strongly during her odious confrontation with Osmond over her desire to go to the dying Ralph. Osmond's assertion to her in the midst of it, "You are nearer to me than any human creature, and I'm nearer to you" (2:356), driving home to her with utmost extremity the nasty situation into which marriage to him has thrust her, seems to drive home as well, as nothing has before, the dimensions of what she describes to herself as "the great undertaking of matrimony" (2:360–61). And she recalls in this moment of reflection, more powerfully than at any moment previously, that "marriage meant that a woman should cleave to the man with whom, uttering tremendous vows, she had stood at the altar" (2:361).[13] She has seen, then, unlike Osmond, who despite his words sees none of it, that the institution of marriage itself, generating an intensity of intimacy unattainable in any other relationship, has an inherent value that cannot be blithely shunted aside, a value that, as the human need to solemnize the relationship with "tremendous vows" shows, may even touch upon the "sacred and precious" (2:356). The very fact that she can see this at all testifies to the validity of her perception. As a result of her marriage and the painful intimacy with Osmond and, eventually, the more painful intimacy with herself that it causes her, Isabel has grown to be the sort of person able to perceive that devotion to things beyond self—to, perhaps, an institution like marriage—can save even a life "thrown away" (2:203), as she has previously regarded her own to be.

Early in the novel, James declares that Isabel is to become "consistently wise" (1:145). Though at this stage of the story, James, to be sure, treats the brash young girl and her longings for the ineffable with a good deal of irony, subsequent events show that James here means exactly what he says. The trial that is her marriage to Osmond leaves her purged of illusions about life and herself and ready to face all with intelligence, compassion, and the quiet courage of which her brashness was merely a crude, transitory manifestation. Saddened by her discovery of Osmond and Merle's liaison but above resorting to the self-demeaning comforts of vengeful tirades against husband or former friend, committed still to the welfare to her pathetically vulnerable stepdaughter, brave, knowing, and loving enough to enter into a beautiful communion with her dying cousin and the spirit of Gardencourt that he and his father have embodied, Isabel proves herself capable of charting the course James doubtless things the finest available to her, that of returning to her marriage. Though, clearly, as she looks at the years ahead, she wishes things had turned out differently, she is wise enough to know that consequences are to be faced and that acceptance of the life that she, others, and circumstances have all had a hand in shaping is what both moral integrity and the imperatives of her situation dictate.

As we all know, there are those who take issue with Isabel's choice. Finding behind her decision motives of which she is largely unconscious that are less admirable than those we have noted and perceiving, perhaps, alternatives for her that are in their eyes less life-denying than the path she chooses, these commentators believe that her behavior at the close of the novel either is abhorrent to James or ought to be.[14] Holding in abeyance for a moment the question of whether James *should* be repelled by her choice, we can, I think, by looking closely once again at Isabel's course at the end of the novel, see the erroneousness of the notion that he *is* so and regards her as driven by self-delusions into the worst of the options available.

Simply put, the notion advanced by some that Isabel's decision to return to Osmond is a crudely self-serving one, growing out of egotism and fear of mature sexuality, is not borne out by the novel. Were Isabel committed merely to an egotistical sort of self-justification in which she seeks only to admire herself and impress others, it is doubtful that James would have presented her profoundly moving last scene with Ralph. To see Isabel in this scene as in the throes of a more subtle form of the egotism she manifested before her marriage is to charge James either with indulging in the most tasteless of ironies at the expense of Isabel, the reader, and even the dying Ralph or with an inadvertent inconsistency of tone, neither of which charges seems justified when one observes the uniformly somber, though not bleak, tone of the concluding chapters of the novel. Further, were Isabel's choice to stay with Osmond motivated by sexual fear, one wonders why James speaks of the "admirably intimate" (2:140) first year of married life she shared with Osmond or why he mentions that the pair had a child who died. (James's inclusion of this latter fact is indeed a skillful touch, for it cuts the ground out from under simplistic assumptions about sexual fears, supplies another source for Isabel's education through marital pain, and does away with any potential a living child might offer for extraneous conflict between Osmond and Isabel or for reasons leading to Isabel's returning to her husband other than the ones James presents.) Nevertheless, commentators point to Goodwood's effect on Isabel, particularly in the final scene with him, as a sign of Isabel's sexual terrors. Obviously, she does fear this man and her response to him. But why on earth should she not? Presented by James as, despite his many virtues, almost a walking phallus, Goodwood is constantly thrusting himself at her, conjuring up visions of a marriage in which she would be not much more than a physical object to him. Her fear as she responds to him physically is not fear of sexuality itself, but of sexuality so overpowering as to carry all that makes for her freedom chaotically before it, including principles, commitments to others, and most of all her identity as one who has lived, suffered, and loved and, in doing so, has found herself.[15]

Moreover, to go off with Goodwood of necessity would involve divorce; and divorce, whether to gain Goodwood, someone else, or some ill-defined liberty, offers Isabel little. It is an enormity that would embarrass not only Isabel herself but Pansy (and thus Rosier) and Osmond. Her refusal to wish the latter pain, a clear manifestation of the wisdom and compassion to which the severe educative process of her marriage has brought her, derives explicitly from the insight that his initial misjudgment of her makeup was in part her fault, from her awareness of the possibility that he might turn on Pansy, who would already be hurt terribly by seeing her father suffering, and, finally, from her feeling that she and Osmond have been too close for too long for her to accept with any equanimity the prospect of damaging him. Further, to go the route of divorce not only implies that surpassing happiness is to be found elsewhere either in or out of marriage, a possibility that Isabel has come to see as illusory, but that happiness is the great good toward which one's life should be directed, a belief of which Isabel has been disabused by the education brought her by marriage. Finally, entering "the great alkali desert of cheap Divorce," as James styles it in *The Golden Bowl*,[16] would represent a repudiation on Isabel's part of an institution that she feels not only to be touched by the sacred but that, as she is fully aware, has taught her a great deal, an institution that she now perceives, in Laurence Holland's words, to be a "form of aspiration and commitment"[17] making the highest demands on those in it and thus opening up possibilities of the greatest victories.[18]

James reveals too, commentators to the contrary notwithstanding, a paucity of alternatives for Isabel should she desire to be right with herself and her circumstances. Divorce out of the question as both she and James see it, there remains nothing for Isabel to do but to return to her marriage and retain the commitment to the institution itself, to Pansy, and, insofar as he lets her, to Osmond. The alternative of staying married to her husband as a different sort of wife, one who finds her pleasures outside her marriage, as Mrs. Touchett does in traveling and residing comfortably alone with no demands on her or as the Countess Gemini does in attempting to avenge herself on her beastly husband by having a string of affairs, offers no chance for Isabel that anyone would seriously think her better off for taking. Mrs. Touchett's prickly, quirky selfishness and the countess's shrill, dotty misery serve, then, both as indicants to the reader of the sorts of folly Isabel avoids by returning, conventionally, to her unhappy marriage and as reminders that because happiness in marriage seems generally rather hard to come by, one might best look for other, perhaps more valuable, rewards in the relationship.

Returning to the question of whether Isabel's course *should* meet with James's approval, as it pretty clearly does, I suspect the answer is not within our purview here. Suffice it to say, as Peter Brooks does, "The theme of renunciation which sounds through James's novels . . . is incomprehensible and unjustifiable except as a victory within the realm of a moral occult which may be so inward and personal that it appears restricted to the individual's consciousness, predicated on the individual's 'sacrifice to the ideal.'"[19] In other words, one either sees beauty in the highly individualistic renunciatory vision shared by Isabel and her creator or one does not; but an inability to perceive it in no way indicates that James does not mean for it to be seen. One for whom Isabel's course would certainly be triumphant is, again, Keyserling, whose statement following might almost have been written as a defense of Isabel's return to Osmond:

> Human life inasmuch as it is superior to that of plants and animals, starts only with the perception of the inevitability of tragedy and its willing acceptance. From this it is evident in what sense a perfect marriage must represent for man the highest achievement of his purpose. In marriage . . . tragic tension is instinctively accepted as the basis of life . . . Thus suffering can mean happiness just as much as satisfaction can; and the most poignant pain can be joyously accepted if it is recognized as the fulfillment of man's destiny.[20]

Tension, indeed, there is aplenty in this marriage with Osmond; and as Isabel resolves it internally in terms of renunciation of self and acceptance of the marital form and its exigencies, the tension is raised to the tragic dimensions of which Keyserling speaks. In her free choice, then, to accept the consequences of an initial decision made in less than perfect freedom and to accept confinement as the price of maintaining character, Isabel, for James, attains genuine tragic grandeur; in a manner not unlike that of the novelist who tells her story or that of the marital institution to which, despite the pain it imposes, she maintains her loyalty, she thus imposes form on chaos.[21]

Like *The Portrait of a Lady*, *The Golden Bowl* focuses on a marriage that is initially as disastrous as any of the irremediably luckless unions to be found in the short fiction; but again, as with the account of Isabel's life with Osmond, James sees this marriage as the rare sort from which, ultimately, benefits of surpassing value are derived. Through her marriage Maggie attains a profoundly tragic vision and the moral courage and compassion James saw as its concomitants. Further, she acquires the devotion to those forms, such as marriage, that seem to partake of the sacred as they impart this tragic vision. All of this, of course, is achieved as well, as we have seen, by Isabel. But for Maggie something else is gained too, something that Isabel and all other sentient protagonists in James's depictions of marriage are not fortunate enough to achieve, and that is happiness. What occurs in *The Golden Bowl*, in fact, is the gradual evolution of the union of a seemingly poorly mated pair into the sort of genuine marriage not only of man and woman but of America and Europe and of worldly and transcendent that Isabel had vague, incomplete intimation of when she decided to wed Osmond and that she continues to see as the informing ideal behind the vows she spoke. Indeed, it is Isabel's allegiance to this very ideal that leads her to stay in her marriage and thus maintain loyalty to the institution that makes the ideal, however rarely attained, a possibility.

When last seen, in loving embrace, Maggie and Amerigo have achieved a marriage unlike any other depicted by James and one by its very nature rarely seen anywhere. It is a marriage in which husband and wife, though devoid through hard experience of pleasant illusions about themselves, each other, or life, can still find happiness together. They find this not through leaving the tragic vision behind but through a constant acknowledgment of it that makes their union, as both they and James perceive it to be, a fragile, beautiful stay against confusion, a commitment to their own and mankind's future despite all they know of pain, and, above all, perhaps, a tribute to love itself, which maintains its redemptive power even amid human imperfection and the awesome mysteries and ambiguities of existence.[22] This sort of solemn yet joyous affirmation of life, one transcending tragedy yet deriving its special beauty from being at the same time grounded in it, is what James hopes the intimate, intense confrontation with experience that marriage affords can lead to. That he sees it doing so only rarely is obvious. The tragic vision itself, without which courageous affirmation cannot be reached, is attained in his marriage works only by Isabel; and though she herself understands what marriage offers, she fails because of Osmond's shortcomings to attain the happiness reached, finally, by Maggie and Amerigo. That they alone in James's marital fiction attain this level in their marriage testifies both to the rarefied character of the ideal marriage as James envisions it and his awareness of how effectually the limitations of human nature keep most from realizing this ideal.

Perhaps James's greatest technical triumph among many in *The Golden Bowl* is the manner in which he makes Maggie and Amerigo's gradual realization in their marriage of this glorious matrimonial ideal convincing by painstakingly delineating its evolution through clearly demarcated stages corresponding to the types of marriages attained by the other husbands and wives depicted in the book. The originally projected title for this novel, *The Marriages*, though not finally as evocative as *The Golden Bowl*, is apt nonetheless as an indicant of the thematic and structural significance of the other marriages. The briefly glimpsed Gutermann-Seuss marriage, the marriages of Adam and Charlotte and of Fanny and Colonel Bob are not merely a means of providing one with scattered insights about the central marriage of the work but are the embodiments, as well, of marital states paralleling those of the prince and Maggie at given stages until this pair moves beyond all of them to a rare conjugal triumph. More specifically, the commercial arrangement of which the Gutermann-Seuss and, at first, the Verver marriages are redolent, the Howellsian "affectionate comradeship" of the Assinghams, and the tragic tension apparent later in Charlotte and Adam's marriage, all correspond to stages of Maggie's marriage with Amerigo, enabling one to understand better where this pair are at any given time, and finally prompting one to grasp that they are moving through these stages to what is essentially another, genuinely transcendent, level of marriage.

Tainting Maggie's marriage from the first is the spirit of acquisition. Underlying both Amerigo's jocular assurance before their wedding that the six months he has spent pursuing Maggie have been "justified" because "capture had crowned the pursuit—or success, as he would otherwise have put it,

had rewarded virtue" (1:4) and Maggie's no less jocular assertion that the prince is "a rarity," an "object of beauty, an object of price," a significant "part" of her father's "collection"
(1:12), is something obviously not humorous at all, an inability on the part of either to conceive of marriage as anything
other than a convenient means of getting something one
wants, be it a pretty, ingenuous little bride of monumental
wealth or an imperially slim husband with impeccable Old
World lineage and charming panache. Before focusing, however, on the intimate confrontation with each other and
themselves that their initial conception of matrimony causes
this pair, James turns to two other marriages, Adam's and
Charlotte's and the Gutermann-Seusses', in order to emphasize more fully the sinister qualities underlying the view of
marriage humorously implied by Maggie and Amerigo.
There are several reasons for this strategy. Were James immediately to focus directly on Maggie and Amerigo's married
life, thereby accustoming the reader to seeing them dealing
with each other, much of the intensity of their intimate confrontation in the second half of the novel might be vitiated.
More, by presenting these other unions James not only
achieves indirectly all the reinforcement necessary to the
characterization he has shaped of the spirit behind the early
stages of Maggie's marriage, but he also establishes something crucial to an understanding of this novel, a sense both
of the timelessness of this spirit and the human susceptibility
to it. Finally, these two other marriages, presenting as they
do an externalization of the false conceptions initially shaping Maggie and Amerigo's married life, implicitly establish a
standard, one of error, against which the development
undergone gradually in the central marriage of the novel can
be measured.

The motivations prompting Charlotte and Adam to marry
are ultimately rather sinister ones, but they are no more sinister than those tainting whatever affection Maggie and
Amerigo feel for each other at the outset of their own marriage. With Adam and Charlotte, they are simply not masked
by the humorous tone and charm with which the prince and
his bride invest the crasser reasons for the pleased anticipa-

tion with which they view their upcoming nuptials. As Charlotte herself is frank to admit, her reasons for wanting to give up her peripatetic single existence and marry have little to do with anything but herself and what she might gain through matrimony. She declares, "I won't pretend I don't think it would be good for me to marry. Good for me I mean . . . because I'm so awfully unattached. I should like to be a little less adrift. I should like to have a home. I should like to have an existence" (1:219). She goes on to confess that she finds "Miss" a term "too dreadful—except for a shop girl" and that she does not want to be "a horrible English old-maid" (1:219). But she notes quite candidly as well that she does not see why "for a mere escape from my state—I need do quite so *much*" (1:219), so much, that is, as get married. Finally, of course, she accepts Adam's offer of marriage, but the spirit in which she accedes to his proposal and that characterizes her sense of what marriage entails never changes, right through her illicit involvement with Amerigo and her transportation, at last, to America, from that which she manifests here. Nor, clearly, does Adam marry Charlotte in any significantly different spirit. If he offers her comfort, stability, and escape from the indignities of poverty and spinsterhood, she offers him, above all, a means of pacifying his daughter's fears that he is lonely.

For all that is wrong here, though, even Charlotte and Adam's reasons for marrying do not see quite so unsavory and dangerous as they actually are, since Adam's apparent guilelessness, Charlotte's beauty, and the relative frankness with which the couple deal with each other impart to their relationship a deceptive aura of innocence. Thus, as Laurence Holland notes, James, seeking to show the ugliness lurking behind the pleasant facade in the impending union of this pair and through it the similar ugliness marring the early stage of Maggie's marriage, provides a brief sketch of the Gutermann-Seuss marriage.[23] This, presented mainly in terms of James's account of the marriage's progeny and the bevy of surrounding Gutermann-Seuss relations—all of whom are in mercilessly full view when Adam and Charlotte call—is, despite being distressingly anti-Semitic, deeply effective in portraying the vulgar essence of acquisitiveness. As Adam deals with Gutermann-Seuss for some precious Damascene tiles, the marital bargain he and Charlotte are on the verge of sealing becomes inextricably associated for the reader with the merchant, his closely ranged offspring of "eleven little brown clear faces, with such impersonal old eyes astride of such impersonal old noses" and his "fat earringed aunts and . . . glossy cockneyfied familiar uncles, inimitable of accent and assumption and of an attitude cruder than that of the head of the firm" (1:213). Hence, the completed transaction with Gutermann-Seuss, marked as it is by the dispensing all round of "heavy cake and port wine" that add to the deal "the touch of some mystic rite of old Jewry" (1:216), ties the upcoming marriage of Adam and Charlotte, no less a product of shrewd negotiation, to what James sees as an avarice timeless in its origins and virtually inexpungible from the human scene.

The unfortunate results of entering marriage with gain for oneself as one's major goal are not long in manifesting themselves. Imperfectly committed to their mates, Maggie and Adam, as all know, spend more time closeted with each other than is good for their marriages. Left too much to their own devices, the prince and Charlotte, themselves devoted more fully to self-indulgence than to their mates or matrimony, are not long in finding illicit mutual solace with each other. What is particularly insidious about all this is, as James shows, its aura of plausibility, even of charm. Certainly, there seems nothing unappealing on the face of it in a daughter and father spending time together, especially time shared with the daughter's child, the handsome little *principino*. And the "noble fairness" of Matcham, where the weekending prince and Charlotte decide to embark on their course of adultery, seems to sound amid the "generous mood of the sunny gusty lusty English April" (1:332) an almost irresistibly enticing "call to the ingenuities and impunities of pleasure," demanding only such "courage and good humor" (1:332) as are readily compatible with its pervasive "wonderful spirit of compromise" (1:354). In such a scene, even the shabby amour of Lady Castledean and Mr. Blint seems

touched by an aura of graceful ease that makes all and anything seem right and acceptable to those for whom the good
is self-indulgence; but as James shows with the Gutermann-
Seusses and the perhaps divorced, perhaps vaguely married
Mrs. Rance, who is seen pursuing Adam before he weds
Charlotte, at the root of the deceptively appealing devotion
to self are blatant rapacity and moral disorder. The failure of
Maggie and Adam, Charlotte and the prince to perceive this
through the first half of the novel manifests James's view
that the pursuit of personal gain at the expense of commitment to principle or to those around one is so intrinsically a
part of the human scene as to seem to many if not right and
natural at least insufficiently appalling to make one fight res-
olutely against it.

The only pair who seem out of place at Matcham are the
Assinghams, a pair about whom critics have long been at
odds.[24] Perhaps the best means of ascertaining their role in
the novel is to begin with Holland's apt assertion that the Assinghams confront the crises in the marriages of their friends
with "terror and compassion, from within the communion of
their own intimate embrace."[25] Indeed, through the first half
of the novel, they are the only married couple in communion
with each other, the only example James offers of a marriage
undamaged by selfishness. Further, their communion, based
less on romantic passion than on an enduring capacity for the
sort of marital partnership so prized by Howells, serves
through the first half of the work, like the Gutermann-Seuss
marriage, as a standard against which other unions may be
measured. Here, of course, the standard is a higher one than
that evidenced by the importer and his family, one, in fact, to
which no other marriage in the first half measures up.
Nevertheless, for all the mutual devotion inherent in the intimate embrace of each other's lives, their marriage is not for
James the embodiment of all that can be hoped for in matrimony. Their happiness, though assuredly not that of shallow, thoughtless folk, still falls short of the state of creative
tension that James believes is the highest form marriage can
attain. Devoid of such agreeable compromise, such good-hu-
mored mutual accommodation as lies at the root of the As-

singhams' union, this higher state of marriage is characterized by a tension not based on conflict finally—though initially engendered by it—but on shared acknowledgement
that oneself and one's mate are deeply loving yet irremediably separate partners, understanding each other, as most
mates do, only imperfectly. The tension in such a marriage as
this is creative because in the unending struggle to be true to
oneself yet devoted to one's mate one finds not ease but continual confrontation with the tragic fact of human frailty in
a difficult world. And this, in turn, can be a constant prod to
struggle to a hard-won, loving communion—beyond tragedy
but grounded in it—with one's spouse. This sort of marriage,
one bringing husband and wife into profound knowledge of
what James here conceives to be love's sacred office as re-
deemer of the human plight, is achieved, as I have noted, by
Maggie and the prince. Thus, if the Assinghams in the first
half of the novel present a standard below which the other
marriages fall, in the second half, this same standard is one
against which the rise of Maggie and the prince can be measured.

However, before Maggie and Amerigo do transcend the
sort of marriage achieved by Fanny and Colonel Bob, the Assingham marriage embodies a state through which they must
pass. Oscar Cargill notes that the Assinghams "preserve the
dignity of the principals by accepting the burden of the mundane in what is, for all of the exquisiteness of Charlotte Stant
and the prince, an exceptionally sordid relationship."[26] But
more, I think, is involved than this. Fanny and her husband
do not merely show through their presence that ugly events,
described here though they be in rarefied terms, are taking
place in a world recognizable as our own. Crucial as this function is, they have others as well. One is to serve as index to
what is taking place between Maggie and Amerigo as they
move from a stage of marriage dominated by personal acquisitiveness through the one marked by partnership that
precedes their further development. The condition of comradeship between Maggie and the prince, only adumbrated
by James as he reserves his most intense and extensive treatment of them for the final stages they attain in their union,

is made more understandable for the reader through his earlier, full delineation of the Assingham marriage. The other pivotal function of the Assinghams is to ground the triumphant final stage of Maggie and Amerigo's marriage in reality. In other words, just as the Assinghams' presence shows that the infidelities in this novel are something to which all too many on less rarefied planes of existence than their four friends are prone, so too their presence shows that the victory achieved by Maggie and the prince, transcendent as it may be, is rooted in the real world and, hence, attainable by at least some.

This "affectionate comradery" of the Assinghams, as Howells might call it, which is closely approximated then by Maggie and the prince during a crucial stage in the development of their marriage, manifests itself in several ways. Despite the fact that Fanny's imagination and capacity for intuiting, and at times overintuiting, the subtlest motivations are unmatched by like faculties in Bob, who, blunt and unimaginative (though not so unimaginative as he lets on) is frequently caught bewilderedly in the rapidly shifting currents of his wife's conjectures, the pair never fall out. The reason for this, apart from the fact that they obviously love each other a great deal, is the ability of each to laugh at his or her own foibles or crotchets and to tolerate with humorous good will those of the other. This and their tongue-in-cheek beratings of each other for either overactive or recalcitrant powers of perception are reminiscent, consequently, of the banter of Howells's Basil and Isabel and tie Fanny and Colonel Bob, then, just as firmly as are the Marches to the quotidian and to what is essentially a pragmatic orientation toward its exigencies. Further, of course, it reveals implicitly that whatever the exigencies, they will face them together. Thus, when Fanny, frightened and shaken by the almost brazen demeanor of Charlotte and Amerigo together at a large party, fears that her efforts at matchmaking will lead her friends into disaster and herself into disgrace, she finds, if not reassurance in Bob's bland pronouncement "They'll manage in their own way" (1:286), at least the comfort of knowing that there is someone who values her enough to seek to reassure her. Similarly, on their arrival home that same evening, Bob's giving Fanny his arm and "their crawling up the stairs together, like some old Darby and Joan who have had a disappointment" (1:287) reveals again the unwillingness of Bob to let his wife suffer alone. Bob, in fact, senses with perfect clarity, for all his supposed obtuseness, that in the matter of their four friends, Fanny finds herself in "deep waters" on a "mystic lake." Though he cannot quite fathom the waters himself, "he hadn't quitted for an hour during her adventure, the shore," and stands ready on the instant to aid her should "the planks of her bark" begin to part. He holds himself, James notes, "so ready that it was quite as if the inward man had pulled off coat and waistcoat" (1:366). Later, when the planks do indeed begin to part, Bob's aid is sure; if it means helping her "save" Charlotte and the prince "so far as consistently speaking of them as still safe might save them" (1:378), he is ready to do so. If it means, even, that he and Fanny must help Maggie rescue the whole situation—including Fanny's peace of mind—by going about "looking like fools" (1:401), professing, that is, not to see anything wrong with their friends' marriages, again this supremely unfoolish if unimaginative man is willing to sacrifice pride in appearance and with his wife take the commonsensical, pragmatic course of doing so. Through all this, doubtless, the support offered in this marriage seems one-sided. One sees Bob repeatedly comforting Fanny, tolerating her flights of fancy and her mild, vicarious involvement with the romantic prince, and finally asking the right, seemingly pedestrian questions that help her steer herself to the correct, pragmatic stance that helps Maggie. However, it is clear from Fanny's own toleration of her mate's sardonic humor at her expense and, indeed, from the whole tenor of this marriage—the only one in the first half of the book in which there is real communication, accommodation, and sacrifice for one's mate—that Fanny would offer similar aid to Bob in this union, which for James shows the best type of marriage attainable on the plane of the commonplace.

The corresponding stage in Maggie and Amerigo's marriage to this sort of union begins when Fanny smashes the golden bowl and Maggie, rather than force immediate confrontation with the prince when he enters and finds the wreckage, allows her "wish for time" to interpose"—time for Amerigo's use, not for hers. . . . " She wants to say to him, "Take it, take it, take all you need of it; arrange yourself so as to suffer least, or be at any rate least distorted and disfigured. Only *see*, see that *I* see, and make up your mind on this new basis at your convenience" (2:184). More, for her own sake and his, she wishes to give him time so that "the dreadful blur, the ravage of suspense and embarrassment" produced in him by his coming on the broken bowl in her presence can be put under the control of his "personal serenity" and "incomparable superiority" (2:184). This decision to give the prince time to compose himself and to consider the implications of Maggie's undeclared but certain knowledge of his infidelity initiates a stage of mutual aid, accommodation, and tacit understanding in Maggie's marriage unlike anything she and Amerigo have achieved previously and the basis for the higher stage of union that they will eventually forge for themselves. In this phase of their marriage, therefore, they enter into a partnership that is, though lacking for obvious reasons in good-natured banter, at least as deep and intense as any of which the Assinghams are capable and certainly deeper and more intense than any relationship they themselves have known, either before or in the course of Amerigo's involvement with Charlotte.

The time Maggie allows the prince enables him quickly to perceive that although "he had used her, . . . had even exceedingly enjoyed her before this," he would now "be *really* needing her for the first time in their whole connexion" (2:186). A "proved necessity" (2:186) to him now, Maggie, he sees, offers him "assuredly a kind of support that wasn't to have been imagined in advance" (2:187). This perception, in turn, leads to an openness between them uncharacteristic of their marriage up to this point. Maggie's explicit confrontation of him with the fact of his "*two* relations with Charlotte" (2:190) prompts not bitter argument and mutual accusation but a long-needed clearing of the air, leading Amerigo to see his newly resolute but still loving wife as more "sacred"

(2:199) to him than he has ever felt her to be. The support that she continues to offer him after the fact of the affair is in the open and that he for his part, as we have noted, sees he needs so desperately is again couched in terms of time— time, in this case, not merely to compose himself and avoid any awkwardness or *bêtise* that would embarrass them both, but time to free himself of the liaison with Charlotte. Nor does he offer nothing in return. Through his quiet efforts, he too provides time and an atmosphere of unruffled calm that establish the opportunity for Maggie to carry out what she must, her own lonely maintenance of the facade of nor- malcy, of the appearance, that is, even in the face of Char- lotte's arrogant hectoring, that the two marriages are undisturbedly pleasant ones. Maggie's work, therefore, not only gives the prince the chance to do his but her courage and love manifested in it inspire him to do so. Also, of course, her work enables Adam to keep his pride and to assert quietly his domination over Charlotte, so necessary to the success of Maggie and Amerigo's plans. Thus, working separately yet intimately together, the pair labor with reciprocal benefits for each other to put their newfound closeness on firmer footing—work, in short, to save their marriage. Like the As- singhams before them, then, Maggie and Amerigo have for- mulated a pragmatic pact. If Fanny and Bob working together must appear a remarkably imperceptive couple to achieve their ends, Maggie and the prince must, though united in aim, work separately and appear to be neither working at all nor anything but a conventionally comfortable man and wife to achieve theirs.

Gradually, in fact, as the Assinghams appear together with decreasing frequency through the second half of the novel, Maggie and Amerigo's marriage becomes James's chief ex- ample of matrimony as pragmatic partnership. However, in- herent in their pact is an unresolved tension between the pair unlike any that is glimpsed between the Assinghams, a ten- sion that, ultimately, both prompts and remains central to the final stage of the younger pair's marriage. Again, it is an- other marriage that helps one perceive fully what is taking place between Maggie and the prince, in this case, once more,

Charlotte and Adam's. The invisible, yet clearly discernible, "long silken halter" that Adam has coolly "looped round [Charlotte's] beautiful neck" (2:286), Charlotte's all too distinct silent shriek, her continuing arrogance and shrill efforts at self-justification, and Adam's quiet, abysmal comment that his terrified wife will know of what life "over there" in the "awful place" holds for her only "when she does know" (2:288), all reveal that although the major problem in terms of plot—that of whether the two marriages will stand and the liaison end—has been resolved, the tension generated within Charlotte and Adam's marriage by the ramifications of the acquisitive terms on which their marriage was established remains thoroughly unresolved. Thus, Adam and Charlotte's union, unlike that of the Assinghams, entails no partnership, no comradeship, only a conflict that cannot be voiced between two personalities that cannot bend and that refuse to accommodate themselves to each other except insofar as it is necessary to keep up appearances. A similar tension, Adam and Charlotte's marriage prepares one to see, is evident in Maggie and Amerigo's marriage, despite all the partnership involved in their effort together to preserve two marriages and the maintenance of correct social forms.

This tension between Maggie and her husband manifests itself increasingly to her as their partnership draws nearer to achieving its desired ends. Her perception that "she was seeing [Amerigo] through—he had engaged to come out at the right end if she *would* see him" (2:322), with which book six, the final section of the novel, begins, drives home to her the fact that she and the prince though helping each other to their goals are also terribly isolated from one another. In part, of course, this isolation derives from a residual uncertainty about each other and from the peculiar demands of their task—unwonted amounts of time with each other would disturb the appearance of unchanged relations that they seek to maintain—but in great measure, too, this isolation arises because they are each markedly different sorts of people. Amerigo's work in their partnership involves, as Maggie comes to see, little more than that he stand, comfortably and calmly, "as fixed in his place as some statue of one of his forefathers" (2:323), a calling for which she realizes he is admirably suited because his "place," his position of ease, "was like something made for him beforehand by innumerable facts, facts largely of the sort known as historical, made by ancestors, examples, traditions, habits" (2:323). Maggie, on the other hand, sees her own work of having to "move indefatigably" toward Amerigo to rescue the situation, while his repose enables her to do so, as involving nothing less than a virtual trek across "new country," on which, like a "settler," a "trader," or even "some Indian squaw with a papoose on her back" (2:323), she lacks even "the most rudimentary map of the social relations as such" (2:324). And, for all its difficulty, she sees herself as eminently suited for this endeavor in a way that the prince could never be; for if, as a quintessential American, a pioneer-aborigine, she lacks the security, the guideposts, the "map" of "examples, traditions, habits," she is free too of the confinement and the reticence to chart new courses to their mutual goal that these would impose on her.

Irremediably, then, for all their increased sensitivity to each other's needs as they work apart yet together, the differences between Amerigo, the knowing, reposeful, Old World nobleman, and Maggie, the aroused New World lamb who seeks to save all "for love" (2:116), are as pronounced, doubtless, as those between Adam and Charlotte. As such, they will never understand each other, much less change each other markedly. Maggie, inevitably, will remain an absolutist, wont to see her life as bound up in choices between good and evil, love and hate, all of which she conceives of as almost tangible realities; and Amerigo will, one suspects, still see most choices as involving little more than the discrimination between pleasant and unpleasant, agreeable or tiresome, and will never quite know what to make of those who do not.

Nevertheless, the loneliness in which their partnership forces each to labor brings home to both, finally, an awareness that existence by its very nature involves terrible isolation and tensions, isolation and tensions felt with particular keenness by such sentient ones as they have come to be. And this awareness, in turn, awakens in Maggie and Amerigo a responsiveness to suffering, a compassion for human frailty, and, through these, a cognizance of their own participation in the human welter of suffering, frailty, and conflict. Hence, Maggie, though unremitting in her pursuit of justice, perceives sadly the silken rope and the silent shriek marking Charlotte's destruction. Having discerned too within herself, not long before this, a capacity for joyous but dangerously chaotic release through open rage, which she envisions vividly as a "wild caravan looming into view with crude colours in the sun, fierce pipes in the air, high spears against the sky" (2:237), Maggie is clearly no longer the young woman whom Fanny once regarded as one who "wasn't born to know evil" (1:78). She obviously knows now with full painful intimacy the capacity for evil lurking in all, even herself. Moreover, when she tells Fanny later that she and her father are "lost to each other really much more than Amerigo and Charlotte" (2:333), she speaks out of a new, no less intimate knowledge of the human capacity for suffering, a suffering in her case made all the more exquisite because she is aware that the loss of her father results from a choice she herself makes, one that is no less painful for being, as she knows, the only right one, the only one that, all sorrowfully, compassionately, knowingly, is "for love." Similarly, the prince through his isolation comes not only to be increasingly attuned to what Maggie requires of him but capable, at last, of seeing that Charlotte is "stupid" (2:348), unaware, that is, of the needs, virtues, and pains of others. Thus, however much he still may see taste as the major touchstone to existence, the prince realizes now that it is not the only one, that a moral vision and commitment to others are not irrelevant to the leading of a tasteful, pleasant life. This heightened sensitivity is evidenced as well in his quiet assertion to Maggie, based on what he has seen of all the major figures of the novel, including himself, that "everything's terrible, *cara*—in the heart of man" (2:349). Consequently, though this crucial development undergone by Maggie and the prince as a result of their lonely yet united efforts is not enough to break down the major differences between them and resolve the resultant tension, it effects sufficient change to enable them to sustain a marriage.

Even more important, of course, in helping sustain their marriage than the changes they undergo is the fact that their partnership confirms powerfully for them both that they do indeed love each other. And, clearly, it is this love that enables them to turn their perceptions of the grimmer facts of the human condition and, closer to home, of the tensions in their marriage that manifest these facts into features that, surprisingly enough, strengthen their union. Too sentient to ignore the tension, too different from one another to resolve it, Maggie and Amerigo are prompted to a deeper love and a new stage in their marital development by it. Unlike Adam and Charlotte, therefore, whose state of tension mirrors their own, they are able to make their differences productive of growth. A constant reminder to them of the pain and chaos inextricably bound up in human existence and, consequently, of the fragility of love, the tension, because they do love each other, makes them cling to each other more fervently. Paradoxically, then, without their differences their love would be less urgent, less strong, something taken for granted and, hence, palling rather than an earnestly chosen stay against confusion and the "terrible" that resides in the human heart. The presence of the *principino* makes clear that their love, again unlike that of Adam and Charlotte, who have a childless marriage, is a vital, procreative one, generating joy and beauty in the midst of the omnipresent darkness.

Maggie and Amerigo's final scenes together in the novel reveal poignantly both the continuing tension in their relationship and the love that asserts itself in response to it. The prince's sexual overture as he draws close to Maggie before their last meeting with Adam and Charlotte engenders a particularly telling example of this. Though clearly drawn physically to the prince, Maggie is disturbed by "the thick breath of the definite—which was the intimate, the immediate, the familiar as she hadn't had them for so long" (2:351), and she refuses, much to her husband's surprise and incomprehension, one suspects, to commit herself fully to physical intimacy with him until the others have been faced one last time and seen off for good. Though her motives are not made entirely clear, one can discern several that may well be at work here: a refusal to surrender to her physical desires the sentience that she will need to see all through this last meeting, a moral punctiliousness that prompts her to refuse all reward till she has earned it through carrying out this last task before her in her overriding effort to sort out the tangled relations among the four, and, lastly, an inability to partake of joy until her pain over her father's imminent departure is assuaged by his actual leaving. These, perhaps linked with a residual distrust of the prince's motives that only makes her want to cling to him more strongly, are reflective of a nature that is, as both realize, more complex, intense, and higher-strung that the prince's; and, patently, this difference between them will remain a constant source of tension for them both in their union. Similarly, Maggie and Amerigo's final scene together, which closes the novel, manifests both this tension of disparate identities and the love that it reinforces. When Maggie, in the last words of the novel, buries her head in Amerigo's breast for "pity and dread" of the light in his eyes as he tells her, "I see nothing but you" (2:369), her response is one of love that has been reaffirmed by the continuing tension in their union that his look and words make her perceive. Her awareness of the total devotion that this relatively uncomplicated man she married will now lavish on her makes her at once pity him for being so fervently committed to an imperfect, limited being in a frightening, pain-ridden world and regard him with some dread because of the very intensity of the devotion he will direct toward her. Confronted one more time, then, with the differences between herself and her husband and with all that this tells her of the strange chaos of life, she realizes once again that there is nothing for her to do but cling to him, find what comfort and order she can with him, and love him fervently in the face of all that seems so capable of driving them apart.

Naomi Lebowitz comments aptly that Maggie's marriage has been "earned in pain."[27] As such, it is, in its final stage, what James belived marriage in its highest form ought to be, a union that in exposing two people to intense experience exposes them, as well, both to the complexity, suffering, limitation, and evil that are the givens of life as James sees it and to a means of triumph over them. Herman Keyserling notes, in this vein, that the "fulfillment of marriage and its happiness entail the acceptance of the suffering pertaining to life. It gives the latter a new and deeper meaning."[28] Doubtless, James would concur with this notion, and throughout the development that Maggie, Amerigo, and their marriage undergo, it is clear that James believes the "new and deeper meaning" marriage imparts to suffering is that the marrieds sentient enough to do so can be brought by marriage to regard suffering as a prompter of love. No one in James's marriage fiction except for Maggie and Amerigo comes to this insight that extends beyond tragic awareness—Isabel might have, had Osmond been a different sort—but this fact makes the insight no less valid and marriage no less sacred for James as a potential means of stimulating people to the moral, spiritual, and emotional growth that renders them capable of attaining it.

Writing of Maggie, Judith Armstrong notes that her "final accomplishment is to restore the moral order of things as they should be,"[29] a comment that calls to mind Laurence Holland's assertion that the marriages in The Golden Bowl "are made symbolic not only of marriages in actual life but of other social institutions and processes which are fused with them."[30] Implicit in both remarks, obviously, is an awareness of the crucial social role James envisions marriage at its best as playing, a realization that such development as Maggie and the prince undergo can never, of course, be without valuable social ramifications. Behind the muted melodrama of their story (and, clearly, of Isabel's too) is a social vision, the memory in a mature author of his father's oft-repeated assertion to him that "we need never fear not to be good enough if only we were social enough."[31] In other words, James hopes that marriage might, in teaching husbands and wives to be more alert to each other's needs, teach them as well to be more alert to human needs generally, more "social" in the largest sense of the term.

As a social institution, one, like the church, calculated to impose spiritual order on the mélange of human life, marriage, James believes, also ought to compel allegiance. What he hopes husbands and wives will maintain in their marriages is an allegiance to the sacred ideal that marriage embodies; and just as the weak priest glimpsed briefly in *The Golden Bowl* seems less than admirable because of his failure to maintain his fervent allegiance to what should be a compelling ideal for him, so too, as we have seen, do the husbands and wives in his marital fiction seem lacking in moral intelligence and sensitivity when they fail to commit themselves fully to marriage, capable as it is of promoting both individual growth and more humane social relations. What he demands then, clearly, in each marriage, and nothing less, is "the golden bowl—as it *was* to have been" (2:216). Particularly apposite here, I think, is F. R. Leavis's comment about the moral demands that James makes on society and its institutions generally. "It is doubtful," Leavis notes, "whether at any time in any place he could have found what would have satisfied his implicit demand: the actual fine art of civilized social intercourse that would have justified the flattering intensity of expectation he brought to it in the form of his curiously transposed and subtilized ethical sensibility."[32] Certainly, James was unable to find this "fine art" in the marriages he saw about him, and he was too honest to purport that he did; but that he continued to hope he might and in one visionary novel created a marriage that attains a surpassing though somber grandeur attests to his highly personal and romantic faith that at least a rare few highly sentient men and women might have the capacity to bring the glorious potential of their best institutions to fruition and make them express and perpetuate—in the very midst of the prevailing darkness—the best in human nature.

1. Tony Tanner, *The Reign of Wonder* (Cambridge: Cambridge University Press, 1965), p. 284.

2. Henry James, *What Maisie Knew* (New York: Scribner's, 1908), p. 9. All subsequent page references to this novel are to this edition, volume 11 in the New York Edition of James's works, and will appear in the text.

3. Among those who see Maisie as failing to grow are Tanner; John C. McCloskey, "What Maisie Knows: A Study of Childhood Adolescence," *American Literature* 36 (January 1965): 485–513; Harris W. Wilson, "What *Did* Maisie Know?"

College English 17 (February 1956): 279–82; and Oscar Cargill, *The Novels of Henry James* (New York: Macmillan, 1961). Some whose view of Maisie's development is closer to mine include James L. Gargano, "What Maisie Knew: The Education of a 'Moral Sense,'" *Nineteenth-Century Fiction* 16 (June 1961): 33–46; Wagenknecht, *Eve and Henry James*; Sister M. Corona Sharp, *The Confidante in Henry James* (South Bend, Ind.: University of Notre Dame Press, 1963); Samuels; and Weinstein.

4. Wagenknecht, *Eve and Henry James*, p. 139.

5. J. A. Ward, *The Imagination of Disaster* (Lincoln: University of Nebraska Press, 1961), p. 91.

6. Dorothea Krook, *The Ordeal of Consciousness in Henry James* (Cambridge: Cambridge University Press, 1962), p. 151.

7. Henry James, *The Awkward Age* (New York: Harper & Brothers, 1899), pp. 261–62.

8. Hermann Keyserling, *The Book of Marriage* (New York: Blue Ribbon Books, 1926), p. 16.

9. Keyserling, p. 21.

10. Tony Tanner, "The Fearful Self: Henry James's *The Portrait of a Lady*," *Critical Quarterly* 7 (Autumn 1965): 207,209–10.

11. Henry James, *The Portrait of a Lady*, 2 vols. (New York: Scribner's, 1908), 2:202. All subsequent page references to this novel are to this edition, volumes 3 and 4 in the New York Edition, and will appear in the text, with the volume numbers cited as 1 and 2. Where variations from the 1881 text occur, I shall cite the original reading in a footnote.

12. Tanner, "The Fearful Self," p. 210. Another significant similarity between the two, David Gervais notes, is that Isabel and Osmond dupe themselves "by loving in each other more the impressions they give of themselves than what they really, secretly, are" (*Flaubert and Henry James* [London: Macmillan, 1978], p. 154).

13. In 1881 this read simply, "Marriage meant that a woman should abide with her husband," the change a clear indication of the increasing significance of the marital commitment for James.

14. Among those who find Isabel's decision to return to Osmond one that James regards with disfavor is Richard Poirier. In his chapter on *The Portrait of a Lady* in *The Comic Sense of Henry James* (New York: Oxford University Press, 1960), he argues that James regards Isabel ironically at the end of the novel. Philip Weinstein argues at the close of his chapter on *Portrait* that James's admiration of Isabel for her return to her husband reflects the severe limitations of his own responsiveness to life. More severely still, Gervais suggests that "Isabel's marriage does not force her into real spiritual growth," only into a self-pity that James "can enjoy . . . unperturbed" (p. 160). Further, Gervais argues, the "sanctity of marriage" theme is James's shabby contrivance for "draping Isabel in a ready-to-wear convention that allows him to explore her fear and her pride while giving them a noble appearance" (p. 194). Gervais asserts, in fact, that this novel is nothing less than "a subtle evasion of the tragic" (p. 149). Annette Niemtzow, in "Marriage and the New Woman in *The Portrait of a Lady*," *American Literature* 47 (November 1975): 377–95, suggests that James, ambivalent about the "New Woman," "on one hand . . . tames the experimental woman and restricts her physical options for her psychic salvation" and "on the other . . . proves bolder than he permits his heroine to be" (p. 395) and undercuts, ironically, the notion that marriage invariably provides a happy ending for any tale.

15. Mary S. Schriber suggests, in "Isabel Archer and Victorian Manners," *Studies in the Novel* 8 (Winter 1976): 441–57, that Isabel also comes to gain as much power for shaping her own destiny as was available to any young woman of her time.

16. Henry James, *The Golden Bowl* (New York: Scribner's, 1909), 1:133. All subsequent page references to this novel are to this edition (volumes 23 and 24 in the

New York Edition) and will appear in the text, with the two volumes cited as 1 and 2. Niemtzow points out that James's distaste for divorce reveals the marked influence of his father's views on the topic. Of course, going off with Goodwood might also involve adultery, and, as Tony Tanner notes, adultery would imply for Isabel "the absolute annihilation of forms," the annihilation, that is, of all that establishes a context in which moral and spiritual growth might occur (*Adultery in the Novel* [Baltimore: Johns Hopkins University Press, 1979], p. 18).

17. Laurence Holland, *The Expense of Vision* (Princeton, N. J.: Princeton University Press, 1964), p. 41.

18. Though Isabel's somewhat disdainful response to Henrietta's marrying Mr. Bantling may show some remnants of her earlier foolish romantic illusions, it more than likely is primarily a reflection of her belief in the grand potential for growth inherent in matrimony and of her disappointment that Henrietta, with the pedestrian, if affable, Bantling, will have no chance to tap this potential.

19. Brooks, p. 5.

20. Keyserling, pp. 18–19.

21. See Holland on this point throughout his discussion of *Portrait*.

22. Holland suggests that Maggie and Amerigo achieve "the full redeeming intimacy of an intense passion" and an "authentic commitment" to the "communion" of their marriage and to "the larger community of purpose it makes possible" (p. 350). Quentin Anderson throughout his chapter on *The Golden Bowl* characterizes their marriage as a wedding of wisdom and love to the world. Keyserling, speaking generally of the sort of marriage that Holland, Anderson, and I think Maggie and Amerigo achieve, characterizes it as a state of "conjugal happiness" in which "partnership is based on the realization of its tragic significance"—that is, on a realization of its vulnerability in a troubled world. This leads the couple to perceive, he asserts, that "life is not a tragedy in the last resort" but "beautiful" because hard-won love can be attained in it (pp. 19, 48).

23. Holland, pp. 359–62.

24. Edith Wharton described the Assinghams as an "insufferable," "dull-witted," and "frivolous" pair of "eaves'-droppers" (quoted in Segal, p. 208). Among the most vehement recent commentators attacking the Assinghams are Fryer, who asserts of Fanny, "If there is a villain in the piece it is probably she, who with her machinations has engineered the whole quartette" (p.119); Anderson, who sees Fanny as an incarnation of the Whore of Babylon (p. 288) and Colonel Bob as an unregenerate servant of Mammon (pp. 295–96); and Sallie Sears, who claims in *The Negative Imagination* (Ithaca, N. Y.: Cornell University Press, 1968) that Fanny is a "puppet master" (p. 165). In addition to Holland and Cargill, cited in my discussion, Segal and Sharp assert the Assinghams' goodness, with Sharp characterizing Bob as a type reminiscent of Conrad's Marlow (p. 246).

25. Holland, p. 375.

26. Cargill, p. 424.

27. Naomi Lebowitz, *The Imagination of Loving* (Detroit: Wayne State University Press, 1965), p. 131. Some who fail to agree that Maggie does grow are Sears, Weinstein, and Tanner in his "*The Golden Bowl* and the Reassessment of Innocence," *London Magazine* 1 (December 1961): 38–49. Besides Lebowitz and those I cite in my discussion, others who see Maggie as attaining significant moral development include Wagenknecht, *Eve and Henry James*, Walter Wright, *The Madness of Art* (Lincoln: University of Nebraska Press, 1962), Anderson, and Cargill.

28. Keyserling, p. 16.

29. Judith Armstrong, *The Novel of Adultery* (New York: Barnes & Noble, 1976). p. 145.

30. Holland, p. 350.

31. Quoted in Cleanth Brooks, R. W. B. Lewis, and Robert Penn Warren, eds., *American Literature: The Makers and the Making* (New York: St. Martin's Press, 1973), 2:1374.

32. F. R. Leavis, *The Great Tradition* (New York: New York University Press, 1963), p. 11.

KATE CHOPIN

*J*N 1894, A LITTLE MORE than a decade after her husband Oscar's death and nine years after her mother's, Kate Chopin reflected, "If it were possible for my husband and my mother to come back to earth, I feel I would unhesitatingly give up everything that has come into my life since they left it and join my existence again with theirs." Although doing so, she says, would mean "I would have to forget the past ten years of my growth—my real growth," she assures herself that she could make this sacrifice "in the spirit of perfect acquiescence."[1] Perhaps she could have. But then again, both the terms in which her contemplation of the return of her loved ones is couched and the bulk of her writing, before and after 1894, lead one to believe that her devotion to husband and mother, though undoubtedly genuine, might not have weighed as heavily with her as her "real growth" and that the "perfect acquiescence" with which she envisions herself turning her back on this progress may well be an unwonted bit of sentimentality in this usually unsparing delineator of things as they are. The realization implicit in her phrasing that existence with the traditionally dominating figures of husband and mother precludes for her the possibility of such personal development as is reflected in her burgeoning literary career and virtually demands self-suppression (note the immediate association of a stance of "acquiescence" with the return of the pair) makes it not entirely unlikely that actually confronted with the choice on which she muses, Chopin would leave husband and mother in the realm of sacred memory. This impression is reinforced by the recurring lesson in her works that, soon or late, people will inevitably seek self-gratification rather than self-suppression. In any case, it is clear that by this time Chopin knew that whatever choice she might make if given the opportunity of which she speaks would be dictated by her desires rather than by convention.

The choice between self-assertion and self-repression posited in Chopin's 1894 diary entry is the central choice posited in most of her significant work, particularly in the marriage stories. Repeatedly, a Chopin tale turns on the question of whether a character is leading an authentic existence, an existence, that is, in which one senses and acts to gratify the deepest needs of his or her nature, those that if denied and unmet keep one from attaining mature identity and a chance for happiness. Though Chopin believes that self-denial can rarely be permanent, for one's nature will almost inevitably assert itself, she regards it as dangerous nonetheless because, so long as denial or repression of self lasts, it engenders pain and frustration. Further, when the drive to self-assertion at last manifests itself after long suppression, it can do so with a force so potent from pent-up pressure as to be exceedingly dangerous. Understandably enough, problems involving the pursuit of authentic existence arise most readily when one is confronted with demands imposed on oneself by others; and it is on such problems that Chopin's best work so often focuses, perhaps nowhere so powerfully as in the marriage stories.[2] Certainly, no other realm of experience so consistently exposes one to the demands of others, and, therefore, none offers such a consistent threat or prod, as the case may be, to self-gratification. This, of course, was in Chopin's day particularly true for women, whose range of experience with the demands of others was, given the nature of nineteenth-century American society, largely limited to marriage.

Leading Chopin to the conclusion that one's pursuit of authentic existence is less a matter of choice than of necessity is her fundamentally deterministic vision of human nature. Though Per Seyersted suggests that Chopin believed that people have "at least a modicum of free will and ethical responsibility,"[3] the bulk of her writings presents a different view, one that Seyersted himself characterizes as perceiving people and society "as forever ruled by the gospel of selfishness which makes basic improvement impossible."[4] Whereas such a vision of human selfishness might conceivably make a writer a moralist, it leads Chopin to an amoral outlook, one emphasizing the folly and futility of seeking to restrain or rail against an impulse as ingrained in human nature as the drive to gratification of the self's needs. As a result, her marriage stories touch little on either the social or moral implications of marriage. For Chopin, morality does not seem to obtain in a context of necessity, and social forms are of little consequence in comparison with the implacable human will to authenticity. What she primarily concerns herself with in her marriage stories is whether the figures she presents find gratification in their marriages. If they do, well and good, the marriage is a success. If they do not, the marriage is a failure, and best left behind.

Despite Chopin's apparent lack of interest, though, in judging whether marriage itself is a good thing, her prevailing doctrine that individual fulfillment is more important than the demands of the institution is inevitably inimical to the social outlook that fosters marriage and is in turn reinforced by it, an outlook that, obviously, emphasizes the maintenance of order, the acceptance of responsibility, and fidelity to commitments made to others. As such, Chopin is, in effect, implicitly attacking marriage itself, which by its very nature does not place individual fulfillment above ties to others. Indeed, it is in her treatment of marriages, even happy ones, that one sees most clearly the essentially anarchic amoralism into which Chopin is led by her deterministic vision of the inexorable drive to self-fulfillment. Its lack of a transcendent dimension notwithstanding, this anarchic amoralism stressing individualistic growth links Chopin less with the realists than with the sort of romanticism espoused by the Emerson of such essays as "Experience," "Fate," and "Power," who promulgates the doctrine that the great good, attained through self-reliance, is self-fulfillment, and that it is not freely chosen but *happens* to an individual who, for some unknown reason, is prompted to growth by the Oversoul. There is for Chopin no vestige of the belief in the possibility of freely chosen moral growth in matrimony that Howells and James sought to maintain. Nor is there here as there is in James and Wharton at least the possibility of such moral freedom as resides in the free choice to accept the limitations of a determined lot. There are only driven men and women here, sometimes finding happiness in marriage, sometimes not, as they are pushed on toward self-fulfillment, a goal that for most realists ought never to be final, but that is all there is here. This rather bleakly deterministic vision Chopin maintains is not nearly so apparent in the nonmarriage stories, for in them there is generally no institution against which her characters may push, always in the name of their own freedom and always, seemingly, with, if not their author's approval, at least her tolerance.

Chopin's earliest stories dealing with marriage, "Wiser Than a God" and "A Point at Issue!" both published in 1889, reveal from the first her tendency neither to defend nor attack the institution but to focus instead on the extent to which marriage enables a given character to attain an authentic existence. That the former story presents marriage as a threat to such existence and the latter, written just two months later, shows it to be an experience fostering authenticity for a newly married pair typifies Chopin's resistance to generalization about matrimony and her concern with questions involving the fulfillment of those confronting it. As I noted, though, such an orientation carries inevitably an inherent judgment of its own, devaluating marriage as character-shaping and society-sustaining institution and seeing it as worthwhile only insofar as those in it perceive it to be a means to their own self-development.

Certainly, were Paula Von Stoltz to marry the young man who proposes to her, she would not be showing the wisdom greater than a god's that the title of Chopin's first story touching on marriage attributes to her,[5] for such a union would mean the end of her self-development. Though the young man has looks, charm, and wealth, and though Paula may well love him, her refusal of his offer is nothing less than an affirmation of her own self and its needs. A brilliant pianist devoted to her music, Paula would, were she to marry George Brainard, a young socialite with a knack for the banjo, be consigning herself to a life spent amid those whose response to her playing cannot go beyond the chorus of "How pretty!" "Just lovely!" and "What wouldn't I give to play like that" (1:43–44) that greets Paula when she completes her hired performance for the society party at which she first meets her importuning suitor. Further, as George's wife and a member of polite society, Paula would not be at liberty to make music her career, a dream long cherished by her and her late parents.

The rightness of Paula's refusal of George is confirmed when Chopin reports that only a few years after the rejection Paula is a renowned pianist while George is perfectly content in his marriage to an inane little chatterbox whose forte when single was dancing Virginia breakdowns at parties. George, Chopin goes on to note, is "as handsome as ever, though growing a little stout in the quiet routine of domestic life," and has "quite lost [the] pretty taste for music that formerly distinguished him as a skilful banjoist" (1:47). Though still single, Paula may indeed end up married herself, for her former teacher, Professor Max Kunstler, is pursuing her with an "ever persistent will—the dogged patience that so often wins in the end" (1:47). Clearly, marriage to Kunstler, one who, as his name presumably signifies, is as dedicated to the creation of beauty as Paula is, would not entail for her a suppression of her nature; rather, it would establish a vital union of two "persistent wills" fulfilling themselves as they nourish each other and the art they serve. Not a story dealing extensively with married life, then, "Wiser Than a God" establishes Chopin's predominant marriage story theme, the idea that wisdom entails avoiding a marriage that will involve suppression of the authentic needs of one or the other of the partners.

In the witty "A Point at Issue!" a newly married couple attempt, perversely enough, to turn their marriage into one that will suppress their natures, and it is only the irresistible assertion of their genuine need for each other that keeps them from succeeding. A man who prides himself on his rationality, Professor Charles Faraday, finding in Eleanor Gale "that *rara avis*, a logical woman—something which [he] had not encountered in his life before" (1:49), decides, as any rational fellow might, to marry her. Marrying, the pair envision a future together spent "looking for the good things of life, knocking at the closed doors of philosophy," and venturing into "the open fields of science" (1:50). Further, with the perfect logic that characterizes them both, they resolve that their marriage is to be a "form," which, "while fixing legally their relation to each other," will in no way "touch the individuality of either." Each will remain "a free integral of humanity, responsible to no dominating exactions of so-called marriage laws." Making possible such union, each believes, is "trust in each other's love, honor, courtesy, tempered by the reserving clause of readiness to meet the consequences of reciprocal liberty" (1:50). In the interest of Eleanor's intellectual development as a "free integral of humanity," the newlyweds decide that she is to stay in Paris "indefinitely" in order to acquire a thorough speaking knowledge of French, with Faraday returning each summer "to renew their love in a fresh and re-strengthened union" (1:50). All goes according to plan until mutual jealousy replaces the mutual trust to which their impeccable logic brought them. Faraday's passing reference in a letter to the charms of Kitty Beaton, the daughter of his friends, awakens bitter suspicions in Eleanor, which are soon paralleled by those aroused in Faraday when circumstances lead him to believe that Eleanor has a lover. Elated and relieved when he discovers both that the supposed lover is merely a painter commissioned by Eleanor to do a portrait of herself for him and that Eleanor herself has been troubled by jealousy, Faraday takes a willing wife back to America to embark on an old-fashioned marriage.

Clearly, the Faradays' scheme for a new-style, purely rational marriage fails because such a union is an attempt to deny the basic need for each other that, whether they know it or not, led them in the first place to marry. The dangers inherent in the effort to live solely in the mind are apparent in this story not merely with the Faradays but also with Kitty Beaton's older sister, Margaret, whose "timid leaning in the direction of Woman's Suffrage" leads her into "the fashioning and donning of garments of mysterious shape, which, while stamping their wearer with the distinction of a quasi-emancipation, defeated the ultimate purpose of their construction by inflicting a personal discomfort that extended beyond the powers of long endurance" (1:52–53). Apparently, Margaret, as Chopin sees it, would be better off overthrowing the joyless yoke of idea[6] and living in her whole being with "bubbling happiness" (1:53) as Kitty does. While rewarding her in the present, this might also assure the girl such contentment in the future as that attained at present by her mother, "a woman whose aspirations went not further than the desire for her family's good" and whose "bearing announced in its every feature the satisfaction of completed hopes" (1:52). Though, indeed, efforts at the denial of the needs of one's nature do inevitably extend, like the discomfort caused by Margaret's clothes, "beyond the powers of long endurance," they can, even in the short run, achieve terrible mischief.

At the beginning of "A Point at Issue!" Chopin notes, curiously enough, that the Faradays' wedding announcement appeared in the newspaper "modestly wedged in between" a statement that subscribers vacationing from home in the summer months might have their papers sent them at no extra fee and a "somber-clad notice" (1:48) from a monument company advertising its stones. The point of this, I suspect, is not to posit any sinister linkup of marriage and death;[7] rather, the linkup involves all three items cited and makes marriage seem as inevitable a part of the nature of things as death and the rhythm of the seasons. Marriage, Chopin implies in this work, has come to seem such an essential part of the natural continuum of things because it answers the needs of so many people; and, consequently, any effort to evade it, such as that made by the Faradays when they seek to have a marriage that, in effect, is no marriage, must be one in response to needs stronger and more authentic than those that marriage can satisfy. Thus, because Paula Von Stoltz's rejection of marriage is indeed just such a response to the most vital imperatives of her nature it carries far greater authority than the rejection attempted by the Faradays, which, in reality, runs counter to the direction of their natures. The decision of the Faradays to end their ill-advised experiment marks an entry into the continuum, an entry prompted by their whole beings. Significantly, Chopin notes that Eleanor's jealousy, which prompts her readiness to adopt a conventional mode of marriage, grows out of her "woman's heart, backed by the soft prejudices of a far-reaching heredity" (1:55). Neither an attack on the conventional woman nor an ironic criticism of man for holding back woman's development, this statement simply suggests that Eleanor Faraday's essential makeup, for whatever reason, does not allow her to be content outside the usual course of a late-nineteenth-century American woman's life. Similarly, Faraday's convenient forgetting of his own jealousy and his condescending thought, "I love her none the less for it, but my Nellie is only a woman, after all" (1:58), entail not an oblique criticism by Chopin of male smugness but merely a late-nineteenth-century American man's comfortable commitment of himself to a conventional pattern of husband-wife relations in which, in this particular marriage anyway, both partners will assuredly find happiness.

More explicit than either "Wiser Than a God" or "A Point at Issue!" in developing Chopin's view of marriage is her first novel, *At Fault*, on which she was already working at the time of the latter story. With *At Fault* she establishes clearly for the first time the context of amorality in which all her subsequent depictions of marriage will occur. When Aunt Belindy, a knowing old black servant on Thérèse LaFirme's plantation, asks sharply of a romantic young girl prating of "leaving the world" to enter a convent, "Religion—no religion, whar you gwine live ef you don' live in de worl'? Gwine live up in de moon?" (1:841), she speaks for Chopin, who portrays throughout this novel the folly of leaving the world behind for a life of fatuous devotion to inapplicable and life-denying ideals. The most damaging of such ideals in *At Fault* is the notion that any marriage—even a hideously unhappy one—must last as long as life. That a marriage should, on the contrary, last only as long as those in it are fulfilled by it is what Thérèse finally learns in this novel and is the lesson behind all Chopin's subsequent marriage fiction.

Because it takes Thérèse so long to learn this lesson, she causes herself and Hosmer, the man she loves, a good deal of mischief and indirectly brings about the death of his wife, Fanny. And, contrary to Per Seyersted's comments that *At Fault* is marred by "a lack of focus due to the many subplots and secondary figures" in it and by Chopin's inability "to fuse her local color with her theme,"[8] every subplot and secondary figure and virtually every detail of local color work to show that life and human nature resist the imposition of such absolutist moral ideals as Thérèse's commitment to the sanctity and indissolubility of marriage.

Typical of the local color details that contribute to Chopin's development of her themes in *At Fault* is "McFarlane's grave," the burial place of a particularly nefarious old villain, whose ghost, according to local legend, haunts the region. The grave itself is used by Chopin as a sinister reminder of a timeless evil, ineradicable even by Christianity. She notes that its "battered and weather-worn cross of wood . . . lurched disreputably to one side—there being no hand in all the world that cared to make it straight . . ." (2:772). Here, Hosmer's sister, Melicent, and Thérèse's nephew, Grégoire, infatuated with each other, stay "till the shadows grew so deep about Old McFarlane's grave that they passed it by with hurried step and averted glance" (2:774). Making this setting so functional in the novel is the fact that Chopin links it with two couples whose relationships end badly when the lesson of the timelessness and inevitability of human weakness conveyed by the gravesite is ignored. Melicent's subsequent rejection of Grégoire because of his frailty and Hosmer's misguided attempt to save Fanny from alcoholism by remarrying her despite his love for Thérèse are both closely tied to the gravesite, the former by the younger couple's stay at the scene (the only time in the novel that this setting is presented) and the latter by Chopin's juxtaposition of Grégoire and Melicent's talk at the gravesite, which closes chapter 8, with Hosmer's surprise return to Saint Louis in chapter 9 to remarry Fanny.

The subplot involving Melicent's rejection of Grégoire and its unhappy result, like the gravesite setting, is an element tangential to the main story of *At Fault* that nonetheless illuminates it. When Melicent, a girl of the foolishly romantic, novel-reading sort, depicted so well by Howells, learns that Grégoire has coolly killed Joçint as he discovered that reprobate in the act of burning down the mill on Thérèse's plantation, she concludes that he is a fiend and refuses ever to talk to him again. Her brother, on the other hand, though certainly not approving of Grégoire's action, is realistic enough to perceive that "heredity and pathology had to be considered in relation with the slayer's character" (2:824), or, to put it as Aunt Belindy shrewdly does, he knows that, as a hot-blooded Creole, "Grégor gwine be Grégor till he die. Dats all dar is 'bout it" (2:833). With this realization that there is an inevitability to people's behavior (a realization, one might note, applicable, as well, to the incurable malignity of Joçint and the blind love for him of his father, Morico), Hosmer has no difficulty in continuing to get along with Grégoire. Melicent, though, ever the unremitting idealist, cuts Grégoire and returns home to Saint Louis, leaving him to the grief that prompts a frenzy of self-destructive behavior culminating in his violent death. When Melicent hears of Grégoire's end, the foolish girl passes her time in bittersweet, romantic reminiscences of him that have as their main function the assuagement of her usual boredom. Her idealism, then, like that of most as Chopin sees it, is fundamentally life-denying, full of all the sterility of self-dramatization and devoid of real self-fulfillment.

The marriages of Fanny's Saint Louis friends, the Dawsons and Worthingtons, which are seen briefly, serve, like the gravesite setting and Melicent-Grégoire subplot, to point up how severely misguided Thérèse is when she rejects Hosmer, whom she loves, and persuades him to sacrifice himself by remarrying Fanny. Neither marriage even resembles a successful one. The coarse wives "were two ladies of elegant leisure," Chopin notes sardonically, "the conditions of whose lives, and the amiability of whose husbands had enabled them to develop into finished and professional time-killers" (2:781). Mrs. Worthington, whose timid, bookish husband is of so little consequence to her that she uses his books to prop up furniture, invariably speaks of the poor fellow "present as of a husband absent" (2:848); and Mrs. Dawson's husband, a crudely convivial traveling salesman, is usually absent in fact. In killing the great deal of time available to them, the wives become gossipy haunters of the more glaring theaters and restaurants, far more familiar than they ought to be with the good-time fellows their brassy looks attract. Chopin's only purpose in bringing this pair into the novel is to emphasize both the inevitability of Hosmer's failure to save Fanny from her alcoholism by remarrying her and the folly of Thérèse for thinking he is morally obligated to try. The vulgarity of Mrs. Dawson and Mrs. Worthington and the failure of their marriages are somehow built into the system of things. Thus, it is in no way surprising that when last seen, Mr. Worthington, sitting quietly, "lost" in reading about "asceticism, martyrdom, superhuman possibilities which man is capable of attaining under peculiar conditions of life" (2:846), is more distant from his wife than ever or that, according to last report, Mr. Dawson shot the man his wife was seeing while he was out of town. Clearly, when Fanny is seen to be an intimate of such women as Mrs. Worthington and Mrs. Dawson, her initial refusal to remarry Hosmer because "it would be the same thing all over again" (2:778) seems far more convincing than his rejoinder, "It will not be the same. . . . I will not be the same, and that will make all the difference needful" (2:778), particularly when one recalls that his proposal to her has been demanded, in fact, by the woman he really loves. In short, Hosmer seems bound and determined to pursue just such a course of "asceticism, martyrdom, and superhuman possibilities" as that of which the ineffectual Mr. Worthington reads so raptly. The results of such an effort by an ordinary man are, unfortunately, all too predictable.

Another secondary figure in *At Fault* whose role is significant in conveying Chopin's theme is Homeyer, friend and adviser to Hosmer. Though Homeyer is never seen (indeed, this fact and the similarity in names makes him seem virtually a symbolic projection of the suppressed commonsensical side of Hosmer's nature), his advice is heard, and it pointedly suggests Chopin's own thinking on denial of self. Warning Hosmer against remarriage with Fanny, Homeyer, as Hosmer recalls, railed at "the submission of a human destiny to the exacting and ignorant rule of what he termed moral conventionalists" (2:777). Hosmer remembers too Homeyer's assertions that "the individual man [must] hold on to his personality," must not sacrifice it for an abstraction or even possible benefit for another, and that, if at all redeemable, Fanny might best be aided through "the capability of [Hosmer and Thérèse's] united happiness" (2:777). Hosmer's rejection of Homeyer's largely deterministic and amoral outlook wins him no plaudits from Chopin and no happiness in his life. On the contrary, it merely leaves him open, as Chopin perceives it must, to unremitting pain.

Inexorably bearing out all that subplots, secondary characters, and aspects of setting reveal about the futility and folly inherent in the quixotic idealism that denies self is Hosmer's second marriage to Fanny. Symbolizing all that is wrong with this union is the "demoniac" and "grotesque" dream Thérèse has on the night Grégoire kills Joçint. In it, "Hosmer was in danger from which she was striving in physical effort to rescue him, and when she dragged him painfully from the peril that menaced him, she turned to see that it was Fanny whom she had saved—laughing at her derisively, and Hosmer had been left to perish" (2:821). Unfortunately, of course, this nightmare is painfully close to the truth, as Thérèse's effort to rescue Hosmer (and herself) from the danger of what her religious and moral convictions tell her is an illicit attraction almost destroys him.

Despite Hosmer's sincere efforts to be a more attentive husband to Fanny than he was in their first marriage, when their basic incompatibility led him to immerse himself in business and her to indulge her constitutional weakness for strong drink, he cannot make a success of their second marriage any more than Joçint could keep from burning down the mill or Morico could refrain from mourning deeply for his worthless son. Sensing the joylessness behind her husband's efforts, Fanny again turns to drink. Her resultant querulous and abusive behavior finally leads Hosmer into pessimism and bitterness that nearly give rise to violence and do lead indirectly to Fanny's death. Reacting viciously to Fanny's taunting him with her suddenly intuited insight that he loves Thérèse, Hosmer grabs her roughly, clutches a clasp knife, and slowly tells her in words "weighted with murder, 'By heaven—I'll—kill you!'" (2:860). When, shocked with himself, Hosmer releases his terrified wife and dazedly hurries away, she, typically enough, needs a drink. Going to an old black's riverside shanty to get it, Fanny dies when the fast-moving current undercuts the bank on which the shanty stands. Hosmer's frantic effort to save her from drowning is as much in vain as his earlier efforts to redeem her from alcoholism by salvaging their marriage. Like the river's eating at the ground under the shanty, to which Chopin purposefully alluded early in the novel, Fanny's alcoholism has a sinister inevitability to it, is productive solely of pain, and is apparently irremediable.

Just as inevitable as the disastrous conclusion of Hosmer and Thérèse's unnatural course of idealism is the fact that after some time they should again turn to each other. Indeed, Chopin closely links their avowal of love for each other with the beautiful new springtime about them, coming in with an inevitability of its own. When Hosmer meets Thérèse again after his long stay in Saint Louis following Fanny's death, "the air was filled with spring and all its promises. Full with the sound of it, the smell of it, the deliciousness of it." Chopin goes on to declare that this "sweet air" is "soft and strong, like the touch of a brave woman's hand" (2:869). Now, like the "brave woman" she really is, Thérèse will no longer allow worn-out conventions to come between her and nature. Aware now of the folly inherent in her attempt to resist gratifying her authentic needs, she can agree with Hosmer's assertion after their marriage that although "the truth in its entirety isn't given man to know," we can "make a step towards it, when we learn that there is rottenness and evil in the world, masquerading as right and morality—when we learn to know the living spirit from the dead letter" (2:872). Presumably, they will now, no longer perceiving themselves to be "at fault" for doing so, pursue that "living spirit" in the marriage that should have come so much earlier, and would have, had not Thérèse and Hosmer forgotten that the only place for them to live, after all, was "de worl'."

At Fault, then, is Chopin's first work to present marriage explicitly as an experience that is valid only insofar as it allows individuals to attain self-fulfillment, an assumption underlying every subsequent marriage story of hers, no matter how dissimilar to each other these stories may otherwise be. Generally, these stories fall into three types, all of which have as a virtual given the notion that marriage, particularly for a woman, involves a certain amount of submission. One group presents characters—all women—who are able to find self-fulfillment solely in submission to the demands their marriages make upon them. A second shows the dangers inherent in refusing to rebel against the demands imposed in marriage when one fails to find an authentic existence in meeting them. And, finally, the third group presents some who, unable to find satisfying lives in their marriages, rebel against them and their demands. Apart from the fact that the last two marriage works Chopin wrote, *The Awakening* and "The Storm," occur in the last group, perhaps betokening an increasing rebelliousness in her, there is no chronological pattern discernible to her marriage stories, and, therefore, I shall discuss them solely in terms of these three groupings.

Chopin's stories that show women who find gratifying, authentic lives in accepting the submission that marriage demands include "A Visit to Avoyelles" (1892) and "Madame Célestin's Divorce" (1893), both of which present women who, surprisingly enough, find contentment with husbands who give every evidence of being curs, and "The Going Away of Liza" (1894) and "Athénaïse" (1896), which depict wives who leave essentially unexceptionable mates but return to them, finally, when they discover that they can only fulfill the demands of their natures within their marriages. Whatever course these women take, be it clinging blindly to mates who are unworthy or finally returning to those who are in fact good husbands, Chopin neither praises nor blames. Again, she merely shows that the inevitable propensity of men and women to seek authenticity renders beside the point conventional moralistic assumptions about matrimony.

Certainly, at first glance, one would not suspect that matrimony offers fulfillment to Mentine, the much put-upon wife of the lazy, impecunious, and arrogant Jules Trodon, in "A Visit to Avoyelles." All that Doudouce, Mentine's rejected suitor, sees on visiting her confirms that seven years of marriage have left her "suffering in a hopeless, common, exasperating way for the small comforts of life" (1:228). Cruelly overworked on her husband's ramshackle farm, hopelessly overburdened with children who seem as numerous and unmanageable as the mangy dogs prowling about the place, the slovenly Mentine that Doudouce sees bears little resemblance to the girl he once asked to marry him: "He would have known her sweet, cheerful brown eyes, that were not changed; but her figure, that had looked so trim in the wedding gown, was sadly misshapen. She was brown, with skin like parchment, and piteously thin. There were lines, some deep as if old age had cut them, about the eyes and mouth" (1:229). Convinced that Mentine cannot be happy in such circumstances, loving her "fiercely, as a mother loves an afflicted child" (1:231), Doudouce leaves, thinking "he would have liked to thrust that man aside, and gather up her and her children, and hold them and keep them as long as life lasted" (1:231). His thoughts in this direction are short-lived, however, for when, in the last lines of the story, he looks back at his lost love, he finds that "her face was turned away from him" and that "she was gazing after her husband, who went in the direction of the field" (1:231).

Seeing Mentine's fixed gaze after Jules cannot, one suspects, fail to clear up Doudouce's own vision, which, both figuratively and literally, has been blinded by love. Indeed, just before he sees Mentine looking after her husband, Doudouce has been stumbling "over the rough ground because of tears that were blinding him" (1:230); and he made his visit in the first place because reports of Mentine prompted a dream in which, in her wedding dress, Mentine was holding out her arms to him, imploring him to save her, clearly a vision of things that is blind to the facts. And the facts are, of course, that Mentine, oddly enough, finds self-fulfillment in submission to Jules. Though it may not accord with the saccharine vision held by the sentimental Doudouce, the simple truth is, Chopin knows, that people *will*, often, be happy doing what others might find to be singularly unproductive of joy.

"Madame Célestin's Divorce" depicts a situation markedly similar to that of "A Visit to Avoyelles." Madame Célestin, a pretty, unpretentious young Creole woman, has been deserted by her husband, an ill-natured lout who drinks and who has abused her. Lawyer Paxton, himself increasingly drawn to Madame Célestin, urges her to divorce the scoundrel; but she continually procrastinates, assuring him that she is on the verge of doing so but is hesitant about flying in the face of the religious convictions in which she was brought up. Finally, her husband returns, promises her, as she relates, "on his word an' honor he's going to turn ova a new leaf" (1:279), and she contentedly gives up all thought of divorce.

Like Mentine, then, Madame Célestin finds self-fulfillment in a marriage that would appall most people. Submission—even to a brute such as her husband—is apparently what her nature demands and thrives on. Always seen "plying her broom" (1:278), tending her rose bushes, or sewing, Madame Célestin is one who feels most herself when caught up in the domestic round and deferring to her husband and to community standards. Though the "deep rings" (1:279) made in the palm of her hand by the broom-handle may well symbolize mutilation, imprisonment, or sexual dependence on her husband, the situation remains the same: Madame Célestin is most herself under the dominion of her marriage. Again, Chopin neither approves nor disapproves; she merely describes an example of things as they are.

Unlike Mentine and Madame Célestin, Liza-Jane Rydon finds happiness in submission to her marriage only after leaving her homespun husband, Abner, and their simple life in Bludgitt Station, Missouri, in a vain effort to seek fulfillment elsewhere. Chronically dissatisfied because, as she grandly declares to one of her acquaintances, she "craves to taste the joys of ixistence" (1:113), an inane, idealized conception of which she has picked up from silly novels of aristocratic life, Liza-Jane, after a series of what one of the townsfolk calls "everlastin' quarrels what's been a imbitterin' their married life" (1:113), deserts her husband. Obviously, the "higher life" for which she leaves Abner and his mother "an' thur life of drudgery what was no ixistence" (11:113), as the same townsman sardonically puts it, eludes her; for as the thoroughly embittered Abner sits quietly with his mother on a stormy Christmas Eve, a tired, sick, and hungry Liza-Jane returns. Once Abner sees her "big dark eyes greedily seizing on every detail of homely and honest comfort that surrounded her" and notes how "whatever sin or suffering [that had] swept over her had left its impress upon her plastic being" (1:114), he yields to the gentle proddings of his mother and the feelings of his heart. "With unsteady hands" he lifts the "wet and tattered" shawl from his wife's shoulders, kneels upon the floor, and takes "the wet and torn shoes from off her feet" (1:115), a gesture that, closing the story as it does, seems to imply, obviously, as does the Christmas setting, that the marriage will be a good one for them both from this time forth.

Every detail of the story makes clear that Liza-Jane's only happiness can come in returning to her marriage. The foolish sound of her high-flown clichés when quoted by her rustic townfolk indicates all of the fatuous pretentiousness underlying her quest for the "higher life," as does the clumsy, folksy sound of her name itself, which stands in comic juxtaposition to her tin-plated visions. Too, the domestic scene to which she returns, significantly in the midst of a storm and, even more significantly, on Christmas Eve (not a subtle story, surely), is one powerfully redolent of the joys of hearth and home. With Abner quietly reading, his mother knitting, and a fire cheerfully giving of its warmth against the storm outside, the Rydon farmhouse seems not only a logical and inevitable, but even a delightful, place to be for a girl with Liza-Jane's background. When her husband kneels before her, it becomes practically unthinkable that this young wife could ever be happy elsewhere. Thus, with all elements of the story working to point up the folly of Liza-Jane's attempt to evade her basic nature and its imperatives, Chopin presents another marriage that will presumably satisfy the needs of those in it. Liza-Jane, though, will not be the last of Chopin's women to leave her marriage, nor will all those who leave return or seem foolish for not doing so.

Markedly similar to Liza-Jane, both in her urgent need at first to leave her husband and in her no less urgent longing at last to return to him, is Athénaïse, a headstrong young woman whose pregnancy leads her to realize that only in accepting the submission and restraints imposed by marriage can she find an authentic existence for herself. Per Seyersted, though accepting that "Athénaïse" is a story with a "happy end" that depicts the "sensuous joys" available to a woman, asserts that it nonetheless "contains a deep protest against woman's condition,"[9] implicit in the newly married Athénaïse's "sense of hopelessness" and "instinctive realization of the futility of rebellion against a social and sacred institution" (1:432) that arise when her parents force her to return to her husband, Cazeau, after an early effort to leave him. However, were Chopin using Athénaïse's early despair as a means of showing the lamentable condition of nineteenth-century woman, she would, one suspects, present the bitter young wife as something other than the callow, histrionic sort she is until she discovers her pregnancy; and she would present Cazeau as something other than the compassionate man *he* is, one who "did not slight nor neglect" (1:434) his wife and whose "chief offense seemed to be that he loved" Athénaïse, a woman who refuses "to be loved against her will" (1:434). Thus, the repugnance Athénaïse feels at first toward her marriage seems prompted less by the poignant desire for freedom felt by a generous-spirited young woman than by her ignorance of her own nature and its deepest needs.

A close look at Athénaïse's makeup and her initial response to her marriage—a marriage she had not been unwilling to make—reveals just how jejune her longing for perfect freedom is. Her loving parents, Chopin notes, "had hoped—not without reason and justice—that marriage would bring the poise, the desirable pose, so glaringly lacking in Athénaïse's character. Marriage they knew to be a wonderful and powerful agent in the development and formation of a woman's character; they had seen its effect too often to doubt it" (1:434). Unfortunately, from the first, Athénaïse, about whose very features and expression "lurked a softness, a prettiness, a dewiness, that were perhaps too childlike, that savored of immaturity" (1:432), is unable to adjust to married life. It is not Cazeau who troubles her, as she tells her hot-spirited fool of a brother, Montéclin, but the intimacy enforced by marriage itself, an intimacy that she finds constricting and nauseating (partly, perhaps, because it strikes her, whether she realizes it or not, as an omnipresent reminder of sexual demands on her):

> "No I don't hate [Cazeau] . . . ; It's just being married that I detes' an' despise. I hate being Mrs. Cazeau, an' would want to be Athénaïse Miché again. I can't stan' to live with a man; to have him always there; his coats an' pantaloons hanging in my room; his ugly bare feet—washing them in my tub befo' my very eyes, ugh!" She shuddered with recollections, and resumed, with a sigh that was almost a sob: "Mon Dieu, mon Dieu! Sister Marie Angélique knew w'at she was saying; she knew me better than myse'f w'en she said God had sent me a vocation an' I was turning deaf ears. W'en I think of a blessed life in the convent, at peace! Oh, w'at was I dreaming of!" and then the tears came. (1:431)

That she had, in fact, rebelled against parents and nuns by having Montéclin spirit her away from the convent that she now recalls so fondly typifies her flair from the first for the histrionic and her inability to accept restraint. More, the very fact that she recalls her sojourn at the convent so fondly is a clear manifestation of her penchant for escaping aspects of reality that she finds unpleasant to acknowledge.

Unable to accept that she is indeed married to Cazeau, Athénaïse repeatedly runs off to her family, seeking escape from commitment, responsibility, and physical intimacy with a man, all of which she finds so disturbing, finally, that she can even convince herself against all evidence that she has a calling to be a nun. Despite her parents' criticism, she enjoys being home and takes uninhibited pleasure, as any unmarried child without a vocation might, in the round of merry parties and dances she finds there and, as well, in the bountiful portions of her mother's cooking on which she gorges herself. When each regressive sojourn ends with Cazeau's coming to take her back to her adult lot as a wife, Athénaïse determines to make a lasting break with him, and, once more delving into her past, she calls on Montéclin to rescue her from imprisonment.

The circumstances in which this last escapade places Athénaïse are all too obviously unsavory ones. Montéclin's excitement as he realizes that "eloping with one's sister was only a little less engaging than eloping with someone else's sister" (1:441) does not quite smack of the incestuous, but it does cast an unwholesome aura over the whole affair, making it seem, at the least, an ill-advised excursion into the irrational, the immature, and the vulgar. Nor does her settling alone in New Orleans palpably improve Athénaïse's situation, for there she becomes increasingly vulnerable to the amatory advances of the genial cynic Gouvernail, a "liberal-minded fellow," in that "a man or woman lost nothing of his respect by being married" (1:444). Though he knows that when Athénaïse hugs him and tearfully pours out her grief he is serving "as substitute for Montéclin" (1:450) and though he suspects too that "she adored Cazeau without being herself aware of it" (1:446), he nonetheless hopes "some day to hold her with a lover's arms" (1:450), an event that, genial fellow as he may be notwithstanding, would be Athénaïse's undoing, consigning her to a life of chaos and prolonged adolescence rather than the mature womanhood that her nature demands she attain.

Only her discovery that she is pregnant brings Athénaïse to herself. Convinced by the maternal and domestic yearnings welling up within her that her place is with her husband, she orders Montéclin to come to New Orleans and take her to Cazeau. Though her call to be brought back is issued to her brother rather than her husband, the implication of this is not that Athénaïse still needs Montéclin more than she does Cazeau but that she feels as if a certain propriety must be observed in the manner of her return. It was Montéclin who took her off; therefore, it must be he who will take her back on what is, in effect, a self-prescribed retracing of her adolescent course in an effort to pass beyond both it and all that Montéclin represents. Her obvious affection for Cazeau on her return and the maternal attention she lavishes on a crying black baby make clear that she has indeed put childish things behind herself and found her identity as a woman.

Throughout the story Cazeau's behavior contrasts strongly with that of Athénaïse, showing invariably the folly of the young wife. A man of quiet dignity, Cazeau refuses to rail either against his fate or his wife when his marriage sours. His suggestion to Athénaïse that although things have gone wrong they ought to see the marriage through as well as they can reveals him to be a mature man who can face facts openly, avoid needless recrimination, and maintain a good deal of affection even for a wife as wayward as his:

> "I married you because I loved you; because you were the woman I wanted to marry, an' the only one. I reckon I tole you that befo'. I thought—of co'se I was a fool fo' taking things fo' granted—but I did think I might make you happy in making things easier and mo' comfortable fo' you. I expected—I was even that big a fool—I believed that yo' coming yere to me would be like the sun shining out of the clouds, an' that our days would be like w'at the story-books promise after the wedding. I was mistaken. . . . I reckon you foun' out you made a mistake, too. I don' see anything to do but make the best of a bad bargain, an' shake han's over it." (1:435)

There is a poignancy to this speech that indicates the kindness and warmth under Cazeau's quiet demeanor. And it is these traits that lead him finally, when Athénaïse goes off to New Orleans, to pursue his wife no more. Remembering the dreadful scene of his father brutally hauling back a runaway slave, Cazeau decides that he cannot put himself any longer in a situation analogous to his father's by bringing back a runaway wife against her will. Cazeau's self-respect and compassion are qualities Athénaïse might well come to emulate as she grows into the womanly identity she has at last acknowledged as her own.

Thus does Athénaïse, like Liza-Jane, ultimately find the self-gratification inherent in learning who she is and what are her needs. Both women seek some vague, ideal freedom, but their pursuit of it leaves them open only to the barrenness, loneliness, and confusion attendant upon suppressing their authentic natures, which seem as much shaped to find satisfaction in married domesticity as are those of Mentine and Madame Célestin. In finding what they want, then, through marriage, these women find themselves. That they do so with these marriages does not, however, bespeak any defense of matrimony on Chopin's part; for many women find authenticity outside marriage, many are, in fact, hindered by marriage in their pursuit of it, and at least two of the women in these four stories find it with mates whom many might regard as less than desirable.[10]

Finding themselves through submission to the restraints imposed by marriage is, as I have noted, an impossibility for some of Chopin's married women. When such women fail either to leave their marriages or to acknowledge their problems to themselves and try forthrightly to seek authenticity somehow, even within the context of their troublesome marriages, the results of such attempts at self-repression can be disastrous. Attempting to resist the imperatives of one's nature, Chopin shows, brings not the inner peace that moralists proclaim comes with the renunciation of self but, instead, all the bitterness of frustration. More, she believes, as we have noted, that, all efforts to the contrary notwithstanding, the repressed desires will ultimately out anyway, perhaps with a directness that is dangerously overpowering, perhaps with an obliquity that can lead dangerously astray.

Virtually a cautionary tale revealing just how troublesome long-repressed desire for gratifyingly authentic existence can be when it finally manifests itself is Chopin's depiction of the folly of self-denial "The Story of an Hour" (1894). In this brief account, Mrs. Mallard, "afflicted with a heart trouble" (1:252), is told gently that her husband has been killed in a railroad accident. After her "storm of grief had spent itself" (1:252), Mrs. Mallard, "pressed down by a physical exhaustion that haunted her body and seemed to reach into her soul," retires to her room to grieve in solitude. Once alone, though, she is surprised to find her grief rapidly dissipating in the face of something else, which is "approaching to possess her" (1:353). Beginning to recognize it, she strives to "beat it back with her will" but finds the latter "as powerless as her two white slender hands would have been" (1:353) and gradually yields. What she yields to, what possesses her, is, of all things, exultation, a joy at the prospect of being "free, free, free" (1:353). So given over is she to this new feeling that she is beyond wondering whether her sudden happiness is "monstrous." A "clear and exalted perception enabled her to dismiss the suggestion as trivial" (1:353). Calmly, she envisions the years to come: "There would be no one to live for . . . ; she would live for herself. There would be no powerful will bending hers in that blind persistence with which men and women believe they have a right to impose a private will upon a fellow-creature. . . . What could love, the unresolved mystery, count for in the face of this possession of self-assertion which she suddenly recognized as the strongest impulse of her being!" (1:353). Happy at last, herself at last, she sits comfortably, whispering repeatedly, in almost incantatory fashion, "Free! Body and Soul Free!" (1:354). Then, answering her worried sister's importunings, she descends the stairs to join her, carrying herself "unwittingly like a goddess of Victory" (1:354), a look of "feverish triumph in her eyes" (1:354). At this moment her husband, indubitably alive and blissfully unaware of the misinformation that has preceded him, lets himself in the front door. Seeing him, Mrs. Mallard falls dead, a victim, say the doctors, of "heart disease—of the joy that kills" (1:354).

An ironical story, certainly, perhaps heavy-handedly so, and what is significant is that the irony is directed so intensely at the unfortunate Mrs. Mallard, whose very name, which conjures up associations of free, far-ranging flight and union with nature, stands in ironic contrast to the constricted life she has forced herself to lead. This is a woman, Chopin implies, who has left herself open to the trick of fate that destroys her by never attempting bravely to seize her own life and live it. Though she leaves her room in response to her sister's call with a sense of having won a great victory, she has, ironically, won nothing; she has merely been granted a prospect of freedom, one to which she cannot cling in the face of her husband's return. Again ironically, the intensity itself with which she grasps for that brief prospect, her fancy "running riot" through a vision of "spring days, and summer days, and all sorts of days that would be her own" (1:355), reflects—as does the melodramatic phrasing, which conveys a sense of how febrile her longings are—just how severely repressed Mrs. Mallard has allowed herself to be. Had she tried to "reach into her soul" long before the inaccurate report and her consequent physical exhaustion, the self-repression might never have taken so strong a hold on her and a sudden prospect of freedom might not, therefore, have engendered so dangerously feverish a response. Clearly, the final irony of the tale—beyond the doctors' crude misinterpretation—involves the fact that the "heart trouble" that kills her is more spiritual than physical. She has lacked the heart, the courage, to assert her real nature in the face of her husband and her marriage.

Though the unnamed wife in "Her Letters" (1894) seems not nearly so repressed as Mrs. Mallard, it is apparent nevertheless that despite entering into an illicit affair she too has never had the requisite courage to follow her deepest longings by leaving her marriage and seeking the freedom her passionate nature desires. Stifled in its normal development, her longing for self-assertion and freedom manifests itself in a frenzied sexual attachment and in a hatred for her husband that is so subtle that she is unaware of it herself. Stricken with a fatal illness after the close of her affair, the woman finds that she cannot bring herself to burn her love letters even though her inability to do so may bring about discovery of the affair after her death, when her husband goes through her papers. Her husband's "tenderness and years of devotion had made him, in a manner, dear to her" (1:399), and she tells herself that she does not wish to cause him possible hurt; but she thinks too "how desolate and empty" her remaining days would be without the letters, "with only her thoughts, illusive thoughts, that she could not hold in her hands and press, as she did these, to her cheeks and heart" (1:399). Consequently, in order to keep her precious letters and, as she tells herself, to spare her husband the possibility of a painful discovery, she appeals to his sense of honor by writing on her packet of letters, "I leave this package to the care of my husband. With perfect faith in his loyalty and love, I ask him to destroy it unopened" (1:400), a behest with which he complies, throwing the packet into the river; but it is not many months later that, tormented ceaselessly by the doubts of his wife's faithfulness that the packet has aroused in him, he follows it into the river as he takes his life by jumping from a bridge.

Close scrutiny of this grim tale reveals that just such a consummation for her spouse may be what the dying woman devoutly wished for, that, in fact, her passion for her lover is not as elevating and her concern for her husband's well-being as sincere as she believes them to be. Indeed, her devotion to her lover seems marked by an almost revolting and finally imprisoning frenzy, seemingly growing out of the suppression of her real identity in order to keep up the appearance, at least, of the conventionally faithful wife. A woman calm and gratified in the assurance of knowing herself and answering the imperatives of her nature would not turn love letters into sexual totems, in what is little less than an obscene parody of the communion service, by taking one of the "most precious" ones, kissing it "again and again," and then, with her "sharp white teeth" tearing off the corner where the name is written and tasting it "between her lips and upon her tongue like some god-given morsel" (1:399). Further, she would not "encircle" the letters in her arms, and lie "breathing softly and contentedly with the hectic cheek resting upon them" (1:399) or regard her former lover so extravagantly as to envision him as one who "had changed the water in her veins to wine" (1:399). Similarly, a woman knowing herself and at peace with herself would never be so self-deluded as to think such a posthumous appeal as this woman makes is intended to spare her husband pain. So fully has she unknowingly committed herself, in fact, to her plan for the exquisite torture of this man who is, "in a manner," dear to her that she dies clutching the key to the desk in which she has sequestered the packet. The virulent hostility she directs toward him, like the virulent passion she feels for her lover and for the artifacts she associates with him, can only come from a desperation so terrible as to be beyond her capacity to acknowledge it even to herself—the desperation of a thwarted life, of a freedom never directly pursued and, thus, never attained.

For Chopin such self-repression as exhibited by Mrs. Mallard and the wife in "Her Letters" is tantamount to self-consignment to death, and in "A Lady of Bayou St. John" (1893), she presents in Madame Delisle a woman who almost literally weds herself to death through her inability to seek mature womanhood. On the verge of running off to Paris with a young man while her husband is away fighting in the Civil War, Madame Delisle receives word that her spouse has been killed. Quickly dismissing her would-be lover, she dedicates the rest of her life to veneration of her husband's memory in the shrine into which she transforms their home. The reason for this sudden decision is neither hard to see nor admirable. Exceedingly childish, young Madame Delisle, before her husband's death, romps with puppies, teases parrots, demands bedtime stories from her maid, stares lovingly at herself in mirrors, and imagines herself capable of great love and sacrifice. For such a woman, ordinary married life holds few attractions, but either elopement with a lover or nunlike self-renunciatory adoration of a fallen hero-husband offers virtually limitless possibilities for self-dramatization. Though both the planned elopement and the endless veneration of the lost husband arise from childish, sentimental romanticism rather than the arousal of a nature seeking to know and fulfill itself, the former course might well have led this fatuous young woman to find her mature identity; for, unlike the similarly childish Athénaïse, Madame Delisle manifests no capacity whatever for finding adult womanhood in her marriage. Such conflicts and difficulties as would have inevitably arisen in an adulterous elopement might possibly have awakened in her impulses toward the development of such an authentic identity. By yielding to convention and channeling her longings for romance into what is merely an extended elaboration of the standard role of the grieving wife, this young woman, who now refuses to acknowledge to herself that she was dissatisfied in her marriage, permanently immures herself in a state of arrested development so deathlike that it precludes for her, alone among Chopin's protagonists, the possibility of any outburst of long-repressed authentic needs. At last report, Chopin notes, she has become "a very pretty old lady" about whom there "has never been a breath of reproach" (1:302), one whose prettiness and spotless demeanor bespeak, one guesses, an insidiously successful job of self-embalming.

More direct than the dissatisfied wives at whom we have just looked, those in "In Sabine" (1893), "A Respectable Woman" (1894), "The Storm" (1898), and, of course, in Chopin's best-known work, *The Awakening* (1898) either pursue authenticity decisively or seem to be on their way to such pursuit. Though such a course may never be successful, may, in fact, leave one vulnerable to a whole panoply of dangers and, perhaps, may not even be a consciously willed one to begin with, failure to pursue it can lead, as we have seen, only to self-deceit and frustration.

"In Sabine," markedly similar to "A Visit to Avoyelles," differs from it in one crucial particular, that being that the much put-upon wife in this story does leave her husband. In each story the husband is an overbearing, shiftless boor and the wife a former beauty now haggard with overwork. But because the wife in "In Sabine," unlike Mentine in the earlier work, finds no happiness with her husband, she rides off at the close of the tale with a dashing Creole rescuer. In the earlier story, Chopin enabled the reader to credit the wife's devotion to her husband by pointing up the sentimental folly of Doudouce in imagining himself a sort of bayou Lochinvar swooping down to gather Mentine up from her misery; but in this work, what she seeks to make plausible is the wife's departure, and she does this primarily by focusing on the brutality of the husband. By emphasizing (perhaps too much so) Bud Aiken's shortcomings—his rootlessness, slovenliness, drunkenness, and his sadism, which manifests itself in his forcing his wife to ride his vicious pony and in his broad hints that he will take her to the wilds of Texas and there desert her—Chopin makes it seem improbable that any woman with self-respect could stay with such a man. Indeed, pointing up just how fully the wife here lacks an authentic identity in being married to Bud is the fact that with him she even lacks her real name. Known, because of her imperious nature, as "Tite Reine" before she was married, she now finds herself called "Rain" by her husband and actually has become as tearful and passive as her new cognomen implies. Her spirited identity stifled, her only recourse is escape; and when she rides off with her rescuer, one's sympathies are just where Chopin wants them to be—with the wife who is unafraid to flout the conventional standards if it serves her deepest needs to do so. Chopin's concern here, just as it is in "A Visit to Avoyelles," is with whether or not her protagonist is fulfilled by the marriage. If so, as we have noted, Chopin believes staying in the marriage is right, even if sentimentalists might think otherwise; if not, she believes leaving is right, though all convention might call the departure waywardness.

Waywardness is something Mrs. Baroda, protagonist of "A Respectable Woman," never finds at all attractive until a dose of moonlight and Whitman with her husband's close friend awakens hitherto dormant elements in her nature that impose demands on her that she seems to find impossible to resist. Though a relatively slight story, "A Respectable Woman" is an interesting anticipation of *The Awakening*. As with the novel, one finds a woman at first singularly unaware of her own boredom and repression, a woman whose marriage, though pleasant and unexceptional, relegates her to a life in which she is merely the object of her husband's affectionate condescension. The arousal of Mrs. Baroda, through a surge of passion for another man, to an incipient awareness of what her conventional training and typical marriage have made her is rendered with a subtlety and ambiguity that mark this story as, at the very least, rich apprentice work for Chopin's extensive treatment of a fuller awakening in her account of Edna Pontellier.

From the first, Mrs. Baroda's response to the visit of her husband's vacationing old college-friend, the journalist Gouvernail (whom we remember from "Athénaïse"), is a complex one. Picturing him before she meets him, she envisions Gouvernail to be "tall, slim, cynical; with eyeglasses, and his hands in his pockets" (1:333), as someone too whom she expects not to like at all. Finding that, except for his slimness, he meets none of her expectations, she discovers that she likes him and, even more, that she is "puzzled" and "piqued" because he makes "no direct appeal to her approval or even esteem" (1:333). What is so intriguing in all this is what it reveals of the depths of Mrs. Baroda's longing to confront a way of life that subverts her own. Knowing that Gouvernail is a journalist and not a "society man" or a "man about town" (1:333) and, thus, not part of the round of "mild dissipation" (1:333) that the Barodas move in when they winter in New Orleans, Mrs. Baroda is exceedingly quick to shape him in her imagination as the virtual cliché of the iconoclastic journalist, a type that she presumably has never known but that she assures herself she would dislike. Though her indulgence in such image-making might seem to bespeak a fervent loyalty to the way of life at which her stereotyped journalist would invariably sneer, the readiness with which she resorts to it and her certainty that she will dislike this fellow she has never seen indicate, as subsequent events in the story show, an uneasy defensiveness about her way of life and an incipient desire to test it against another vision of things. When she finds that Gouvernail, though not the odious cliche she has convinced herself he would be, is someone nevertheless whose very nature calls her own way of life into question, the uneasy but strong interest she manifests in him reveals just how powerful her underlying need to scrutinize her life has been.

It is exactly Gouvernail's lack of concern for appealing for her approval and esteem that reveals to Mrs. Baroda, apparently, an independence in him that sets him apart from the type of man she knows and understands. More, it seems to reveal a respect for her own independence because such attempts to appeal for her approval and esteem as she has known have doubtless been all too like those of her husband—based, that is, on the assumption that what women most approve and esteem are men who genially repress them by treating them with the patronizing air that one would direct toward a generally amiable child. Disturbingly typical, one suspects, of Mr. Baroda's behavior to his wife is his response to her assertion that something about Gouvernail disturbs her. Taking her "pretty face" between his hands, he looks "tenderly and laughingly into her troubled eyes" and tells her jocularly, "You are full of surprises, ma belle . . . . Even I can never count upon how you are going to act under given conditions" (1:334). Used to such treatment as this, Mrs. Baroda is, not surprisingly, both drawn to, and unsettled by, Gouvernail because of his behavior.

Finally, she is charmed intensely by Gouvernail when, alone with her one evening, he recites—typically enough, more to the night than to her—Whitman's apostrophe, "Night of south winds—night of the large few stars! / Still nodding night—." Aroused physically by the passion in the poetry, the beauty of the night, and her nearness to this man who, unlike all others, does not patronize her, she "wanted to reach out her hand in the darkness and touch him with the sensitive tips of her fingers upon the face or the lips. She wanted to draw close to him and whisper against his cheek— she did not care what—as she might have done if she had not been a respectable woman" (1:335). At last, as the impulse grows stronger still, she draws away from him. Shaken, she is tempted to tell her husband of "this folly that had seized her" (1:336). But she does not yield to this temptation, for "beside being a respectable woman she was a very sensible one; and she knew there are some battles in life which a human being must fight alone" (1:336). When, months later, another visit from Gouvernail is proposed by her husband, her response to his stated hope that she has overcome her initial dislike for his friend is, "I have overcome everything! You will see. This time I shall be very nice to him" (1:336).

It is difficult to accept Seyersted's contention that these last words of Mrs. Baroda, which end the story, are "wonderfully ambiguous to the reader."[11] Strictly speaking, of course, they are ambiguous in that one cannot be totally sure of what Mrs. Baroda means by "nice,"[12] and this obviously adds to the resonance of the story. Nonetheless, all indicates that such niceness as she will show Gouvernail is far from what one might normally expect of a "respectable woman." Indeed, the repeated emphasis itself on Mrs. Baroda's respectability finally strikes the reader as more than a little ironic, particularly when the respectability yields so readily before the onslaught of Mrs. Baroda's "sensible" desire to keep her fit of passion from her husband. Further, because she is a "sensible woman," one suspects that the "everything" that Mrs. Baroda has "overcome" is every restraint that might hold her back from what Chopin conceives to be the eminently sensible course of gratifying her passionate longing to become intimately involved with the first man to speak to the authentic, mature woman long latent in her. What ambiguity there is in this story resides not so much in the immediate import of Mrs. Baroda's last words as in their ultimate import. One does not know just how far Mrs. Baroda's incipient rebellion against her "respectability" will go or what its consequences will be. Will the affair with Gouvernail that seems to loom ahead be the culmination of a quest for authentic selfhood or at least the springboard to such a quest, or will it lead to some new form of entrapment, some personal disaster? Such questions as these are clearly unanswerable within the framework of this story, but, because of Chopin's skill in showing the early stages of the arousal of what was ostensibly a permanently conventional woman to a sense of her own needs, they are inevitable and fascinating.

Though one can only speculate about Mrs. Baroda's destiny, what ultimately becomes of that other aroused conventional wife, Edna Pontellier, in *The Awakening*, is well known. It is what motivates her and what one is to make of her that are open to speculation. From the early reviewer who, self-professedly baffled by the novel, asked "*Cui bono?*" in concluding his discussion of the work to more recent commentators, who disagree about such matters as whether it is a "problem" novel or a detached account of one troubled woman and whether Edna's suicide is an act of childish regression or one of heroic renunciation,[13] *The Awakening* has been a work unsusceptible to easy interpretation. As a result, "*Ah! si tu savais,*" the snatch of song that so haunts

Edna, becomes increasingly resonant, haunting the reader as well. If one only knew what, then what? What, one asks, does Edna know, if anything, that might explain her and perhaps many another? And if she knows nothing significant in this line, is she merely a pathetic victim of a vague malaise of no intrinsic consequence that she allows to precipitate in her a course of irresponsible and self-destructive behavior or is she a courageous quester after identity and understanding? Clearly, as the diversity of critical response indicates, Chopin's account of this desperate woman who, almost in response to the parrot's call of *"Allez vous-en! Allez vous-en! Sapristi!"* (2:881) that opens the novel, swims farther than most women ever do from the safe shores of domesticity is not without its ambiguities, ambiguities that finally seem irresolvable. There is, in short, no evidence in the novel to indicate whether or not Chopin admires Edna; nor is there any conclusive evidence that Edna herself either understands fully the implications of her behavior or fails to do so. All that *is* clear in this difficult work, as it is so often clear in other Chopin works, is that Chopin believes that people will generally do as their authentic natures demand that they do—this is as true of the other characters as it is of Edna—and that she thinks moral judgment of a situation such as Edna's, in which a woman is driven implacably by the imperatives of her aroused deepest needs, is an indulgence in egregious irrelevancy. Indeed, not just Edna's behavior and motivations but the cultures to which she has been exposed—her marriage, her husband, her love, lover, and friends, and even some of the key imagery—are presented in terms so redolent of ambiguity as to suggest that Chopin means to drive home upon her readers the realization that examination of complex human behavior involves one inevitably in so many tangled strands as to make moral judgment impossible. Difficult to attain, certainly, but not beyond human reach, though, are understanding and sympathy; and it is these, Chopin implies, toward which one should strive in looking at the case of Edna Pontellier.

Though Edna's difficult, complex, perhaps incomplete, awakening is keyed by a marriage that is not without its own complexities, it actually finds its origins in the days of her youth. That there is a marked influence on Edna of a girlhood in a Kentucky that was not long past frontier exigencies and of a Presbyterianism that still rigorously maintained hardest-line Protestant doctrines is undeniable, but whether that influence is on the whole a good or a sinister one as Chopin sees it is a great deal harder to ascertain. Repressive though they were, the Presbyterian training Edna received and the narrow Kentucky context in which she received it were, for better or worse, crucial factors in fostering her "awakening" years later. As a Calvinist religion, Presbyterianism, particularly in the time of Edna's youth, by its very doctrine thrust one back upon oneself into an intense, unending drama of self-scrutiny that for many—as it does for Edna—might outlast the hold of the dogma itself. Also, such repression as the Presbyterianism of that time and place might have enforced could well have had the opposite effect of exacerbating a rebellious streak of individualism in one, like Edna, who may be rebellious by nature to begin with. This might be all the more likely in nineteenth-century Kentucky, permeated as it still was by the frontier propensities for a potentially chaotic code of rugged individualism and for romanticizing the self's struggle for fulfillment in a difficult world—propensities implicitly evident in Edna's strait-laced father's un-Presbyterian love of betting on horse races. Such, at any rate, is the situation with Edna, as the particular form of repression with which she was faced in her girlhood prompted a rebelliousness and a heightened sense of the drama of her existence that resulted in her marriage to Léonce and then, after lying dormant for years, precipitated the "awakening" with Robert.

Unmistakably, Chopin shows, the latter stages of rebellion are implicit in the first. Thus, one of Edna's sharpest early memories has her, significantly, "running away from . . . the Presbyterian service read in a spirit of gloom by my father that chills me yet to think of" (2:896) into a meadow in which the grass was so high as to make her feel as if she were swimming. She cannot recall whether she was "frightened or pleased" (2:896), but remembers that she felt an exhilaration akin to nothing she had ever felt before. This sense of strange, lone voyaging, with its concomitant sense of drama and romance into which her repugnance for Kentucky Presbyterianism brought her, clearly stayed with her long thereafter, sparking infatuated longings for a somewhat elderly, "sad-eyed" cavalry officer (who looked something like Napoleon), for a young man engaged to a lady on a neighboring plantation, and for a "great tragedian," whom she had never met but whose face and figure nonetheless "began to haunt her imagination and stir her senses" (2:898). Indeed, even her marriage to Léonce, stultifying as it now seems to Edna, grew out of reaction against her background. All that was needed to make Edna accept Léonce, "who pressed his suit with an earnestness and an ardor which left nothing to be desired" (2:898), was such "violent opposition" as she received from her father and her sister to the notion of "marriage with a Catholic" (2:898). Clearly, then, without such prodding to her innate tendency for individualistic rebellion as that exerted by Kentucky Presbyterianism, Edna might never have begun her long process of striving for the forbidden, one that culminates only with her death. The specific embodiments of the forbidden change, of course; but the ultimate goal, full self-definition and complete self-fulfillment through hard-won triumph over conventional restraints—a goal of which she might not ever be completely aware—is constant. Hence, be the object of her immediate longing an older man, a spoken-for man, a man of disreputable calling or of unsanctioned religious background, or, be it, as it is after her marriage, soul-mate or merely bed-mate, what Edna is finally seeking, though perhaps known to herself only at the last, is an ineffable state of perfect freedom, of unadulterated authenticity. Her search culminates in the waters of the Gulf of Mexico, but its origins in the sealike meadows of Kentucky are, as we have seen, presented by Chopin as multifaceted, complex, and, thus, no less impervious to moral judgment than are the final stages.

Just as unsusceptible to easy moralistic evaluation is the Creole culture in which Edna's potential for "awakening,"

implanted in her by her nature and background but long dormant, becomes aroused. Obviously, it is not merely gratuitous that it is in precisely *this* culture that Edna awakens to
her obscure personal quest. By its very nature, Creole life,
particularly in the relaxed form in which it presents itself to
her at the resort at which she is summering, is an unsettling
experience for Edna, with its "freedom of expression" and
"entire absence of prudery" (2:889) at first striking her as "incomprehensible" and then as nothing short of a "shock"
(2:889). Consequently, although Adéle Ratignolle's relation
in company of "the harrowing story of one of her *accouche-
ments* withholding no intimate detail" (2:889) and the propensity of Creole women for free discussion of such books as
Edna "felt moved to read . . . in secret and solitude" (2:889–
90) are not difficult for her to reconcile with the "lofty chast-
ity which in the Creole woman seems to be inborn and unmistakable" (2:889), they do nevertheless contribute to an
atmosphere of repose and lack of restraint so different from
anything to which her early background exposed her as to
shake her and thereby prompt long-somnolent forces deep
within her to sudden and profound stirring. Had Edna never
come into contact with Creole ways, then, her "awakening"
might never have taken place; but whether the fact that it is,
in large part, keyed by the Creole way of life somehow for
Chopin legitimizes Edna's quest is again impossible to say.
Creole life as Chopin presents it here is at once appealing and
distasteful. Easygoing as it may be, devoted to good conversation, light entertainment, and the maintenance of the
pleasant order of things as it may be, it is also devoid of passion or aspiration and hedged about with restraints and hy-
pocrisies that, unfortunate in themselves, are particularly
onerous to a woman of romantic spirit. In violating the pre-
cepts of the very culture that keys her quest, Edna, consequently, is leaving behind what may be both a pleasant order
and an insidiously comfortable form of repression for anyone
who seeks more than unexamined repose. Such a studiously
balanced picture as Chopin presents here of Creole life is obviously calculated to show how difficult monolithic judgment

of life as it is really lived is and, implicitly, how exceedingly difficult judgment of Edna becomes once one perceives the complexity of the influences that shape her course.

In no way geared to making judgment easier is Edna's marriage. Though it becomes increasingly intolerable to Edna as her "awakening" develops, her marriage to Léonce is not depicted as an experience that the vast majority of women in her time would find a hideous one. Léonce, manifestly, is no monster. Affectionate to his wife and children, free with gifts, chary of complaints, blatant demands, and threats, Léonce is, with some justice, regarded by most who know him as a good husband, "the best . . . in the world" (2:887), as the group at the resort declare. Be that as it may, however, there is also much in this marriage that might lead others to believe, again with some justice, that escape from union with Léonce and the Léonce type generally is an entirely legitimate option for a woman who needs to awaken to herself. The marriage, like Creole life itself, may be altogether too passionless, too freighted with conventional usages, and, finally, too dominated by the husband to meet the authentic needs of one such as Edna Pontellier. Typifying, perhaps, all that a woman of awakening authentic needs might find onerous in such a marriage is the scene, early in the novel, in which Léonce, returning in high spirits from a jolly evening at Klein's with some of his gentleman friends, clumsily awakens Edna from a deep sleep and despite her drowsiness bores her by recounting the insipid gossip and anecdotes he picked up through the evening of hilarity. As he talks on, absolutely oblivious to the desire of his wife for rest, he casually empties his pockets, pulling out "a fistful of crumpled banknotes and a good deal of silver coin, which he piled on the bureau indiscriminately with keys, knife, handkerchief . . . " (2:885). The act, innocuous as it seems, is a significant one; for these items, so nonchalantly tossed upon the bureau, are little less than the symbols of Léonce's domination of his wife and marriage. Money, possession, power (the knife), and decorum (the handkerchief) are the tools of Léonce's control. Were these contents of his pocket meant to have less sinister associations here, one suspects that Chopin would not have linked them in this scene with Léonce's total lack of concern with his wife's manifest desire to be left alone at this point or to the grating reproaches he soon delivers to her about her care of the children; nor, it is obvious, would their enumeration so closely precede Chopin's reference to the terrible sense of "indescribable oppression" (2:886) that Edna feels as, now thoroughly unable to sleep, she lies beside her contentedly sleeping mate.

Such a scene as this, soon followed as it is by one in which Léonce tries insistently and irritatedly to assert his authority by ordering Edna to come to bed (one assumes for sexual relations) when she lies in her hammock, feeling the lure of the nighttime sea, makes it difficult for one to condemn her rebellion out of hand. The lure of the sea with all that it represents in terms of compelling quests, freedom, beauty, and mystery seems, consequently, not as outrageous an alternative as it might at first to a life spent in meeting the demands of Léonce Pontellier. Then, of course, one must remind oneself that Léonce's criticism of Edna for neglecting the children is not baseless and that a man is not necessarily a beast for wanting to chat with his wife or to be physically intimate with her—particularly when he does not, as Léonce does not, force himself brutally upon her. Nothing is one-sided in this novel; nothing is easy; nor, obviously, does Chopin want anything to be.

Fully as shrouded in ambiguity are the physical changes Edna undergoes as she rebels against Léonce, her marriage, and conventional restraints. The voracious appetite she develops and her increasing need for long naps may well betoken that she is living now with such vigor and intensity that she needs more nourishment and rest than she has ever needed in the past. Or, less admirably, they might be the manifestations, as Cynthia Griffin Wolff suggests, of a regressive longing for an unencumbered childlike state, a yearning that is only gratified with Edna's self-destructive immersion into the seductively womb-like sea.[14] Still another possibility is that Edna's ravenous appetite for food and sleep is indeed childlike but symbolizes not regression but rebirth and new identity. All these explanations seem plausible, as might others, with the result that certainty again eludes us, save for the certainty that, whether admirable or not, deep forces are aroused in Edna that she is powerless to resist as they drive her increasingly into behavior strikingly unconventional for a wife and mother.

Similarly manifesting childlike tendencies is the immediate object of the "aroused" Edna's longings. Charming, devoid of stuffiness and pretension, refreshingly unconventional, Robert is also, perhaps, more than a little flighty. Seen posing as an inconsolable lover with Adéle, planning vaguely to go to Mexico to make his fortune, being casually dismissed by Pontellier as nothing but a slight playfellow for his bored wife, Robert seems not at all out of place "surrounded by a troop of children" and followed by "two nursemaids" who look "disagreeable and resigned" (2:889). Nor does it seem merely gratuitous that at one point Robert "sat down upon a stool which the children had left out upon the porch" (2:925). Significantly too, the most recent photograph taken of Robert shows him about to leave for college, "with eyes full of fire, ambition, and great intentions" (2:928)—none, presumably, carried out. Robert may well strike the observer, then, as a case of arrested development, alternately playful and full of the romanticism of the perennial freshman, stopped short of adulthood. Such childlike tendencies as he manifests can, like Edna's, be construed as betokening either liveliness, charming authenticity, and a winning nonconformity or, less flatteringly, weakness, puerility, and lack of adult development. One's view of Edna must in part hinge on one's view of this man who means so much to her, but here as elsewhere the information necessary for shaping one's vision is complex, contradictory, irremediably ambiguous.

Nor is there sufficient evidence for clearcut judgment on the other person to whom Edna is most drawn at the resort, Adéle Ratignolle. Preeminently a "mother-woman" (2:888), Adéle seems at first a faintly bovine, blind adherent to convention, one so caught up in submitting to the demands of husband and family that she fails to have an identity of her own. Further, her major choices seem to involve such matters as which chocolate to choose from a proffered box, and her major worries seem typified by her concern about how the candy she finally chooses will affect her "condition" (pregnancy), about which she is "always talking" (2:889). Nonetheless, this woman is perceptive enough to warn Robert that Edna's lack of understanding of Creole ways makes his flirting with her a dangerous matter. More, she is courageous and selfless enough to think of Edna in the midst of her own difficult labor in childbirth and, using her pain as a vivid reminder of what she sees as the sacred office of motherhood, warn her, "in an exhausted voice" to "think of the children!" and "Remember them!" (2:995). Thus, both limited and fulfilled, unthinkingly devoted to the conventions and sharply perceptive, absorbed in her familial sphere and devoted to the welfare of her friends, Adéle Ratignolle is a character whose presence in *The Awakening* adds to the difficulty of passing moral judgment on Edna's quest. Edna's own inability to paint what she considers to be a likeness of Adéle indicates, one suspects, her inability to understand Adéle's essential character. Whether her inability to grasp the makeup of this "mother-woman" is something Chopin believes admirable or unfortunate in Edna is impossible to say. Similarly, the outcropping of latent hostility toward Adéle and her way of life that may be inherent in Edna's crumpling-up of her attempt at Adéle's portrait could well be construed as a sign of childish petulance or as poignant manifestation of Edna's frustration as she dimly perceives her friend's sort of happiness, knows she does not want it, but does not know what she wants in its stead. If, as Lewis Leary notes, the other characters in *The Awakening* "appear only in their relation to Edna Pontellier,"[15] the light they project from their own complex natures is so multihued as not to clear things up but merely to shroud them in further ambiguity.

Three lesser figures in the novel whose presence makes judgment of Edna's behavior no less difficult are Robert's brother Victor, Alcée Arobin, and Mademoiselle Reisz. Victor, a loudmouthed, self-indulgent buffoon, and Arobin, a crude womanizer, are, unlike the others in the book, figures lacking in complexity. Both seem to be used, however, for a relatively complex purpose. Calling into question as they do by their very natures the commitment to self-gratification, they seem set off by Chopin against Mademoiselle Reisz, who, by and large, seems to legitimize the pursuit of self-gratification. Obviously, this setting-off or balancing does little to clear up ambiguity. Nor is Chopin's portrayal of Mademoiselle Reisz merely a one-sided one, for Chopin seeks, apparently, to compound ambiguity with ambiguity. Thus, Mademoiselle Reisz, the brilliant pianist, seems to show what a free woman, on her own and assured of her identity and needs, can accomplish, and thereby seems calculated by Chopin to make one more sympathetic to Edna's quest for authenticity. But, as soon becomes evident, Mademoiselle Reisz has one thing that Edna, like most people, lacks—and that is real talent, even genius. Therefore, her irascibility and self-absorption, her tastelessness and isolation from life, as typified by the "rusty" black lace and artificial violets she wears, though certainly not admirable are excusable, deriving as they probably do from the very forces and tensions that make her the artist she is. When Edna, on the other hand, manifests similar traits, such as in her refusal to go to her sister's wedding, the effect is not to make her seem akin to Mademoiselle Reisz but to point up the major difference between them and make Edna seem merely petulant. Moreover, even the pianist is shown to be partially limited by her self-absorption, at least insofar as it leads her to underestimate others. For example, when she plays for the group at Klein's, she is positive that of them all only Edna can appreciate her work; but, in fact, "she was mistaken about 'those others.' Her playing had aroused a fever of enthusiasm" (2:907), one typical comment being, "That last prelude! Bon Dieu! It shakes a man!" (2:907). Her obvious undervaluing of commonplace folk and her habitual self-imposed isolation from them, then, may serve as an implicit criticism of Edna, who seems to reveal the same failings without such extenuation as Mademoiselle Reisz's genius provides. Then again, though, it may simply show that by their very makeup large natures, unfortunately, are unable to fit comfortably into the context of usual life. As a result, neither the presence of the woman of genius nor that of the two blocks of banality, Victor and Arobin, makes judgment of Edna any easier to formulate.

Finally, working with Chopin's depiction of Edna's background, Creole culture, and the other characters to convey fully the complexity and ambiguity of Edna's experience is the imagery Chopin associates most vividly with the "awakening." Though the sun and the sea that lure Edna so powerfully have an undeniable beauty, that beauty is not without its sinister overtones. The "slimy lizards" that Edna hopes to see "writhe" (2:915) in the sunshine at Grand Terre, the sun to whose "mercy" (2:1000) she consigns herself when, naked, she walks to the sea for her final swim, the "foamy wavelets" that "curled up to her white feet, and coiled like serpents about her ankles" as she steps into the water for the last time, all seem to imbue her quest with an aura of the insidious as well as of the free and inviting. Too, is the bird with broken wing "reeling, fluttering, circling . . . down, down to the water" (2:1000) meant to convey a sense of Edna's weakness, of her bravery in fighting against all the odds, or of her foolishness in fighting what is inevitably a losing battle?

Because Edna's behavior is so unconventional, one's immediate impulse is to judge it somehow; but all in *The Awakening*, as we have seen, is calculated by Chopin to show how difficult, even impossible, it can be to make moral judgments about complex behavior. What appreciation of the ambiguity pervading this novel does, ultimately, is push the reader away from Edna to the requisite detachment that makes understanding, if not judgment, possible. From this position of detachment, one sees that, for Chopin, Edna, like all others perhaps, cannot, by virtue of the dominant needs within her, do other than what she does. "Fate," Chopin notes, "had not fitted" Edna for the "responsibility she had blindly assumed" (2:899) of being a mother. Similarly, when Edna refuses to leave her hammock and come to bed as Léonce demands, Chopin states, "Edna perceived that her will had blazed up, stubborn and resistant. She could not at that moment have done other than denied and resisted" (2:912). Later Chopin declares of Edna, "She was blindly following whatever impulse moved her, as if she had placed herself in alien hands for direction, and freed her soul of responsibility" (2:913). When, still later, Edna yields to Arobin, Chopin's phrasing makes clear that what takes place grows not from any decision that Edna freely makes but from an unavoidable answering to the irresistible imperatives of her nature. When Arobin kisses her, "it was the first kiss of her life to which her nature had really responded. It was a flaming torch that kindled desire" (2:967). Finally, even Edna's last walk to the sea is presented almost entirely in terms of her physical actions, never in terms of a decision consciously reached by a woman in control of her destiny. Thus, although Edna asserts herself aplenty in the course of her quest for authenticity and self-fulfillment, the drive to assertion is itself not a freely chosen course but an inevitable response to voracious demands aroused within her.[16] As inexorably as the happiness of the young lovers briefly seen at the resort will ultimately give way to the grimmer reality represented by the woman in black who seems invariably to shadow them, Edna, like most, as Chopin views it, must yield to the reality of her nature. To resist its demands is impossible, and to think that some moral or social code can enable her to do so is, for Chopin, the rankest folly. Hence, for two reasons, then, one cannot pass moral judgment on Edna as Chopin perceives it. First, her self-assertive behavior itself can seem, like the behavior of virtually all in this novel, either justifiable or reprehensible depending on one's angle of vision; and second, it is determined behavior anyway, beyond the realm of ethical choice, in a universe that Chopin apparently regards as devoid of moral absolutes. Judgment out of the question, consequently, one can only observe, learn, and sympathize in response to Edna's plight.

Thus does *The Awakening* become Chopin's fullest depiction of the irrepressible power of the drive for authenticity. As such, it becomes, implicitly at least, her strongest attack on marriage. Though she once again offers no overt criticism of the institution and once more shows a distinctly happy marriage—that of the Ratignolles—in terms that are only slightly, if at all, deprecating, her emphasis on the impossibility of repressing authentic impulses to self-gratifiction, even if yielding to them may destroy a marriage, certainly constitutes no defense of matrimony. Further, when Chopin links this emphasis to an essentially deterministic vision, as she does here, the result is an outlook that tends to undermine almost every assumption on which marriage—and, I might note, the outlook informing literary realism as generally conceived—is based, assumptions involving beliefs in free will, moral responsibility, and the virtue of compromise with those around one. This cutting of the ground from under marriage is, of course, evident in Chopin's earlier work, but it is more pronounced here because of the greater length and force of *The Awakening* and because the determinism is more explicit and extensive than in the earlier works.

Chopin's last marriage story is "The Storm," in which Calixta and Alcée, two young Creoles strongly attracted to each other before their marriages (as seen in the earlier tale, "The 'Cadian Ball"), meet again when Alcée takes refuge at Calixta's house during a tempest and cannot resist going to bed together as they had longed to do years before. Here, unlike in *The Awakening,* no one seems to be hurt by the surrender to authentic needs. Calixta is jovial and deeply loving to her husband and son when they return after Alcée's departure. (Apparently, unlike the wife in "The Letters," an interlude of sexual authenticity is all Calixta needs to be herself, not a complete break with her marriage.) Alcée's wife, receiving word from her husband that she and her child may stay a bit longer at the resort to which she has gone for a rest, is not at all displeased by the prospect of a brief extension of her respite from "their intimate conjugal life" (2:596). Thus, all seems to go well with these four marrieds when Calixta and Alcée finally surrender to the deep proddings within themselves. Coincidentally too, as they near the climax of their lovemaking, the storm increases in its fury, abating and passing only when they reach satiety, an indication, one suspects, that, for Chopin, their act has all the naturalness and inevitability of an elemental force of nature. When Chopin closes the tale with the quiet comment "So the storm passed and everyone was happy" (2:596), she leaves one with the unescapable impression that both marriages would have been somewhat less happy had Calixta and Alcée had to endure the frustration of never gratifying their longings for each other. An unconventional impression to convey, certainly, but, as we have seen, convention for Chopin ever has little to do with the facts of human nature.

Chopin once stated that her main interest as a writer was in depicting "human existence in its subtle, complex, true meaning, stripped of the veil with which ethical and conventional standards have draped it."[17] The "true meaning" that she believes these standards cloak, one suspects, is the central human truth that one ought not to attempt the futile endeavor of repressing the drive to authenticity. It is in her marriage stories that she presents this doctrine most tellingly. Here people are in the most intimate contact with others, tied to them in presumably lasting commitments—for most women of her day the most pressing social commitments they will ever know—and when Chopin thrusts that contact and those commitments aside as impotent in the face of the individual's will to self-assertion and self-gratification, one sees how little her outlook is in accord with the prevalent literary realist thought of her day. Indeed, as I noted at the outset, one is forced, in taking an overview of Chopin's work, to speak of its romantic tendencies, for certainly the propensity to set convention at naught compared with the demands of the individual is something many romantics would fully understand; but nonetheless, there is in Chopin's work something else, something that sets her apart finally, from most romantics as well as most realists, and it is most apparent in the very marriage works at which we have been looking. It is a fundamental inability on Chopin's part, ultimately, to see people as anything more than automata. Though it is clear that Chopin has it in mind to assert the unique worth of each individual in the face of the restraints and repressions of convention, the effect of her work is invariably to do otherwise. Instead of a world in which people and the choices they make matter, she presents a bleak scene in which they bounce off one another chaotically in unending, unthinking response to impulses over which they have no control and little understanding. Nor does she maintain the ethical framework that redeems from moral chaos those essays by Emerson such as "Experience," "Fate," and "Power" of which her work is in its emphasis on the deterministically ordered pursuit of self-fulfillment more than a little reminiscent. Her very insistence that moral questions are irrelevant to the ways in which people live undercuts her obvious effort to point up that individuals count for something and makes for an implicit condescension to her characters and their dreams that comes through in everything she wrote. No intellectual, apparently unable or unwilling to think her impressions through, Chopin, in spite of herself, presents in her pieces on married men and women as bleak a picture of the human conditions as one can find in late-nineteenth-century American writing.

1. Kate Chopin, diary entry, 22 May 1894, quoted in Per Seyersted, *Kate Chopin: A Critical Biography* (Baton Rouge: Louisiana State University Press, 1969), pp. 58–59.

2. Some stories not depicting marriage that deal with the necessity of self-assertion include "The Maid of St. Philippe" (1892), "A Shameful Affair" (1893), and, most notably, the powerful tale of a young priest's inability to forget his past and suppress his passion for a certain woman and the freedom she represents, "A Vocation and a Voice" (1902).

3. Seyersted, p. 85. Chopin's poem "Because" supports Seyersted's contention here, but the belief in free will and its concomitant moral responsibility expressed in this poem is clearly atypical of the outlook usually expressed in Chopin's work.

4. Seyersted, p. 90.

5. Chopin uses as epigraph to this story the Latin proverb "To love and be wise is scarcely granted even to a god." The text of Chopin's works that I am using is Per Seyersted's edition of *The Complete Works of Kate Chopin*, 2 vols. (Baton Rouge: Louisiana State University Press, 1969). All page references to Chopin's work are to this edition and will appear in the text.

6. Seyersted speaks of Chopin's intense "irritation with moral reformers" (pp. 90–91). Note too that Margaret's commitment to reform seems merely an intellectual one, not a reflection of the needs of her whole being. Hence, she makes the same mistake that the Faradays do.

7. Seyersted, ignoring—wrongly, I think—the subscription notice, sees here a "surprising juxtaposition of marriage and death," which seems to him to imply that Chopin regards marriage as an institution that represses women and that "she wishes the Faradays success in their venture to live as perfect equals" (p. 107). Though it is clear that Chopin often did see marriage as repressive, it is apparent nevertheless that in this story she regards the Faradays' experiment as ludicrous and as more repressive than their marriage ever could be.

8. Seyersted, pp. 119–20.

9. Seyersted, p. 113. Another who sees the conclusion in somber terms is Lewis Leary, who regards it as depicting the forced submission of a young woman who has been involved in a "battle against becoming only a useful household possession" (Introduction, *The Awakening and Other Stories by Kate Chopin*, ed. Lewis Leary [New York: Holt, Rinehart & Winston, 1970], p. x).

10. "Désirée's Baby," more a story of race relations than of marriage, presents a woman who *would* find happiness in submission if her husband's racism did not intercede and destroy them both.

11. Seyersted, p. 111.

12. Chopin's choice of the word "nice" here is a marvelously apt one. In addition to its prevalent meanings of "fastidious" and "agreeable," modes of conduct that, of course, might in some contexts be at odds with each other, "nice" once meant "foolish" or "wanton." Though both of these latter meanings were probably obsolete in Chopin's day, she may well have been aware of them.

13. The full range of critical views to which I have alluded is well represented in the essays Margaret Culley reprints in her edition of *The Awakening* (New York: Norton, 1976). The early reviewer I quote is an anonymous commentator for the *Mirror*. His review, originally published in the *Mirror*, 4 May, 1899, is reprinted in Culley's edition, pp. 145-46.

14. Cynthia Griffin Wolff, "Thanatos and Eros: Kate Chopin's *The Awakening*," *American Quarterly* 25 (October 1973): 449-71; rpt. Culley, pp. 206-18.

15. Lewis Leary, *Southern Excursions: Essays on Mark Twain and Others* (Baton Rouge: Louisiana State University Press, 1971). The quotation is from reprinted chapter on Chopin in Culley, p.197.

16. Adding to the sense of inevitability surrounding Edna's death is the bit of foreshadowing provided by the duet from "Zampa" played on a piano early in the novel. This romantic opera, as Margaret Culley notes, "includes a lover's death in the sea" (Culley, p. 4).

17. Quoted in Chopin, *Complete Works*, 1:17.

EDITH WHARTON
THE MARRIAGE OF ENTRAPMENT

*I*N EDITH WHARTON'S SHORT STORY "The In-
troducers" (1905), Tilney, a supremely knowing fellow, asserts in his most knowing manner, "It takes a
pretty varied experience of life to find out that there are
worse states than marriage."[1] As a paean to domesticity, this
is hardly in the same league with old chestnuts of the "it
takes a heap of living to make a house a home" variety, but it
is as close to an impassioned defense of marriage as Wharton
ever presents explicitly in her fiction. At least once in her
conversation, though, she went well beyond Tilney's tepid
affirmation. Percy Lubbock reports that he was present one
day when Wharton in the course of a discussion of *Middlemarch* "*spoke out*, 'Ah, the poverty, the miserable poverty, of
any love that lies outside of marriage, of any love that is not
a living together, a sharing of all!' "[2] Such an outburst is, of
course, more than a little surprising given the failure of
Wharton's own marriage, the predominantly bleak tenor of
her work generally, and the fact that the bleakness inheres
most strongly in her marriage stories, which, as Geoffrey
Walton notes aptly, convey "a stronger feeling of pathos and
even tragedy"[3] than do her other works. Clearly, a glance at
most of the marriages Wharton presents, a group that includes such infelicitous matings as those of the Fromes, Dorsets, Marvells, and deChelleses, might lead one to find even
Wharton's wry avowal of faith in matrimony in "The Intro-
ducers" a bit improbable. Yet neither Tilney's comment nor
the emphatic assertion recorded by Lubbock is finally at odds
with the overriding outlook on marriage that Wharton presents in her works. Though she knows that all too few marriages offer the perfect "living together" and "sharing of all"
that she so passionately envisions—and, to be sure, presents
no marriages of this sort—she also knows full well that there

are indeed "worse states" outside marriage, states verging on the "miserable poverty" of emotional, moral, and spiritual chaos. And her defense of marriage is not merely negative, for she stresses throughout her career that even unfortunate marriages can have worth for the individual and society. Positive as it tends to be, though, her defense is almost invariably a somber one, as even her best marriages are successful usually only insofar as they lead married folk to see the bleakness of life and the depth of human folly.

Wharton's rather Jamesian vision of marriage as invariably imperfect but invariably of potential value as well is apparent in her first works depicting married life, the early stories "The Fullness of Life (1893) and "The Lamp of Psyche" (1895). Both works merit a close look because between them they define a stance toward marriage from which Wharton never departs during her long career to come. Though the wives who are protagonists in both stories find their marriages exceedingly disillusioning experiences, neither sees any other valid possibility for herself than continuing in the union she has chosen. In accepting their disillusionment, they foreshadow the similar acceptance by a goodly number of Wharton's marrieds and act in a manner that Wharton never fails to admire as one that leads to personal growth and social stability.

"The Fullness of Life" is a fantasy in which a woman whose taste is impeccable and whose longing for beauty unquenchable finds exquisite satisfaction at the point of death in knowing that she will never again hear "the creakings of her husband's boots—those horrible boots—and that no one would come to bother her about the next day's dinner . . . or the butcher's book . . . (1:12). With these serene awarenesses, she passes away and finds herself in an afterlife of surpassing loveliness. There she tells the presiding "Spirit of Life" that she has missed the "fullness of life" and that in large measure this failure derives from her marriage. Merely "fond" of her husband, she confesses that she could not abide his flaws: "His boots creaked, and he always slammed the door when he went out, and he never read anything but railway novels and the sporting advertisements in the papers—

and—and, in short, we never understood each other in the least" (1:14). Too typical for her of their life together was the moment in the tabernacle of Orcagna when she was so smitten with all the beauty about her that she wept because "the joy, the mystery . . . seemed too intolerable to be borne," and turned to her husband, only to hear him say "mildly: 'Hadn't we better be going? There doesn't seem to be much to see here, and you know the table d' hote dinner is at half-past six o'clock'" (1:16). With a whole catalogue of such memories, the woman finds her death a heavenly escape from her marriage indeed.

Her happiness seems assured when she is told by the Spirit "that every soul which seeks in vain on earth for a kindred soul to whom it can lay bare its inmost being shall find that soul here and be united for eternity" (1:16). Exultant, she meets her perfect soul's mate and realizes that for all time they will see everything "with the self-same eyes and tell each other in the same words all that we think and feel" (1:17). So close are they, in fact, that she finds to her joy they admire not merely the same art, literature, and music but even the same aspects of each revered work. Her vision of a blissful eternity is dispelled, however, when she hears of the less than sanguine prospects awaiting the poor fellow left behind with his creaking boots. He, alas, she is told, will have no boon companion through eternity because he has foolishly imagined his wife to be that "kindred soul" for whom all seek, and "for such delusions eternity itself contains no cure." Learning this, she realizes that she cannot blast the man's hopes: "If he had come here first," she insists, "*he* would have waited for me for years and years, and it would break his heart not to find me here when he comes" (1:20). To the Spirit's warning that she is "choosing for eternity," she replies "with a half-sad smile, 'Do you still keep up here that old fiction about choosing? . . . How can I help myself? He will expect to find me here when he comes, and he would never believe you if you told him that I had gone away with someone else—never, never.'" Consequently, the story ends with her resignedly "seated alone on the threshold" of the afterlife, listening "for the creaking of his boots" (1:20).

At first glance, Delia Corbett in "The Lamp of Psyche" seems a good deal more fortunate than the unnamed woman in "The Fullness of Life." She believes she has found in this world the soul's mate that the earlier woman found only too late. Delia's first husband, "poor Benson," was a crass moral weakling, but his convenient death allowed Delia to attain "the one portion denied to all other women on earth, the immense, the unapproachable privilege of becoming Laurence Corbett's wife" (1:42). Having dreamed even while Benson was alive of becoming helpmate to the most gracious and refined man of her day, the romantic, idealistic Delia sees nothing ahead but tasteful joy and "noble leisure" (1:53). Her happiness is marred, however, when she discovers that her new husband sat out the Civil War. Having lost relatives and friends in the fighting, Delia is shocked not merely by Corbett's failure to serve but by his insouciance in accounting for it. His initial explanation, "I don't think I know," casually yields under her prodding to another: "Well—it all happened some time ago, . . . and the truth is that I've completely forgotten the excellent reasons I doubtless had at the time for remaining at home" (1:56), a response so unsatisfactory to Delia that it leads her to accuse him of cowardice. After an hour, though, she apologizes, because as "a woman of sense she could do no less." Corbett, as is his wont, is "perfectly charming; it was inevitable that he should go on being charming to the end of the chapter." No less inevitable is it that "she should go on being in love with him." However, "for the passionate worship which she had paid her husband she substituted a tolerant affection which possessed precisely the same advantages" (1:57).

Neither "The Fullness of Life" nor "The Lamp of Psyche" is a terribly happy story, of course, but each does offer an affirmation of sorts in the midst of its grimness. The affirmation, a somber one to be sure, and reminiscent of James's affirmation in *The Portrait of a Lady*, posits marriage as an institution that can enable people to grow by making them confront the pain Wharton saw as central to existence, a confrontation in Wharton's work that often leads one to be disabused of pleasant but fatuous illusions. In both stories one sees what is to become a typical Wharton marriage situation, one in which a person of some sensitivity who is prone to the self-deception of believing that perfect bliss and beauty are within human reach is yoked to another incapable of appreciating such sensitivity, much less of manifesting it, and too pedestrian ever to have harbored any longing for an illusory perfection of bliss or beauty. In "The Fullness of Life," death itself offers no real escape from the entrapment; and in "The Lamp of Psyche," a second marriage proves no more liberating, ultimately, than the first. And certainly this paucity of actual alternatives to the imperfect marriage is also to become a standard element in Wharton's marital fiction. But a third factor that is to be a feature in a number of Wharton's accounts of such dreary marriages as these is also evident—one that at least palliates the grimness somewhat: the redemptive capacity of the sensitive mates here to put aside delusory hopes and grimly accept what must be accepted. Thus, for Wharton, the decision of each woman to go on with her flawed husband is the only sound one, and her approval of these two who bear what might have once seemed to them the unbearable is manifest.

For either woman in these two stories to do other than what she ultimately does would be, for Wharton, to pursue a course of self-indulgence and frivolity. Were the unmarried initiate into the tastefully appointed afterlife to allow her husband to go through eternity without her, she would not only be hurting him but would, in effect, be consigning herself to an endless conversation with herself. Her soul's mate is studiously rendered by Wharton with such colorlessness that he seems little more than a reflector of the woman's aesthetic sensibility; and over the years, one suspects, even self-admiration and self-congratulation for one's impeccable taste would pall. What the woman's clumsy, plodding husband offers her, on the other hand—the opportunity for commitment to another and for growth through loving accommodation to that other—is a better bet for lasting fulfillment. Similarly, by quietly accepting her second husband as he is, Delia Corbett overcomes the unfortunate propensities in her own nature. Foolishly romantic previously, convinced that perfection not only is attainable but indeed is to be found in her second husband, Delia is living in a fool's world, caught up, like the woman in "The Fullness of Life," in an orgy of self-admiration because of her ostensible refinement and sensitivity. Perceiving at last that no marriage offers perfect bliss because life offers no perfect bliss, Delia learns a good deal. Though she will live with less idealism, she will live more intelligently, more aware that life, as the wife in the earlier story acknowledges, is less a matter of grand choices than of accepting what has been thrust upon one. With such knowledge one is not only more at peace with oneself but more likely to be at peace with others.

No less, then, than Melville's Urania in "After the Pleasure Party" does Wharton acknowledge that "such the dicing of blind fate / Few matching halves here meet and mate." But rather than a justification for bitterness and flight, Wharton, as we have observed, sees the unhappy marriage as itself a potentially educative if never joyous experience. In this connection Blake Nevius states, "In the antiromantic tradition none of the love affairs in Edith Wharton's novels acquires interest or significance until one or both of the partners is married. Once she has her characters ensnared as a result of their sentimental miscalculations, she is able to introduce a second, contingent theme." This theme, notes Nevius, involves Wharton's inquiry into "the extent of one's moral obligations to those individuals who, legally or within the framework of existing manners, conventions, taboos, apparently have the strictest claim on one's loyalty."[4] The conclusion Wharton reaches invariably in her marriage works, whether novels or stories, is that there is indeed a compelling moral obligation to see through one's commitment to one's mate, even if the commitment was undertaken with minimal experience and awareness. If one can honor such a commitment, as do the two women in the stories we have looked at thus far, it indicates the presence of a finely developed moral sense, one that may well have grown out of the truth to which marriage brings so many in Wharton's world—the truth that the world is a hard place, indifferent if not inimical to our desires. Consequently, in Wharton's austere vision, marriage presents one with the chance to dwell with the wise in the house of pain rather than amid the fools who flock to the house of mirth. There in the darker house, purged of illusions, no longer seeing fulfillment in frivolity or freedom in irresponsibility, one achieves not happiness, perhaps, but the clear vision and the moral awareness that link one to the great continuum of civility and order that Wharton hopes will persist even in the face of what she sees as ever-increasing chaos and stupidity.

Certainly, Wharton knows that one need not marry to come to the threshold of the house of pain, that other paths are available. But for Wharton marriage is infallibly an experience that will bring one to the choice of entering or turning back to the other house. Why this should be so for her is not hard to discern. Wharton has few sentimental illusions about human nature. One looks in vain through her work for any characterization in which the human potential for virtue is overestimated. With this less than sanguine perception, it naturally follows for Wharton that any relationship that demands of an individual capacities for sharing, sacrifice, and endurance is going to be a terribly difficult one, one that can force a confrontation with hard questions about oneself and about life. Marriage, of course, is such a relationship, in some ways the epitome of such relationships; and, therefore, to Wharton the marriage ceremony is usually nothing less than the first step in the direction of the looming house of darkness.

Many marrieds, needless to say, retreat from a confrontation with the hard questions to which marriage can bring them; but even many of this weaker sort are, as Wharton notes wryly, well served by marriage, for the experience *can* keep them from manifesting the worst flaws in their natures. By generating a routine, a round of things that come between a couple—"children, duties, visits, bores, relations"— matrimony can "protect married people from each other" (1:123), as a character in "Souls Belated" notes sardonically but accurately. Or, as Wharton notes elsewhere in the same story, a couple's "common obligations . . . make the most imperfect marriage in some sort a center of gravity" (1:108). Drawn to this center of gravity, then, this buffer of the routine, the partners have less time or inclination to attack each other or to indulge those traits that might ultimately injure their mates. Though one might hope that marriage would offer more than this, offer if not love at least the wisdom that comes with experience and disillusionment, its capacity for keeping men and women from hurting one another or embarking on the courses bound to lead to folly and suffering that they might have followed had they stayed single is, for all her sardonicism here, not, finally, taken lightly by Wharton. More than a little cynical about human nature, Wharton, like James, has no reason to believe, as Howells tried to, that marriage somehow can secure one from pain and fatuity. Marriage, to Wharton, is, like all other areas of existence, a grim undertaking. But if in the very midst of the grimness that marriage itself helps perpetuate it also provides some mitigation, *any* mitigation, Wharton does not see this as a negligible benefit—even if the benefit involves little more than the creation of a marital routine so boring that those who might otherwise be dangerous are stultified sufficiently to forget the use of fangs and claws. Of course, there are still other married folk—most, actually, as far as Wharton's works show—who, unable to grow in understanding through matrimony, cannot even avail themselves of this opportunity to be stultified by the marital routine into something approximating security and stability. These attempt ill-advised escapes from marriage, become involved in sordid liaisons, or use their marriages as weapons in a fight for social status and power. Because there are so many of this sort in Wharton's work, there are numerous bad marriages, marriages lacking even the slightest mitigation of the badness; but for Wharton the evil here resides far less in the institution of matrimony itself than in those husbands and wives who do not avail themselves of its somber possibilities for growth through pain and for palliation through unquestioning loyalty to the routine.

But again, whether benefits are derived in the marriages Wharton depicts or not, one must remember that her mar-

riage works are never entirely untinged with grimness because matrimony is inescapably part of a world that Wharton
saw as far more bleak than otherwise. Wharton's third marriage story, "A Journey" (1899), presents a marriage marked
by a horror that may be more extreme than that found in any
other union depicted by her but that certainly is reflective of
a darkness that touches virtually all her accounts of wedded
life. In this work a recently married young woman finds that
her sickly husband has died in his train berth as she is taking
him home to New York after a futile trip to Colorado for his
health. Her great concern is that no one know of his death,
for she fears being put off the train with the corpse before
she can get to New York and the solace and support of family
and friends. She succeeds in convincing everyone that her
husband is resting quietly behind the drawn curtain, but the
strain finally tells on her, and she faints as they enter New
York, "striking her head against the dead man's berth" (1:87).
Adding to the general unpleasantness of the story is the fact
that the marriage itself was nothing like what the bride con-
fidently expected it to be. Shortly after the wedding, her husband's health failed, turning him into an irritable, demanding
invalid rather than the exciting man she thought she was
marrying. Thus, as in the stories before, though more horribly, and as in so many stories to come, does Wharton show
bright hopes for wedded life turn to the darkest of dross.

There are, as I noted, no other marital situations in Wharton's work quite as horrible, perhaps, as that in "The Journey," but there are so many sufficiently distressing to show
kinship with it as to make one wonder *why* marital misfortune and the terrors and grim triumphs that mark it should
so prompt Wharton's creative energies. In part, of course, the
failure of Wharton's own marriage might have led her to
turn often to the bad marriage as a subject; but, more importantly, the subject may have attracted her as well because
characters' failures to make the most of marriage could serve
as a potent and ready means of indicting them and their society. In other words, given the opportunities Wharton sees
marriage as offering, failure to make a go of one's marriage
or to derive benefits from it is often the clearest indication of

moral shabbiness. Moreover, the polite society that is usually Wharton's fictional milieu is one in which marriage would naturally present itself as a chief means of establishing the conflict and complication that generate the serious moral inquiry she seeks to undertake. After all, gunfights, battlefields, whale hunts, and skirmishes between striking workers and police take place far from comfortable New York drawing-rooms. Deep personal anguish, however, is no stranger even in the best of society, and there it often is intimately tied up with the unfortunate marriage—hence, the prominence of the subject of Wharton's work.

Because there is no change over the years in Wharton's attitude toward marriage, a chronological overview of her marriage tales would not be as fruitful as a discussion of them in terms of the major types of marriage stories she presents. Basically, Wharton's depictions of marriage fall into three major categories. There are works depicting marital entrapment (or, more specifically perhaps, one partner's sense of entrapment) that show how frightening an experience marriage can be, works that present marital problems but subordinate them to the human and social failings of which the problems are manifestations, and, finally, works that focus on the benefits that can be derived from marriage. As I have noted, not only do stories of the first two types predominate, those of the third type, despite Wharton's belief in marriage as an institution of potential benefits, are almost always somber affairs marked by Wharton's omnipresent awareness of human failings.

The grimness in Wharton's stories of marital entrapment—perhaps the grimmest stories she ever wrote on any topic—resides most tellingly in the paucity of pleasant alternatives available to one who feels imprisoned by his or her mate. Worse, Wharton sees a sense of imprisonment as an all too probable occurrence in marriage given the ignorance about one's mate and the institution of marriage with which most are wed and given the dearth of virtues that most people can bring to bear on difficult marital situations. Invariably, Wharton advocates, at least implicitly, endurance as the course to be followed should one feel trapped in one's marriage, but she never suggests that it is easy or that it leads to happiness. Rather, she recommends it, simply, as the line of duty—duty to one's family, to society, to oneself.[5] Whatever affirmation that may arise in these tales from the ability of some to do their duty is, however, highly muted at best. Far more powerfully perceived is the misery of the unfortunate marriage itself, which is all the more palpable in those stories in which the unhappy protagonist, unable to take advantage of marriage's stern opportunity to grow through endurance, attempts an ill-advised escape. None of this, of course, constitutes an indictment of marriage on Wharton's part; one must remember that she saw the pain in life generally as outweighing the happiness. That the pain can be more acute among those who feel oppressed in their marriages argues no failure in the institution itself; rather, it bespeaks, once again, an opportunity to grow through enduring what must be endured.

In the early stories "The Line of Least Resistance" (1900) and "The Quicksand" (1904), the protagonists come to the realization that their mates are beastly. Nevertheless, both stay in their marriages and in doing so achieve results that, without mitigating significantly the ugliness to which they know they are inextricably bound, are less destructive than those that would have come about were they to leave their mates. In the former, Mindon, a befuddled and pompous but generally good-natured dyspeptic, finds that his selfish, extravagant wife has been having an affair with the arch young fellow she has inflicted on him as a family friend. Furious, Mindon, with "all the consecrated phrases—'outraged honor,' 'a father's heart,' 'the sanctity of home' " (1:221)—coming rapidly to mind, takes a room in a hotel, determining to end the marriage. However, it is not long until his determination falters before the persuasive shabbiness of his hotel room and the nastiness of the hotel food and crumbles in the face of arguments from his minister, his uncle–business partner, and his jaded old friend, whose past as a roué has led him to become "the consulting physician of injured husbands and imprudent wives" (1:223). These worthies, men of the world,

assure Mindon that the pain of accepting his dubiously peni-
tent wife (who, because never seen by the reader, seems to
loom all the more ominously) pales before the pain that
would ensue from messy divorce proceedings and the attendant publicity. The "shadow of obloquy" that he would lay
over his children and the ridicule to which he would subject
himself must, they urge him, be avoided at all costs. Frightened, he yields to their arguments, stammering that "it's for
the children" (1:226) that he is doing so.

That his children are spoiled brats who have little use for
him, that his wife is almost undoubtedly going to continue
being a difficult mate to tolerate, and that the three self-
styled comforters are tired old hypocrites does not mean for
Wharton, finally, that Mindon's decision is the wrong one.
Clearly, the society he lives in is fraudulent in many ways;
nevertheless, it is stable, providing for the continuity of the
little that is admirable in the human condition, and the alternative can only be chaos and such dinginess as he finds in his
hotel room. One can readily envision a better society than
this, but certainly not for these people, given their background and training. Were Mindon to leave his wife, there
would inevitably be obloquy and turmoil for the children, ridicule for Mindon himself, and ostracism for his wife, leading
her into a demimondaine's existence and, one suspects, a
chain of sleazy affairs. By keeping up appearances and staying in the marriage, Mindon avoids this and thus benefits all.
Small affirmation of marriage this, but it is an affirmation in
the midst of ugliness nonetheless.

Grimly affirmative too in its vision of marriage is "The
Quicksand," in which the widowed Mrs. Quentin, remembering her painful life with her husband, convinces her son's
fiancée to break her engagement to this young man who is so
disturbingly like his father. The nasty work of the elder
Quentin, who published *The Radiator*, a scandal sheet that
makes its fortune by presenting daily "some miserable bleed-
ing secret that a dozen unhappy people had been struggling
to keep out of print" (1:408), is now being pursued by his son
with a vigor that rivals that of his fallen predecessor. A
woman of refinement, Mrs. Quentin found the shame of

being linked with *The Radiator* almost intolerable and, more, found to her horror that not only could she not change her husband or shield her son from the "contamination" of his influence but that with every effort to do so she herself "sank deeper" (1:408) into the noisome quagmire that had opened under her when she accepted her husband's lie that the paper was only a temporary expedient to meet financial exigencies. Consequently, she warns the fiancée that the son, like the father, will never change and assures her that "it's you who would have to change—to die gradually, as I have died, till there is only one live point left in me," an "aching nerve of truth" (1:410). Obviously, it is that "aching nerve," inflamed by the virulent infection that ravaged her marriage, which has prompted her to spare an innocent girl by hurting her own son. What is apparent in all this is that by staying in a hideous marriage, Mrs. Quentin has gained more than she would have had she sought to escape it. Brought by her marriage to an awareness of the intransigence of evil in human nature, including her own, Mrs. Quentin has been purged of illusions. She has won her way into the house of pain and from its vantage point can see her way clear to shielding another from a dark triumph like her own. Though in Wharton's world the chances for happiness are slim indeed and such a victory as Mrs. Quentin's may be the best for which a sensitive person ought to hope, it speaks well for Mrs. Quentin's capacity for growth and reveals the darkly educative effect her marriage has had on her when she commits herself so bravely to allowing this girl at least an opportunity for happiness.

Both "The Reckoning" (1904) and "Joy in the House" (1933) present women who, unlike Mrs. Quentin, believe that something better than the house of pain does exist for them and, therefore, leave their marriages to find it, only to incur disastrous results. In the former, Julia Westall, finding her first husband "impossible," enthusiastically gave herself over to "The Marriage Law of the new dispensation," which is "*Thou shalt not be unfaithful—to thyself!*" (1:421). Consequently, she divorced her "impossible" mate, whose chief failing resided as she saw it in his living in a "climate in which only his own requirements survived" (1:420), ironically enough the very sort of climate in which she herself clearly desired to live; and she married Clement Westall, one whose commitment to the "new dispensation" was every bit as complete as her own. Both agreed that marriage need no longer engender entrapment, that "there would be no further need of the ignoble concessions and connivances, the perpetual sacrifice of personal delicacy and moral pride, by means of which imperfect marriages were now held together," for, both acknowledged, "the new adultery was unfaithfulness to self" (1:427). Now, after ten years of marriage, Westall concludes that faithfulness to himself demands that he shed Julia and marry a younger woman. Deeply hurt, Julia suddenly realizes how badly she herself had hurt her first husband years before, and in tears, she stops by her old home to apologize to him. As she apologizes, she breaks out tearfully and haltingly in a vehement defense of marital responsibility: "If we don't recognize an inner law . . . the obligation that love creates . . . being loved as well as loving . . . there is nothing to prevent our spreading ruin unhindered . . . " (1:436; Wharton's ellipses). With this she leaves, finding herself "outside in the darkness" (1:437). Thus, as Wharton shows, nothing has been gained by Julia's following a doctrine of irresponsibility save suffering and the furthering of such social chaos as Westall promotes when he lectures on his marital theories to large gatherings of dangerously impressionable women. To be sure, Julia has herself been jolted into some painful insights, but only by having wilfully and wantonly hurt another ten years before. Again, escape from an unhappy marriage brings no lasting happiness, love, freedom, or moral strength.

In "Joy in the House," published thirty-three years later, little has changed for Wharton except that there is an increase in the intensity of suffering involved in both the bad marriage and the effort to escape it. Before the story opens, Christina Ansley, we learn, found herself unhappily married to a relentlessly gregarious small-town realtor, whose cloying iteration of "New Morality" clichés about "self-realization" (2:709) betokens no largeness of heart or questing intelligence but merely an inability to feel deeply or think intelligently. Unlike Wharton, however, Christina took such clichés seriously and was disturbed by Ansley's failure to live in accordance with them. Instead, "*his* life was one of bedroom slippers and the evening paper by a clean gas fire, with his wife stitching across the hearth, and telling him that the baby's first tooth was showing" (2:709). Unable to bear such a marriage, one that she felt deprived her of the "self-realization" about which her husband canted, Christina deserted him and her son to run off to Europe with a talented painter, who left his own wife to go with her.

Predictably, given that Wharton's distaste for "self-realization" achieved at the cost of responsibility exceeds her scorn for stultifying marriages, Christina's action precipitated misery instead of leading her to happiness. Five and a half months of dreariness in Europe with the impecunious painter, who, despite his passion, too often "solicitously nursed those sacred objects, his 'painting things' and forgot about everything else, herself included" (2:710), have led Christina to long now for the heretofore rejected comforts of those evenings by the hearth with her husband. Consequently, she avails herself of the "New Morality" promise he made on her departure that she can return within six months from what he calls insipidly her "trial marriage" and be accepted with no recriminations. On her return her husband's effusive welcome and the no less effusive giant floral display proclaiming "Joy in the House" seem to augur well for the marriage. However, her lover's bitter wife soon informs Christina that the painter, despondent over losing her, has killed himself. Christina's immediate realization that her husband must have known this before his warm welcome to her and apparently regarded it as little more than the "providential solving of a problem" (2:721), leads to a frantic desire to "get away . . . from this stifling atmosphere of tolerance and benevolence, of smoothing over and ignoring and dissembling. Anywhere out into the live world, where men and women struggled and loved and hated, and quarreled and came together again with redoubled passion . . . "(2:721).

Mrs. Ansley soon perceives, however, that she has tried this before, with horrifying results. So, she decides this time to accept her lot. Ordering the maid to remove the ludicrous and now withered floral display and reminding herself "But there's the boy—" she walks "slowly up the stairs to find her son" (2:722). Thus does she finally put aside childishness and accept what Wharton believes she should have accepted long before: the necessity of staying with her odious husband so that she might counter as much as she can his potentially unhealthy influence on their son and might also keep herself from causing again such misfortune as that which ensued with the painter when she sought to avoid the house of pain to find one of unalloyed joy.

Nothing in any other stories Wharton wrote about those who leave marriages in which they feel trapped fails to confirm the lessons glimpsed in "The Reckoning" and "Joy in the House." Lydia Tillotson, in "Souls Belated" (1899), forced to carry out an aimless and apparently endless tour of shabby, even at times sordid, out-of-the-way European watering places with her lover—a writer who is so bored and depressed by their promiscuous, vagabond existence that he can no longer write—learns to her surprise that, as noted earlier, the "center of gravity" (1:127) provided even by "the most imperfect marriage" generates a complex of social relationships that can keep two shallow people from seeing the "nakedness of each other's souls" (1:123). As a result, Lydia and her lover, though no longer devoted to each other, marry, entering willingly into a less than promising union in order to gain that "center of gravity." Another runaway wife, Kate Clephane, in *The Mother's Recompense* (1925), returns to New York from Europe some twenty years after deserting her husband and daughter and finds that by a horrible coincidence her most recent lover has become engaged to the daughter. Because she has not seen the girl in twenty years, Kate has forfeited all influence over her and so cannot work subtly to change her mind. Further, simply revealing the truth to her would entail giving what Kate's minister tells her is merely "sterile pain,"[6] pain, that is, that would serve no purpose, since the young couple apparently love each other. Thus, Kate can do nothing but hope that her daughter will find happiness in marriage or, short of that, at least stay in it so she will not run the risk of incurring a lonely grief like her mother's.

Moreover, Wharton shows in "The Pretext" (1908) and "Atrophy" (1930) that there are even terrible dangers in being unfaithful to one's spouse by fantasizing about a more rewarding relationship with another. In the former, Mrs. Ransom, married to a colorless fellow who is lawyer for a small college, becomes infatuated with a glamorous young visitor from England. Convinced that he cares for her, she makes him an impassioned speech in which she at once avows her love for him and renounces it dramatically as something that cannot be. Her scene played out, she feels that the memory of it will redeem the sad wastage of the years to come with her husband. Later, she is pained to learn that the young man regarded her as little more than an acquaintance, and even used her name on returning to England as a convenient cover, or "pretext," so that he could disguise his love for another and deceive his disapproving family. Similarly making something of a fool of herself because of her illicit longings for another is Nora Frenway, who is disillusioned to find just how strong the old social conventions can be even in times of "tolerance, laxity and ease" (2:501). Feeling imprisoned in her marriage, she decides impulsively to rush to the deathbed of the man she has secretly loved for years and declare at last her love for him. Instead of getting a touching final moment with him, though, she has to endure an embarrassing confrontation with his spinster sister, who, clearly guessing why Nora is there, keeps her from her brother's room with cool politeness and then efficiently sends her back to her train with a cordial but pointed promise to "write and thank Mr. Frenway" (2:510) for his wife's kind visit. The squalor and filth of the train and the sinister image of a trapped fly in it buzzing against a windowpane confirm that one commits oneself to ugliness and desperation when, like Nora or Mrs. Ransom, one seeks to flout convention and gratify an extramarital romantic longing.

Wharton's fullest treatment of the disasters that can occur when one attempts to leave even a repellent marriage is *Ethan Frome* (1911). Perhaps no other character in Wharton's work is tied to a more insensitive mate than is poor Ethan. Indeed, so unremitting is his pain throughout his long marriage that some have suggested that this work is not much more than a nasty little horror show. Lionel Trilling, for one, asserts that it "presents no moral issue at all" and merely reveals Wharton's limitation of heart.[7] Though Trilling's reading is admirably responsive to Ethan's suffering, it seems to miss the point when it implies that the loveless Frome marriage is only a means by which Wharton indulges virtually sadistic tendencies in herself by tormenting her protagonist. Actually, Wharton's tale does present a discernible counsel on how best to face life in a universe that apparently cares little for those who inhabit it.

In Ethan's small New England town, one sees a way of life with none of those genteel trappings that in polite society shelter people from a daily confrontation with the grimmer facts of existence. Perhaps the grimmest of these is that people are often victimized irremediably by forces over which they have no control. Gary H. Lindberg, in fact, sees Wharton as essentially deterministic in her outlook in that her characters generally seem to be caught up in a "flow of destiny" in which their private schemes "generated by personal lines of intention are simply dwarfed." It is not, he notes, a "scientific formulation of biological and environmental determinism but rather a configuration of moral inevitability posited by the conjction of a given choice and the social world within which that choice is made."[8] Lindberg's point about Wharton's determinism is well-taken, though in this particular case the crucial conjunction is not that of a "given choice" and the "social world" but of a choice (itself not quite freely made) and the very nature of things, of which the dense social world usually seen in Wharton's works is merely a manifestation. Though the context here is cosmic rather than social, the configuration of moral imperatives that inevitably takes shape is no different from that to be seen in Wharton's tales of marital entrapment that are set in circumstances less bereft of social relations.

That Ethan's marriage is an unhappy one for him is well known and needs no rehearsal here. What may be less obvious, though, in the narrator's account of things is that both his decision to marry Zeena and his subsequent attempt to escape the marriage through suicide with Mattie grow out of a deep, almost childish fear of loneliness, a fear instilled in him, in great measure, by the bleak landscape itself and all that it seems to symbolize about the bleakness of the universe. Ethan proposed to Zeena because he had an "unreasoning dread of being left alone on the farm."[9] This dread evoked, substantially, by the wintry scene around him led him to overestimate Zeena's capacity for human feeling. Reflecting on his error, Ethan "often thought since that it would not have happened if his mother had died in spring instead of winter . . . " (p. 76). Showing more fully that Ethan was a good deal less than a free agent when he married are the references to the landscape about him as having been shaped by the huge, timeless pressures exerted on it, these references serving as an implicit reminder that those who people this landscape are similarly shaped by elements larger than themselves. Thus, the "ledge of granite thrusting up through the ferns," which seems to unroll the "huge panorama of the ice age and the long dim stretches of succeeding time" (p. 37), forces one to see Ethan's story in a larger context than the one in which one normally thinks Wharton's tales operative—forces one, in other words, to see Ethan in a universe of powerful and inevitably enigmatic forces that buffet people about uncaringly and probably unknowingly.

Positing implicitly this central vision, then, the narrator's account of the disaster of Ethan establishes as a central issue the problem of ascertaining how one is to confront life in a bleak, indifferent universe in which one's options are severely limited. The young Ethan's inability to cope with the pressures in his life in no way indicates that means of coping cannot be found; rather, it is an index to his own sentimentality and immaturity as he childishly sees Mattie as embodying virtues and as linked to a happiness that are, quite obviously, well removed from the world we all know. As Cynthia Griffin Wolff notes, "It is always easier for Ethan to retreat from life into a 'vision'" than to face what must be faced. He is, Wolff goes on to say, invariably too receptive to the "appeal of passivity and a life of regression."[10] The childishness of his attempt—typically bungled, of course—to regress to a state of ultimate passivity through suicide is brought out by the very form that the attempt takes: a down-hill ride on a sled. One can imagine few others in Frome's village who would have chosen such a ride. The Powells, Hales, and their ilk, glimpsed briefly through the narrative, are there, in part, to offer an instructive contrast to the dreamy, dissatisfied Frome. They go quietly about their business and in the routine they establish create a little realm of order and responsibility in the midst of a stark wintry scene, an order that Ethan's crack-up crudely violates.

One possibility in this work that cannot, of course, be overlooked is that the facts as presented by the narrator may not accord with the events that occurred. The narrator's vision of Ethan's past is just that—a vision, and Joseph X. Brennan suggests, therefore, that *Ethan Frome* must be judged "in terms of the special character of the narrator's mind" and, further, that "since the narrator has had to imagine almost the whole of Ethan's history and the most important traits of his character as well, in many respects, inevitably, the sensibilities of the two are indistinguishable."[11] So indistinguishable might they be that one cannot be sure that the real Ethan Frome ever felt anything akin to what the narrator attributes to him or did the things he did for the reasons the narrator either consciously or inadvertently offers. What *is* objectively verifiable does not necessarily reinforce one's sense of the narrator's accuracy. For example, the picture of Ethan, Mattie, and Zeena with which Wharton closes the work calls into question much of what has been offered previously as a probable version of the past. Though Mrs. Hale asserts that before the crash she "never knew a sweeter nature than Mattie's" (p. 194), whereas Zeena was, she says, "always cranky" (p. 194), in evidence nevertheless as the narrator enters the Frome farmhouse are Mattie's "querulous drone" (p. 187) and Zeena's quiet patience in ministering to this irritable invalid. Inevitably, this makes one wonder whether Mattie was ever quite so good or Zeena quite so bad as the narrator envisions them to have been. On this central question as elsewhere, the narrator may well be indulging his propensities for the exaggerated and the romantic that he reveals throughout the work. Indeed, were the narrator not an exceedingly romantic fellow, even something of a sentimentalist, he would not involve himself in an extensive reverie about thwarted dreams and longings in the first place, nor would he construct the monolithic (and perhaps reductive) image patterns he does in contrasting Mattie and Zeena before the sledding disaster. As Brennan notes, the narrator consistently links Mattie with lovely and delicate objects in nature, such as birds and field mice, whereas he characterizes Zeena throughout with stifling imagery of the indoors and the artificial and through ties to such predators as cats and owls[12] (which, of course, have an innate yen for field mice and small birds). Moreover, the narrator's liking for such phrasing as "in a sky of iron the points of the Dipper hung like icicles and Orion flashed his cold fires" (p. 28) and "[Ethan] had found Mattie's lips at last and was drinking unconsciousness of everything but the joy they gave him" (p. 130) further reveals the presence here of an exceedingly romantic sensibility and, consequently, must lead one to question the accuracy of his vision of the past.

Whatever the case, however, whether the narrator's vision is a valid one or not, Wharton's allegiances are clear. An accurate telling implies, whether the perhaps too romantic narrator is aware of it or not, that Frome was, as I have noted, a sentimentalist who could not face up to the facts of his existence. If it is an inaccurate account, then it is the narrator who stands indicted as a mawkish sentimentalist (or, as Wolff puts it, one with a "ghastly" mind)[13] who indirectly and inadvertently makes a powerful argument for living up to such commitments as those he envisions the young Ethan as trying to escape. Finally, if one concludes, as one well might, that *Ethan Frome* is irresolvably ambiguous, Wharton's position is no less clear. In a world in which the truth is nebulous, perhaps impossible to glean with certainty, one must, she teaches, strive for order, even self-imposed order; and this must be carried out even in the face of the determinism that she sees as operative, for, rightly or wrongly, she does not regard moral responsibility as incompatible with a restricted will. The establishment of routine, of order, by carrying out ordering responsibilities imposed by the severe demands of marriage is thus a goal to strive for, one that either Ethan or the narrator (or both) could not perceive as valuable. Without such order, Wharton believes, a difficult existence can only be made more difficult.

1. Edith Wharton, *The Collected Short Stories of Edith Wharton*, 2 vols. (New York: Scribner's, 1968), 1:547. For this and all other Wharton works cited, all references after the first to each will be to the edition cited and will appear in the text. All page references in my discussions of the short stories are to this two-volume collection.

2. Percy Lubbock, *Portrait of Edith Wharton* (New York: Appleton-Century-Crofts, 1947), p. 103.

3. Geoffrey Walton, *Edith Wharton: A Critical Interpretation* (Rutherford, N. J.: Fairleigh Dickenson University Press, 1970), p. 102.

4. Blake Nevius, *Edith Wharton: A Study of Her Fiction* (Berkeley: University of California Press, 1953), p. 110.

5. E. K. Brown notes, in this connection, "Divorce has always been bitterly opposed in her fiction: it appeared to her to be an unwarrantable sacrifice of the group to the individual . . . " ("Edith Wharton," *Etudes Anglaises* [Paris, 1938]; rpt. Irving Howe, ed., *Edith Wharton* [Englewood Cliffs, N. J.: Prentice-Hall, 1962],p. 66).

6. Edith Wharton, *The Mother's Recompense* (New York: Appleton, 1925), p. 265.

7. Lionel Trilling, "The Morality of Inertia," in Robert MacIver, ed., *Great Moral Dilemmas* (New York: Institute for Religious and Social Studies, 1956); rpt. Howe, ed., *Edith Wharton.* Also see Walton, who views the work as having "no real moral any more than social conflict" (p. 82).

8. Gary H. Lindberg, *Edith Wharton and the Novel of Manners* (Charlottesville: University of Virginia Press, 1975), pp. 47, 48. Somewhat less deterministic is David Eggenschwiler, "The Ordered Disorder of *Ethan Frome*," *Studies in the Novel* 9 (Fall 1977): 237–46. Eggenschwiler suggests that "Wharton will have it both ways, showing that man does determine his life in a universe that is not chaotic, but also showing that his lot is hard, his choices difficult . . . and the consequences of his actions often different from what he had expected" (p. 245).

9. Edith Wharton, *Ethan Frome* (New York: Scribner's, 1911), p. 76.

10. Cynthia Griffin Wolff, *A Feast of Words* (New York: Oxford University Press, 1977), pp. 176–77.

11. Joseph X. Brennan, "*Ethan Frome*: Structure and Metaphor," *Modern Fiction Studies* 7 (Winter 1961–62): 356.

12. Brennan, pp. 349–50.

13. Wolff, p. 165.

EDITH WHARTON
MARRIAGE IN AN IMPERFECT SOCIETY

*T*HE STORIES at which we have just looked present entrapment or one's sense of being trapped as problems that develop because marriage makes demands that the mismated, the weak, the unintelligent cannot meet. Even *Ethan Frome* with its stark backdrop of cosmic indifference focuses primarily on marriage, marriage as a catalyst slowly bringing to fruition all the worst potentials in Frome's makeup and thus initiating a chain of events that evidences much of the bleakness of life. In other significant depictions of marital discord, however, one notes a shift of emphasis. Such works as *The House of Mirth* (1905), *The Fruit of the Tree* (1907), *The Custom of the Country* (1913), *Twilight Sleep* (1927), and *Hudson River Bracketed* (1929) all portray unhappy marriages but focus more on the failures of society and of human nature generally that mar those unions than on the demands prompted by marriage itself. A key means by which she attacks these failures, obviously, is to show their pernicious effects on marriage.

In *The House of Mirth*, certainly, one sees little that is not pernicious in the set that Wharton depicts. The prevalent atmosphere of menace and disorder conveyed through the pervasive ocean metaphors and through striking metaphors of war and earthquake establishes Lily Bart's world as one that for all its material comforts, is almost Hobbesian in the ruthlessness of its inhabitants and the consequent necessity in it for power in order to survive. Moreover, it is a world that allows one few options in charting one's course through the threatening landscape. Lily, who, fittingly enough, "always carried an Omar Khayam in her travelling-bag,"[1] is presented throughout as so victimized by her training that she virtually lacks free will. In the very first chapter, Selden muses aptly that Lily "was so evidently the victim of the civilization which had produced her that the links of her bracelet seemed like manacles chaining her to her fate" (p. 10). Nor is this situation peculiar to Lily; for Selden realizes later that "he was, as much as Lily, the victim of his environment" (p. 245), and throughout the work one sees little evidence that the other denizens of the house of mirth have much say in the courses they follow.[2] If they did, they probably would not choose the existence of social climbing, hypocrisy, illicit relationships, repression, and conspicuous consumption that they lead. But, products as they are of the crass, monied society that has been erected on the foundations of an earlier, somewhat less imperfect New York, they do not have the self-awareness to do much more than perpetuate the failings that played such a large part in shaping them. Ultimately, "good" turn-of-the-century New York society looks like nothing so much as a world in which a spurious gentility masks imperfectly a Schopenhauerian existence in which all are blindly driven to self-aggrandizement at the expense of others, and the real freedom of a morally educated will is rarely to be seen.

Though Lily's case reveals poignantly how vulnerable the singles in her world are, there is nonetheless little glimpsed among her married acquaintances in upper-class New York that seems to recommend matrimony except the power that it conveys. Marriage in Lily's circle is, Lindberg notes, "primarily a means of securing social power."[3] Married, Lily could with impunity do those things that lead ultimately to her destruction when she does them as a single woman. "All turned," thinks Lily herself, "on the tiresome distinction between what a married woman might, and a girl might not, do" (p. 127). Hence, although it is "shocking" for a married woman to borrow money (especially from a man), "still, it was the mere *malum prohibitum* which the world decries but condones, and which . . . does not provoke collective disapprobation of society" (p. 127). When Lily, however, borrows money from Gus in the form of an investment he ostensibly makes for her, she sets in motion a chain of events that helps bring about disaster for herself. Similarly, the ugly criticism directed at Lily when she poses in a revealing costume for Mrs. Bry's *tableaux vivants* would be muted were she married. Ned Van Alstyne's comment is a telling one here: "When a girl's as good-looking as that she'd better marry; then no questions are asked. In our imperfectly organized society there is no provision as yet for the young woman who claims the privileges of marriage without assuming its obligations" (p. 254). Finally, as a single woman, Lily has no champion, no protector. Thus, when Bertha Dorset orders Lily not to return to her yacht, insinuating thereby that Lily is having an affair with George, Lily's social destruction is virtually assured. A married woman, though, is far less vulnerable to such insinuations. Wharton notes, "The code of Lily's world decreed that a woman's husband should be the only judge of her conduct: she was technically above suspicion while she had the shelter of his approval, or even his indifference" (pp. 167–68). That Bertha Dorset herself *is*, unlike Lily, having an affair, as most, in fact, know, and is doing so with impunity, so long as her timid husband does nothing about it, is obvious confirmation of Wharton's observation.

Marriage, then, does offer power and security in Lily's milieu, particularly a marriage that unites one to money. A sense of the necessity of making such a marriage was, of course, drummed into Lily by her mother, but somehow, perhaps because of Lily's memory of her mother's own marriage, the lesson never really took. Though a rich and therefore ostensibly happy couple until their financial downfall, Lily's parents had a relationship that as Lily recalls it can only strike her as chilling: "Ruling the turbulent element called home was the vigorous and determined figure of a mother still young enough to dance her ball-dresses to rags, while the hazy outline of a neutral-tinted father filled an intermediate space between the butler and the man who came to wind the clocks." (p. 45). Her father was "down town" all day, a dray horse making the money to support his frivolous but demanding wife's extravagances; and when his business failed, all that remained of the marriage were Mrs. Bart's recriminations and Mr. Bart's illness and early death. Doubtless, such memories have had their effect on Lily by getting in the way whenever she is on the verge of making a marriage that bids fair to be as "successful" as that of her parents before her father's financial reverses. Her inchoate longings for something better, including beauty and love, lead her from the prospects of such a marriage but are not sufficiently strong to lead her far enough from her social circle so that she will no longer even halfheartedly seek a marriage of this sort or be damaged by her refusals to make one.

Further keeping Lily from rushing into the marriage that confers social power may well be an awareness of the obvious ugliness of the marriages of her friends. The marriages in Lily's circle presented at greatest length by Wharton are those of the Trenors and the Dorsets, both of which are odious for the unlucky persons in them and exceedingly dangerous for those, like Lily, lacking in social power who come into contact with them. In each case husband and wife exacerbate each other's failings, bringing about an increasingly volatile situation. Judy Trenor's belief that Gus is nothing more than a vulgar but unfortunately necessary source of funds for her lavish entertainments forces him into excesses in which he might not otherwise indulge. Judy even resorts to the expedient of encouraging women to flirt with her husband so that he will be in a sufficiently pleasant mood not to question what she spends his money on. Gus, on the other hand, realizing full well his wife's contempt for him, indulges in his amatory escapades with all the vigor of a man constantly seeking to throw his wife's disgust with him back in her face. Needless to say, every new episode of misbehavior merely confirms Judy's contempt for him, leading her to throw herself into spending his money with renewed energy. No less trapped in a cycle of increasing spiritual and emotional decay are the Dorsets. The promiscuity of the waspish Bertha chronically provokes the neurasthenic self-pity of George, which, in turn, prompts further licentiousness in Bertha. In both marriages, though, it is not the partners who suffer most but Lily. Unmarried, she is the powerless bystander who is ground down by the complex social machinery set in motion by the marital discord around her.

The power that this complex social machinery confers on those who make the right marriages and thereby help maintain the order of things is conveyed graphically through

Wharton's depiction of the Van Osburgh nuptials, which she characterizes ironically as "the simple country wedding," one "to which the guests are convoyed in special trains, and from which the hordes of the uninvited have to be fended off by the intervention of the police" (p. 139). She goes on to note, no less ironically, that while these "sylvan rites were taking place, in a church packed with fashion and festooned with orchids, the representatives of the press were threading their way, note-book in hand, through the labyrinth of wedding presents, and the agent of a cinematograph syndicate was setting up his apparatus at the church door" (p. 139). Obviously, this is no quiet ceremony before a harried justice of the peace and his drowsy wife. It is, instead, one means by which a rich and strong social class seeks to perpetuate itself. While flaunting its wealth and power as it bestows its approval upon a young couple who seek full initiation into its ranks, it impresses upon all participants the attractiveness of its way of life and the concomitant necessity of working to maintain it. The febrile efforts to which those such as the Brys and Simon Rosedale must resort as they attempt to break into this world reveal its imperviousness to change and its implacability, both factors that ultimately serve to destroy the unmarried and financially embarrassed Lily.

Little as there is in the depiction of marriage in *The House of Mirth* that seems to recommend the institution to anyone not seeking power in the polite New York society at the turn of the twentieth century, the novel does not condemn marriage. Certainly, Wharton sees no valid alternatives to it even in this society. Selden's bachelorhood consigns him to a life of emotional as well as aesthetic dabbling and, as a result, finally, to regret for a life misspent. Though Gerty Farish finds a certain contentment in devoting her spinster's existence to charitable works, Wharton makes clear that few have the large stores of serenity and benevolence to make acceptance of such a lonely lot seem anything other than what Lily would call "dingy." Nor does escape from a marriage that one finds onerous bring either contentment or a worthwhile life in this novel any more than it does in other works by Wharton. The divorced Carry Fisher is reduced to a hanger's-on existence on the periphery of upper-class society, where, thought useful though not entirely savory, she is tolerated as one who can swell a progress, enliven a party, or keep a saturnine husband in a good mood and away from a wife who does not care to be under his scrutiny. Ugly as are the lives of many of the married in *The House of Mirth*, then, there is definitely no real happiness ascertainable here outside marriage.

That happiness, though, can be found in marriage, however rarely, is affirmed in Wharton's depiction of the lower-class couple, Nettie and George Struther. Implicit in their union is, for Lily finally, the "central truth of existence." She sees that their life, though "meagre enough" and "on the grim edge of poverty, with scant margin for possibilities of sickness or mischance, . . . [has] the frail audacious permanence of a bird's nest built on the edge of a cliff—a mere wisp of leaves and straw, yet so put together that the lives entrusted to it may hang safely over the abyss" (p. 517). Doubtless, this "central truth of existence" that Lily sees as bound up in their union is one of human continuity, of a tenuous but lasting, timeless order established by love and mutual commitment. Significantly, it is only the Struther marriage in this novel in which there is a visible child. The Struther baby, so appealing to Lily, becomes the palpable symbol for her and for Wharton of the unending, procreative order that love and a good marriage can help sustain.[4] Unfortunately, though, not only is such a marriage as this rare in Wharton's work but it is unconvincing. Rendered only briefly, with little detail, the Struther union is largely an expression of uncharacteristic sentimentality on Wharton's part, as she trots out the comforting cliché that the poor attain a surpassing contentment, since they live more lovingly, more sincerely, more rewardingly than others. As such, this marriage is little more than an unachievable ideal, less something to strive for in matrimony than a means solely, whatever Wharton's intentions, of heightening the bleakness of the rest of the marriages in *The House of Mirth*.

In *The Fruit of the Tree* as in *The House of Mirth*, Wharton depicts marital discord as a manifestation of problems larger than those inherent in marriage itself. Just what those problems are and where they reside has frequently been misunderstood by commentators, leading them to believe that it is a work that lacks clarity of purpose, one in which Wharton burdened herself, as R. W. B. Lewis suggests, with "too many subjects."[5] Certainly, subjects abound in the novel; labor reform and reformers, marriage, euthanasia, the mores and foibles of upper-class society, and the repression of women are topics that, among still others, Wharton develops in *The Fruit of the Tree*. But the apparent plethora of subject matter notwithstanding, Wharton does manage to hold the novel together admirably, in terms of both theme and plot, as each subject ultimately is developed to one conclusion: the revelation of the human propensity for folly. Social failings exist, Wharton teaches, because of human failings; reforms rarely succeed because these failings are profound and ineradicable. This is most apparent in marriage, the subject on which Wharton focuses most intensely here, using it as a chief means of revealing the implications of the others. Through her depictions of the failed marriages in this novel, Wharton makes clear that the inability of two people who know each other intimately to forge a lasting, worthwhile union bespeaks a fundamental inability in most to overcome the selfishness, the egotism that are impediments to the achievement of happiness. More specifically, the flawed marriages in this work fail, as Wharton sees it, for the same reasons that millworkers are downtrodden, upper-class types are often supercilious and parasitical, mercy-killers occasionally selfserving, women repressed, and reformers ineffectual and frequently driven by purely personal motives.

Wharton notes at one point in *The Fruit of the Tree* that "compromise is the law of married life,"[6] a lesson consistently flouted by the unyielding reformer John Amherst with disastrous results for the two marriages he makes. A mill foreman whose feverish devotion to bettering the lot of the millhands is motivated in great part by a desire for such "personal ascendency" (p. 127) as may be attained through shaping others to work toward his ends, Amherst is totally unaware throughout the novel that, as Wharton asserts, "man can commit no act alone, whether for good or evil" (pp. 605–6). More, this man striving so single-mindedly to realize his ideal is unaware, as well, of another truth central to Wharton's outlook, the fact that "human relations . . . [are] a tangled and deep-rooted growth, a dark forest through which the idealist cannot cut his straight path without hearing at each stroke the cry of the severed branch: '*why woundest thou me?*'" (p. 624). As such, Amherst, who combines his unremitting zeal with a consummate lack of tact or ability to compromise in dealing with others, is eminently deserving of Cynthia Griffin Wolff's sharp criticism that his "insensitivity to the feelings of others would make him unfit to be the companion of anyone in any context."[7] Certainly, one context for which he is unfit is, of course, matrimony, as both Bessy Westmore and Justine Brent learn to their grief.

Although Amherst does not marry Bessy solely to control her and her mills, "he would scarcely have contemplated marriage with a rich woman," Wharton notes, "unless the source of her wealth had offered him some such opportunity as Westmore presented" (p. 184). And certainly *this* rich woman does seem to be a perfect choice for Amherst. Not only is she a physically attractive millowner but she exhibits a childlike tenderheartedness in her charity to needy individuals that Amherst believes he can shape into a lasting commitment to his program of reform. Unfortunately, when Amherst learns that Bessy's largesse to a millhand or two is in no way symptomatic of a desire to oversee the decimation of her family fortune on behalf of the community of millhands and, worse, finds that she is a querulous child-woman who, though capable of isolated acts of generosity and flashes of idealism, is incapable of sustained benevolence, he withdraws from her, inevitably destroying the marriage and making it clear that from the first the mills meant, if not everything to him, at least more than the woman did.

Perhaps an understanding husband might in the course of continually reinforcing Bessy's better traits effect a gradual improvement and maturation in her. Amherst, of course, is unable to be this sort of husband. Instead of fostering her good traits, he aggravates her bad ones. When, early in the marriage, Bessy, totally under Amherst's sway, is caught up in an "eager adoption" of his ideas and is organizing a "Mothers Club" for the mills, planning a "recreation-ground," an emergency hospital, and the "building which was to contain the night-schools, library, and gymnasium," Amherst regards her efforts condescendingly as childish ones geared to "minor projects which he had urged her to take up as a means of learning their essential dependence on his larger scheme" (p. 181). Sensing her husband's monomania and his lack of respect for her and warned by her father and her trusted lawyer that Amherst's devotion to his vision will drain her wealth, Bessy begins to limit the scope of Amherst's philanthropic endeavors. For Amherst this means only one thing: his wife is "surreptitiously . . . giving aid and comfort to the enemy, who were really defending her own cause" (p. 183). Rather than assuage her fears, he throws himself more deeply than ever into his work, spends days and weeks apart from her on mill matters, and turns their relationship into a continuous battle of wills over money in which, through what amounts to a sort of emotional extortion, he invariably wrests more funds from her. Eventually he accomplishes just what his mother feared he might when she warned him, early in his marriage, against "sacrificing your wife to the mills" (p. 176). Bessy retreats into childishness, embarking on an endless, petulant quest for pleasure amid a horde of shallow socialites. Finally, when her money is seriously depleted by Amherst, she panics and makes him give up management of the mills and control of her property. The apparently final separation prompted by this leads Bessy into the reckless behavior that culminates in a fatal horseback ride on the aptly named Impulse, resulting in her painful, almost certainly mortal injuries and then in the euthanasia she persuades Justine to carry out on her. That there was much good and love in her nature that might have been fostered by a less selfish man than Amherst is driven home by her will, in which she left all to her husband.

No less a sacrifice to the mills and, of course, to Amherst's commitment to self from which his devotion to the mills largely derives, is Justine Brent, who from the first has been

strongly drawn to him by his strength of purpose. Unremittingly an idealist herself, she sees him as one "whom no gust
of chance could deflect from his purpose" (p. 274); and after
she moves into the Amherst household at Bessy's request,
she is overwhelmingly "conscious . . . of the quiet strength
she was absorbing from his presence, of the way in which his
words, his voice, his mere nearness were slowly steadying
and clarifying her will" (p. 275). Not surprisingly, then, when
Amherst proposes marriage to her, nearly two years after
Bessy's death, she is quick to accept although the offer is
couched in terms that might give many pause. No conventionally ardent swain, Amherst "abruptly" asks, "Wouldn't
you marry if it . . . offered you hard work, and the opportunity to make things better . . . for a great many people . . . ?" (pp.464–65). To Justine this is manifestly the call
for which she has been waiting her whole life, a call to a
union in which the perfect love of an idealistic couple for each
other will spur them on to ever greater heights of philanthropy. To her dismay, she learns how little capacity for love
Amherst really has and how misguided and ineffectual much
philanthropy can be.

Commenting on Amherst's two marriages, Blake Nevius
suggests that "Amherst's failure to raise . . . Bessy to his
level of moral insight and conviction is followed by Justine's
near failure to raise Amherst to hers; the disaster which concludes the first experiment is narrowly averted in the second."[8] Clearly, however, there is no such aversion of disaster.
Though Justine does at last grow, her moral growth is
prompted by the effectual destruction of her marriage and in
no way serves to pull her husband out of his bondage to self.
At first their marriage does indeed seem so successful that
one suspects Amherst may well be humanized by it, but their
happiness, Wharton reveals, is deceptive. She notes that the
pair view themselves as voyaging together on seas "studded
with happy islands: every fresh discovery they made about
each other, every new agreement of ideas and feelings, offered itself to these intrepid explorers as a friendly coast
where they might beach their keel and take their bearings"
(p. 472). Perhaps the key words in this lush account are

"every new agreement of ideas and feelings." Obviously, any marriage will be a happy one as long as husband and wife are in total accord, as Amherst and Justine are at first. Just as obviously, though, the test of a marriage comes when there arises a significant lack of agreement between the pair.

In this marriage that test is precipitated when Amherst learns that Justine gave Bessy the fatal dose of morphine. It is a test, ultimately, that the marriage cannot withstand, as Amherst turns from his wife, finding especially odious her declaration that in giving Bessy the death for which she begged she was only following his own advice and his own example by pursuing a course of independent behavior in the face of conventional belief. That this plausible assertion makes Amherst recoil so powerfully from Justine, particularly in the light of his own implicit defense earlier of euthanasia in the case of a cruelly hurt millworker, is attributable, one suspects, to his own vague guilt feelings as he perhaps realizes unconsciously not only that he indirectly brought about Bessy's injury but that Justine acted virtually as his surrogate, unwittingly carrying out his own deep-rooted wishes to have Bessy out of the way so that he might gain unhindered control of the mills. Not given to probing scrutiny of himself, however, Amherst apparently feels only the faintest proddings of the culpability he is so quick to project upon his second wife, whom he now finds so tainted. More any lingering guilt he might still feel after this projection he assuages grandly by (probably willfully) misconstruing Bessy's blueprint for a pleasure dome for herself to be her plans for a lavish gymnasium for the millhands. Secure in his perception that he is carrying out his first wife's fond wish, which, of course, he now sees as identical to his own, he can indulge in the unadulterated pleasures of extended self-congratulation. That his second wife has no place in this scheme of things bothers him not at all; the needs of those close to him never have.

Thus, like the first Amherst marriage, the second turns out badly. In this case, though, Wharton does find something salvageable, and that is Justine's moral intelligence. Until Amherst's revulsion from her, Justine seems little more than a female counterpart to the strong-willed reformer. With it, and the jolt to her egotism that it provides, what R. W. B. Lewis calls her "intense if uncertain moral seriousness"[9] gives way to serentiy and moral maturity.[10] Voluntary confession to Bessy's father makes her vulnerable to his hatred, scorn, and possible desire for revenge; but it also leads, as she knows it will, to total exoneration of Amherst. Her realization that her husband, now alienated from her, is unconsciously expiating his unacknowledged sense of culpability arouses no bitterness in her, merely a calm acceptance of her own partial responsibility for his self-deception and a willingness to let him find what reassuring illusions he may. Aware too that he is beyond the reach of any help she can offer, she directs her efforts where there seems to be more hope that they will be effectual and devotes herself lovingly and selflessly to the welfare of Bessy's daughter, Cicely. No longer, one suspects, will she be prey to the proddings of a restless and relentless ego.

Through Justine's development of a profound moral awareness, then, Wharton manages to provide at least a qualified affirmation in this otherwise bleak novel. The overly comfortable and selfish society of Bessy, her father, Lawyer Tredegar, and professional family friend Mrs. Ansell will not change, nor will such unreformed reformers as Amherst whose efforts to improve that society even at the risk of bringing it down are often more dangerous than what they are combatting. Meanness and folly we shall, apparently, always have with us. To purge ourselves of these, and, having done that, to work to help one or two others within our immediate ken is perhaps the best any of us ought realistically to hope for, as Wharton sees it. Hence, the "compromise" that, as we have seen, she asserts "is the law of married life" is also, she seems to feel, the law of all social life—not compromise in the sense of lack of principle, certainly, but compromise in the sense of a willingness to accept the fact that one cannot achieve all one might wish to. This sort of compromise, this acceptance of the limitations of one's powers, is a quiet triumph over egotism. It is this lesson that Justine ultimately learns as she enters the house of pain, a lesson that

Wharton hoped might often come through marriage, as, ironically, it does here. Thus, even in this account of two desperately flawed marriages, Wharton refuses to indict the institution itself. When marriages fail, it is people who fail, not the darkly demanding institution of marriage itself; and, as one sees in Justine's case, even when marriages fail, in the process of loss something of enduring value can be gained.

The Custom of the Country, unlike *The Fruit of the Tree*, has never been regarded as having a bewildering surfeit of subjects. Nevertheless, it presents quite as many as the earlier work does. Among these are the enervated, anachronistic quality of old-line, upper-class life in New York, the neglect of wives by business-obsessed husbands, the powerlessness of women and the evils to which it leads them, the rise of parvenus, and the decline of business probity with all that it indicates about a general moral decline on the American scene. That this array of subjects has never suggested thematic incoherence to commentators derives primarily from Wharton's success with Undine Spragg. So strikingly conceived is she as virtually the embodiment of insatiable, vulgar appetite that Undine not only draws the subjects together by the sheer force of her characterization but symbolizes in herself, as well, the corrosive egotism and corruption that pervade every area of modern American life that Wharton explores in the novel.

Though the strength of their portrayal of Undine is sufficient to bring about thematic unity, *The Custom of the Country* is not a novel with unity of tone.[11] Wharton's intent seems mainly to be satirical, but there are crucial moments when emotional detachment is forgotten and Wharton's detestation of Undine and of all that she represents for modern America breaks through, with the invariable effect of turning the novel closer to melodrama than to satire. What is significant in this for our discussion is that Wharton's emotional involvement is most apparent in her depiction of Undine's disastrous marriage to Ralph Marvell. The reasons for this are not hard to see. Ralph's destruction at Undine's hands is, for Wharton, symbolic of the destruction of the lingering vestiges of an old and valuable way of life. More, it illustrates the modern American loss of veneration for marriage, so integral a part, as she saw it, of the maintenance of that old way of life. Wreckage of such magnitude is obviously something she cannot regard with equanimity. Thus, despite the dearth of good marriages in this work (unlike *The House of Mirth*, it lacks even one appealing marriage), *The Custom of the Country*, like Wharton's other depictions of marital difficulties, constitutes no attack on matrimony. Implicit in her bitter, melodramatic account of Ralph's marriage is a defense of the relationship that Undine scorns.[12]

In portraying the failure of Undine's marriage to Ralph, Wharton, like Howells with Bartley and Marcia or Herrick with many of his unfortunate couples, sees the misfortune as ultimately deriving from large failings on the national scene. Undine, notes Ralph's perceptive friend, Charles Bowen, is "a monstrously perfect result," the "completest proof of [the] triumph" of a modern "system"[13] in which the "average American looks down on his wife" (p. 205), turning from her to the business world, which is the real focus of his interest. In the process, Bowen comments, he inevitably turns his wife into little more than the most self-indulgent of consumers, as "money and motors and clothes" become "simply the big bribe she's paid for keeping out of some man's way!" (p. 208). Moreover, this "system," obviously not conducive to marital happiness at best, has particularly disastrous effects for Ralph and Undine. "Monstrously perfect result" as she might be, Undine represents as well, as Bowen does not perceive, a new stage in its development. Come from the West, where Wharton believes, the pernicious "get ahead" spirit is even stronger than in the East—strong enough, indeed, to infect even women—Undine represents a hitherto unseen force on the national scene, one that will make itself felt increasingly in both East and West: the new woman who wants power on a scale that previously has been accessible only to men and is as unscrupulous as the worst of them in her efforts to attain her ends. Barred because of her sex from the sources of power available to men and incapable of understanding the underlying causes of her resultant sense of frustration in the role of consumer forced on her by her training in modern

America, she is chronically restive, dissatisfied, grasping—seeking feverishly in possession, social position, and men the power for which, largely unbeknown to herself, she really longs. No less discontent, clearly, in this modern marital "system" is Ralph, who, unlike Undine, has not been shaped for it by his training. As one of the last of the old-line New Yorkers, Ralph lacks the energy, the ruthlessness, the unscrupulousness requisite to survival in the modern American business world and, increasingly, as Wharton sees it, in America itself. Perhaps the most telling evidence of this is his pathetic belief that, Pygmalion-like, he can fit Undine to the mold of the vanishing codes and values of Old New York. That he will be unable to do so is as much a foregone conclusion as is the failure of a marriage in modern America between persons of their backgrounds.

Such a perception of both Undine and Ralph as illusion-ridden and even faintly comic victims of shaping national forces they do not understand might readily evoke here, as similar perceptions do elsewhere in Wharton's work, a stance of authorial detachment, but this is not the case. Instead, Wharton's portrayal of Ralph, despite its pointed delineation of his enervation, his delusions, his essentially effete egotism, is not without a good deal of sympathy. One sees no Gilbert Osmond here, balefully contemplating an Isabel who refuses to conform to his narrow specifications; nor does one see an essentially satirical figure like Waythorn, who is caught up in somewhat similar circumstances in Wharton's "The Other Two," a story at which we shall look later. Rather, one finds oneself involved in the travail of this sensitive though feckless young husband who finds to his growing horror that behind all his wife's energy and physical beauty lie a spiritual emptiness and voracity for self-aggrandizement that are of frightening dimensions. There is little of the satirical and little to promote detachment when one sees this poor fellow frightened to "broach the subject of money" with his wife because "he had too keen a memory of the way her lips could narrow and her eyes turn from him as if he were a stranger" (p. 158) or when one sees his hope of becoming a writer wither under the blast of Undine's total lack of sympathy with his literary efforts and refined sensibility. Now, this sort of material, of course, can be the stuff of satire, even of comic strips. But Wharton does not work it this way. Instead, she heightens its emotional appeal by linking it to a plot line that is essentially melodramatic and to a tone that has little of the urbane, sardonic restraint one often sees in her work, including, even, sections of this one not tied to this particular marriage. Thus, Undine's faithlessness to Ralph and her young son, which eventually drives her husband to suicide, smacks of melodrama that is not suggested by such satirical touches as Undine's conversation with her hairdresser, which opens the novel.

Nor it is merely in terms of melodrama that Undine's marriage to Ralph is removed from a context of satirical detachment. Ralph's slow realization early in the marriage that Undine shares little in his interests and tastes is replete with a pathos that is not encountered elsewhere in the book. Sitting with his new wife on a charming hill near Siena, moved by the setting and the beauty of the young woman next to him, Ralph tells her she looks "as cool as a wave," lovingly fondles her hand, and thinks to himself that at this moment "earthly dimensions were ignored and the curve of beauty [was] boundless enough to hold whatever the imagination could pour into it." Inspired, "Ralph had never felt more convinced of his power to write a great poem" (p. 142). Undine's response to the setting and to Ralph's evident passion is first to stir "uneasily" and then to remark with "a faint accent of reproach, 'I don't feel cool, you said there'd be a breeze up here'" (p. 142). When he suggests that they go to Ucceto, from which the "drive back by moonlight would be glorious," Undine makes "a slight show of interest" and grants, "It might be nice—but where could we get anything to eat?" (p. 143). Again, this is material that could be rendered satirically, but despite the probability that Wharton's overriding intentions in the novel are satirical, such is not the case here. The poignancy inherent in Ralph's illusions and blighted hopes ultimately is not meant to prompt in the reader the detachment requisite to satire. Apparently, Wharton herself cannot maintain the pose of detachment when the despoliation she is depicting involves, as we have noted, not merely marriage but the last remnants of that Old New York sensibility, which, for all its shortcomings, she sees as preferable to the depredations of Undine, of her first and fourth husband Elmer Moffat, and of their modern ilk.

The detachment that eludes Wharton in her portrayal of Undine's marriage to Ralph is achieved by her in the account of Undine's next marriage, her ill-fated union with the urbane French aristocrat Raymond de Chelles. In terms of Wharton's story line, there is really very little reason for this marriage, for the confrontation between the reckless dynamism of a crass, modern America as embodied in Undine and the staid way of life of a long-entrenched aristocracy has already been delineated fully in Undine's marriage to Ralph. And although Raymond's defeat at the hands of consummate American vulgarity propped up by money and power is less complete than Ralph's, the point about Undine and her destructive impact on social stability has already been made. What Wharton is seemingly attempting to do here is turn the novel back in the direction of satire. From the first, when Undine reflects that her new husband "was really charming (it was odd how he reminded her of Ralph!)" (p. 480), through her growing realization, as Raymond tries to interest her in the life of the mind, that he "had again developed a disturbing resemblance to his predecessor" (p. 506), until her divorce from him, which simply culminates her systematic violation throughout the marriage of long-held Chelles traditions,her marriage to Raymond is essentially a repetition of her marriage to Ralph, only now rendered satirically. Though Raymond is stronger than Ralph and, unlike his predecessor, can coolly withdraw into his protective shell of aristocratic disdain when Undine becomes particularly difficult, the fundamental patterns of the two marriages are decidedly similar. All that is changed is the tone with which they are presented by Wharton. The two strong-willed but essentially limited combatants in the Chelles marriage are finally so impervious to the thrusts of each other but nevertheless so unwilling to compromise that their conflict finally becomes ludicrous. With no one deeply hurt as Ralph was and with no neglected child as a counter for Undine to manipulate as she did in the earlier marriage, there is in her union with Raymond little to engender emotional involvement on either Wharton's part or the reader's. Though such sources of contention between the couple as the sale of heirloom tapestries, Undine's desire to spend more time in Paris, and her difficulties in getting along with her in-laws might in other contexts be matters of serious import, the lack of real emotional depth in either combatant rules out gravity as the fitting tone in all this.

The reestablishment of a satiric tone through Undine's marriage to Raymond is sustained through the close of the novel, as Undine remarries Elmer but finds that, despite his money and power, her divorce precludes the possibility that she will ever be an ambassador's wife, a position for which she suddenly finds herself longing because she believes "it was the one part she was really made for" (p. 594). Clearly, one's sympathies are not aroused. Dissatisfied though she will always be, her schemes and goals are so shabby as to evoke little concern for her welfare in the reader. She and Elmer, who will, presumably, spawn between them a progeny of Babbitts, may well be disturbing and frightening people; but they are so contemptible to Wharton that they are, finally, objects of humor and scorn as, like so many modern Americans, they pursue a worldly success that Wharton, like Herrick, knows is thrust before them as a promise by modern America itself, but which, even if attained, can never satisfy. That Wharton's account of Undine's career departs from contemptuous satire in the treatment of her marriage to Ralph indicates just how fully Wharton valued marriage as a relationship that, by bringing a pair into intimate confrontation with the onmipresent darkness, has a capacity for nurturing just those values—tradition, order, and a sense of commitment to others—that Undine spurned.

In *Twilight Sleep* Wharton presents a society in which the values of the Undine Spraggs and the Elmer Moffats have been roundly accepted as those by which all shall live. A conversation between the frantically "modern" socialite Pauline Manford and her daughter, Nona, establishes both the dominant system of values that Wharton observes in 1920s

America and a poignant reminder of the earlier, better system now largely discarded. Pauline, a well-meaning woman but a shallow and foolish one nonetheless, assures Nona that "being prepared to suffer is really the way to create suffering" and that "creating suffering is creating sin, because sin and suffering are really one." She goes on to declare to her daughter, "We ought to refuse ourselves to pain. All the great Healers have taught us that." Nona, lifting her eyebrows "in the slightly disturbing way she had," quietly responds, "Did Christ?"[14] an answer that does not please Pauline and that doubtless, would not please the other devotees of the cult of self-indulgence that Wharton believes dominates modern American life.

The dangers of this new way are shown in *Twilight Sleep* to be particularly potent in marriage. Unable to sustain the commitments that might entail pain, the modern New Yorkers, who help set the tone for the whole nation, have made the marriage of long standing a rarity. Thus, the Jim Wyants, a young pair who have been married not quite two years, have come "to be regarded as one of the 'old couples' of their set, one of the settled landmarks in the matrimonial quicksands of New York" (p. 12). Pauline, herself married to Dexter Manford for twenty years since her divorce from Arthur Wyant, Jim's father, is appalled when she thinks of an Italian relation of hers who cannot get a divorce because of his country's laws. She "could conceive of nothing more shocking than a social organization which did not recognize divorce, and let all kinds of domestic evils fester undisturbed, instead of having people's lives disinfected and whitewashed at regular intervals, like the cellar" (p. 19). Such an attitude, shared by almost all of those about her, leads to the sort of situation described caustically by Nona when, speaking of her mother's dinner parties, she asks her, "Doesn't Maisie always have to make out a list of previous marriages as long as a crossword puzzle, to prevent your calling people by the wrong names?" (p. 29).

Convinced though Pauline is that a determinedly followed course of self-indulgence will lead to freedom and happiness, such has not been the case in her own circle, in which it has fostered only aimlessness, ennui, and discontent. Typically, Pauline's divorce from the ineffectual, old-line New Yorker, Wyant, so that she might marry the energetic Midwestern businessman, Manford, has brought neither her nor Manford the contentment both envisioned as within their grasp. Dexter's feverish pursuit of money he no longer needs and Pauline's slavish devotion to her reputation as a fashionable hostess as well as to any quack health faddist or self-styled transcendentalist guru who promises for a fee to keep her from pain evidence their dissatisfaction with the valueless way of life they have chosen.

Though unable to grasp exactly where things have gone wrong, Dexter, unlike Pauline, at least realizes that once he saw something better, more substantial, than the life he now leads. Contemplating the self-indulgent Pauline, "he had a vision of his mother, out on the Minnesota farm, . . . —saw her sowing, digging potatoes, feeding chickens; saw her kneading, baking, cooking, washing, mending, catching and harnessing the half-broken colt to drive twelve miles in the snow for the doctor, one day when all the men were away, and his little sister had been so badly scalded" (p. 79). This prompts a yearning dream of an ideal life far different from what he now has with Pauline, one, that is, which is inherently more peaceful and family-oriented, more akin to the life of the "common lot" as envisioned by Herrick, than the isolated, self-absorbed lives he and his wife lead as wealthy New Yorkers in the 1920s:

> What he really wanted was a life in which professional interests as far-reaching and absorbing as his own were somehow impossibly combined with great stretches of country quiet, books, horses and children—ah, children! Boys of his own— teaching them all sorts of country things; taking them for long trudges, telling them about trees and plants and birds— . . . and coming home in the dusk to firelight, lamplight, a tea-table groaning with jolly things all the boys and girls (girls too, more little Nonas) grouped around, hungry and tingling from their long tramp—and a woman lifting her calm face from her book. . . . (Pp. 80–81)

Frustrated by the realization that such a marriage is beyond the reach of one, like himself, who too long has been caught up in his wife's circle, Dexter casts about desperately for anything that will take his mind off his failure to find a worthwhile mode of life. Not surprisingly, given his weakness, the distractions he finds are all too much a part of the modern pattern of things. He enters into a vapid affair with Pauline's friend Gladys Toy (whose buxom figure reminds him hauntingly of the strong farm women of his youth but whose name shows how seriously one need take her as a woman), and then, finally, into an ugly liaison with his stepson Jim's chronically bored little vamp of a wife, Lita. The latter relationship prompts Arthur Wyant's accidental wounding of Nona as he attempts vainly to kill Manford and thereby defend his vacillating son's honor. Honor, then, like a strong sense of family ties, is rarely to be seen in the world of *Twilight Sleep*, and the effort to achieve it can be as dangerous and abortive as are Manford's yearnings for a lost, better life.

As Nona's wounding indicates, this is a society in which, for all its avoidance of pain, people do get hurt. Unfortunately, the hurt that Nona receives is far more serious, ultimately, than that caused by a bullet in the arm; it is the destruction of her moral vision. Until the shooting it is Nona alone who maintains a sense of principle and a devotion to values larger than self. Unlike her mother, whose "moral muscles" Nona regards as "atrophied" (p. 307), Nona regards divorce as something a good deal less than a panacea, particularly when children are involved; "Nona always ached for the bewildered progeny suddenly bundled from one home to another when their parents embarked on a new conjugal experiment; she could never have bought her happiness by a massacre of innocents" (p. 211). So troubled is she, in fact, by the corrosive effects of divorce on society that, even though he is childless, she turns down the man she loves rather than allow him to break up his loveless marriage for her. This rigorous commitment cannot, however, survive in the face of the corruption around her; and after the shooting and her discovery that her father has been having an affair with her half-brother's wife, Nona is terribly changed. When her mother urges her to forget her sorrow and get married, Nona answers bitterly, "Married? Do you suppose being married would make me happy? I wonder why you should! I don't want to marry—there's nobody in the world I would marry. . . . Marry! I'd a thousand times rather go into a convent and have done with it." To Pauline's horrified reply, "A convent—Nona! Not a *convent*?" she wearily answers in the closing words of the novel, "Oh, but I mean a convent where nobody believes in anything" (p. 373).

Wharton's comment on *The House of Mirth* that "a frivolous society can acquire dramatic significance only through what its frivolity destroys"[15] is applicable to Nona's case just as fully as it is to Lily Bart's. From a devotion to value, Nona is brought to nihilism, to the commitment to the "none" that is echoed by her very name. Her refusal ever to marry is nothing less than a refusal ever to believe in or care for another.[16] Thus does Wharton reveal how a society whose spiritual impoverishment is shown most blatantly by the ephemerality of its marriages spawns only more valuelessness in an increasingly sordid America. If the rendering of this situation in *Twilight Sleep* careens wildly from the farcical to the melodramatic, as commentators have noted, this failure to achieve unity of tone grows, like the similar failure in *The Custom of the Country*, out of a moral outrage so pronounced that she cannot hold it in check as she tries to satirize the scene about her, a moral outrage engendered by what she perceives to be a loss in modern Americans of a sense of social responsibility. And this loss, she believes, is felt nowhere so devastatingly as in the decline of the American marriage.

The scene Wharton depicts in *Hudson River Bracketed* is little different from the one that destroys Nona. As George Frenside, a shrewd commentator in the work, notes of the difficulties being undergone by the protagonist, Vance Weston, "It's a bad time for a creator of any sort to be born, in this after-war welter, with its new recipe for immortality every morning."[17] Though the "after-war welter" does not destroy Vance, it hinders his development as an artist, increases his tendency toward self-indulgence, and leads him into a miserable marriage. In short, Vance is, in Blake Nevius's words, "the victim of postwar confusion and the currently unstable values in conduct as well as art."[18] Thus, although Vance's marriage—like most of the marriages in this work—is a failure, and although Wharton does perceive that the artist has special problems that may well be exacerbated by marriage, *Hudson River Bracketed*, like *The Custom of the Country* and *Twilight Sleep*, indicts not marriage but the cultural disruption that causes so many marriages to fail.

Vance's ill-advised marriage to Laura-Lou Tracy is a direct result of the aesthetic and spiritual deprivation he has undergone in his Midwestern youth, spent in such environs as Pruneville, Hallelujah, and the College of Euphoria. "Born into a world in which everything had been, or was being, renovated" (p. 3), he has no sense of tradition, no example of stability that will give his romantic, febrile yearnings after absolute beauty the ballast they need in order to find adequate expression in life or art. Certainly, his family provides no guidance; Vance's father is a small-town go-getter realtor, who simply pulls his wife in his wake as he lives out the code of Babbittry he joyfully proclaims. Nor is there much help from Vance's grandparents: "Perfection was grandma's passion—ladies were grandpa's" (p. 6). Because of this dingy background, Vance's innate thirst for beauty is increased, since he can find nothing in the sterility around him to satisfy it. As a result, he seizes almost in desperation upon his pretty but not terribly intelligent Eastern cousin, Laura-Lou, transforms her in his own mind into the virtual embodiment of transcendent beauty and artistic inspiration, and marries her, with horrendous results for them both. Had the postwar Midwest been less of a wasteland peopled by money-chasers, skirt-chasers, and chasers of panaceas for the spirit, Vance never would have made the mistake he does.

Inevitably Vance finds that Laura-Lou in no way approximates his prenuptial vision of her; and, frustrated in his literary career by the politics of New York publishing and reviewing, bewildered and troubled by the spurious, ostensibly avant-garde pontifications of the poseurs and hacks who comprise most of the New York literati, he has diminishing patience for his clinging and increasingly sickly wife. Indeed, he himself brings about the tuberculosis that finally destroys her by his foolish and selfish efforts to transform this simple girl into the muse he envisioned her to be. Forcing her to climb a snow-covered mountain with him so that she can be suitably inspired by the prospect from the summit, he succeeds only in turning her into a fatally ill consumptive as he reenacts unwittingly the pathetic end of the marriage between another driven romantic artist and his mortally stricken child-bride. Like Poe and Virginia, Vance and Laura-Lou move to the Bronx, where they live in a desperate poverty that speeds the death of the girl. With little thought for his failing wife, Vance pursues his work compulsively; and at her death, significantly, it is Bunty Hayes, the pleasant but crude suitor she gave up for Vance, who draws down the poor girl's eyelids. Misled, then, into a bad marriage by the romantic longings in him that are ungratified by his background, disheartened and turned inward by the corrupt literary world about him in New York, Vance finally has come to care less for his wife than does her spurned suitor. He has, again like Poe, seemingly lost concern for the mundane and those who people it, not necessarily a damaging happenstance for the imaginative artist, who can create a world of his own, but a dangerous occurrence for a husband.

Like the marriage of Vance and Laura-Lou, the other union seen at any length in this novel, that of Halo Spear and Lewis Tarrant, is one that never should have taken place. That it did is, as with Vance's marriage, less the fault of either partner than of the temper of the times. Halo's parents, who, like many of their contemporaries, pride themselves on being advanced, even revolutionary, thinkers, are merely vapid hedonists, whose "heresies were too mild to cause any excitement outside of their own circle" (p. 62). Too selfish and weak to support themselves and their children, they pass on to Halo only poverty and their propensity for self-dramatization, lack of direction, and weakness of purpose. Moreover, Halo's marriage itself is part of their unfortunate legacy. Grateful to Tarrant for his huge loans to her parents and thus too quick to see him as a contrast to both her father and her wastrel brother, Halo tells herself that "she ought to be able to love him" and that, even if she cannot, she will, "at any rate . . . never willingly cause him any pain" (p. 190). Entering into her marriage with Tarrant, consequently, with nothing motivating her that is quite so potent as her desire to get away from her parents, Halo finds it difficult to maintain any sense of obligation to the marriage when she discovers that her husband, himself too much a product of the times, is cold, selfish, and as immature as her parents. Halo and Lewis's childlessness, representative for Wharton perhaps of the emptiness of their marriage, aggravates the situation. Halo herself believes that things might have gone better "if between her and her husband there had been a presence, warm and troublesome and absorbing, to draw them closer yet screen them a little from each other" (p. 195). Lacking such a presence, each is thrust against the other's faults and turns away, Halo to Vance and the encouragement of his work, through which she gains a vicarious gratification, and Tarrant, petulantly, to his growing self-absorption—both, finally, victims of an age unconducive to real personal growth and to marriage, which Wharton, of course, sees as so often linked to such growth.

Hence, despite the Weston and Tarrant marriages, Wharton's faith in matrimony itself as providing potential benefits along with its pain remains. In *The Gods Arrive*, Frenside, again serving as Wharton's wise observer, notes that becoming lovers, as Halo and Vance do in this sequel, offers none of the advantages of marriage; he asserts, "We most of us need a framework, a support—the maddest lovers do. Marriage may be too tight a fit—may dislocate and deform. But it shapes life too, prevents lopsidedness or drifting."[19] None of Wharton's works, however bleak any marriage presented may be, contradicts this view. The failures Halo and Vance undergo in marriage are ascribable to shortcomings in them imparted by their backgrounds and not to weaknesses in matrimony itself.

1. Edith Wharton, *The House of Mirth* (New York: Scribner's, 1905), p. 104.

2. For additional comments on determinism in *the House of Mirth*, see Nevius, p. 56; Lindberg, pp. 45–48; and Margaret B. McDowell, *Edith Wharton* (Boston: G. K. Hall, 1976), p. 52.

3. Lindberg, p. 62.

4. Wolff sees Nettie's baby in less affirmative terms, regarding "Lily's powerful identification with the baby [as] silent testimony to the infantilizing force of the mutilating image of women that society fosters" (p. 130). Also apparently unimpressed by the Struther marriage as a means by which Wharton expresses faith in matrimony is Judith Fetterley, who asserts that in *The House of Mirth* "marriage is deadly because it is an economic transaction in which the beautiful object [woman denied her indentity] becomes the possession of the man who has money enough to buy her" (" 'The Temptation to be a Beautiful Object': Double Standard and Double Bind in *The House of Mirth*," *Studies in American Fiction* 5 [Autumn 1977]: 205). Certainly both Wolff and Fetterley make valid points here. Lily *is* infantile, marriage in her milieu *is* often ugly; but one must add too that Wharton had faith in the institution, believing it could be better than it is through much of this work and could help women grow.

5. R.W. B. Lewis, *Edith Wharton: A Biography* (New York: Harper & Row, 1975), p. 181. Other commentators who have regretted what they perceive to be the blurred focus of this novel include Henry James, Edmund Wilson, E. K. Brown, Q. D. Leavis, Margaret B. McDowell, Louis Auchincloss, and Geoffrey Walton. For a fuller discussion of *The Fruit of the Tree* than I have undertaken in this chapter, see my "Wharton's *Blithedale*: A New Reading of *The Fruit of the Tree*," *American Literary Realism* 12 (Autumn 1979): 330–37.

6. Edith Wharton, *The Fruit of the Tree* (New York: Scribner's, 1907), p. 292.

7. Wolff, p. 143. Geoffrey Walton notes that Amherst, "an intense individualist," has "little real feeling for other individuals" (p. 94).

8. Nevius, p. 101.

9. Lewis, p. 181.

10. Wolff suggests that Justine fails to reach this serenity and moral maturity because she has inchoate sexual longings that find no adequate outlet or satisfaction (p. 142). The question of Justine's sexual needs does not seem to me to be an issue in this novel. Rather, like Marilyn Jones Lyde, I am inclined to believe that the issue is whether Justine will learn the value of "balancing individual idealism and social necessity." Clearly, Justine seems to. See Lyde's *Edith Wharton: Convention and Morality in the Works of a Novelist* (Norman: University of Oklahoma Press, 1958), pp. 91–92. Also, Elizabeth Ammons notes aptly that Wharton would create few other characters as "splendid as Justine Brent, or as betrayed" (*Edith Wharton's Argument with America* [Athens: University of Georgia Press, 1980], p. 55).

11. Though most commentators regard the novel as a satire, many see elements in it that bring about a clear departure from the satirical tone. Louis Auchincloss asserts that "Wharton hates Undine too much" (*Pioneers and Caretakers* [Minneapolis: University of Minnesota Press, 1965], p. 38). Nevius sees the situation in similar terms (p. 152). McDowell suggests that the "intensity" of Wharton's portrayal of Ralph is an exception to "the consistency of tone in this satirical comedy" (p. 81).

12. Elizabeth Ammons notes that it is "not Undine Spragg, self-centered and insensitive as she is, but the institution of marriage in the leisure class [that] constitutes the main target of Wharton's satire in *The Custom of the Country*"("The Business of Marriage in Edith Wharton's *The Custom of the Country*," *Criticism* 16 [Fall 1974]: 327). Certainly the marriages one sees here are just as unsuccessful as those glimpsed among the leisure-class marrieds in *The House of Mirth*, but, as with the earlier work, it is clear that criticism of these marriages does not constitute an attack on the institution of marriage itself, in whatever class it exists.

13. Edith Wharton, *The Custom of the Country* (New York: Scribner's, 1913), p.206.

14. Edith Wharton, *Twilight Sleep* (New York: Appleton, 1927), pp. 324–25.

15. Edith Wharton, *A Backward Glance* (New York: Appleton, 1934), p. 207.

16. Lyde notes that Nona's "loss of belief in life" represents "the negation of Mrs. Wharton's primary moral values: truth and belief" (p. 57).

17. Edith Wharton, *Hudson River Bracketed* (New York: Appleton, 1929), p. 392.

18. Nevius, p. 227.

19. Edith Wharton, *The Gods Arrive* (New York: Appleton, 1932), p. 311.

EDITH WHARTON
MORAL GROWTH AND MARRIAGE

HE BENEFITS that Wharton sees as deriving potentially from marriage are austere ones to be sure—so
austere, indeed, that they might make marriage seem
to many a less than enticing prospect. But Wharton, obviously, is not writing for the many. Rather, she aims at
those who can understand with her that the realities of life
and human nature preclude the possibilities of perfect happiness and long-sustained romance. Understanding this, they
can see, she hopes, the somber compensations that marriage
can offer: a stabilizing and solacing routine in a shifting
world, moral growth through committing oneself to another's well-being, and a sense of social responsibility through
learning to see oneself as a significant part of a functioning
society.

Largely comic in tone, "The Mission of Jane" (1904) is,
nevertheless, a story that conveys poignantly Wharton's
view about the solace and growth derived from marriage by
showing that however unhappy a marriage may be, it can allow two people to comfort each other in the face of any
greater unhappiness the world may heap upon them. Certainly, this is the lesson Lethbury learns after his wife, longing for the child they are unable to have, brings home the
exceedingly troublesome foundling Jane. Up until this time,
Lethbury, convinced "his marriage had been a failure" and
unpleasantly aware that "the world is surprisingly well
stocked with the kind of women one ought to have married
but did not," has slowly drawn away from his wife. Though
"he had preserved toward his wife the exact fidelity of act
that is sometimes supposed to excuse any divagation of feeling," for years "the tie between them had consisted mainly in
his abstaining from making love to other women" (1:368).
More intelligent than his wife, he amuses himself at her ex-

pense by making ironic jokes that pass over her head; colder than she, he fails to see her goodness, her sensitivity, and the pain that her loneliness causes her. However, as Jane, difficult from the first, grows up to be a humorless, overly assertive but not overly intelligent bluestocking, the Lethburys draw closer through trying to cope with her and to find someone imperceptive enough to marry her and take her off their hands. And when they do, at last, get her married off, they do not grow apart again. After the wedding Lethbury, with his hand on his wife's, asks her to "go off and have a jolly little dinner at a restaurant." In times past "such a suggestion would have surprised her to the very verge of disapproval," but now she "agreed to it at once." On this pleasant note, Wharton closes the story, commenting, "Jane had fulfilled her mission . . . she had drawn them together at last" (1:379). One might suggest, obviously, that marriage, even as depicted here, presents no real benefits; for without a marriage to begin with, there would have been no problem between the Lethburys and, hence, no need to adopt Jane, but this is to miss Wharton's point. As she sees it, there are always cold, self-isolated people such as Lethbury, whether married or not; but if they are married and, consequently, intimately exposed to the needs of others, they have more of a chance to grow and even find a bit of warmth in a frigid world than they would have were they single.

That this possibility should not be dismissed as negligible is revealed in *Summer* (1917). Though the marriage of Charity to her guardian, the elderly Lawyer Royall, which closes the work, is obviously not the sort of marriage one envisions as the most appealing for an attractive young woman to make, it does not "ominously darken the ending," as one commentator has suggested.[1] One must not forget that Charity's fate should she not marry Royall would be far more "ominous" and "dark" than it is with the marriage. The daughter of a prostitute and an alcoholic felon, Charity, pregnant and abandoned by her lover, has no family to turn to. Royall himself has been the source of the only stability she has known. Seeking her mother's aid in an outcasts' community in the mountains near her town, she finds the woman, whom she barely remembers, lying dead on a rank, unmade cot, surrounded by raucous, drunken louts, who carouse as the corpse bloats and corrupts. This is the world from which marriage to Royall rescues her. She can, with the marriage, have her baby—the compassionate lawyer accepts the situation—and thereby avoid what Wharton sees as the horror of abortion; moreover, she can be sure that she and the child can live comfortably in a settled community. Finally, Royall, himself a reformed alcoholic and womanizer, will, to all evidence, be a devoted and understanding husband. His delicacy in not getting into bed with the exhausted and frightened Charity on the first night of their marriage and in pretending instead to fall asleep in a chair inspires gratitude and affection in the girl and a deep realization that "she was safe with him."[2] Her last words to Royall in the novel, "I guess you're good, too" (p. 291), are not, to be sure, romantic ones; but they indicate her confidence in this man toward whom in the past she has had an aversion, confidence that augurs well for their marriage. Doubtless it will lack the passion of her illicit relationship with Harney, but it offers something Wharton sees as more valuable and longer lasting: a modicum of security and mutual trust in a world in which disorder and mistrust are too often the rule.

In "The Other Two" (1904), "The Letters" (1910), and, most significantly, The Age of Innocence (1920), Wharton shows in detail the sort of moral growth that marriage can inspire. In the first, Waythorn, a refined New Yorker of the old school, finds that his marriage to a twice-divorced woman leads him to question some of his narrower time-honored assumptions. Heretofore, "Waythorn was an idealist. He always refused to recognize unpleasant contingencies till he found himself confronted with them, and then he saw them followed by a spectral chain of consequences" (1:391). With his marriage to Alice, however, Waythorn comes to see that idealism is suspect and that unpleasant contingencies abound but that their train of consequences can be both diminished and rendered less frightening if one approaches them with common sense, an awareness of one's own fallibility, and a sense of humor.

At first, Waythorn's idealism leads him into two serious mistakes with regard to his marriage. Unable to see his new bride initially in anything but sentimentalized terms redolent of "some old trail of verse about . . . garlanded nuptial doorposts" (1:380), he has convinced himself that her first two husbands were totally to blame for the failures of their marriages to Alice. He conceives of the first, Haskett, as some sort of brute who "remained in the outer darkness from which his wife had been rescued" (1:382) and of the second, Gus Varick, as a genial but boorish and promiscuous sort to whom no woman of refinement would wish to stay married. Also, Waythorn believes that marriage can exist far removed from the world and its often unseemly influences. Through his marriage he becomes disabused of both of these notions. It is not long before he learns that neither Haskett nor Varick is a bad sort and that his marriage, rather than isolating him from the world, not only brings him into close contact with it but teaches him, as well, the folly of seeing himself as above it.

Through his unavoidable meetings with both of his wife's former husbands, Waythorn discovers not only that neither is a scoundrel but that each has played an ineradicable part in shaping his wife's character. More, he is troubled to perceive that the tact with which she copes with finding herself and her husband thrown into contact with her former mates grows out of an innate "pliancy" that "was beginning to sicken him" (1:393). She is, he observes, "'as easy as an old shoe'—a shoe that too many feet had worn . . . Alice Haskett—Alice Varick—Alice Waythorn—she had been each in turn, and had left hanging to each name a little of her privacy, a little of her personality, a little of the inmost self where the unknown god abides" (1:393). Knowing now that it is this pliancy that attracted him and to which he owes the domestic contentment he has previously found with Alice, he tries sardonically "to trace the source of his obligations . . . he perceived that Haskett's commonness had made Alice worship good breeding, while Varick's liberal construction of the marriage bond had taught her to value the conjugal virtues; so that he was directly indebted to his predecessors for the devotion which made his life easy if not inspiring" (1:394). Finally, though, the bitterness implicit in this line of thought gives way to something else. As the story ends, with Alice serving tea in Waythorn's library to each of her three husbands, Waythorn accepts with a wry appreciation what he cannot change, and takes "the third cup with a laugh" (1:396).

His laugh at the close betokens more, though, than humorous acceptance of his wife's pliancy and his enforced and seemingly inescapable intimacy with her former mates. It seems to manifest as well his sense of a joke at his own expense for his former delusions.[3] No more, apparently, will he see himself as immune to buffeting by the indignities of life. No more will he be quick to look with the Olympian disdain of the well-bred New Yorker at the Mr. and Mrs. Hasketts of the world, whom he had condescendingly envisioned sitting, before their divorce, in a "'front parlor' furnished in plush, with a pianola, and copy of *Ben Hur* on the center table" and going, perhaps, "to a 'Church Sociable'—she in a 'picture hat' and Haskett in a black frock coat, a little creased, with [a] made-up tie on an elastic" (1:389). He knows now from contact with him that those in Haskett's milieu have their virtues, and he knows from contact with his wife that the barriers that separate that milieu from his own are not nearly as insurmountable as he thought. One can infer, further, that he is aware too from his acquaintance with both of Alice's former husbands that in their divorces, as in most, neither mate is alone to blame for the failure of the marriage, a perception that is a powerful corrective to the romantic speculations in which he has indulged. Thus, with the knowledge that his marriage brings him, Waythorn can now laugh at his earlier snobbishness, sentimental idealism, and fear of facing unpleasant realities. More open, tolerant, and at home in the world, he is a better person as a result of his marriage.

Similarly, Lizzie West, in "The Letters," grows through her marriage to a less than perfect mate. In this sardonic reworking of the Jane Eyre story, the exceedingly romantic Lizzie not only gets to marry her former employer after the death of his neurotic semi-invalid first wife but comes into a fortune as well. Unfortunately, as she learns after three years of marriage, there would have been no wedding had she not come into the money first. Though her three years with her husband have brought her to see that he is merely a charming, dilettantish loafer who lounges about in "smiling irresponsibility" (2:198), they have neither shaken her love for him nor prepared her for the realization of his cool duplicity to which she comes when she learns that he did not read the passionate love letters she wrote him before their marriage. Rather than being touched by them as he claimed to be, he never even opened them, totally forgetting Lizzie until learning that she had become wealthy.

Lizzie's first impulse on discovering the unhappy truth is to reject her husband. Lifting their baby son, she finds that "for the first time no current of life ran from his body into hers. He felt heavy and clumsy, like some other woman's child; and his screams annoyed her" (2:201). Worse, "the mere thought of [her husband's] caress was hateful" (2:205). Nevertheless, as she considers the romantic expedient of walking out on him, she wavers because she realizes that although "according to the laws of fiction" her husband, "having deceived her once, would inevitably have gone on deceiving her" (2:204), such has not been the case and he has deceived her in nothing else. While she wavers, her unmarried friend, Andora Macy, enters. As romantic as Lizzie herself has been up to this point, Andora, whose initial theory on learning about the letters is that some dark conspiracy launched against Lizzie's husband kept him from reading them, soon urges Lizzie to leave her monstrous spouse immediately. Seeing reflected in her foolish friend the folly of her own now-shaken romanticism and sentimentality, Lizzie quickly resolves to accept the situation in which she finds herself. To turn her back on marriage she now sees would be to turn her back on her identity, which is that of a married woman who, knowing her husband's faults, loves him anyway. Consequently, she rejects Andora's advice and, seeing her husband approaching, reflects, "The [three] years had not been exactly what she had dreamed; but if they had taken away certain illusions they had left richer realities in their stead." Her husband, she realizes, "was not the hero of her dreams, but he was the man she loved, and who had loved her." Finally, "she saw now, in this last wide flash of pity and initiation, that, as a comedy marble may be made out of worthless scraps of mortar, glass, and pebbles, so out of mean mixed substances may be fashioned a love that will bear the stress of life" (2:206). Such "richer realities" as the quiet wisdom and intelligent love reflected here, then, are what marriage, as Wharton sees it, has to offer to those perceptive enough to take them. Consequently, when Lizzie, in the last words of the story, tells her feverish friend, "Oh, poor Andora, you don't know anything—you don't know anything at all!" (2:206), she speaks for Wharton as well, to whom all the romantic Andoras of the world are just so many illusion-ridden fools who would do well to get married.

Another brought by marriage to perceive the folly of romanticism and, as well, the value of social forms—even restrictive ones—is Newland Archer in *The Age of Innocence*. By the close of the novel, Archer himself might praise, as Wharton does in *A Backward Glance*, "the value of duration" and all that "the traditions of three centuries have contributed to the moral wealth of our country."[4] By accepting the fact of his marriage to May, Archer accepts also the community and traditions to which it links him and the responsibility of working to maintain order even at the cost of his own personal pain. Wharton's evident approval of Archer's acceptance links *The Age of Innocence*, as Nevius notes, with her other late novels, which advocate "a strict sense of individual responsibility, regardless of the mitigating factors that may be involved." Moreover, as Nevius goes on to say, "the clearest suggestion that carries over from *The Age of Innocence* to *Hudson River Bracketed* and *The Gods Arrive* is that the pain of life must be accepted."[5]

At first there is little to lead one to believe that acceptance of the "pain of life" is indeed Wharton's lesson in *The Age of Innocence*. All, in fact, seems to point in the opposite direction, as anything—such as his rebelliousness in linking himself with Ellen—that would lead Archer from the world of the Sillerton Jacksons and Larry Leffertses appears to be an unmitigated good. But this clearly is part of Wharton's strategy in the novel. By leading one first into close involvement with Archer and his plight and then gradually distancing one from the agitated young man, she drives home skillfully how enticing yet finally how troublesome the rebellious impulses for perfect freedom and fervent romance can be.

Although the fifty years that, as Wharton occasionally reminds the reader, separate the events of the story from the time of the telling serve to distance one from Archer's emotional turmoil, the first half of the book, which closes with Archer's wedding to May, virtually forces the reader to identify closely with this young man in his quest for romance and freedom in a society that seems like nothing so much as an opulently appointed prison. Here, as Wharton comments caustically at the start, "what was or was not 'the thing' played a part as important . . . as the inscrutable totem terrors that had ruled the destiny of [Archer's] forefathers thousands of years ago."[6] Here too the series of formal scenes with which the first five chapters are replete—the operas, balls, ceremonial visits, and dinners—define, in Gary H. Lindberg's words, a way of life "so formalized as to become a ritual,"[7] so formalized, one might note, as to seem at this stage of the novel nothing short of stifling.

Seemingly no less stifling are the marriages briefly glimpsed in the first half of the novel. Archer's prospective in-laws, the Wellands, have an amiable enough union, but one in which wife and children are devoted to ministering cheerfully to every whim provoked in Mr. Welland by his hypochrondria. This rather healthy valetudinarian has, as Archer reflects subsequently, apparently put aside any "escapes and visions" he might ever have had and fearfully "conjured up all the hosts of domesticity to defend himself against them" (p. 295). The troubling vision of Mr. Welland constantly aided and abetted by loving family in a lifetime process of self-suppression stands before Archer all through his engagement to May as an extreme example of all that his culture seems to encourge and all that he seeks to avoid. Any misgivings the Wellands stir in Archer pale, however, before those awakened in him by the van der Luyden marriage. This coldly correct old couple, at once arbiters and embodiment of the values New York society holds dear, strike Archer, as he contemplates them in their mausoleum of a home, as being "gruesomely preserved in the airless atmosphere of a perfectly irreproachable existence, as bodies caught in glaciers keep for years a rosy life-in-death" (p. 50). Clearly, for Archer the loss of vitality inherent in Mr. Welland's self-willed invalidism is epitomized by the van der Luydens, whose approval of his plans to marry May strikes him increasingly as tantamount to a death sentence.

Were May herself presented differently in the first half of the novel, one's sympathy for Archer in his longing for freedom and romance would diminish appreciably, but such is not the case. Seen only briefly, May, in striking contrast to Ellen, seems merely to be what Archer considers her to be: one more in a long line of women in her family who, having gone through their youths with their eyes bandaged, never did look about them and "descended bandaged to the family vault" (p. 81). Consequently, she seems to offer him nothing but the prospect of an insipid marriage that will lock him into the ritualized social patterns and values of Old New York, a marriage, that is, which will inevitably become what Archer believes "most of the other marriages about him are: a dull association of material and social interests held together by ignorance on the one side and hypocrisy on the other" (p. 41). Certainly, this is the impression May herself conveys when, in response to Archer's desperate urgings that they stop being "like patterns stencilled on a wall" and somehow "strike out" for themselves, she replies laughingly, "Mercy—shall we elope?"; and it is quickly reinforced when in response to his taking this seriously as a sign of life in her and his begging her indeed to elope with him, she, a "litle bored," answers, "But that kind of thing is rather—vulgar isn't it" (p. 82). May's closing off the discussion by assuring Archer "I do love you, Newland, for being so artistic" (p. 82), only confirms one's impression that she is simply as empty-headed and dull a young woman as Archer fears New York society has shaped her to be.

Through the first half of the novel, consequently, the prospect of marriage to May strikes one as leading to nothing else but "the pitching down headlong into darkness" (p. 174) that Archer envisions as ahead for himself. The insipidness of the Welland way of life, the chill of the van der Luydens, May's apparent lack of imagination, and the pernicious silliness of Sillerton Jackson and Larry Lefferts all combine with the recurring occasions of stuffy formality to convey a sense of a society inimical to life and growth. As a result, one finds oneself close to Archer in his efforts to escape the nefarious clutches of this milieu. With Archer's wedding to May, however, a subtle change begins to take place; and though the third-person limited narrative point of view that prevails through most of the novel is still restricted mainly to Archer's vision, one's involvement with his quest and dissatisfactions wanes. Gradually one comes to regard him with a good deal of detachment, perceives the shortcomings inherent in his romanticizings, and, surprisingly enough, finds much that is admirable in the New York society that seemed so reprehensible in the first half of the novel.

Perhaps it is the solemnity of the wedding ceremony itself that fosters the change in one's perceptions. Though Wharton's account of the wedding as "a rite that seemed to belong to the dawn of history" (p. 177) and a "prehistoric ritual" with its "sacred taboos" (p. 180) is reminiscent of her sardonic depiction early in the work of "the thing" as a "totem terror," the tone here has no tinge of the sardonic. Instead, it apparently reflects Wharton's own wonder at the continuing power of the timeless ceremony to strike one with reverence. The door swinging "majestically open," sending the "murmur" of "the family" running through the large, expectant gathering, the best man's nervously whispered "Newland—I say: she's here!" the "music, the scent of the lilies on the altar, the vision of the cloud of tulle and orange-blossoms floating nearer and nearer, the sight of Mrs. Archer's face suddenly convulsed with happy sobs, the low benedictory murmur of the Rector's voice, the ordered evolutions of the eight pink bridesmaids and the eight black ushers" (p. 185)— all these time-honored elements of the ancient ceremony convey a sense of solemn grandeur that moves even Archer himself. For all his misgivings about the step he is taking, he lapses into the bridegroom's traditional nervousness, asking himself, "My God, *have* I got the ring?" as "once more he went through the bridegroom's convulsive gesture" (pp. 185–86). Observing this strangely moving rite, an event that does not neatly fit into the simplistic thematic framework of freedom versus repression within which one initially regards the novel as set, the reader can no longer view Archer as justifiably longing for liberty while being victimized by a mindlessly restrictive society. Such a reading, one begins to perceive, is a reductive and sentimental one in that it ignores the power of traditions to enrich lives and establishes the individual's emotions as the major guide to action. Moreover, as a result of Wharton's rendering of the striking power of this nuptial ceremony one can never forget through the rest of the novel that Archer's actions must, at least partly, be judged in terms of their effect on his wife, a perception that never allows the reader the virtually unlimited involvement with Archer's quest that heretofore obtained.

Indeed, from this time on, one's perception of May gradually becomes quite different from Archer's view of her, again increasing one's distance from him and from his perspective generally. Wolff's comment that May offers her husband "a true and honorable life"[8] because she embodies what Archer himself perceives to be "peace, stability, comradeship, and the steadying force of unescapable duty" (p. 208) is increasingly borne out as Wharton depicts the Archer marriage. May's good taste in avoiding scenes and bitter conflicts over Archer's behavior, her compassion for Ellen, and the quiet courage with which she goes about bringing her husband to a sense of his marital commitment and to an awareness of his responsibility for the maintenance of social order all win the reader's admiration, hence removing one farther from involvement in his febrile longings. This distancing from Archer becomes pronounced as one is increasingly aware of the pain to which May is being subjected by him, such pain, for example, as is particularly apparent on the night Archer is sent to pick Ellen up at the station on her return from Washington. As he sits with May later that evening in the library, lost in his thoughts of Ellen, Wharton notes, "he had taken to history in the evenings since May had shown a tendency to ask him to read aloud whenever she saw him with a volume of poetry" (p. 297). One senses, as he does not, May's hurt as, rebuffed once more, she turns quietly to embroidering a cushion for him, a task she does not like but performs anyway "since other wives embroidered cushions for their husbands" and "she did not wish to omit this last link in her devotion" (p. 297). Convinced as he regards her that May will never surprise him "by an unexpected mood, by a new idea, a weakness, a cruelty, or an emotion" (p. 298), Archer fails to perceive what May's "wan and almost faded face" at dinner earlier and "strained laugh" when (dreaming longingly that she might die) he patronizingly calls her "poor May" (p. 299) bespeak in the way of suffering.[9] Finally, the image of May, after the farewell dinner for Ellen, going to bed alone with head aching and with her "torn and muddy wedding-dress" (damaged on a carriage step) "dragging after her across the room" (p. 329) provides a poignant finishing touch to one's impression of her as a woefully undervalued, deeply hurt woman. Awareness of such suffering as hers, needless to say, precludes the possibility of one's caring terribly deeply about the romantic longings of the man causing her the pain.

Working with the wedding ceremony and the changing impression of May to distance one from Archer is the increasing shabbiness with which he is linked as he pursues Ellen. Following her to Boston, Archer emerges from the train station on a "steamy day" to enter streets "full of the smell of beer and coffee and decaying fruit," and with a "shirt-sleeved populace" moving through them "with the intimate abandon of boarders going down the passage to a bathroom" (p. 230). He speaks to Ellen briefly in an "untidy sweltering park" (p. 235) and then goes with her on a steamboat through the "oily undulations" of the bay in search of cool breezes. In the private room they take on the boat for their quiet discussion, they sit down at a table "covered with a coarse checkered cloth and adorned by a bottle of pickles and a blueberry pie in a cage" (p. 240). Such dingy circumstances, of course, undercut ironically Archer's notion that his devotion for Ellen is imbued with an aura of high romance. Instead, Wharton uses these features of the setting to symbolize the moral shabbiness of this illicit infatuation he nurtures. Ellen, far more worldly than Archer, realizes, as he does not, that this shabbiness of both environment and moral vision inevitably awaits all who embark on liaisons such as he longs for with her. She declares of the realm of true love, which he hopes they can find together, "I know so many who've tried to find it; and, believe me, they all got out by mistake at wayside stations: at places like Boulogne, or Pisa, or Monte Carlo—and it wasn't at all different from the old world they'd left, but only rather smaller and dingier and more promiscuous" (p. 293).

Nor is the shabbiness to which Archer is tied in the second half of the novel merely one of environment. Increasingly one finds him linked with characters whose rebellion against social norms renders them dangerous or foolish. In one of Archer's more ludicrous moments, he devotedly kisses the handle of a parasol that he believes is Ellen's. Instead, it belongs to the "largest of the Blenker girls, blonde and blowsy, in bedraggled muslin" (p. 226), who, seeing that her sister had dropped it, declares proudly, "We Blenkers are all like that . . . real Bohemians!" (p. 227). To Wharton, however, "Bohemian" is little more than a term redolent of carelessness, slovenliness, and silliness. Similarly "Bohemian," one supposes, is Ellen's Aunt Medora, a pathetically romantic decadent, who, by the end of the novel, has "worn out the patience of all her other relations [apart from Ellen] just at the time when she most needed looking after and protecting from matrimonial perils" (p. 241). Clearly, should Archer succeed in getting Ellen to run away with him, it is the Aunt Medoras of the world with whom he would find himself invariably associating. More sinister than the Blenkers or Aunt Medora but nonetheless someone whose course is not terribly far-removed from that which Archer persists in following is Julius Beaufort. Though this womanizer and embezzler is obviously a more sordid type than Archer ever is, his rebellion against the rigorous standards of polite society is a cautionary reminder of all the ugliness with which one involves oneself when one begins to indulge in shoddy behavior. Significantly tying the roguish Beaufort intimately to Archer is the fact that Beaufort too manifests a strong illicit longing for the beautiful Ellen. Linked, then, by his infatuation to such people as these, Archer, Wharton implies, is embarked on a course that is a hideously misguided one.

Once the reader's sympathies are tied to May rather than to her husband, they become increasingly tied as well to the society that shaped her. Though one can never see this society as a perfect or even a very interesting one in which to live, one does come to see that it has its worth; and when Gary Lindberg asserts that "Old New York is obviously not a satisfactory social order, but it is a social order,"[10] he gets precisely at what Wharton perceives that worth to be. By the very virtue of being an "order," Old New York society, as Wharton presents it, does promulgate and enforce certain values, and those particular values that it promotes are not ones she takes lightly. Business probity, family loyalty, marital fidelity, and the maintenance of decent appearances make, she believes, for a stable and humane if somewhat stuffy and unadventurous society. Perhaps lacking in romance, this society is also lacking in the shabbiness and wrecked lives in which romance often ends.

The life Archer leads when he finally gives up his dream of Ellen and resignedly takes his place in this society is anything but shabby or wrecked. As concerned citizen, affectionate husband, and attentive father, "his days were full, and they were filled decently" (p. 350). Though lingeringly aware that he has missed "the flower of life," he has come to see "it now a thing so unattainable and improbable that to have repined would have been like despairing because one had not drawn the first prize in a lottery" (p. 350). Unlike the Julius Beauforts, Aunt Medoras, and "Bohemian" Blenkers, he has worked to hold things together and to provide a framework of civility in which the young, including his own unexceptionable and loving children, might be nurtured. Moreover, although he has never really been able to love May or to value her properly, "their long years of marriage together had shown him that it did not so much matter if marriage was a dull duty, as long as it kept the dignity of a duty"

(p. 350). By maintaining that "dignity," Archer never lets his marriage lapse into the "mere battle of ugly appetites"(p. 350) that such a marriage as his might otherwise become. Thus does Archer grow through his marriage. Forced by his wife's pregnancy to give up his rebellious quest for unattainable romance, he finally accepts his marriage and, accepting it, gradually comes to admire the society that his marriage helps maintain, so much so, in fact, that by the end of the novel, the now elderly Archer can reflect, one assumes with Wharton's full agreement, that "after all, there was good in the old ways" (p. 350).

In a few stories—and given what James called Wharton's "fine asperity," one need not be surprised that they are just a few—Wharton does see a greater good than solace or even moral growth as possible in marriage, and this is the possibility of love. Though she generally avoids depictions of marriage characterized by perfect love,[11] she closes two works with weddings that serve as deeply felt affirmations of marriage as nothing less than the embodiment of the hope that lasting unions characterized by beauty and intimacy can be established in a grossly imperfect world. Thus, in "The Last Asset" (1908), even the cynical newspaperman Garnett perceives this after managing to bring together for their daughter's wedding his dissolute acquaintance Mrs. Newell and the misanthropic husband she deserted so that she might carry out her itinerant course of promiscuity in Europe. Though the groom's conservative family would not have allowed the marriage to take place had they known of the separation of the bride's parents, Garnett still wonders, until the marriage ceremony, whether his role in bringing about the wedding is worthwhile. Observing the nuptial rites, however, he comes to realize the value of what he has done: "Through the glow of lights and the perfumed haze about the altar, Garnett's eyes rested on the central figures of the group, and gradually the others disappeared from his view and his mind. After all, neither Mrs. Newell's schemes nor his own share in them could ever unsanctify Hermione's marriage. It was one more testimony to life's indefatigable renewals, to nature's secret of drawing fragrance from corruption . . ." (1:615).

A similar affirmation of marriage as one of "life's indefatigable renewals" occurs in the novella *The Old Maid* in Wharton's *Old New York* (1924), when Tina's marriage redeems at least partially the wasteland of her mother's existence. Such affirmation seems not to be in the offing, however, when the story opens with Delia Ralston's grim musings on the stifling nature of marriage, particularly marriage in "good" society. Looking back over her own transition from fearful newlywed to bored wife, Delia finds little to commend in marriage:

> . . . There was the large double-bed; the terror of seeing him shaving calmly the next morning, in his shirt-sleeves, through the dressing-room door; . . . a week or a month of flushed distress, confusion, embarrassed pleasure; then the growth of habit, the insidious lulling of the matter-of-course, the dreamless double slumbers in the big white bed, the early morning discussions and consultations through that dressing-room door which had once seemed to open into a fiery pit scorching the brow of innocence.
>
> And then, the babies; the babies who were supposed to "make up for everything!" and didn't—though they were such darlings, and one had no definite notion as to what it was that one had missed, and that they were to make up for.[12]

Reinforcing the sense of suffocation conveyed by Delia's thoughts are some of the artifacts decorating her bedroom and drawing room. In the former an ormolu clock representing a rural swain surprising a shepherdess with a kiss is a vivid reminder of the romance that slips farther from Delia with every stroke of the minute hand. On the wall of the drawing room, the steel engravings of Cole's "Voyage of Life" and a life-size statue of "A Captive Maiden" symbolize a destiny of imprisonment that Delia feels only too keenly. Not surprisingly, when Delia learns that her cousin Charlotte has given birth to the illegitimate daughter of the romantic Clem Spender, to whom Delia herself has always been attracted, she responds with envy as well as concern. Indeed, jealousy as well as family responsibility motivates her when she intercedes to stop Charlotte from marrying her husband's cousin. In like manner her decision to adopt the "foundling" who, in reality, is Charlotte's child grows out of a mixture of motives, with generosity mingling with a bored married woman's longing for vicarious romance as she assumes for herself Charlotte's legitimate role as mother of Clem's child.

With such a beginning, *The Old Maid* might seem another of Wharton's tales of marital entrapment, but it is not. Delia's sense of entrapment is real, of course; however, it is more than offset finally by Wharton's affirmation of the beauty that marriage can involve. The process of affirmation begins when, years after her husband's death, Delia learns that he knew all about the deception and was nonetheless quietly willing to give Charlotte's child, Tina, a good home as his adopted daughter. He knew that "somebody always has to foot the bill" (p. 151) for irresponsible romantics, and realizing, apparently, that as a married man he had a stake in maintaining civility, he chose to be that someone. This process of affirmation culminates when Wharton shows that Tina's own marriage, with which the story ends, will not only lead to a life of stability for her (which her background as a foundling jeopardized) and her husband (a young man whose family believes he needs to get "settled"), but will rescue her as well from the querulous, old-maidish behavior that has overtaken the unmarried Charlotte. Also, Tina's marriage will be for Delia the "compensation for all she has missed and yet never renounced" (p. 169) and will end for Charlotte long years of pain and silent anguish, as she sees that the legacy of her illicit love will not be a painful one. The kiss that Delia, in the last lines of the novella, urges Tina to bestow on her "Aunt" Charlotte at the wedding is at once a tribute to the long-suffering mother and a reminder of the generosity and compassion that marriage with its timeless but only rarely realized potential of joy and beauty can instill.

For all of the affirmation that attends the marriages in "The Last Asset" and *The Old Maid*, few marriages, assuredly, in Wharton's work are happy ones. None brings to full fruition the potential for lasting bliss or love that Wharton sees as the compelling promise of the institution. Granting this, as one looks over her numerous stories of marriage, one still sees a faith in matrimony that never wavers. Through all her writings, whether dealing with marriage or not, Wharton depicts the folly of purely personal quests after perfect freedom, untainted beauty, never-palling romance, and the like; and she teaches that such quests inevitably end in the chaos and shabbiness of mere self-indulgence. Against this she continually advocates the virtues of loyalty to family, to community, and to the lasting principles that make for a humane social order. And, as we have seen, imperfect as she knows it to be, she perceives marriage to be a major means of inculcating these virtues.

Early in this discussion of Wharton's fiction of marriage, I suggested that her belief that one can undergo moral growth through enduring a painful marriage was similar to James's thinking as reflected in *The Portrait of a Lady*. Clearly it is, but it is different too, because the moral growth that James envisions sets apart the one who grows—not, certainly, from relations with others and the commitments to them that must be honored, but apart in the sense of coming to a capacity for selfless love that transcends all mundane conceptions, that somehow partakes of the genuinely supernal and at the same time is so personal as to be essentially untranslatable save as partially manifested in behavior. For Wharton, on the other hand, the moral growth has no dimension for the individual that transcends social relations. It makes one a better person because it makes one a better citizen, a better member of the human community. Despite the difference, however, there is a romantic dimension to this teaching of Wharton's as there is for James's, because the humanely responsive community to which she seeks to exact loyalty from her characters is nonexistent, an ideal that grows out of her idealized remembrance of the "Old New York" of her youth, and as such every bit as removed from the reality of her time as James's imaginatively conceived vision of selfless love is from his. Like James, then, and, as well, like Howells in his frequent return to idyllic conceptions of marriage as a socially redemptive comradeship, and like Chopin in her belief that men and women are caught up in the irrepressible drive to authenticity, and, as we shall see, like Herrick in his highly idealized visions of what marriage in an increasingly corrupt America ought to be, Wharton's faith in marriage reflects a continuing penchant for romanticizing, surprisingly strong even in an age of ostensible realism.

Hence, largely unproductive of joy as they are, marriage and marriages, Wharton believes, must last; and, undoubtedly, she would find it not too much to ask of husbands and wives that they commit themselves to such an austere ideal of matrimony as that set forth by Howard Nemerov in "The Common Wisdom" when he asserts wryly of the enduring marriage,

Their marriage is a good one. In our eyes
What makes a marriage *good*? Well, that the tether
Fray but not break and that they stay together.
One should be watching while the other dies.[13]

1. McDowell, p. 70.

2. Edith Wharton, *Summer* (New York: Scribner's, 1917), p. 284.

3. Wolff asserts that Alice now seems to Waythorn "a grotesque, some specialized form of monster, endlessly mutating—willing to please, not malicious, but not—not quite—human" (p. 109). She misses, I believe, the tone of the ending. Waythorn regards the whole situation now—and particularly himself—from the saving standpoint of humor.

4. Wharton, *A Backward Glance*, p. 5.

5. Nevius, p. 218.

6. Edith Wharton, *The Age of Innocence* (New York: Appleton, 1920), p. 2.

7. Lindberg, p. 162.

8. Wolff, p. 325.

9. Lindberg notes that "all these ought . . . to be telling signs, but for Archer they are mere appearances" (p. 106) as he forgets the uncanny way in which people brought up in the world of Old New York as May has been can infer a great deal more than one ever shows explicitly and, similarly, can convey a great deal more than they state explicitly.

10. Lindberg, p. 109.

11. One exception might be *New Year's Day*, a rather silly and unconvincing novella in *Old New York* (New York: Scribner's, 1924) depicting Mrs. Hazeldean, who enters into a distasteful affair simply to get money to support the impecunious and fatally ill husband to whom she is so devoted.

12. Wharton, *Old New York*, p. 82.

13. Howard Nemerov, *The Western Approaches* (Chicago: University of Chicago Press, 1975), p. 28.

ROBERT HERRICK

*J*N 1919, AS HE SURVEYED HIS WORK, Robert Herrick asserted, "The one subject always to be found in my books is the competitive system—its influences upon men and women. Whenever I look back into these books, I find the one insistent question implied in almost every chapter, 'What is success?' "[1] Through most of his career, Herrick assured himself that he answered this question and in the process pointed up the pernicious folly of the "competitive system." Real success, he preached, resided in giving up the feverish pursuit of wealth and position in which so many Americans were caught up and in accepting the "common lot" of honest toil and warm human relations. He emphasized further, in several of his most significant novels, that a chief means, perhaps a crucial one, of bringing his countrymen to this more rewarding vision of success is the good marriage, one in which husband and wife continually reinforce each other's best impulses, thereby fostering generosity, honesty, industry—all, in short, that makes for contentment in people and health in nations. In espousing this doctrine, Herrick had one major problem, however, one that damaged his books both as literature and message: try as he might, he could not believe fully in what he was saying. The simple pleasures of the "common lot," the role of marriage in bringing about contentment, might all be very attractive to William Dean Howells; but ultimately they were far less enticing to Herrick, who once noted of himself, perceptively, "There was something within me, as in every pure-blooded New Englander, of the mystic, the transcendentalist, the idealist."[2] Though characterized by Larzer Ziff as one who "rose to continue the Howellsian grind"[3] and by Alfred Kazin as "one of the most serious and neglected pioneer realists of the Progressive era,"[4] Herrick was as much the romantic as the realist, yearning for a "success" that was, in fact, ineffable and transcendental, one that could never be found within the ostensibly realistic context in which his stories and themes were most often delineated.[5] Nonetheless, he long persisted in his halfhearted insistence that happiness could be found most readily in the Howellsian commonplace, never entirely convincing himself or the reader of the validity of what he was saying. That he did continue in this line results, one suspects, from an uneasy, incompletely understood concession on his part to the literary temper of his day. A novelist interested in the moral improvement of his or her compatriots, it was clear to Herrick's contemporaries, must, virtually by definition, focus on social issues and offer socially oriented theories of how improvement might be achieved, a judgment that Herrick, who must have felt in any case that his visions had to be grounded somewhere on the real American scene, found difficult to quarrel with if not entirely convincing.[6] Whatever the cause, though, Herrick's continuing effort to deny his deepest impulses in order to promote what he conceived to be the good of society imparts to his work a peculiar poignance; and nowhere, perhaps, is that poignance more apparent than in his portrayal of marriage, an institution about which he had grave personal misgivings, but which, until his last major novel, he forced himself to see as the cornerstone of the doctrine he espoused.

It may be that it was only to be expected that Herrick would have misgivings about American marriage. Certainly, neither the intellectual tradition from which he sprang in New England nor his own experiences with the institution were likely to imbue him with much faith in the redemptive power of matrimony.[7] Indeed, only the opposite could have resulted from his extended exposure to the traditional New England imperatives that personal growth is more significant than social accommodation and that such growth depends less on relationships with others than on an individual quest for a spiritual fulfillment that cannot be attained in society or shared with others.[8] Moreover, the influence on Herrick of this regional emphasis on going it alone in the search for spiritual values was doubtless reinforced by what he himself saw of his parents' marriage and went through in his own. His parents' union was a terribly unhappy one that blighted his childhood. As Blake Nevius notes, Herrick's father, "like the husbands in so many of Herrick's novels, . . . sacrificed himself, almost meekly, to his wife's ambitions" and allowed himself to be drained of money and health by the "count- less . . . modes of conspicuous consumption that his wife adopted."⁹ The unhappiness of Herrick's own marriage, which ended in divorce, was manifested in his extramarital relationships and in his grim comment after the divorce that his former wife "would be really happier" if "she could only be convinced that she had done me all the harm possible— that mine is an *oeuvre* completed and finished."¹⁰ There was little in either marriage, clearly, that would not join with the New England background in leading Herrick to suspicion of the institution he attempted to promote through most of his career.

Indications of Herrick's lack of an abiding faith in marriage as a means to both individual salvation and national spiritual recovery are as apparent in his works advocating matrimony as they are in *Waste* (1924), the late novel in which he implic- itly disavows his longtime advocacy of the institution. One obvious sign, of course, is the preponderance of dismal mar- riages he presents in these works. However, the mass of un- happy husbands and wives is as much a sign of Herrick's be- lief that the competitive pursuit of wealth blights all aspects of American life, including marriage, as it is an indicant of his lack of faith in matrimony itself. More revelatory is the man- ner in which the good marriages in Herrick's work are pre- sented. They are rarely seen from the inside, rarely shown, that is, with the wealth of particularizing detail that makes a number of the marriages, both good and bad, delineated by a Howells or a Wharton seem fully realized ones. Instead, Her- rick usually presents his happy marriages in such vague, idealized terms as to remove them from any recognizable so- cial context—not, ultimately, to create a compelling Jamesian romantic vision of marriage as a realm of tragedy that spurs painful growth nor to establish a no less compelling romantic vision, such as Wharton's, of a society tied to eternal principles of civility and order, but simply to blunder into vapid romanticizings that are not compelling, only implausible. Further, Herrick's presentation of his good marriages in idealized terms is part of a general tendency in his presentation of virtually all marriages toward such undue simplification of the makeups of his marrieds, the conflicts that embroil them, and the moral issues involved and toward a prose style so portentous in tone, inflated, and, at times, even feverish as to impart to his marriage novels qualities of both the crudely melodramatic and the crudely allegorical. Though melodrama and allegory are not out of place in such visionary, nonrealist novels as *The Healer* (1911) and *A Life for a Life* (1910), which Herrick described as "idealistic romances so-called . . . where I deal with large spiritual themes, and the characters are types, the action almost always symbolical, etc.,"[11] they are greatly at odds in the marriage novels with his insistence that happiness resides in accepting the "common lot."[12] For one to embrace this "common lot," he must, of course, dispense with the impulse toward ideality, which involves transcending or ignoring the actual social context, and which for Herrick typically manifests itself in the allegorical and melodramatic modes, which can only seem clumsy, blatant, and crude when imposed on novels ostensibly celebrating the commonplace. Unable, in fact, to find value in restricting himself to the commonplace realm in which marriage typically operates, Herrick is inadvertently arguing against himself in his novels espousing marriage, for the lessons he is supposedly asserting are undercut by the very manner in which he asserts them. Not surprisingly, the result is invariably to make these works something less than convincing.

Herrick's uneasy avowals of faith in marriage and his long-withheld subsequent disavowal can best be explored by focusing on four novels that mark clearly delineated stages in his thinking on the subject. In *The Gospel of Freedom* (1898), Herrick's first extended treatment of marriage, he explores at length two factors that make so many American marriages unhappy ones and offers a glimpse of an idealized marriage that is meant to serve as an alternative to what he saw actually taking place between most American husbands and wives. In *The Common Lot* (1904), Herrick attempts to show how an unhappily married pair can fight off the corrupting influences of the American competitive system and turn their marriage into a perfect amalgam of virtue and contentment. *Together* (1908), Herrick's major marriage novel, presents both his most vehement indictment of marriage as it exists in modern America and his fervent vision of how it might be. Finally, in *Waste* (1924), Herrick's last significant novel, there is no longer evident even a pretense of faith in marriage as a means of offering a sensitive person or, ultimately, a troubled nation an opportunity for fulfillment. *All* marriages he now regards as either inextricably bound up in corruption or, at the very least, as a hindrance to the development of all that is best in the individual.

The major theme in *The Gospel of Freedom*, Herrick's first novel,[13] is one that would be central to his career, intimately tied to his attempt to define real "success." It is, essentially, the struggle between the individual's desire for personal liberty and the "conditions of life."[14] Herrick seeks, in other terms, "the new religion which could touch the spirit of modern man"[15] and resolve the question of whether man ought to "retreat from the world into the self . . . or to accept the world as it comes to hand."[16] This "new religion" or resolution of the conflict between commitment to self and commitment to others is embodied in Adela Anthon's long-delayed realization that true freedom consists not in striving egotistically for some personal attainment of transcendent and ineffable beauty, grandeur, and achievement that are inherently unrealizable but, instead, in an immersion of oneself into the commonplace and in a willing acceptance of responsibilities and commitments to others. Crucial in bringing Adela to this realization are the failure of her own marriage and the contentment that she knows is inevitably to be achieved in the marriage of her friends Thornton Jennings and Molly Parker. Had Herrick been able to make the success of the latter marriage as convincing as the failure of the former, *The Gospel of Freedom* would not only be a far more effective statement of where happiness is to be found and of how a good marriage is central to such happiness but it would have been, as well, a far better novel than it is.

The fundamental weakness of this novel lies, then, in Herrick's inability to make its affirmation, based largely on marriage, either believable or compelling. This, as I noted, would be a problem too with Herrick's subsequent marriage novels, deriving from a basic lack of faith in the institution he was attempting to promote. In this novel the affirmation not only fails to convince but its impact on what is effective in the book is harmful. Nowhere is this more apparent than in Herrick's portrayal of Adela's marriage with John Wilbur. In delineating the background of the marriage, John and Adela's unhappiness together, and their breakup, Herrick makes the Anthon-Wilbur union a telling example of all too many American marriages of his day as he sees them, marriages that are at once the result and perpetuators of the corruption pervading the national scene. Unfortunately, much of the power of this portrayal is diminished by the vapidity of the moralizing strain that runs through the work in the pious speeches of Jennings and Molly and that culminates in their marriage, a union that ostensibly drives their lessons home to Adela, thereby providing the story with its affirmative conclusion. The one-dimensional nature of Herrick's portrayal of this relentlessly virtuous pair and the cloying vision he implicitly conveys of what their marriage will entail ultimately force the novel into a context of ideality in which the salience of the unpleasant facts of American life revealed through the Wilbur marriage is eroded. If such unpleasantness can be dispelled so easily by leaping into ideality, one wonders why it ought to be presented extensively or taken seriously in the first place. Thus does Herrick's predilection for an idealized vision of marriage detract from the authority of what is best in *The Gospel of Freedom*, which is his skillful presentation of an unhappy marriage as what Howells would have called a "modern instance"—a symptom, that is, of a malaise afflicting a great many American marriages.

Much of Herrick's success in portraying the unhappy marriage of Adela and John as both a reflection of their personal failures and of national shortcomings resides in the care with which he establishes that their reasons for marrying each other are not only all wrong but wrong, in large measure, because of the influence on them of the national outlook. Both Adela and Wilbur are presented as typical of a sort of young American prevalent in their era. The obvious similarities of each to James's Isabel Archer and Caspar Goodwood, respectively,[17] are symptomatic less of imitativeness on Herrick's part than of the prevalence in late-nineteenth-century America of highly promising yet uneasy and dissatisfied young men and women. Like Caspar and like Isabel before she marries Osmond, Adela and Wilbur are intelligent, aggressive, and exceedingly restless, as their relentless egotism, perhaps prodded by the seeming limitlessness of American possibility itself, forces them to resist confinement in the commonplace. Again, as with James's pair, the provoking egotism is manifested in different ways by men and women. Wilbur, like Caspar, throws himself into business competition. Adela, like Isabel lacking such ready outlet, is, like her, led by her egotism into more subtle combats. The main difference, of course, between Herrick's pair and James's is that Herrick's young couple marry each other. This is far more usual than what befalls Isabel and Caspar; and in his account of the disastrous results of this typically American mating, Herrick presents a provocative indictment of the national scene.

If the egotism of Adela and Wilbur makes the failure of their marriage an inevitability, it also makes virtually inevitable their decision to marry each other, since each is unhealthily attracted to the other's aggressive self-assertiveness. Adela is wealthy, pretty, and the "impulse of life" is "throbbing in her generously";[18] but as the product of an unhappy marriage between a power-hungry tycoon and a querulous snob, she is flawed by her legacy of "intolerance," an "iron will," and an insatiable thirst for "practical power," an inheritance that has been sublimated into a fitful quest after surpassing beauty and freedom. More, this legacy has made her so dissatisfied with her prospects as a woman that she is capable of declaring, giving "her egotism rein recklessly," that she, like all women, has only two bleak opportunities before her—"a husband, or a vocation badly filled" (p. 40). In John Wilbur, however, she sees another alternative, a means of satisfying her egotism by entering a relationship that will combine marriage and vocation. Wilbur, a rugged young inventor-businessman, seems to Adela not only to embody all the romance and procreative power of the American West itself but to offer her a chance to partake of this romance and power. A loan Adela advances him helps him complete his "Water-Hoister," an irrigation device that, according to one newspaper account, will "open up an era . . . when the desolate plains of the mighty Rockies shall flow with milk and honey, and the seat of the national capital shall be moved westward to the centre of a new civilization" (pp. 78–79). Convinced that her restless energy can find direction in prodding him to new achievement, the now-successful Wilbur asks Adela to marry him, assuring her that their marriage will be constructed along the most approved modern lines as a "partnership"; he asserts, in fact, "We have worked along shoulder to shoulder, like real partners, through the first big crisis I have had [and] marriage would be a closer partnership, longer . . . and more intimate" (p. 89). Not surprisingly, Adela finds this a most attractive offer. Though it entails marriage, about which she is, as we have seen, dubious, it is a marriage that is perceived by both as a pleasant businesslike arrangement, with room for affection, certainly, but devoid of the necessity for emotional commitment or for giving of oneself. As such, this marriage strikes her as not too large a price to pay for the chance to exercise power. Thus, Herrick reveals how the American identification of success with commercial and social force leads to the distortion of personal relations, with the effects nowhere more damaging than in marriage.

By establishing his newlyweds in Chicago, a city that, for Herrick, presents a landscape of unrestrained voracity and vulgarity, epitomizing all that is destructive in the headlong pursuit of worldly success, Herrick further makes them seem national types. Significantly, too, it is Chicago, embodying in extreme form the lust for power that brought Adela and Wilbur together, that most effectually drives the pair apart. For Wilbur, "Chicago was like a congenial Alpine air, which stimulated his appetites. From the very first the strife for advancement summoned all his virility. . . ." Adela, "on the other hand, remembered for many a day the sudden depression the fierce city had given her spirits that first March morning of their arrival" (p. 104). Herrick's point here, clearly, is not that Adela is somehow too morally fine to be at home in Chicago. Rather, it is that Chicago typifies egotism stripped bare of all the ideality with which Adela invested it by linking it in her own case with a vague longing for transcendence or in John's with the glory and romance of the fertile American West. Therefore, Chicago cannot be pleasant for her. As Herrick notes pointedly, Chicago is indeed "the first *fact* she had ever known" (p. 104); and this fact, that the lust for personal power is in its essence crude, ungovernable, and ruthless, is one from which Adela instinctively recoils, for it brings the insight that a marriage such as her own, founded on the ostensible partnership of powerful egos, is a very vulnerable relationship.

Any lingering illusion Adela may have after seeing Chicago and, worse, her husband's admiration of it, that her marriage to Wilbur is to be a lasting partnership is dispelled with crushing swiftness when Wilbur sells out his holdings in the "Water-Hoister" business, undercutting his associates in the struggling enterprise, and enters the world of Chicago high finance. The significance of this is not lost on Adela, who recalls that "their partnership was based upon faith in the idea of the "Water-Hoister" (p. 120), a device that by very virtue of its procreative function seemed to symbolize for her the promise she has imagined to be closely tied to power. Soon, the whole notion of partnership goes the way of the "Water-Hoister." Instead of being Wilbur's confidante and cohort, Adela finds, as she declares, that she is simply a wife whom he regards as having a "fine presence in dress" and as a singularly "clever woman" (p. 183) whose assignment is to "'make the home,' cultivate persons whom it is well to know; even entertain horrid, stupid people because her husband's interests are involved" (p. 108). Try as she will to "invest her new home, her clubs, and acquaintances with importance" (p. 120), she is unable to do so, and the birth of her child only makes her feel farther apart from her husband and the "partnership" she envisioned. Though Herrick believes it incumbent on a wife to struggle to improve even such a marriage as this, finding joy with her child and home until she can perhaps bring her husband to a humbler and more humane vision of success, this course is not one Adela is able to follow. Instead, she can only wail bitterly to Molly, "No! there is no freedom for women: they are marked incapable from their birth and are supported by men for some obvious and necessary services. Between times they have a few indifferent joys dealt out to them" (p. 110). With this realization comes a longing only for freedom and a fear that no commitment to another can be anything but imprisoning.

Accentuating Adela's disgust with her situation is Wilbur's increasing corruption. If Chicago strips the egotistical of what genteel restraints they may maintain, it also strips the greedy of any lingering ethical misgivings about their avarice and the ways they seek to appease it. Adela is revolted to find that Wilbur has participated in a deal that is little more than "a common swindle on the public brought about by a dicker between a knave and a gang of venal county legislators" (p. 125). Even more repellent to her is Wilbur's shamelessness about what he has done. Confronted by her on the issue, he airily replies that "a woman *can't* understand [that] business is like life" and one must "play *hard* all the time" rather than be "dainty" (p. 126). With her abhorrence of Wilbur's business chicanery, though, comes Adela's first perception that he alone is not to blame either for his own shortcomings or those of the marriage. Though she is not yet able to see that the fundamental difficulty confronting both herself and Wilbur is their egotism, she does at least perceive that they have both been shaped by a corrupt culture that led them into an idea of marriage that was all wrong. More, the source of the difficulty between her and her husband, she now sees, "dated some generations back, and it mattered little when the breach declared itself" (p. 165). Thus, Adela now views Wilbur as "not a bad man" (p. 126) but one "merely heartily of his times," to whom commercial scruples were "unintelligible" (p. 126). He is, in short, "the American peasant," a man whose quick rise to wealth "suddenly placed him in a world for which he had no traditions ready to assist him" (p. 180). Most significantly, she admits to Wilbur and to herself that she too is not blameless in the wreck of their marriage (which, with the death of their child through illness, now has nothing at all left holding it together). Trying loftily to lecture Wilbur on what marriage entails, she suddenly confesses, "I don't know. I have done you a wrong somehow" (p. 184).

Despite this awareness of her own share in the failure of the marriage and of the limits of Wilbur's culpability, Adela is still incapable of breaking out of her thralldom to egotism, still unable to see the truth of Molly's assertion to her that she is foolish to take her life and marriage as "a thorough course in self-development" (p. 99). Still desperate for perfect freedom and the attainment of some imperfectly conceived transcendent beauty, Adela goes to Europe and enters the tutelage of Simeon Erard, a Gilbert Osmond-like sterile dilettante whose appreciation of art is little more than a cover for his adoration of himself. Only the examples set by Molly and Jennings's selflessness and their marriage keep Adela from succumbing to Erard's subtle blandishments and entering into an affair or, perhaps worse, a marriage with this man whose interest in her resides chiefly in the opportunity he perceives for gaining not only a good deal of money but control over a beautiful woman whom he regards as little more than an *objet d'art* to be collected for his personal gratification. With her escape from Erard, who lures her with a vision of a life free of responsibility and commitment spent solely in the pursuit of pleasure and beauty and who seems virtually an allegorical representation of pure selfishness, Adela achieves her final growth in the novel. She is at last capable of realizing, through the influence of Jennings and Molly, that real freedom and beauty consist in overcoming egotism and are most fully manifested in forging lasting commitments to others.

Thematically apposite as it may be, the account of Adela's relationship with Erard severely diminishes the impact of *The Gospel of Freedom*. Though the decline of the Wilbur marriage is for the most part described in general terms rather than enacted, it is nonetheless a relatively convincing account of the increasing unhappiness of two misguided people, one made all the more compelling by the aura of inevitability surrounding their descent into misery, as the culture of which they are such consummate products channels them to a "success" that is terribly akin to the most painful of failures. From the recognizable social context in which the Wilbur marriage is depicted, however, Herrick veers into a framework of clumsy, unconvincing melodrama when Adela comes under the influence of Erard, a man who lacks even the veneer of social grace that makes an Osmond such a plausible villain. Shameless, blatantly vulgar for all his ostensible taste in art, Erard, unconcerned even with appearances, blithely roams through Europe while his long-suffering brother literally works himself to death supporting their indigent parents (and even sending Simeon money now and again to help finance his museum-hopping). Moreover, apart from his longing for power over Adela and her money, he seems incapable of passion. In essence, then, Herrick's characterization of Erard and his portrayal of Erard's dealings with Adela turn *The Gospel of Freedom* into the clumsiest of melodramas, reducing, unavoidably, the credibility of the depiction of the Wilbur marriage to which Herrick incongruously ties them.

The Erard characterization is unfortunately of a piece with those of Molly and Jennings, who do little more than deliver themselves of homely platitudes. The most telling of these in Adela's quest for fulfillment comes near the conclusion of the novel with Jennings's assertion that "there is no freedom and everyone is free. It is all a matter of feeling. And that feeling you cannot command" (p. 268). With this, Adela realizes that freedom is, "like love" (p. 268), not a matter of striving but of receptivity. From this time on, she will no longer grope for the unattainable but accept life as it comes, acknowledging the beauty of the commonplace. There is obviously nothing wrong with Jennings's notion here, or with anything else he and Molly declaim through the novel. The problem is, quite simply, that their moral maxims divorced from believable characters become mere saccharine commonplaces. Similarly, their marriage, meant to symbolize vividly the home-spun joys available to those who give up the ego-driven quest for transcendence, seems little more than a vapid contrivance because this pair has never been depicted in believable terms. Their marriage, then, smacks of the very ideality against which Herrick warns in his account of Adela.

Thus, the cumulative impact of Erard, Molly, and Jennings on *The Gospel of Freedom* is to render it a novel that fails to compel belief. The relatively interesting account of a failed modern American marriage is smothered by an overlay of ideality and heavy-handed melodrama. One senses that Herrick, no less than Adela, is grasping for a beauty that is ineffable and unattainable, one that he knows, whether he will admit it to himself or not, cannot be found in marriage. This conflict between what Herrick wants to believe is possible in marriage and what he actually knows to be the facts recurs in subsequent works, never failing to mar, as it does here, what is good in them.

Neither *The Web of Life* (1900) nor *The Real World* (1901), Herrick's next works of any note in which marriage figures significantly, breaks any new ground. In each a dissatisfied quester (Howard Summers and Jack Pemberton, respectively) finally finds happiness by giving up his grandiose aspirations and entering into a marriage that brings him into closer and more comfortable relations with the commonplace than he has heretofore known. *The Real World* also portrays a marriage (that of Elsie Mason) that is destroyed by the aggressive egotism of both husband and wife. There is little in either novel that is not seen with Adela, Wilbur, Jennings, and Molly. Moreover, as with *The Gospel of Freedom*, the aura of ideality Herrick establishes in both of these novels detracts from the credibility of the characterizations of marriages that are depicted in only relatively scant detail to begin with. In *The Common Lot*, however, Herrick, though unwilling to dispense with his penchant for ideality, attempts to provide a more extensive presentation of marriage than is evident in any of the previous novels. Almost by its very nature, however, the attempt fails, for marriage and ideality make an uneasy mix unless handled by one with the genius of a James for grounding the ideal (and the melodramatic mode through which it is often conveyed) in the real. Nonetheless, it is an interesting novel because it is Herrick's most extended effort up to this time to explore the commonplace in detail and a further revelation of his continuing lack of real faith in marriage as a means of ameliorating shortcomings in either individuals or society. The latter, of course, grows out of his underlying lack of faith in the value of the very commonplace about which he is so prone to wax eloquent and vitiates inevitably the effectiveness of any such exploration of the "common lot" as he attempts here.

Indeed, if Herrick had been able to dispense with the context of ideality in which he sets it, his account of the vicissitudes of the Hart marriage would not seem terribly out of place in a Howells novel, so close to Howells's views on marriage are the ones to which Herrick is ostensibly committed here. In *The Common Lot*, for example, Herrick for the first time shows, as Howells did, that marriage itself can change the people in it. Thus, unlike Adela and Wilbur, whose flaws remain constant and wreck their marriage, and unlike Molly and Jennings, whose unfailing virtue will surely make their marriage a good one, Jackson Hart in this novel finally becomes a better person because of the influences exerted on him through his marriage. Further, in *The Common Lot*, Herrick, again like Howells, attempts to show in far more detail than he did in *The Gospel of Freedom* the reciprocal effects exerted between a given marriage and its social context.

Nor is it merely in terms of Herrick's views on marriage that *The Common Lot* strikes a Howellsian note. The overtones of *A Modern Instance* and *The Rise of Silas Lapham* are unmistakable in Herrick's account of Jackson Hart's internal conflict and its impact on his relations with his wife. Hart, a promising young architect, must choose between prostituting his abilities in pursuit of a rapid rise in social status and wealth and developing them slowly in order to become a genuine creator and a benefactor thereby of society. At first he follows the path of corruption, doing showy and shoddy but highly remunerative work in which he often departs from agreed-upon specifications in order to increase the profit margin. However, the fire that destroys one of Hart's cheaply built hotels, killing many of the guests, destroys as well his greed and egotism. Shattered by what he has wrought, he turns, finally, to his wife, whom he has long neglected and who has left him on learning of the corrupt practices in which he has been engaging. Under the aegis of her integrity and healing love, Hart expiates his guilt and returns to humble work for the honest architect with whom his career had begun. He accepts now the "common lot" of devotion to home and craft that will make him a happier man and a better citizen. Thus through the fruition of marriage's potential for good does a Bartley Hubbard type assume the moral grandeur that a Silas Lapham finally attains—a Howellsian consummation the validity of which Herrick devoutly wished to assert.

But, as I noted, Herrick is ultimately *not* writing Howellsian novels or, whatever his intentions may have been, maintaining faith in a Howellsian vision of matrimony. Every aspect of his depiction of marriage that might seem reminiscent of Howells's work is undercut, as *The Gospel of Freedom* was, by ideality and one of its major manifestations in Herrick's marriage novels, as we have seen, crude melodrama. Clearly Herrick is trying to make a good marriage seem all the more attractive by presenting it in idealized terms and a bad one all the more appalling by setting it in the context of melodrama, but nevertheless the result is to make the vision of marriage he seeks to present here less convincing than it might otherwise have been. Marriage, he wants us to believe, is preeminently of this world, a means to fuller participation in the nourishing communion of ordinary folk. However, the vapory ideality and blatant melodrama into which his romantic impulses propel him deal in broad, even lurid, colorings and, hence, distortions of the world we know, unlike the subtly internalized melodrama one finds in James, which heightens and intensifies our perception of the world about us although seemingly departing it and rarely professing explicitly devotion to it. Consequently, although Herrick goes to some lengths in *The Common Lot* to provide a more "realistic" and affirmative vision of matrimony than he offers in *The Gospel of Freedom*, the very fact that he feels he must depart from commonplace reality to do so limits the effectiveness of his effort.

Hence, as a result of Herrick's one-dimensional, melodramatic rendering of it solely as a means to the ultimate avowal of an idealistic vision, Hart's decline into moral degradation is a bit too redolent of the *Ten Nights in a Barroom* school of writing. The evil tempting Hart is too crudely portrayed, too devoid of complexity and subtlety, even too obviously unappealing to convince one that a man like Hart, who is intelligent and who can love such a virtuous woman as the transplanted New Englander, Helen Spellman, could so readily succumb to it. Unconvinced by this, the reader is unable to believe that Herrick is indeed presenting the real world as he purports to be doing, and as a result finds Hart's subsequent redemption, involving as it does his resolve to accept the commonplace lot we know, difficult to credit. By this late stage of the novel, one can no longer quite bring oneself to believe that either Hart or Herrick knows what the "common lot" entails—knows, in short, that it is not without its failings just as the lives of the wicked who lust after mere self-gratification are not entirely without attractiveness and at rare times, perhaps, even value. Certainly, one becomes dubious about Herrick's gifts for observation after seeing him present Hart as drawn to a way of life embodied most sharply and typically in the vicious, social-climbing widow, Mrs. Phillips, who drove her decent husband to drink and an early grave, who coldly ignores her troubled, sensitive daughter, and who desires nothing more from her flirtations with Hart than to pull him down because "she considered all men base,—emotionally treacherous and false-hearted, and would take her amusement wherever she could get it."[19] Similarly, Hart's partner, the heavy-handedly named, dishonest contractor, Mr. Graves, has no existence save as an unremittingly corrupt money-grubber. Presented even in that role in the palest of terms by Herrick, he, like Mrs. Phillips, fails to be believable, therefore, either as a lure for Hart or as a character drawn from actual observation, such actual observation, that is, as would lead one to believe Herrick knows full well what he is speaking of when he lauds the virtues of the "common lot." Even Chicago, here as in *The Gospel of Freedom* virtually a metaphor for unrestrained egotism, is presented one-dimensionally and, consequently, uncompellingly and unconvincingly. The city, Herrick declares febrilely, has a "titanic, heartless embrace" (p. 189). Those trapped in its grip alternately drive themselves at "top speed" or, in rare interludes of quiet, fall together, "worried, fagged, preoccupied" (p. 52), often in fashionable restaurants "smutched" with a "soot" and "a thick sediment of ashes and coal dust" (p. 191) that are all too clearly symbolic of the moral filth of the city. Still, we are to believe that "the noise, the smell, the reek of the city, touched [Hart], folded him in, swayed him like a subtle opiate" (p. 63). What is wrong with all this, of course, is not the notion that men can be attracted to what is life-denying. We all know that they can be. The difficulty here is that Herrick's rendering of this one instance of this attraction is lacking in what James characterized as "felt life," lacking, that is, in vivifying detail derived from sensitive observation, in credibility, and, thus, in interest—lacking in all, really, save the moral outrage of one who is more the unremitting idealist than the artist. As such, as I have noted, none of this establishes a context in which Hart's triumphant self-immersion into the commonplace can be taken seriously.

Unconvincing for much the same reasons is Herrick's depiction of the Hart marriage. Both the decline of the marriage, as Hart falls headlong into corruption, and its subsequent renewal, as Helen helps him to expiation and regeneration, are rendered in the most monolithic terms. In neither phase of the marriage does anything occur that brakes either Hart's descent into the nadir of degradation or his rapid acceleration to the peaks of moral affirmation. Nor are there any moments in either phase in which Hart, like most people, manifests any real doubts about the course he is pursuing or even in which he sits down and talks in human terms to himself, his wife, or to anyone else about his motivations. With none of the psychological and emotional complexity of a real human being, he simply moves too rapidly from consummate despicableness to unadulterated virtue—neither of which is convincing in this context in the first place. Herrick, once again then, is sacrificing the credibility of both his characterizations and his portrayal of marriage as he resorts to the unabashed melodrama that is his invariable mode of conveying his idealized vision of reality in the marriage novels.

Consequently, from Herrick's portentous question at the time of the Hart wedding, "Did the woman know now that the man who stood there face to face with her, her husband, was yet a stranger to her soul?" (p. 115) to the moment when Helen leaves her husband, all one sees is a decline in Hart and the marriage, one that ostensibly takes place over years, but that seems nevertheless incredibly precipitate because of Herrick's single-minded devotion to focusing only on instances of degeneration in Hart. Almost immediately after the wedding, or so it seems, Hart is living well beyond his means and concluding that it is "just self-indulgence to build houses" (p. 149), as he and Helen had fondly dreamed he would. Rather, he declares, with neither compunction nor even an attempt at face-saving rationalization, that he will devote himself to "a larger business,—factories, mills, hotels,—work that could be handled on a large scale, roughly and rapidly" (p. 149). Of course, Hart's refusal to build homes obviously parallels his refusal to make his own home a happy one, as with dispatch he turns Helen, as much as Wilbur did Adela, into a mere appendage in his pursuit of worldly "success." Because the fashionable crowd would look askance at Helen's working in a settlement house, Hart compels her to give it up. Even Helen's innocuous, democratic habit of riding in streetcars rather than cabs is finally too *outré* for one with Hart's aspirations to allow it to continue. Thus, it is only to be expected that before long Helen realizes unhappily that she has been forced to become a "mere spender and enjoyer . . . of the money which came out of these ephemeral and careless buildings, whose pictures dotted the walls" (p. 187). This realization and the subsequent revelation that Hart has not only connived to get the contract for a trade school building funded by his late uncle's estate but is, further, actually cheating with Graves in failing to meet the construction specifications prompt Helen to take their children and walk out on this marriage to which her husband feels no real commitment and which Herrick has rendered in only the most simplistic of terms.

Epitomizing Herrick's failure throughout his account of the breakup of the Hart marriage is the scene in which Helen confronts Hart with her knowledge of his unethical practices. Sensitively rendered, the scene might have been a telling one, showing poignantly the futile efforts of an honorable wife to save her marriage by bringing her misguided husband to some sense of his errors. Such a rendering could have easily grown out of Herrick's conception of Hart as one who is weak rather than evil and is at last vaguely "troubled" and "distressed" that Helen has become "less loving, less passionate" toward him when, after all, as he finally resorts to rationalizing, it was "largely" for his family's "advancement in the social scheme of things" (p. 259) that he threw in with the Mrs. Phillipses and Mr. Graveses of Chicago. Sadly, this potential for building a powerful scene out of this briefly gimpsed, human, bewildered side of Hart does not come to fruition, as Herrick once again resorts to heavyhanded melodrama. Confronted with his dishonesty by Helen, Hart, "warmed by . . . liquor," becomes "insolent" (p. 288) and resentful of "her new tone of authority to him" (p. 290). He mutters accusingly, "You'd like to see me get into trouble" and "You make me out a thief at once" (p. 291). This Timothy Shay Arthur brand of luridness diminishes the effect of Helen's unhappy rejoinder, "I wish you were a clerk, a laborer, a farm-hand,—anything, so that we could be honest, and think of something besides making money" (p. 294). Her fervent declaration could in another context have been a moving one; but in this scene it seems merely sentimental, another melodramatic excess in a work irremediably marred by them.

Hart's regeneration after Helen's departure and the holocaust at the shoddy hotel he constructed is rendered as unconvincingly by Herrick as was Hart's decline. After the fire, Hart, acknowledging to himself that Helen left him because

297

"she had felt the leper taint, which had been eating at his heart all the years of their marriage" (p. 339), rushes to his late uncle's Vermont farm, where Helen and the children have gone to live. He is seeking not merely a renewal of Helen's love but the moral regeneration that she asserted was within his reach and that now seems to him almost as palpable as the New England landscape itself. As helpmate to Hart in his rise, Helen is depicted, unfortunately, as less a woman than as a part of the New England springtime scene, a setting that for Herrick symbolizes a lingering vestige of honor and moral courage in the American wasteland. Full of a rare "charm, like the delicate first bloom of Puritan women" (such women, presumably, as Helen herself, whom Mrs. Phillips called a "cold Puritan"), the New England spring gives promise of a "hidden, reticent beauty" (p. 360). Just as the scene with which she is identified suddenly blooms gloriously, Helen warms as she realizes that Hart is ready to be reclaimed, and she guides him along the "hard road" (p. 394) to expiation. (Too coincidentally, perhaps, one of their children recovers from a nearly fatal illness—the health of a couple's children often being for Herrick too convenient a means to be avoided for symbolizing the health of a marriage.) A better man, Hart returns to Chicago, testifies truthfully at the coroner's inquest on the fire, and decides that he and his family will be happier accepting the "common lot" in life rather than aspiring to what the world deems "success": "The woman and the child! These were the ancient, unalterable factors of human life; outside of them the multitudinous desires of men were shifting, trivial, little. For the first time in his life an indifference to all else in the world swept over him in gratitude for these two gifts . . ." (pp. 408-9). Acting on this decision, he goes back to his first employer, the honest Mr. Wright, and contentedly designs homes again—good homes for decent working folk. Thus does Herrick, like Howells before him, show how a good marriage while engendering a sense of commitment to wife and child can also develop in one a sense of social responsibility or "complicity," to use Howells's term once more. Fully aware now of his own complicity in the deaths of innocent people, Hart, under Helen's guidance, assumes in his career a sense of social responsibility that heretofore has been grievously lacking in him. (Presumably, such a sense of complicity will also be developed in Mrs. Phillips's daughter, Venetia, and Doctor Coburn, as Herrick, holding nothing back in his effort to build an affirmative ending, brings an otherwise extraneous subplot to its conclusion by ushering this pair to the nuptial altar.)

The problem, of course, with Herrick's affirmative conclusion to *The Common Lot* is the same one perceived throughout the novel. By resorting, in a work ostensibly set in a realistic framework, to unrestrained idealization, blatant melodrama, and such crude allegory as is inherent in the use of names like "Graves," and "Wright," and even "Hart" in lieu of vital incident to define character, Herrick sacrifices credibility and literary effectiveness, finally, for turgid, moralizing, sentimentality, and incongruous romance. Consequently, he fails to make a convincing case for the doctrine that a simple, unpretentious marriage and acceptance of a sense of social responsibility are the best means available of attaining happiness. Realism of the Howellsian stamp, such as Herrick is, at least in part, trying to deal in here, clearly does not mix well with his propensity of ideality. Unaware of this, Herrick often writes badly flawed novels; and, too much the romantic individualist ever to value marriage as much as he apparently wanted to, he inevitably depicted wedded life in ways that fail to convince.

The Memoirs of An American Citizen (1905), probably Herrick's most successful novel, offers in its accounts of the marriages of the Harringtons and Drounds a picture of the emptiness of far too many marriages in a society dominated by egotism; but this novel has far less to do with marriage than it does with the business world in Chicago and what that world reveals about the modern American lust for power. It is the panoramic vision of modern American matrimony *Together*, published three years later, that is Herrick's fullest treatment of the intimate, reciprocal relationship between the spiritual health of a society and the health of the marriages in it. In the course of this portrayal, he offers his most extensively developed and fervent attack on the tenor of many American marriages and his most idealized vision of what marriage could be were it not for the selfishness pervading the American scene. Moreover, in the course of his idealization of the institution, Herrick attempts to imbue marriage with a sense of mystery lacking in his portrayal of it in earlier works. He characterizes it here as a timeless, divinely sanctioned, even divinely inspired, means by which people attempt to accommodate themselves to each other and to their society.

As before, what keeps Herrick's vision of marriage as it is and as it might be in America from being terribly convincing is his inability or refusal to present marriages that bear much resemblance to those we know. This is evident, to be sure, with the bad marriages, which, as elsewhere, he presents one-dimensionally, often verging, as in *The Common Lot*, on melodramatic excess; but it is particularly marked with the happy ones, which are so idealized as to be positively cloying. The latter are made all the more alien to our experience by Herrick's insistence that they are linked to some benevolent, all-powerful transcendent force grounded in Nature (Herrick typically capitalizes this word in *Together*), a sort of Oversoul, apparently, that manifests itself as joy and procreative energy only to those who have rejected the lure of worldly success and have, by accepting the "common lot" as Jackson Hart did, aligned themselves with Nature and Spirit. This transcendent energy, which might almost have swept over into *Together* from Frank Norris's *The Octopus*, has devastating effects on the novel, for the attempt to link a portrayal of modern marriage to such a phenomenon inevitably runs the risk of sliding into the sentimental, even the bathetic; and sentimentality and bathos are morasses into which *Together* blunders with an unhappy facility. Further, such a notion as this type of "Life Force" is cannot do other than undercut Herrick's avowal of faith in marriage because, finally, it compels him to envision a beauty and dynamism that are difficult for the reader to conceive as graspable within the confines of a real marriage in the modern world. One can see, consequently, that even the best marriages in *Together*, idealized though they are by Herrick, fail to have his deepest commitment. In spite of all his best intentions to make them compelling embodiments of vital joy, they seem somehow not only too good to be true but also vaguely anachronistic and, worse, plodding and uninteresting, as if Herrick is revealing his belief that anyone with real spirit who seeks this divine energy will not find it in bonds of matrimony. Once again, therefore, difficulties arise because Herrick's romantic predilections make it difficult for him to carry out his obvious purpose, which is to present accurately, and ultimately to defend, an institution that is the very antithesis of romance. In the course of describing one of the marriages in *Together*, Herrick notes that to the knowing observer "the most commonplace household created by man and woman would be a wonderful cosmography."[20] Clearly, Herrick is committed to revealing this "wonderful cosmography," but he fails to do so by immediately leaping beyond the commonplace into the ideal and therefore never forging the union between simple households and transcendent value that he set out to establish.

Herrick's failure in *Together* to carry out a convincing portrayal of modern American marriage is all the more disappointing because of the effectiveness of the opening of the novel. *Together* begins with the marriage ceremony of Isabelle Price and John Lane, which Herrick uses tellingly to establish his vision of what is wrong with marriage in contemporary America. Though he shows that the ceremony is not without its awe-inspiring solemnity and grandeur as it enacts a timeless "mystery" (p. 4) in which the bride, like her mate-to-be, "stood before the veil of her life, which was about to be drawn aside" (p. 3), he skillfully reveals nevertheless that there is much in the present scene that detracts from the beauty of the ancient ritual. Thus, patrolling among the rich array of presents on display are "soft-footed detectives . . . examining the guests" (p. 15). No less discordant a note is struck by one of the fashionable guests, the worldly, cynical Fosdick, who comments chillingly that "Love and Marriage are two distinct and entirely independent states of being. . . . I have observed that few make them coalesce" (p.21). He objects, moreover, to the "savage glee" over marriage:

> "It's as though a lot of caged animals set up a howl of delight every time the cage door was opened and a new pair was introduced into the pen. They ought to perform the wedding ceremony in sackcloth and ashes, after duly fasting, accompanied by a few faithful friends garbed in black with torches." (P. 23)

Most devastating are the bride's own misgivings. Troubled by what she perceives as Lane's "look of mastery" (p. 5), she asks herself, "What was he, this man, now her husband for always, his hand about hers in sign of perpetual possession and protection?" (p. 5). She thinks too of her parents' "happy" and "very peaceful" marriage and reflects ominously that "hers must be different, must strike deeper" (p. 4). With the family of the bride distrusting the honesty of those at the ceremony, a guest (perhaps speaking for many) vocalizing his distrust of matrimony, and, worst, the bride herself distrusting her commitment and seeking a happiness that may well be unattainable in marriage, there is ample reason to suspect that the old words of the marriage ceremony merely cloak an emptiness at the core of most modern marriages and of a large part of modern life.

This suspicion is confirmed most fully in the novel by Herrick's depictions of the marriages in the Lanes' circle of friends. Though Blake Nevius suggests that all the marriages in *Together* were initially intended by Herrick principally to provide implicit "commentaries" on the Lane marriage,[21] they are there as well to establish that the difficulties confronting the Lanes are not peculiar to them but are typical of the problems arising in many marriages in modern America. More, Herrick shows, as Howells did in *A Modern Instance*, that such marriages, flawed as they are by the pernicious cultural forces about them, in turn become themselves part of the virulent national infection and damage other marriages. More specifically, Herrick shows here as he did in earlier works, though now on a grander, more panoramic scale, that the egotism, the lamentable drive for a personal, essentially tawdry "success" manifests itself in marriage as an inability to sustain ties of love and responsibility to mate and children, a failing with grave repercussions, Herrick believes, for all the marriages around the troubled union and finally for America itself.

Prime examples in *Together* of marriages marred by such selfishness are those of Isabelle's friends, the Falkners and Poles. The sexual desire that prompted their marriage sated, neither Rob nor Bessie Falkner is content in their union. Bessie's greed for possession and status (encouraged by her proximity to the overly fashion-conscious Lanes) turns Falkner into little but a chronically dissatisfied workhorse. As the marriage declines, the restless Bessie has, in turn, a powerful impact on Isabelle, heightening the latter's own restlessness and longings for some vague romantic fulfillment, the substance of which eludes even her but which she feels certain marriage cannot bring her. The strongest repercussion of the failure of the Falkner marriage is felt, however, in the marriage of Margaret Pole, as that discontented seeker's inertia of unhappiness with her vapid, selfish, clubman husband is broken by the availability of the no less discontented John Falkner, prompting their affair. Though Herrick presents this affair in highly idealized terms as a real union of a deeply loving pair, he describes it, ultimately, as injurious to the family and to social stability. An appealing relationship, therefore, and one that shows, ironically, what is lacking in all too many marriages, it is nevertheless a dead end as far as Herrick is concerned here. Thus do flawed marriages work to destroy each other and perpetuate forces of egotism that are socially harmful.

The unfortunate effects of the Falkner and Pole marriages on those who come within the compass of the unhappy couples are mirrored throughout *Together*, as other marriages pull down not only husband and wife but also friends and even those barely known into a maelstrom of misery, corruption, and even violent death. Early in her marriage, Isabelle meets the brooding Kentuckian Tom Darnell and his wife. Fascinated by the romantic Darnell, Isabelle is titillated to learn that he is having a particularly lurid extramarital affair.

Though she is suitably horrified when Darnell kills himself and his wife, she continues to be captivated by this man's unrestrained passion in pursuit of his own ends, and this leads to her unhealthy relationship with the *soi-disant* Byronic type, the self-indulgent, self-pitying Tom Cairy, a relationship that in turn results in the violent death of her brother, Vickers, who seeks to save her from falling into corruption with the odious Cairy. Similarly engendering an unhealthy influence is the marriage of Conny Woodyard. An extremely ambitious, restive woman, Conny is a threat to all around her, not only driving her husband into misery and immorality but carrying on a flirtation with Tom Cairy that makes him seem all the more attractive to Isabelle, with, of course, disastrous results. Driving home his point that bad marriages set up a network of unfortunate influences, Herrick comments, "Cornelia Woodyard . . . was becoming for Isabelle a powerful source of suggestion, just as Isabelle had been for Bessie Falkner in the Torso days" (p. 247). Glimpsed briefly is another unhappy and, hence, dangerous marriage, that of the Conrys. Observing the beautiful Mrs. Conry's apparent helplessness in dealing with her brutal husband inspires such sympathy in the suggestible young romantic, Vickers Price, that it leads him to run away with her, resulting in the ruin of his prospects, in his chronic depression (when Mrs. Conry, less helpless than he thought, runs off with another man), and in his subsequent decision to redeem himself and save his sister by goading Cairy into killing him.

For Herrick, though, as I noted, bad marriages damage society as well as individuals, engendering nothing less than cultural suicide. Politics become debased: Conny Woodyard, for example, virtually compels her weak, uxorious husband into political corruption. Literature becomes degenerate, as idle, bored women seek unhealthy diversion: "Gay little books, saucy little books, cheap little books, pleasant little books. . . . A literature composed chiefly by women for women,—tons of wood pulp, miles of linen covers, rivers of ink,—all to feed the prevailing taste, like the ribbons, the jewels, the candy, the theatre tickets!" (p. 521). Ultimately, too, procreative power atrophies among the native-born Americans, those Herrick feels are inherently fittest for leading the nation. The perceptive Alice Johnston declares to Isabelle, ". . . The people who made the country are dying out so rapidly, giving way before Swedes and Slavs and others,—because these people are willing to have children" (p. 158). More bitterly, Herrick himself comments blatantly on the rising power of the immigrants: "We chatter of the curse of Castle Garden, unmindful that in the dumb animal hordes, who labor and breed children, lies the future. For THEIRS WILL BE THE LAND, when the blond hunter of the market and his pampered female are swept into the dust heap" (p. 518).

This last statement by Herrick, disturbing in its bitterness and its distrust of the newcomers, culminates a chapter that is nothing less than a diatribe lamenting the unfortunate impact on society of the decline of marriage in modern America. In it, as he presents an extended account of the healthier marital patterns he insists once predominated on the national scene, he is trying to set up a standard toward which, he hopes, his contemporaries will aspire. Unfortunately, his propensities for grandiose idealization, lavish generalization, and the ponderous tone of the jeremiad hinder his effort to convince one either that such marriages as he envisions once were the American rule or that, even if they were, they are worthy of emulation.

Originally, Herrick declares in the course of this essay-chapter, marriage in America was a "primitive body-wracking struggle of two against all," with the "Man and Woman . . . free and equal"; and this, he asserts, "remains the large pattern of marriage to-day whenever sound. Two bodies, two souls are united for the life struggle to wring order out of chaos,—physical and spiritual" (p. 513). With the Civil War sending the husband off to fight, the pattern changed, but this also made for "the perfect type of Marriage—comradeship, togethership,—and yet larger than before because the two share sacrifice and sorrow and truth,—things of the spirit. Together they wage War for others" (p. 514). Similarly, the postwar period brought a new but no less perfect marital relationship. The returned soldier "goes down into the market-place to sell his force . . . ; while his woman waits behind the firing line to care for him,—to equip him and to hoard his pelf." Of this sort is the marriage of the Prices, Isabelle's parents. Her mother proudly asserts, "He made the money, I saved it" (p. 514). In each of these stages, claims Herrick, the "union of Man and Woman is based on effort in common, together; . . . not on individual gratification of sense or soul" (p. 514). Among the fashionable on the contemporary scene, however, those whose way serves as an example to be followed by the many, Herrick sees only selfishness. The husband works not in the "hope of hard-won existence for woman and children"; he works only for gain, for self. So "Woman," notes Herrick, "no longer the Pioneer, no longer the defender of the house, no longer the economist, blossoms—as . . . The Spender." She is "the fine flower of the modern game, of the barbaric gamble" (p. 515), the "mistress rather than the wife" (p. 516). Like all mistresses she is selfish and restless, longing for a legitimate fulfillment that her debased marriage cannot bring her and, consequently filled with ennui, experiencing a vague sense of malaise and inchoate yearnings that she seeks to gratify in social climbing, adherence to silly fads, and, worse, in affairs.

In order to show that modern marriages need not be corrupt, that there is, in fact, an alternative to the way of the Falkners, Poles, and Woodyards, Herrick focuses on several happy marriages that have attained a real success in conforming to the earlier American marital patterns he extols. These are marriages involving people who seem virtually untouched by the contemporary infection of devotion to worldly conceptions of success—devotion, that is, to self. Among these people are, as we have noted, the Prices. Mrs. Price, a loving homemaker, Colonel Price, a fair, enterprising businessman, are, Herrick notes, "the best aristocracy that this country has seen" (p. 111). That their daughter Isabelle is as misguided as she is, is testimony not to the failings of the Prices and their sort but to the power of the modern corruption that undermines their influence.

Another marriage that is a happy one in the old way, bringing contentment to those in it and benefit to society, is that of Isabelle's cousin Alice Johnston and her husband Steve. Though Isabelle at first cannot bring herself to emulate this couple who can be satisfied with few possessions and no social position to speak of, she does see nonetheless that there is something fine in their marriage. Herrick notes, "Isabelle could understand that Alice's marriage was quite a different thing from what hers was—something to glorify—something to glorify all the petty, sordid details, to vivify the grimy struggle of keeping one's head above the social waters" (p. 101). If the marriages of those such as Conny Woodyard damage those around them and society as a whole, the Johnston marriage and those like it have an opposite effect. Steve Johnston, his selflessness and integrity constantly reinforced by his closeness to his strong wife, gives up his job rather than participate in the shady dealings his employers demand of him, and later sacrifices his life rather than stand by and let a motorcar run down a woman and child. In acting as he does, he leaves behind himself a legacy of courage and decency not only for his wife and children and the pair he rescues from the car but for others too, including John and Isabelle Lane, whose lives are drastically changed, even redeemed, by the example of Steve Johnston.

Similarly, though glimpsed only briefly, the marriage of the Shorts, a humble New England farm couple, benefits all who come into contact with it. Their marriage, says Margaret Pole, "is the figure of perfect marriage, interlocked activity, with emotional satisfaction" (p. 491). She observes that they have a perfect union: "Mrs. Short's climax of the day is her hot supper laid before her lord. . . . Do you see how they talk without words across the table? They know what the other is thinking always. So the Shorts have found what so many millions miss,—a real marriage!" (p. 491). Isabelle too is impressed by the Short marriage; along with the Johnston marriage and, perhaps, the lingering influence of her parents' marriage, it encourages her to return to John and try to salvage their union.

Significantly, all three of these happy marriages seem not merely in the earlier American tradition of matrimony but positively anachronistic. All are linked with an earlier, pioneering America and with a primitivistic conception of life close to nature rather than with the modern, increasingly urban landscape. The Shorts are farmers, the Johnstons become truck farmers when Steve leaves his job, and the Prices are remnants of an earlier, more rugged way of life. By his refusal, or inability, to portray a successful marriage functioning in a complex, modern, urban society, Herrick is not only portraying modern America as corrupt but implicitly revealing his lack of faith that marriage can mitigate the shortcomings of a decadent age. He is, then, pushing marital happiness into the past and into the realm of sentimentality.

This is precisely what happens with Herrick's portrayal of the central marriage in *Together*, that of the Lanes. Ostensibly, the salvation of their marriage through their rejection of the shabby contemporary values that have stunted them and their relationship is to serve as Herrick's affirmation of marriage as an institution in which people can attain rare happiness and through which society can perpetuate virtue and the desire for real achievement. Unfortunately, Herrick, as in his earlier marriage novels, fails to convince one that he really believes this to be the case. Shallow and generalized as his account of the marital difficulties of the Lanes is, it is far more credible than his vision of their redemption and subsequent happiness. As unhappy moderns, the Lanes are not implausible. Their weaknesses are not rendered with Herrick's usual tendency to melodramatic excess when dealing with marital discord; rather they are shown, within a generally realistic context, to be like those of Wilbur and Hart, the natural products of the unfortunate influence of the age.

The grip of their time upon the Lanes is apparent from the first. Their honeymoon, significantly, is in the vacation lodge of a blatantly corrupt United States senator. During the honeymoon Isabelle, shaped by a *zeitgeist* that discourages giving of oneself, finds that she is repelled by sex and fearful of motherhood. Herrick notes, "The idea clutched her like fear: she would defy this fate that would use her like any other piece of matrix, merely to bear the seed and nourish it for a certain period of its way, one small step in the long process. . . ." Thus, "lying there in full contemplation of this new life that might already be putting its clutch upon her life, to suck from her its own being, she rebelled at it all" (p. 39). From this time on, she is an indifferent wife and, as time passes, an indifferent mother, giving herself over solely to her modern marital role as "Spender," which engenders such concomitant roles as blind adherent of foolish self-improvement fads, neurotic semi-invalid, and potential mistress of wastrel dilettantes such as Tom Cairy. Nor is her spiritual decay hindered by her husband, who, like her, fails to resist the worst pressures of his day and thereby fails, as she does, to align himself with the vital, transcendent force that Herrick in this work perceives to be at the core of existence. Beginning his career as a junior executive for a large railroad, he soon reveals himself to be only too willing to rise by ruthlessly carrying out the monopolizing company's most unsavory schemes. A poor boy originally, Lane, like John Wilbur and Jackson Hart before him, is driven by the American "success" ethic, so alluring, Herrick knows, to clever poor boys; and he is willing, no less than Wilbur and Hart and Van Harrington, to give up his integrity and ignore his wife in the process of carrying out his financial and social rise. Starting in the oddly named small town of Torso (signifying paucity of spirit?), Lane becomes a power in railroading, but only at the cost of everything that counts, the cost demanded by the times.

Though the Lanes' decline is, as I noted, credible enough, the redemption they and their marriage undergo presents some difficulties for the reader. Several factors are put forth by Herrick as initiating the change in John and Isabelle. Vickers's self-sacrificial death prompts Isabelle to question the whole tenor of the life she has been leading. Putting herself under the influence of the psychologist-cum-guru Doctor Renault, she learns from him not only that "Life is GOOD—all of it—for every one" (p. 468) but that there is within the reach of all "the Vision that abides within apart from the teasing phantasmagoria of sense, the Vision that comes, now dim, now vivid, as the flash of white light in the storm, the Vision by which he may learn to live and endure all!" (p. 501). All that keeps one, Renault teaches her, from seeing and following the Vision is "Egotism . . . the pestilence of our day" (p. 497). Such egotism might well be overcome by making a wholehearted commitment to another in marriage, but, Renault tells Isabelle, she and others like her "make marriage a sort of intelligent and intellectual prostitution" (p. 498). He goes on to declare vehemently, "Man is given you to protect, and you drive him into the market-place," and then he asks her pointedly, "What have *you* done for your husband?" p. 499). Shaken, Isabelle is ready for regeneration. Though previously convinced that she is irremediably different from such types as the Johnstons and Shorts, she now longs deeply to emulate them, to be able to say of John as Alice Johnston says of her devoted, honorable husband, "It's Steve—and I wouldn't have him different for all the success in the world." Finally, she perceives that "such was marriage,—perfect marriage,—to be able to say that in the face of worldly defeat" (p. 554). Coincidental with this sincere longing of Isabelle's for a better marriage there comes a change in John. An ugly trial in which the railroad officers are prosecuted for graft and the subsequent suicide of one of his powerful associates lead John to a realization of the unsavory turn his life has taken. Moreover, like Isabelle, John finds Steve Johnston's life and death and the Johnston marriage inspirations that finally cannot be ignored. Consequently, the Lanes decide to go to the West, where John will manage a small railroad line, which he will run fairly, for the benefit of the farmers of the region. All indications point to the genuine success of the railroad, the region, and the marriage. Thus, as the novel closes, it is apparent that the Lanes have found happiness by foreswearing the "cult of the ego" (p. 587) and by aligning themselves with the "vision," or, those "forces other than physical ones, beyond,—not recognizable as motives,—self-created and impelling, nevertheless; forces welling up from the tenebrous spheres in the depths" of one's being, welling up, in short, as "something higher than Judgment" (p. 589).

The difficulties with such an ending to the novel lie less with the plausibility of the Lanes' regeneration—though the plausibility *is* suspect—than with Herrick's insistence that their regeneration reveals the intercession of transcendent impulses. Blake Nevius notes that Herrick here as elsewhere is attempting to express "a truth beyond the visible facts, which could be embodied in appropriate symbols drawn from the reality of everyday life."[22] Such a task, obviously, cannot be an easy one, and a writer is bound to fail at it if he cannot effect a union of all-encompassing "truth" and "everyday life," if he fails, that is, to find his "appropriate symbols." And, unfortunately, this is what occurs in *Together*.[23] Even if the Lanes' regeneration were unquestionably plausible, they are not sufficiently large or sufficiently developed characters to sustain all the symbolic significance Herrick loads upon their change of values. Thus, Herrick's grandiose claim that there is a sort of divine energy, grounded somehow in the "common lot" to which the Lanes, like the Harts, turn, driving all irresistibly to the good seems little more than a bombastic exercise in wish-fulfillment. Nothing in the novel itself makes such an affirmative, romantic vision credible. In fact, all seems to point the other way. If Goodness is driving all before it, then the evil and shabbiness that pervade America in *Together* are ultimately inexplicable and presumably ephemeral. Hence, Herrick's frequent moralizing—either as narrator or through mouthpieces such as Renault—is beside the point.

Therefore, in *Together* social criticism yields to vapid romanticism. Marriage, ostensibly regarded by Herrick as a crucial means of overcoming the national malaise, is left behind, as the novel leaps into the cloudlands of a vaguely conceived transcendentalism. In fact, it is clear that for all of Herrick's supposed faith in marriage, he is writing the institution off as a means to a gratifying life in modern America. Revealingly, the most fulfilling union in the work is that of Margaret Pole and Rob Falkner, the affair that Herrick disavows in the interest of social order but that he renders in more detail and with deeper emotional commitment than he does any of the marriages. Further, as I touched on earlier, the successful marriages, those of the Prices, Johnstons, Shorts, and the Lanes after their redemption, are tied inextricably not so much to the possibilities of modern American life as to an earlier America that may not even have existed save in the sentimental imaginings of Herrick—a proud, young land filled with the perfect marriages of pioneering men and loyal, submissive, protective women. Clearly, for Herrick, marriage can function only in a context of primitivism and ideality, not in the complex modern world in which *Together* is presumably set. More, it is a work that argues against itself and is thereby irresolvably incoherent. We are back with the failings of *The Common Lot*, but the incoherence is more potent here, for in *Together* both the supposed faith in marriage and the contradictory commitment to a vague transcendental romanticism are established more fully and explicitly than they ever were in the earlier work. Such incoherence, revealing Herrick's desperate discomfort with marriage and the "common lot" he so wanted to promote, finally marks *Together* as, in spite of its own affirmative trumpetings, a work of virtually unremitting bleakness.

Herrick's disavowal of faith in marriage, which is largely inadvertent in *Together*, becomes more conscious and explicit in his next three novels that present notable depictions of marriage. In *One Woman's Life* (1913), Milly Ridge, a foolish and egotistical romantic, destroys her first husband's career as an artist by pressuring him to do merely commercial work, and will presumably injure her second mate, a man far too good for her. What women need in order to grow, Herrick concludes, is not marriage so much as the practical training that will prepare them for any course they choose to follow, be it matrimony or a career. Adelle Clark, in *Clark's Field* (1914), marries an ineffectual fellow who turns to drink and finally starts a fire accidentally that kills their little boy. Though she may at some time in the future marry her capable, virtuous second cousin, it is significant in any case that Herrick makes no attempt here to offer marriage itself as a means either to personal development or the social reform that he believes a nation spawning such slums as Clark's Field needs so desperately. Similarly, marriage offers little of worth in *Homely Lilla* (1923), in which Lilla's marriage to the pompous, vicious Gordon James ends in her desertion of him. Though Gordon refuses to divorce her, she effects a lasting union anyway with a rugged western rancher (himself formerly married unhappily), thereby manifesting that Herrick has come round to the belief—earlier rejected, though with difficulty, in *Together*—that a man and woman might find permanent happiness with each other although unmarried. However, the novel that shows Herrick's loss of conscious commitment to marriage most fully and intensely is *Waste*, his last major work after *Together*. An unrelievedly grim book, *Waste* delineates Jarvis Thornton's futile search for value in a tawdry society. In an America given over to pursuit of possession and social status, Thornton learns that seekers after real value are only deluding themselves if they look for understanding, comfort, or inspiration through a lasting union with another. Apparently Herrick believes that in the Vanity Fair that is modern America as he sees it the chances of a questing idealist finding a kindred soul are so slim that he had best go it alone. Obviously such a view reflects little commitment to marriage, and certainly the marriages that Herrick portrays in *Waste* do not inspire faith in the institution. At the close of the novel, after years of looking vainly for understanding from another, Thornton sees marriage as out of the question for himself. Like Herrick, he has come to believe that marriage offers little of value to either the sensitive individual or the cause of social reform.

The marriages portrayed in *Waste* are at worst hellish and at best stultifying. Jarvis, a sensitive boy, grows up, as Herrick himself did, in a home in which the mother, a nasty snob, berates the ineffectual father for having developed "no proper ambition in life."[24] "Stamped indelibly on his memory" is the scene in which his mother, barely prevented from throwing a great pan of hot water over his father, managed to get a few scalding drops on the poor man as he sat "dumbly, head bent, at the kitchen table" (p. 13). Despite this hideous background, Jarvis does not recoil immediately from marriage. Glimpses of other marriages—that of his friend's parents and of his kindly aunt and uncle—lead him to believe that happiness is perhaps attainable in matrimony. However, his own marriage to a whining, greedy social climber, a girl who reveals herself to be little different from his mother, goes a long way toward disabusing Jarvis of this notion. Never marrying again, Jarvis drifts into relationships with two unhappily married women, Juliana Laurence and Cynthia Walton, both of whom appreciate his sensitivity and honesty but are finally hindrances, too weak to perceive the value of Jarvis's efforts to attack various manifestations of American commercial and social corruption. This confirms Jarvis's realization that he must fight on alone, as he apparently perceives that if lovers restrict his efforts for reform, a wife certainly will.

Even the happy marriages with which the mature Jarvis comes into contact are, unlike those in the earlier novels, not without sinister overtones; for example, the comfortable union of Jarvis's sister, Susan, with the thoroughly likable Forest turns them into a smug, overly comfortable pair, totally impervious to any awareness of just how corrupt American life has become. When Jarvis, after losing his son in the World War and seeing its horrors firsthand, fails to join in the abrasively jingoistic sentiments of his community and consequently inspires anger and distrust, his sister, formerly bright and sensitive, is unable to understand his refusal. Similarly, the Gerson marriage, a generally happy one, succeeds only because Gerson's perceptive wife shuts her eyes to his greed, his shady business practices, and his chauvinistic, home-front brand of patriotism. The tendency of a happy marriage, then, as Herrick sees it, to encourage Americans to follow a pattern of mindless conformity to the worst motives of the powerful on the American scene makes it impossible for Thornton, or Herrick, ever to advocate marriage as a means of ameliorating unfortunate social conditions. Finally, then, for Herrick, to be married in America, even in what may be a relatively happy marriage, is to make oneself merely part of a group of "huddling, little animals, pressing blindly towards some center, for the warmth of contact with their fellows" (p. 213).

After reading *Waste*, one ought not to be surprised when looking at Herrick's subsequent work that the crucial lesson learned by the widower-protagonist in *The End of Desire* (1932) from his protracted affair with a woman long separated from her husband is of the futility inherent in "the fatuous belief that at last he might achieve the perfect union" or that Herrick in his utopian novel *Sometime* (1933) should envision his perfect society of the future as one in which the government sponsors free love.

Writing of *Together*, William Dean Howells noted that Herrick "may be painting moods . . . where he seems to be painting lives, when he portrays so many women loathing their husbands in the first moments of marriage, or getting sick of them as marriage keeps relentlessly on, and breaking from them at last in open or covert rebellion."[25] The observation is a shrewd one, for Herrick's marriage novels never delineate the actual pedestrian course most marriages follow. Without being grounded in portrayals of marriage that seem credible, the dissatisfactions expressed by Herrick's married characters do indeed seem as unsubstantial, as lacking in authority, as are mere moods. Ultimately, though, the "moods" that pervade these works find their origins less in the characters themselves as they respond to marital exigencies than in the psyche of Herrick. Prompted by a romantic impatience with the commonplace, which he has little inclination to observe closely or depict accurately, Herrick is unable to offer either a careful examination of the manner in which many modern American marriages fail or a clearly thought-out theory of how good marriages might be fostered.

There is little, therefore, that is "realistic" in the Howellsian sense in Herrick's vision of marriage. The bad marriages are simplistic, often lurid, melodramatic portrayals. The good ones (except for those in *Waste*, in which even the ostensibly good marriages come off badly) are rendered in such primitivistic, idealized terms as to be inherently unconvincing; for one just does not find credible Herrick's panoply of husbands who, despite youth, energy, and intelligence, turn their backs on modern life or his wives who find fulfillment in unquestioning submission to their men.[26] If this is what good marriage entails for Herrick, it is clear that real marriage, that mixture of sweets and sours, of accommodations and skirmishes, had little appeal for him. Conveyed inadvertently by

Herrick in *The Gospel of Freedom, The Common Lot,* and *Together,* this fundamental distaste for marriage becomes overt and consciously expressed in *Waste,* with its emphasis on self-reliance for one with intelligence and integrity.

As they show Herrick, consequently, struggling to offer social criticism and social remedies while clinging to a residual romanticism, his marriage novels exhibit not only the poignant situation of a writer stymied by internal conflicts that he does not fully understand but a striking example of the persistent hold of romanticism in the midst of what is ostensibly a time of realism. Though, as we have seen, a greater writer, such as James, could fruitfully combine romantic and realist impulses, Herrick could not; and his work suffers accordingly, never delineating convincingly what Herrick took real success to be. That he should as a realist attempt to write accurately and even admiringly of marriage as a means to such success is understandable. No less understandable, though, is the fact that as a romantic he would simultaneously suspect marriage to be an impediment to individual growth and, not unlike many an earlier New England romantic, finally conclude that "the tragedy of living . . . was not the recognition of . . . isolation, but the vain efforts after union" (*Waste,* p. 444). Apparently well on the way to this conclusion all through his career, Herrick found himself, nonetheless, trying to write novels that would show compellingly that such union was possible through matrimony in a social context embodying all the homespun, commonsensical, domestic virtues espoused by a realist such as Howells. That he failed in his efforts to write against his own deep convictions should surprise no one.

1. Robert Herrick, quoted in George Gordon, *The Men Who Make Our Novels* (New York: 1919); rpt. Walter Fuller Taylor, "The Humanism of Robert Herrick," *American Literature* 28 (November 1956): 291.

2. Blake Nevius, *Robert Herrick: The Development of a Novelist* (Berkeley: University of California Press, 1962), p. 114. In speaking of his visionary novel *The Healer* (1911), Herrick describes the work as manifesting "a mingling of my two moods—realism and idealism" (Nevius, p. 115). George Spangler notes that Herrick's affirmations all "share the quasi-mystical quality of intuited truth" ("Robert

Herrick's *Waste*: Summary of a Career and an Age," *Canadian Review of American Studies* 2 [Spring 1971]: 28).

3. Larzer Ziff, *The American 1890's* (New York: Viking, 1966), p. 347.

4. Alfred Kazin, *On Native Grounds* (New York: Doubleday, 1956), p. 94.

5. Nevius comments that "although three-fourths of his fiction, according to his own estimate, is conventionally realistic in method, Herrick resented being typed as a realist." Herrick, in fact, declared, "Consistent realism can be found only in the work of inferior and unimaginative artists, because they are more easily satisfied with surfaces. . . ." Herrick noted, though, that "conversely . . . consistent romance easily becomes nonsense . . ." (Nevius, *Herrick*, p. 199). Thus, again does one see the mixed and often conflicting tendencies in Herrick's work.

6. Herrick commented of the critics, "If [an author] has shown that he can do 'realism' of a certain sort fairly well, they pigeon-hole him forever as a 'Realist' . . . and woe to the author who ventures to disturb their conviction about himself." The segment of his work that, as Herrick described it, "does not conform to the harsh lines of Realism" was, as Nevius puts it, "nearest to his heart." Unfortunately, though, Herrick well knew, notes Nevius, that it "held no appeal for the public" (Nevius, *Herrick*, p. 200).

7. Kenneth Lynn notes in this connection, "Cheated by his parents out of a happy childhood in the golden age of success, Herrick the man concluded that he had been cheated again, that the success society in which he was fated to live did not at all resemble the glorious world which he was sure had existed in the past but was a horrible facsimile of his own family life" (*The Dream of Success* [Boston: Little, Brown, 1955], p. 213).

8. Kazin notes, "[Herrick] could not place his faith in makeshift laws and the politics of the moment; he believed too completely, out of the fullness of a great sensibility, in individual perfection" (p. 97).

9. *Herrick*, p. 10.

10. Nevius, *Herrick*, p. 259.

11. Quoted in Nevius, *Herrick*, p. 204.

12. That melodramatic elements can be used fruitfully in fiction set in a realistic context is, of course, evident in a number of Henry James's works. However, the melodramatic aspects of James's better works are handled with a subtlety that eludes Herrick and are never linked, as they are in much of Herrick's work, to an incongruous insistence that happiness is to be found in the "common lot."

13. *The Man Who Wins*, a novella by Herrick published in 1897, is of some interest for its portrayal of a scientist who is kept from doing his best work by his neurotic, egotistical wife. The bleak marriage here is, of course, an anticipation of many to come in more significant works by Herrick.

14. Nevius, *Herrick*, p. 75.

15. Lynn, p. 218.

16. Bernard Duffey, *The Chicago Renaissance in American Letters* (East Lansing: Michigan State University Press, 1956), p. 117.

17. Nevius, *Herrick*, (p. 18) and Louis J. Budd touch on these similarities, Budd asserting, further, that Adela "is a New Woman, a role that dwarfs her similarities to James's Isabel Archer, whose name she echoes" (*Robert Herrick* [New York: Twayne, 1971], p. 34).

18. Robert Herrick, *The Gospel of Freedom* (New York: Macmillan, 1898), p. 11. All subsequent page references to *The Gospel of Freedom* and to all other Herrick novels after the identification of the edition of each will be given in the text.

19. Robert Herrick, *The Common Lot* (New York: Macmillan, 1904), p. 175.

20. Robert Herrick, *Together* (New York: Macmillan, 1908), p. 199.

21. Nevius, *Herrick*, p. 169.

22. Nevius, *Herrick*, p. 191.

23. One who concurs with this view is Warner Berthoff, who notes that Herrick "had a weakness . . . for furnishing vaguely transcendental solutions to the dilemmas of the characters he favored" (*The Ferment of Realism* [New York: Free Press, 1965], p. 140).

24. Robert Herrick, *Waste* (New York: Harcourt, Brace, 1924), p. 14.

25. William Dean Howells, "The Novels of Robert Herrick," *North American Review* 189 (June 1909): 813.

26. One who is troubled by the latter, seeing Herrick, in fact, as a misogynist, is Katherine M. Rogers, *The Troublesome Helpmate: A History of Misogyny in Literature* (Seattle: University of Washington Press, 1966), pp. 226–30.

CONCLUSION

*T*HOUGH TWAIN SUGGESTS in the statement with which this study began that marriage is the logical place to end a book about "grown people," he offers no advice about just where to end a book about the depictions of the marriages entered into by such people. Because no line so distinct as that separating the marriage fiction of Howells and James from all stories of wedlock that came before in America divides it and the marriage stories of Chopin, Wharton, and Herrick from all that came after the careers of these five were under way, there is a temptation to strike on farther into the twentieth century. The marriages depicted by Cather, Glasgow, and Sinclair Lewis in the realist tradition, by Farrell in the naturalist, by Fitzgerald and Dos Passos, and, closer to our own day, by Updike and Bellow among many others since the days of the five authors scrutinized here all show that possibilities for significant delineation of married life did not end with these five. Yet there is, nonetheless, ample reason to stop where we do. As the first writers of fiction in America to depict married life extensively, thereby manifesting the freshest of literary responses to it, and as the realists who, of all those writing in the forty to fifty years regarded as the heyday of literary realism, look at marriage most intensely, they obviously form a natural unit of scrutiny.

As one studies the five, one sees similarities among them that link them to a common literary outlook—realism. Not only do all concern themselves with depicting an extremely significant social relationship, but they depict it in a world neither fantastic nor exotic, one at least meant to be recognizable as the one inhabited by most of their contemporaries. They are committed as well to accuracy of detail in depicting whatever specific area of this world they choose to describe.

Further, they all write with a consciousness, however vague it may be and however tenuously held, that their task of inspiring readers to be more aware of the possibilities in their own world of human suffering, human grandeur, human behavior generally, can have worthwhile social effects.

One sees too, however, significant differences among the five as they develop their views of what marriage as an institution and married life as actually lived have to offer. Thus, both Howells's fond wish that marriage could be a little realm of civility and affection that might have beneficial effects for society at large and his ultimately irrepressible fear that it would not be bear little resemblance to James's view of marriage as a particularly intense form of experience that usually leads the sensitive into pain and, far more rarely, into hard-won, personal, strangely sacred triumphs not unmixed with pain. Nor do the views of either have much in common with Chopin's view of marriage as a relationship in which, for better or for worse, for the success of the marriage or not, one's authentic needs will inevitably assert themselves, or with Wharton's dominant belief that marriage, like many another institution, is a horribly imperfect but nonetheless necessary check on the folly of no less imperfect human beings. Finally, Herrick's portrayal of married life as at its best an escape from the turmoil of an acquisitive society into the calm, sanity, and quiet joys of the "common lot," though bearing some superficial similarity to Howells's vision of matrimony, is essentially a product of romantic idealization. Consequently, it is as far removed from Howells's notion of matrimony as are some of the bitter depictions of bad marriages Herrick presents that Howells could not bring himself to credit. Taking into account such differences as these on a topic like marriage, which is presumably of central interest to anyone who has a realistic orientation in literature, it becomes apparent that realism and realists are perhaps far less easy to define and categorize than one might think.

Moreover, the one major similarity that is manifested in their views on matrimony—the recurring pessimism all show about the prospects for most men and women to find happiness or undergo significant growth in marriage—reflects, I suspect, more of a continuing influence on all of them of the highly individualistic strain in American romanticism than any ties to an outlook of realism. One's thoughts about marriage inevitably reflect one's thoughts about a great many other things. And certainly one common component of the fundamental outlooks of all five whether they are depicting marriage or not is a deep commitment to individualism. Be it Howells's pragmatism or his sense of existential chaos and terror, be it James's "imagination of disaster" and devotion to renunciatory gestures such as Isabel's, or be it Chopin's anarchic determinism, Wharton's wry, terrible conviction of human limitation and folly, or Herrick's transcendental idealism, all five present highly personal visions of life that are informed by no prevailing social doctrines of their time and are built usually on the belief that men and women must ultimately struggle alone as they confront issues involving moral and social dimensions.

Because of this, they focus, more often than not, on men and women who even within marriage are exceedingly alone as they cope with, or fail to cope with, the demands exerted on them by this social relation. The defeats endured by James's characters and the triumphs they achieve are lonely ones—as lonely as any of the sufferings and victories one finds in Hawthorne's or Melville's accounts of American isolatoes. If Isabel Archer's folly is a purely American one of quirky individualism and egotism, her moral grandeur at last is no less in the earlier nineteenth-century tradition of the self-defining, self-justifying, individualistic quester. If Maggie Verver's struggle in the web of deceit in which she finds herself brings her at last to sacred union with her husband, the struggle itself, despite the silent partnership she has with Amerigo, is a lonely one. Moreover, the poignance permeating the union that closes the book arises from this pair's awareness, as well as the reader's, that such moments as this of perfect communion are all the more beautiful for their rarity and transitoriness in a world in which, as James's marriage works show, loneliness is the rule and will continue to be so, even for these two. Similarly, Chopin's driven men and women may, indeed, occasionally find themselves in liaisons or even marriages that fulfill them; but such fulfillment as they find is purely personal, for the prevailing rule of human existence for Chopin is that individuals cannot help but embark on a lonely pursuit of such gratification as may involve another but that ultimately has as its sole raison d'être the meeting of one's own authentic needs and nothing, at last, to do with the well-being of others. Both Wharton and Herrick, obviously, did seek to tie their marriage fiction to a concern for the well-being of others, endeavoring to show in their depiction of failed marriages the errors of the society about them and in the successful ones the embodiment of the values that they hoped American society might some day manifest. However, Wharton's contempt for what modern America had become, her realization of the limitations of the best society she might envision—that of "Old New York"—and her unflagging awareness of the ineradicable human capacity for folly led her almost invariably to present her social values as vague ideas rather than as compelling delineations of functioning societies. Indeed, what is most striking in her marriage works—reflecting always her own personal bitterness over the failings she saw rampant on the modern American scene—are her delineations of lonely, valueless men and women swept along in the tide of corruption and of the no less lonely individuals sentient enough to envision something better than the goals thrust before them by their society but too powerless to do so. One might note too that an exception like Newland Archer, who does achieve a triumph of sorts by acquiescing at last to a legitimate sense of social duty in a less than perfect but defensible society is himself so alone in his struggles as to make clear that even in a work like *The Age of Innocence* relatively untinged by bitterness, Wharton's essential focus is still on the struggles of the lonely. Herrick too was generally unable to overcome his contempt for the social scene about him, but his inability to do so led him, as we have seen, not into bitterness but into a highly personal visionary idealism clearly within the tradition of Emersonian transcendental individualism native to the New England in which Herrick was born and raised. What is unmistakable here, though, is that like Wharton, and, for that matter, like James and Chopin as well, Herrick in his marriage fiction does not come near cutting himself off totally from the individualism evident in the earlier nineteenth-century American fiction.

Nor does Howells, perhaps the most explicit of the writers here in his fear that commitment to self is destructive of a sense of social commitment, cut himself off from this individualism. Even he, reacting against the absolutism and idealism associated with individualism, is, by grounding his social commitment in the pragmatic outlook, finally throwing the individual back on himself for the determination of what is the most effectual course to pursue in trying to achieve humane ends. Thus, whatever social themes may be evident in the fiction in which marriage figures prominently, the works ultimately resolve themselves into Howells's delineations of highly individual pursuits of understanding and right conduct. Atherton, the Reverend Mr. Sewell, Silas Lapham, Basil and Isabel March, whether pragmatically inclined or not, are on their own as they struggle to discern what acting well involves and what the human difficulties they observe or are caught up in can reveal about the nature of existence. To be sure, Basil and Isabel are together, indubitably a benefit accorded them by their marriage; but such conclusions as each reaches often differ from the other's, and nothing in the major works in which they figure or in the other marriage fiction ever changes the fact that the pursuit of truth for Howells's characters is finally as lonely a one as that undertaken by any characters of Hawthorne, Melville, or Poe, though certainly carried out in less *outré* circumstances, indeed, usually in the midst of polite society.

Hence, study of the marriage fiction of these five reveals that realism may be at once far more pessimistic and far more closely tied to romanticism than has heretofore been perceived. Obviously this does not imply that there are no differences between these writers and the major figures preceding them. After all, the realist traits that they do manifest set them to some degree apart from their predecessors. But the residual individualism one sees in the works of these five does clearly establish a link that ought not to be ignored. Perhaps it is this continuing concern with isolated figures and lonely pursuits of value and courses of right conduct that makes the realists in their marriage fiction as relatively unconcerned as they are with the advocacy of specific social reforms involving marriage. Such matters as liberalization of divorce laws, more control for married women of their financial situations, equitable chances for careers for married (or unmarried) women, fairness in child custody decisions, and the like are usually touched on tangentially if at all by these writers. Thesis fiction is no more what they are about, clearly, than it was what Melville, Poe, Hawthorne, Brown, Irving, or the Cooper of the adventure novels had in mind. Perhaps too the preponderance of unhappy unions in realist marriage fiction also grows out of the traditional American individualist leeriness of confinement through conventional commitments. Happy marriages do not usually make for likely fictional subjects to begin with, but the real paucity of happy marriages in the works at which we have looked may require such further explanation as is offered by the supposition that it grows out of the residual individualism of which we have spoken. Finally, this lingering individualism may also be at the root of the conscious or unconscious tendency glimpsed among the five writers at whom we have looked to impute—either with faint contemptuousness or admiringly—pedestrianism to the happier marriages they depict. By its very nature, the individualistic outlook seems to concern itself with ideals and, rarely meeting the ideal in its observations of the world about it, may well see such happiness as it marks as the refuge of inferior sensibilities. One need only remember Ishmael's comments on happy men in "The Try-Works" chapter of *Moby-Dick* or recall how cloying and unconvincing Hawthorne seems to become in works like "The Great Carbuncle" and "The Ambitious Guest," in which he seems almost trying to force himself to believe that the happiness he posits really is worthwhile, to see the operation of this tendency in the individualistic mentality.

Such similarities as we have touched on between the realists and their predecessors are also apparent when comparing their marriage fiction to that of the American writers following them. Again, one sees a preponderance of unhappy marriages and the lingering American commitment to the depiction of lone characters in pursuit of individually defined goals. The Dick Divers, Henderson the Rain Kings, Rabbit Angstroms, and battling Mr. and Mrs. Tate are all figures no less driven than Isabel Archer, Ethan Frome, or Edna Pontellier were by deeply personal needs—needs, I might add, that finally have little to do with any particular social issues of their day and that cannot be gratified by any particular reform that would right any social injustice. Though writers such as Philip Roth and Mailer, among others, deal far more explicitly, of course, with the physical relations in marriage than the writers whom we have studied and focus more explicitly, as well, on conflicts between husband and wife in terms of power struggles between husband as Man and wife as Woman—a type of conflict only anticipated in the realist period—they ultimately are still more concerned with the destiny of their characters as individuals than as reflections of sexual, political, or social types. Again, old American tendencies of thought die hard. The concerns of those writers we style romantics and those we style realists are still our concerns, and their thoughts on marriage are still ones that bear on our own lives.

Also dying hard, apparently, if dying at all, is marriage itself, which has a knack for remaining on the scene even in an era such as ours when many are writing it off. One lawyer remarks, in fact, "Perhaps the most impressive lesson one learns from exposure to divorce courts is that people generally are extremely loath to terminate their marriages; in fact what most people endure during marriage before finally resorting to divorce is practically unbelievable."[1] Moreover, the statistics continue to tell us that although the divorce rate climbs, the great majority of those divorced do indeed try marriage again. That Howells, James, Chopin, Wharton, and Herrick were the first to look at this remarkable institution is certainly not the least of their achievements.

1. Donald J. Cantor, quoted in Epstein, p. 24.

INDEX